**Implementing Employee and Manager
Self-Services in SAP® ERP HCM**

 PRESS

SAP PRESS is a joint initiative of SAP and Galileo Press. The know-how offered by SAP specialists combined with the expertise of the Galileo Press publishing house offers the reader expert books in the field. SAP PRESS features first-hand information and expert advice, and provides useful skills for professional decision-making.

SAP PRESS offers a variety of books on technical and business related topics for the SAP user. For further information, please visit our website: *www.sap-press.com*.

Ben Hayes
E-Recruiting with SAP ERP HCM
2008, ~300 pp.
978-1-59229-243-1

Brian Schaer
Time Management with SAP ERP HCM
2008, ~500 pp.
978-1-59229-229-5

Manuel Gallardo
Configuring and Using CATS
2008, 162 pp.
978-1-59229-232-5

Greg Newman
Discover SAP ERP HCM
2008, ~500 pp.
978-1-59229-222-6

Jeremy Masters, Christos Kotsakis

Implementing Employee and Manager Self-Services in SAP® ERP HCM

Galileo Press

Bonn • Boston

ISBN 978-1-59229-188-5

© 2009 by Galileo Press Inc., Boston (MA)

1st Edition 2009

Galileo Press is named after the Italian physicist, mathematician and philosopher Galileo Galilei (1564–1642). He is known as one of the founders of modern science and an advocate of our contemporary, heliocentric worldview. His words *Eppur si muove* (And yet it moves) have become legendary. The Galileo Press logo depicts Jupiter orbited by the four Galilean moons, which were discovered by Galileo in 1610.

Editor   Jenifer Niles
Copyeditor   Mike Beady
Cover Design   Jill Winitzer/Silke Braun
Photo Credit   Getty Images/Paco Serinelli
Layout Design   Vera Brauner
Production   Kelly O'Callaghan
Typesetting   Publishers' Design and Production Services, Inc.
Printed and bound in Canada

Contents at a Glance

Contents

4 The Foundation of Employee Self-Service (ESS) and Manager Self-Service (MSS) 49

5 ESS and MSS Installation and Setup 71

6 Functionality Available in ESS 85

7 Functionality Available in Manager Self-Service 163

10 Enhancing Self-Service Applications 361

11 Self-Service Case Study 375

12 Lessons Learned 385

13 Resources 409

Acknowledgments

This project draws inspiration from the efforts and support of many individuals. Without these friends and colleagues, this book would not have been possible.

Thank you to our friends at Galileo Press — for their guidance, patience, and support. We would especially like to thank Jenifer Niles, who made this book possible and has encouraged us to get the words onto the printed page (again).

We owe the utmost gratitude to our families, who supported us during the writing of this book. Juad and Nicholas as well as Paola, Nicholas, and Michael — thank you for your love and patience throughout this project.

We would also like to recognize some of our most loyal colleagues who have been a key part of our successes throughout the years. Without their hard work and innovation, we could not have delivered on our projects time and time again. A big thanks to: Venkat Challa, Rinaldo Condo, Matt Miller, John Wunderlich, Brad Chilcoat, and Vidyasagar Guntur.

We hope you find this book informative and easy to read. We are hopeful that we will provide you with new perspectives, practical anecdotes, and "food for thought" as you embark on your self-service implementation.

Foreword

Whether it be learning about the search for life on Mars on the Discovery Channel, picking up some fashion sense from "What Not to Wear" on TLC, or seeing "How It's Made" from the Science Channel, Discovery's over 1.5 billion cumulative subscribers around the globe enjoy some of the most captivating topics on their television sets and computer screens each day. Cable television has never been the same since programs like "MythBusters," documentaries like "Shark Week," and enduring mini-series like "Planet Earth" enchanted imaginations and piqued curiosity. Online resources from *www.discovery.com* provide adults and young adults alike with intriguing interactives and an excellent outlet for research.

For some readers, you may be reading this book to help you with your own "exploration" of sorts. You may be considering to start – or on the verge of starting – your own employee self-service and/or manager self-service implementation using SAP ERP HCM. Excitement is probably high among your project teams and senior leaders. Probably a combination of nerves and suspense is mixed in as well. Perhaps you have already defined your scope – or maybe you still need to go through a scoping exercise.

In some respects, an implementation of employee and manager self-services is like exploring the "unknown" on a Discovery Channel special. Much like the specials and learnings available within our network, this book is aimed at helping you understand these unknowns, eliminate confusion, and offer solutions and insights to great mysteries and problems. With a focus on the core concepts of self service, its strategetic direction, implementation pain points, as well as lessons learned, the authors' provide rich content that will prove extremely valuable for your implementation.

Here at Discovery, employees and managers currently have timekeeping functionality in their HR self-service portal. Timekeeping provides our organization with transparency in our time recording practices. Time submission metrics are collected and analyzed to understand how to improve the process and the overall service delivery.

Service delivery is one of the most important considerations when implementing this functionality. Although bringing self service down to the lowest delivery tier will reduce "administrivia" for the Human Resources function and free up its professionals to help with more strategic initiatives, it also underscores the importance of how the services are delivered to employees in your organization. Just as our company places extreme focus on how we can transmit effective learning to our subscribers, we have and will continue to place importance on the experience to our own employees.

Probably much like you, big plans are ahead of us at Discovery in the years to come for leveraging our SAP HCM self-service framework. With the latest releases – especially in the area of talent management and analytics – we are soon looking for functionality to allow managers to submit personnel change requests as well as allow them to submit/review compensation recommendations on the portal. We have decided to follow a phased-approach to our implementations (an approach the authors fully support and discuss as well) as opposed to a "big-bang" implementation.

At Discovery, we want to retain our title as the #1 non-fiction media company in the world – for both our subscribers as well as our employees. Best of luck as you begin your own journey. Let's hope this book busts a few myths itself!

Ralph Beidelman
VP, Compensation and HRIS
Discovery Communications

Preface

SAP customers have been implementing self-service applications for many years now, but there's been a lot of excitement recently. The latest enhancements to the SAP system's self-service platform (including the introduction of Web Dynpro technologies to support the SAP NetWeaver infrastructure) has accelerated its maturity so much that industry analysts now place SAP's Employee Self-Service (ESS) and Manager Self-Service (MSS) solutions beside many standalone point solutions in terms of viability and effectiveness. Customers have been responsive to SAP's focus on usability — recent attention has been focused on delivering an intuitive user experience. Concepts, such as the Homepage Framework and the Floorplan Manager (FPM) have proven to be invaluable. In many customers' eyes, SAP's self-service platform has "come into its own" with the latest versions of ESS and MSS.

As a result of these developments, we decided to embark on a book that would satisfy both the functional and technical needs of any SAP ESS and MSS implementation. We will review the business case for self-service as well as review some lessons learned about implementation. A case study is also reviewed that will provide the reader a better context in which to support the functionality both during and after deployment. Throughout the book, we have highlighted leading practices based on our experiences with customers. We have paid special attention to explaining common pain points experienced when deploying ESS and MSS processes. Mitigation steps to alleviate these pain points are provided as well.

This book provides an overview of the self-service functionality for employees and managers. It does not provide a thorough explanation of HCM Processes and Forms, though we will make mention of accommodating a Human Resources (HR) Generalist and Compensation Specialist within the design. Adobe Form functionality for Processes and Forms (available in ERP Central Component (ECC) 6.0, Enhancement Pack 2) is covered at a cursory level. Focus is placed more on the other standard applications available within the standard business packages of ESS and MSS.

Christos Kotsakis & Jeremy Masters
New York, NY

Human effectiveness and process efficiency have become a top priority on corporate agendas. Companies continue to redefine how services are delivered and how to better leverage integrated systems to augment their approach for service delivery. This book explains how to improve Human Resources (HR) service delivery with SAP software's latest Employee Self-Service (ESS) and Manager Self-Service (MSS) functionality. This chapter gets us started on our journey — here we introduce the book, its target audience, and its layout.

1   Introduction

In the last decade, companies have implemented, expanded, and progressively leveraged major Enterprise Resource Planning (ERP) systems such as the SAP system. The integrated and reliable transaction-processing capabilities of the ERP have provided companies with a foundation for optimizing processes, leveraging the integration capabilities to improve business dynamics, and, in many cases, reducing costs. Companies have also taken advantage of the real-time update and validation capabilities to seamlessly integrate critical business processes on top of a standard central data and process model.

Savvy companies are now starting to look beyond platform integration and basic self-service and thinking about how to increase effectiveness. They are investing more time focusing on the underlying process, administrative tasks, and the overall user experience to make employees and managers more effective and efficient, and to achieve enterprise collaboration. Corporate chat rooms, wikis, and blogs are becoming commonplace within companies. Online knowledge harvesting is becoming a must-have for today's businesses as an aging and more competitive workforce underscores the need for companies to protect their intellectual property.

Over the past few years, self-service for employees and managers has matured and is now being used by many organizations in one form or another. The maturity of the technology and underlying systems has positioned companies to continue to take advantage of increasingly complex self-service applications. Advanced delivery of self-service for non-managers and non-employees (e.g., HR Generalists, Compensation Specialists, and Executives) is now providing online dashboards to facilitate and influence their day-to-day activities and help them make more informed decisions.

1.1 Target Audience

This book is written for HR professionals, Information Technology (IT) professionals, and SAP ERP HCM consultants interested in understanding the steps needed to deliver a successful ESS/MSS implementation using the latest SAP versions. Other topics that will prove valuable to our target audience include: how to develop a business case for ESS and MSS, lessons learned from previous implementations, and a case study on implementing self-service applications. These topics will help set up the appropriate framework for deploying a sound technical solution.

Project managers of ESS and MSS implementations will also find this book helpful, because we will share things that "went right" and things that "could have gone better" in past projects. As we all know, nothing is more valuable than experience. We expect that the information in this book will resonate with project managers and project team members alike.

1.2 Book Layout

We have organized the book to tell a logical story from project birth through design and implementation. The first part of the book sets the stage for why self-service is important to organizations. An introduction and background on ESS and MSS as well as an outline on how to develop a business case are covered. From there, the book moves on to explain some of the more fundamental elements of self-service, including its installation and setup, followed by a full review of the components available within the standard SAP ESS and MSS Business Packages. More advanced topics are discussed later in the book, including key areas such as Object and Data Provider (OADP) framework, workflow, and security. A case study and lessons-learned section are discussed as well. The book concludes with a resources section that contains useful information for reference.

Now let's take a look at what will be covered in each chapter:

Chapter 2 presents an overview of self-service, including a definition of the self-service application, a breakdown of ESS and MSS, and an explanation of a basic service delivery model (inclusive of self-service).

Chapter 3 provides a business case for implementing ESS and MSS. Discussion is focused on the value proposition of self-service as well as self-service myths. The business case covers all aspects of the strategic decision to move forward with such an initiative, including the identification and exploitation of its benefits, both short and long term.

Chapter 4 focuses on some of the essential, baseline components needed to support self-service, including the "chief" manager relationship, the organizational structure, and workflow.

Chapter 5 discusses installation and setup procedures for ESS and MSS, including the business packages and initial configuration needed to get the out-of-the-box functionality operational.

Chapter 6 discusses the functionality available within ESS. Topics include the ESS Homepage Framework (SAP software's standard portal navigation framework), the ESS portal role, ESS portal iViews, and tips and tricks with the configuration in the portal and in the backend SAP system.

Chapter 7 focuses on the functionality available within MSS. Topics include the MSS Homepage Framework, the MSS portal role, MSS portal iViews, and tips and tricks with the configuration in the portal and in the backend SAP system.

Chapter 8 presents advanced concepts in ESS and MSS. Topics include the OADP, workflow and the portal inbox, delegation (including substitutions), and guided procedures (checklists).

Chapter 9 reviews the important topic of authorizations. Both standard backend roles (in ERP Central Component (ECC)) as well as SAP portal roles are discussed. Special attention is placed on structural authorizations and when and where structural authorizations should be implemented within an ESS and MSS context.

Chapter 10 discusses how to enhance self-service applications through development using the SAP standard development environment. The "how-tos" on development procedures (including the NetWeaver Development Infrastructure -

NWDI) within ESS and MSS Web Dynpro applications are reviewed. This chapter is technical in nature.

Chapter 11 provides a case study on a large, enterprise-wide ESS and MSS implementation. Emphasis is placed on how this self-service functionality supported the new service delivery model for the company.

Chapter 12 reviews lessons learned from previous ESS and MSS experiences. The chapter is divided into four sections, including ESS processes and applications, MSS processes and applications, change management, and system implementation.

Chapter 13 reviews helpful resources for your implementation, including where to search for common problems, such as SAP Developer Network (SDN) and Service Marketplace.

1.3   Product Releases

This book is based on the SAP ERP 6.0 system (sometimes referred to as ECC 6.0). However, because some clients have not yet upgraded (at the time of this publishing), we have made sure to mention functionality available starting from Enterprise 4.7 Extension Set 1.1. Although most screenshots in this book were taken on an ERP 6.0 system, many are still relevant for the earlier releases. Many iViews in Enterprise 4.7 and ERP 5.0 are similar to those available in ERP 6.0, but may vary due to technology choice (e.g., ITS versus Web Dynpro for Java versus Web Dynpro for ABAP) or enhanced functionality (e.g., enhanced Leave Request functionality in ERP 6.0). Throughout the book, we will be sure to call out the differences between versions (if needed) so that you are made aware of any future enhancements available within the standard framework.

1.4   Summary

This book serves as a comprehensive guide to SAP's ESS and MSS solutions. We place self-service within the overall service delivery model and try to help you develop a business case to justify its implementation. We also highlight all of the implementation components and provide Best Practices for implementation. We hope you enjoy the book!

Self-service technologies and applications are becoming critical elements in helping organizations define and develop cost-effective service delivery strategies that enhance the availability and quality of service for its employees and customers. This chapter provides an overview of self-service and its benefit to the organization's overall service delivery.

2 Self-Service Overview

Self-service applications continue to be the primary focus of Human Resource (HR) departments as well as other parts of organizations as they try to control costs and deliver increased services and efficient processes to both employees and customers. Due to the recent evolution of self-service technology, the adoption of enterprise portals, and the potential impact to the bottom line, this focus is now greater than ever. Self-service applications and technologies have also taken center stage as companies have attempted to transform how they do business and increase productivity at all levels.

The expectation from HR leaders and senior management is that self-service strategies will help streamline the organization and HR processes while reducing costs. More important, senior HR leadership is looking to find ways that will help the organization recruit, hire, engage, manage, and retain key talent.

In this chapter, we will discuss what defines a self-service application and how it benefits the overall service delivery strategy. To demonstrate the value of the self-service approach, we will define a basic service delivery model. Using the basic service delivery model, we can show the direct impact that self-service has on service delivery. We will also discuss some key concepts in self-service and review some of the most common applications delivered in a self-service system.

2.1 What is a Self-Service Application?

A self-service application defines any functionality that delivers a service (information or the completion of a transaction) that would otherwise be delivered by a service center or individuals within a business function.

Self-service applications came of age in the last decade when most companies moved critical functions to a centralized Enterprise Resource Planning (ERP) system such as the SAP system. Having all of their information and transactional capability in one centralized system enabled many organizations to take the next step in exposing that functionality directly to employees and managers. The integration and reliability of these systems made it possible to give employees and managers information that was not readily available in the past.

> **Example**
>
> One popular example of a self-service application is benefits enrollment. Employees can log into the system and view their current elections and, depending on the event, make new elections from the available plans. They can add dependents and, if eligible, enroll them into available plans. The employee is in complete control and can complete an enrollment without any human intervention. Once the enrollment is complete, the employee can receive immediate feedback in the form of a confirmation letter highlighting the plans they elected and the associated costs.

In some companies, this service is delivered by calling into a service center, internal resources from the benefits department, or an outsourced provider. In this case, the actual enrollment is completed by someone who interacts with the employee and gathers the information needed to enroll the employee in the selected benefit plans. Optionally, some organizations collect the bulk of the enrollments in paper forms that are subsequently entered into the system.

Having applications that replace the need for the service center or eliminate the redundant effort involved in collecting, validating, and entering the forms into the system of record is the main idea behind self-service.

2.2 Employee Self-Service

Employee Self-Service (ESS) is effective in driving transactions to the lowest level. More and more companies make basic employee self-service transactions available, realizing significant benefits to both the organization and the employee.

As discussed in the previous section, ESS transactions are holistic in nature and eliminate the need for the employee to access a call center for information or to complete a transaction. What is even more important is that as employees gain access to personal and organizational data, they become empowered to make it accurate. Greater accuracy resulting from a single input source and higher employee awareness reduces back office administration, making the entire process more satisfying for the employee and more cost effective for the organization.

Most organizations have implemented basic ESS transactions and have already started to reach the limit on benefits that can be achieved. These basic transactions include pay statements online and benefits enrollment. Having implemented basic transactions and realizing their value, HR and IT are teaming up to upgrade these basic transactions with newer, more advanced versions offered by SAP, and they are preparing for more complex transactions that were once only possible with the help of an HR Generalist.

The trend continues to be positive as organizations around the world invest in ESS and realize savings in reduced workloads for HR Service Centers, HR Generalists, and employees. Now, let's switch gears a bit and discuss Manager Self-Service.

2.3   Manager Self-Service

Manager Self-Service (MSS) applications are based on the processes and information needed to empower a manager so that he can effectively manage his organization. As managers assume more and more responsibilities, their success is tied to the people they manage. Fundamentally, managers will be successful if they effectively attract, hire, develop, and retain key employees.

Managers find it complicated and, in some cases, tedious to manage the employee lifecycle, which results in poor execution on key people objectives. MSS aims to empower managers to take control of their organization and efficiently manage the employee lifecycle.

MSS is a compelling application of self-service technology but has yet to become common place in organizations. Several reasons are to blame for the lack of adoption and effectiveness. The following are some of the key reasons:

▶ **Process Redesign:** In order to create an effective MSS solution, companies must be willing to review and change existing processes and substitute the manager for many of the HR tasks.

▶ **Technology:** For the most part, MSS applications are not mature enough to handle the types of processes that organizations need to create. It is also difficult for many implementation teams to understand how to build these processes into solutions using the available technologies.

▶ **Complex Transaction and Approvals:** Manager transactions tend to be more complex because they encompass many variations and business rules. These transactions include promotions, transfers, terminations, etc. The overall complexity in initiating one of these transactions and the associated approval flow have been an obstacle of MSS implemenations.

▶ **Global Standardization:** Many MSS implementations try to accomodate regional variations in processes making it vastly more complex to rollout a standard solution. All too often these variations do not offer enough business value versus the complexity that they add to the delivery of the solution. Lack of standardization is increasingly the reason for lower adoption of MSS.

▶ **Change Management and Training:** Many organizations underestimate the change management needed to deliver MSS along with the reluctance for managers to adopt the applications.

2.4 Self-Service Delivery Model

Self-service applications change the way an organization delivers its services. Most service delivery models have a tiered approach that handles the requests or cases in the first tier and adds additional tiers to support more complex requests.

Companies have increasingly augmented service delivery models to include self-service so they can lower the cost of delivering these services. Nowhere is this more common than in HR. HR services have come under increasing scrutiny in the past decade as companies race to expand and compete in a global landscape. This focus has put pressure on HR departments to reexamine how they deliver HR services and the impact it has on the organization.

In self-service delivery models, knowledge becomes an enabler because it allows users to make key decisions and complete important transactions. The relationship with the target user replaces the human infrastructure necessary to complete transactions. Additionally, it increases the transfer of information and knowledge across corporate boundaries, replacing much of the personal communication that takes place in a non-self-service environment.

HR service delivery models that include self-service components improve HR services by addressing four variables that affect employee and organizational value:

- **Service availability goes up:** Self-service improves the service level that an employee receives by providing an interactive service that is personalized, is quicker to access, increases the accuracy of transactions, and enhances the ability to track requests — all with 24/7 availability.

- **Cost goes down:** Because self-service applications do not require human intervention, they are typically lower in cost. The more transactions executed and information disseminated using self-service the lower the total cost of ownership and cost per employee interaction.

- **Quality goes up:** The overall quality improves as employees and managers have control of their information and can improve accuracy. Additionally, employees and managers are presented with only the relevant information that is personalized to them and to the context of the transaction they are completing.

- **Completion time goes down:** With self-service applications, employees and managers can complete transactions quickly and often see the results of the transactions immediately. The amount of time it takes to complete a transaction is reduced as compared to calling a service center and waiting for a representative to help complete the transaction.

Self-service applications and service delivery are not just for HR services. Although our focus will be on HR services for this book, consider that the value chain of many other areas can benefit from self-service technology and applications. Many companies have adopted a wide array of self-applications to improve service delivery to customers by improving the value-chain from the initial customer order of a good or service to delivery of that order.

Let's define a basic service delivery model so that we can better demonstrate and understand how self-service applications can impact the service delivery model.

2.4.1　Basic Service Delivery Model

Depending on the services being delivered, service delivery concepts and practical implementations can vary greatly and be fairly complex. Every aspect of a customer interaction is mapped out, measured, and tracked for efficiency and overall customer satisfaction.

For the purposes of this book, we will define a basic service delivery model that we can refer to. We will base the service delivery model on the context of the HR function of delivering services to employees. Our service delivery model depends on a call center staffed with key resources that can help resolve issues. Our model also supports the processing of transactions requiring that our first line of support be able to execute specific transactions on behalf of employees and managers. Figure 2.1 shows a tiered model that handles requests or inquiries made by employees and managers.

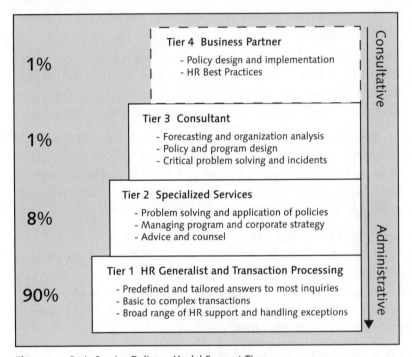

Figure 2.1 Basic Service Delivery Model Support Tiers

Tier 1 is the most cost effective and is designed to handle the majority of the requests. Requests can range from basic information to conducting a transaction in the backend system. An example would be employees calling in to change their home address or request information about employee benefits. This tier is usually staffed with generalists that have a broad range of knowledge that is not deep in any one area. The interaction at the first tier is highly scripted. If the request or inquiry cannot be handled by the first tier, it will be handed off to the second tier.

Tier 2 handles all of the requests that the first tier cannot handle and the interactions are usually not scripted. The second tier is usually staffed with resources that have deeper knowledge and are segregated to a specific area, such as benefits or payroll. Conceptually, the second tier of support should receive far fewer requests than the first tier and maintain a process that reviews incidents and determines how they could be handled at the first tier. If an incident calls for very specific knowledge or management intervention, the second tier will hand off the incident to the third tier.

Tier 3 is the least cost-effective tier to resolve an incident or request internally. It handles very specific issues that may require management intervention or an interpretation of policies and is usually staffed with experts, or subject matter experts (SMEs), in the respective area. Depending on the function, the third tier may also be the same resources that execute the daily work.

Tier 4 is reserved for the business partner. Policy design changes and industry Best Practices are frequently sought after from this group, as outside assistance can give perspective on how competitors are doing things better. This is the least cost-effective service delivery channel and is typically "as needed."

Based on the size of the organization, the model could be deployed in many different configurations. The implementation can range from the complete service delivery taking place in the HR department, various functions being outsourced to specific vendors, or the complete service delivery being outsourced. A mix of these can also occur, across — as well as within — functions.

2.4.2 Adapting Service Delivery with Self-Service Applications

In our basic service delivery model in Figure 2.1, employees can only make requests or inquiries to tier 1, which often requires a staff of employees. We can adapt our service delivery model by introducing a new, more cost-effective tier called tier 0. Instead of using employees to staff tier 0 we can introduce a set of self-service applications that is available 24/7 and allows employees and managers the ability to execute transactions and get a wealth of information.

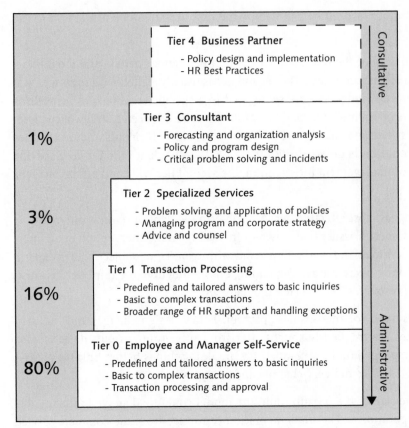

Figure 2.2 Service Delivery Model with the Introduction of Self-service Applications

By adapting the service delivery model with self-service applications, we can lower the amount of calls that are required at tier 1, which will significantly lower the overall costs of our service delivery model and provide better service to the employee and manager (Figure 2.2).

2.4.3   Employee and Manager Benefits from Self-Service

In addition to providing benefits to the overall organization, self-service delivers many benefits to the individual employee. Employees can personalize and customize the information they receive — making it easier to obtain and understand information relating to policies and procedures. Employees can also find the tools that make it easier for them to manage life events and perform their jobs. Employee life and career events are discussed in more detail in Chapter 8, "Advanced Concepts in Employee and Manager Self-Service."

Allowing employees to gain access to important information and deal with personal matters increases their well-being and improves job performance. Job performance can also be improved if self-service applications are linked to collaboration software that enables employees to find each other, communicate more effectively, and work together toward a common goal.

The reality when introducing self-service is that it adds an additional burden on the employees and managers than they have today. Managers especially complain about the introduction of self-service because it is perceived to be more time-consuming and requires that they understand more of the process than is necessary. Depending on the application or process, this has a grain of truth; however, the burden quickly turns into a benefit when employees and managers realize the control they have over information and executing transactions as well as the ability to track progress without the need to go through other channels.

2.5   Delivering Self-Service Applications

The self-service framework is based on a platform of several technology components. This "technology mix" has proven to be one of most challenging aspects in its successful delivery. In this section, we discuss the main layers within the application, including the core HR system (ECC), the portal, and integration with a corporate Lightweight Directory Access Protocol (LDAP).

2.5.1   The Role of the Underlying HR System

The underlying HR system and the data it contains is the foundation on which all self-service applications are based. A successful self-service strategy and effective processes will be based on the availability of key data and corresponding configuration in the underlying HR system.

Although self-service applications help to increase data quality in the underlying system, some data is critical to deliver the functionality to users. As each self-service application is reviewed for implementation, you will want to review the underlying functionality in the HR system to determine how suitable the underlying configuration and data are.

An example of this would be the introduction of MSS applications that require a way to derive the manager relationship and their span of control. The SAP system offers powerful technology to manage organizational information, such as the "chief" manager relationship and span of control; however, it is a prerequisite that you have managed the data and set up the organizational structures with the intent of determining manager relationships and span of control. The topic of chief manager relationships and the organizational structure is discussed in detail in Chapter 4, "The Foundation of Employee and Manager Self-Service."

2.5.2   The Role of the Enterprise Portal

Self-service applications can be applications within themselves, such as online banking or a collection of applications that make up the various services, including address changes, adding a dependent, and enrolling in benefits. Because ESS and MSS applications are distinct applications, they are usually related by life or company events.

> **Example**
>
> When an employee experiences the birth of a child, this life event may require the employee to add the child as a dependent, enroll him in benefits, and review the leave policies that apply for maternity leave.

The practice for delivering these distinct yet connected applications is done using an enterprise portal. Implementing an enterprise portal enables the information and transactions to be performed in a single, common, and integrated environment that is tailored to the employee using roles. Portals are designed to bring together a large amount of information and distinct transactions in a common way that is both easily accessible and intuitive to the user. The portal can replace the call center that would normally represent the single point of entry for getting information or conducting a transaction.

SAP NetWeaver Portal has evolved over the years (under the SAP Enterprise Portal name) into a robust and user-centric application. Throughout the book, we will discuss its capabilities as well as some of its limitations.

2.5.3 Role-Based Access

Role-based access is an important component in delivering self-service applications. Roles allow users to be segregated into groups that can be assigned specific functionality within the enterprise portal. For example, employees can be grouped into the employee role. They can be assigned this role once they are hired into the system and as a result, gain access to all of the ESS transactions and information.

Roles work like building blocks allowing the assignment of multiple roles to one user. For example, an employee who is a manager can be assigned to both the employee role and the manager role. The assignment to the manager role can be made once the employee is promoted to manager and removed once the employee is no longer responsible for managing others.   Once the employee is assigned the manager role, they can access MSS transactions and see information related to their employees. Roles remove much of the administration required to manage each individual user and provide a way for abstracting users to a higher level, making it easier to target functionality.

2.6 Common Applications for ESS

Employees primarily use self-service applications to complete transactions related to life events, such as the birth of a child, or a career event, such as performance management and development planning. Table 2.1 highlights the most common ESS applications that companies implement. These applications are explained in detail in Chapter 6, "Functionality Available in Employee Self Service."

Self-Service Application	Description	Category
Benefits Enrollment	Employees can enroll in benefit plans that they are eligible for	Benefits and Payment
Participation Overview	Employees can view what plans they are enrolled in and print a statement	Benefits and Payment
Pay Advice (Salary Statement)	Employees can view the current and previous pay statements generated by the payroll processing. Widely used to reduce mailing statements.	Benefits and Payment

Table 2.1 Most Common Employee Self-Services

Self-Service Application	Description	Category
Total Compensation Statement	Employees can view a total compensation statement that aggregates various compensation components such as base pay, bonuses, and stock awards as well as other compensation, such as benefits and training. Prerequisites, like tuition or fitness club reimbursements, can also be listed on the statement.	Benefits and Payment
Leave Requests	Employees can view and request time away from work based on a configured reason.	Time Management
Time Statement	Employees can view a company time statement, which could include information on overtime and vacation or sick time quota balances.	Time Management
Universal Worklist (Workflow Inbox)	Employees can view workitems that need to be approved or require an action.	Workflow
Tax Withholding	Employees can update tax-relevant information, such as number of withholdings and marriage status.	Benefits and Payment
Personal Data	Employees can maintain personal information, such as name and Tax ID information.	Personal Data
Address	Employees can maintain various addresses, such as mailing and home addresses.	Personal Data
Bank Information	Employees can maintain their bank information for their primary and "other" banks (if necessary).	Personal Data
Dependents (Family Data)	Employees can add family members. These family members are then available to other processes, like Benefits Enrollment.	Personal Data
Appraisals and Development Plans (Performance Management and Development)	Employees can set objectives and conduct self-evaluations. Employees can also complete individual development plans.	Career Information

Table 2.1 Most Common Employee Self-Services (Cont.)

Self-Service Application	Description	Category
Skills Profile	Employees can maintain a skills profile by selecting competencies and providing a skill level.	Career Information
Employee Directory (Who's Who)	Employees can use multiple search criteria to find users throughout the organization.	Company Data
Travel Request and Expense Reports	Employees can request approval for travel and can complete expense reports that are submitted for approval and subsequent payment.	Travel

Table 2.1 Most Common Employee Self-Services (Cont.)

2.7 Common Applications for MSS

For managers, self-service applications represent a way to effectively manage employees, departments, and the processes for which they are responsible. Managers have specific objectives that they need to execute as part of their job. Most managers need to attract and retain key talent, create and measure department goals, and reduce costs. Accomplishing these objectives is a difficult task and managers increasingly need self-service applications to reduce the time required to effectively manage employees.

Table 2.2 highlights the most common MSS applications that companies implement. These applications, and other applications available in the MSS business package, are explained in detail in Chapter 7, "Functionality Available in Manager Self-Service."

Self-Service Application	Description	Category
Approve Time Sheet	Managers can review and approve employee time sheets.	Time Management
Check-In/Check-Out Corrections	Managers can make corrections to clock-in and clock-out entries submitted by the employee.	Time Management
Approve Leave Requests	Managers can review and approve leave requests.	Time Management

Table 2.2 Most Common Manager Self-Services

Self-Service Application	Description	Category
Personnel Change Requests	Mangers can manage their organization by initiating transactions like promotions, salary increases, transfers, and terminations. Personnel change requests can also be customized by organizations to add additional transactions, for example, security requests and vacation payments.	Employee Transactions
Appraisals	Managers can evaluate employee's objectives and conduct reviews with a final evaluation. Evaluation ratings can then be used in compensation to provide suggested merit increases and awards.	Employee Evaluations
Reminder of Dates	Managers can view current and future dates, such as birthdays and anniversary dates. This functionality can replace custom reports that many organizations provide to managers on a regular basis.	Department Information
Team Viewer	Team viewer provides managers a view of the direct and indirect employees in their organization. Team Viewer also allows managers to select an employee and view additional information specific to that employee.	Department Information
Phone List	Managers can see a quick list of employees and contact information making it easy to contact the employees.	Department Information
Attendance Overview	Managers can track absences and attendances (including vacations, sick days, and training courses) for their direct and indirect reports.	Department Information
General Data (Employee Profile)	Managers can see basic information about an employee, such as name, organization, and location.	Employee Information
Emergency Contacts	Managers can get access to emergency contact information for an employee in the event of an emergency in the workplace.	Employee Information

Table 2.2 Most Common Manager Self-Services (Cont.)

Self-Service Application	Description	Category
Compensation Adjustments (Employee Profile)	Managers can get a history of compensation adjustments.	Compensation
Salary Development (Employee Profile)	Managers can view a salary history showing an employee's progression in the organization.	Compensation
Awards (Employee Profile)	Managers can view a history of awards for an employee.	Compensation
Compensation Planning	Managers can use a customizable compensation worksheet to make merit adjustments and provide bonus or stock award recommendations. Managers can also view the compensation budget that can be distributed to employees.	Compensation
Position Profile	Managers can view position-related information (such as vacancies, cost center assignments, and "holders") for employees within their span-of-control.	Department Information
Reporting	Managers can use an intuitive interface to execute reports that have been made available to the portal.	Department Information

Table 2.2 Most Common Manager Self-Services (Cont.)

2.8   Summary

With the adoption of a self-service strategy, the service delivery model can become more efficient and lower the total cost of operation while delivering high levels of service that are available 24/7. The delivery of these services and the overall user experience becomes more consistent — allowing users to use the services when it is convenient for them.

Using a self-service strategy can also position the organization to become more strategic. As we discussed earlier in our sample service delivery model and the impact to the organization, resources that once catered to completing transactions and providing information to employees can now be redeployed toward more strategic initiatives, such as employee development, recruiting, and employee retention.

In the next chapter, we will construct the business case for self-service and look at both the tangible and intangible benefits.

A business case is the foundation for which intelligent decisions are made and serves as a baseline by which future operations can be measured.

3   Value Proposition for Self-Service

Before investing in an online workplace that delivers self-service applications, you should make an attempt to calculate the return on the investment. To do this, you need to construct a business case that clearly explains how the effort will enhance corporate value. The business case is not just to benefit the C-level executives or to get funding for the project. The goal of the business case is to clearly define the value proposition and serve as a reference for those implementing the project and managing future operations. Once the project is completed and the system is implemented, your business case should serve as a baseline of planned efficiencies or metrics to measure corporate value.

Creating a business case is not always straightforward and many organizations wrestle with the business case for self-service. Although the value to the business is clear; it may be challenging to articulate this value in the form of a business case with a solid Return on Investment (ROI).

This chapter is dedicated to the creation of a business case for Employee Self-Service (ESS) and Manager Self-Service (MSS). Because companies vary in size and can be very different in terms of markets, types of employees, and reliance on shared services, we will focus on highlighting possible value propositions. You can take each value proposition alone or link it with others to create a business case that will resonate with your company.

3.1   Self-Service Myths

Before we start building a business case for self-service, we need to delve into some of the myths that surround the approach and the technology. It is important to understand these challenges to conventional thinking so that you can address them in your company.

Myth #1: Self-service delivered over a web channel will dramatically reduce, or even replace, phone calls to service centers

The first myth is not necessarily a myth; it definitely challenges conventional thinking because it is predicated on the fact that every web self-service interaction is represented by a phone call to a service center. The reality is that web interactions are no longer directly linked to a phone call and in many cases are never measured against the introduction of web interactions.

Let's examine this closer. In some very specific cases a self-service transaction will drive calls lower. For example, using an application to request a forgotten password can dramatically reduce the number of calls to the help desk. Does this not validate the myth? Yes, but if you simply look at targeted self-service applications, you will get a different result. If you step back and look at a holistic self-service solution that encompasses many transactions across multiple functions, you will quickly realize that the same dramatic results may not materialize. Why is this the case?

The reality is that self-service applications will expose a hidden demand that exists across the organization. The processes that can be moved to self-service on the web happen in many forms. Participants in the process use a variety of methods to accomplish the work including paper, email, and fax. The hidden need becomes greater as the organization grows with more processes and as it expands globally with variations in the process.

The other factor that comes into play is adoption. In order for your organization to dramatically reduce calls, you would need an increase in the adoption of self-service transactions for the majority of the organization. Although calls to the service center will be reduced to some degree, try to think broader than just reduced calls to the service center when making your business case. Focus on the increased productivity by channeling commonly defined processes with automated data collection and centralized processing.

Myth #2: Implementing self-service is fast and easy

Sometimes this is a true statement because companies choose to implement a simple self-service transaction and limited policy information, but for the most part it is neither fast nor easy. SAP software has dramatically improved both the usability of self-service applications and the underlying technology making it simpler to implement self-service applications more quickly, but if this is your company's first attempt at self-service transactions, consider that the underlying data may need to be cleansed, a proper communication plan needs to be created, and all the accompanying processes may need to be reengineered.

Myth #3: Self-service technology will reduce headcount

The reality is that you might be able to save headcount, but it is not a guaranteed result of implementing self-service technology. Most organizations believe they can decrease personnel in specific areas, such as phone support. With well-engineered self-service applications, users will not need to call for information because it is available in tandem with online transactions. Although this is predominately the case, the higher level support required to handle the escalation of issues are rarely affected, and with the addition of higher skilled workers to support the system the intended cost savings may not materialize.

Companies can expect to achieve an overall curbing of headcount as they adopt self-service applications. They can handle more transactions without the need of adding resources in each support tier and can also tailor the support interactions to provide a higher quality of service.

Myth #4: Introducing self-service to employees and managers will be perceived negatively

This myth comes from the common argument that managers will not accept having to do additional administrative work that is currently being executed by Human Resources (HR). The reality is that all users appreciate the ability to have a well-designed process and system for executing transactions. This applies to almost every aspect of self-service transactions. Managers who are properly trained in the process and application are far more effective in completing administrative processes with less effort and more immediate feedback.

Companies that make the effort to design effective processes that consider self-service components, implement effective self-service applications, and communicate the change will realize very high adoption rates and little resistance from managers who now have to complete administrative transactions.

3.2   The Business Case

Self-service strategies help companies attain business value by reducing transaction and business process costs, improving data accuracy, and by shifting the focus of service centers and HR to a more strategic focus that produces business value. So let's first discuss some key benefits of self-service.

3.2.1   Key Self-Service Benefits

As we discussed in the previous chapter, self-service implementations change the service delivery model by driving transactions to the lowest level and improve each of the four variables that affect employee and organizational value:

▸ Service availability goes up

▸ Cost goes down

▸ Quality goes up

▸ Completion times go down

The following self-service benefits define the high-level groupings that you can use in your business case and link to the four variables listed previously:

Benefit #1: Redefined processes that increase HR effectiveness

Self-service expands a company's reach and enables it to better address the employee lifecycle. Companies can move beyond the normal processes and become more competitive in recruiting, hiring, onboarding, training, and rewarding employees.

With self-service in place, companies can move to dramatically change the role of the service center as well. Current service centers typically walk employees through transactions, conduct transactions that are triggered by a phone call to the service center, process paper-based transactions, and process data entry requests. Service centers within a self-service strategy shift to a more strategic role as the service employees can answer more sophisticated policy-oriented questions and handle specific questions related to the self-service process.

The real value sought after by companies implementing a self-service strategy is the reduction of workload and the creation of more bandwidth for strategic business objective-aligned efforts. The reduction in time is very small with respect to employees but it becomes fairly significant for HR Generalists and HR Specialists, such as compensation and benefits personnel.

Benefit #2: Reduced transaction processing time

Additional business value is derived from process transaction time. Employees and managers can see a dramatic decrease in the time it takes to process a transaction — especially with ESS, where the transaction is completed instantaneously and the employees see immediate confirmation.

Benefit #3: Increased data accuracy

Data accuracy is also improved by having the transactions completed by the employee and manager, thereby eliminating the need for reentry of data by a service center or HR resources.

Benefit #4: Reduced transaction costs for commonly executed transactions

Each time a transaction is executed, it carries an internal (and sometimes external) cost. From our assessment of various clients, we found that internally executed HR transactions can carry an average cost of approximately $17 and can be reduced by approximately 50% with the introduction of self-service transactions that divert the workload away from HR.

3.2.2   Employee Value Equals Corporate Value

Much of the value that companies realize when implementing self-service is difficult to measure and most likely falls into the category of intangible benefits. When it comes to corporate value, intangible benefits are as important as tangible ones. It is critical to understand the positive impact that effective processes and well-defined tools have on an organization. Employees experience less frustration, are more apt to comply with administrative processes, and reduce overall workload for everyone involved in the process.

This may not lead to headcount reduction, but it can lead to higher productivity levels and additional focus on more critical business objectives.

Additionally, companies can extend their reach to potential employees and business partners allowing them to feed directly into the central Enterprise Resource

Planning (ERP) systems. Potential employees can find important information about the company and culture, making them more likely to join the company. The onboarding process can be streamlined by having new employees fill out forms before they start employment.

3.2.3 Building the Business Case

Building the business case for self-service strategy and implementation typically involves these four steps:

1. *Identify processes, applications, and participants:* List the processes that you want to expose via self-service and the roles that are affected in the organization.
2. *Identify potential cost savings:* Determine cost savings considering process improvement, reduction in processing times, and data accuracy.
3. *Assess project parameters:* Determine project approach, timeline, and estimated cost for software and implementation.
4. *Decide whether to pursue the project:* This involves determining the company's internal metrics, matching costs to business goals, identifying costs associated with human components, and the opportunity costs of not pursuing the project.

Identify Processes, Applications, and Participants

The core of the business case needs to include the processes that you will redesign, the applications that you will introduce to make the processes more efficient, and the roles that are affected. We typically categorize this section in our business case by breaking down ESS and MSS into three main categories with each category offering more complexity and a greater opportunity for ROI.

The first category of self-service is the publishing of policies, procedures, links to forms, and HR checklists that provide the foundation for self-service processes and applications. Employees can quickly find information about policies that affect them and reference the procedures and forms for executing transactions.

The second category of self-service is the simple transactions that can be completed in their entirety, change underlying data in the source HR system, and provide the employee with immediate feedback. It also includes the availability of HR data, such as remuneration statements for employees, compensation and organizational data for managers, and reports for HR Generalists.

The last category of self-service is the complex transactions that require the collaboration of various people to successfully complete the process via workflow. This category includes transactions like promotions, transfers, salary changes, and terminations. These are fairly complex transactions and originate with employees or managers, reviewed by HR, and can ultimately be processed by an administrator or service center.

3.2.4   Aligning Your Self-Service Strategy

Another element in the business case is the alignment of the self-service strategy with the corporate and HR service strategies. The business case should attempt to link the processes that are being enhanced or implemented by showing how they support the underlying service delivery strategy or business objectives.

The following are some client examples that we used when linking self-service strategies to HR service strategies and business objectives:

▸ The company is experiencing high growth globally and is expected to add between 20% and 30% more employees and contractors in the next year. Standardized onboarding and talent management processes will be required to quickly onboard employees and measure, develop, and reward them in order to retain key resources and reduce turnover.

▸ HR is moving to a lower cost provider for benefits processing and will need to implement an online benefits center where employees can enroll in benefits, review policies, verify participation in plans, and submit benefits claims. This will enable HR to reduce the overall costs associated with delivering benefits administration, increase employee satisfaction, and decrease the number of service center calls associated to policy inquiries.

▸ Investments are being made in global research and development that require a higher degree of collaboration amongst employees. Self-service applications will be introduced to capture employees skills and qualifications to better leverage talent on a global scale. Additionally, metrics and processes will be put in place to enable specific projects to leverage the qualified resources that are most cost effective.

▸ Employee retention has become a critical component to maintaining a competitive advantage in our primary markets. HR will implement an extension to compensation administration that will enable managers to view employee's holistic compensation and make direct compensation recommendations for merit, bonus, equity, and market adjustments in one cohesive and intuitive tool. Additionally, employees will be provided with an online total compensation statement that shows a summarized view of their direct and indirect compensation.

Identify Benefits and Potential Cost Savings

Once you have identified which processes you will be enhancing and the roles that are affected, you can begin to identify the benefits and potential cost savings that will be realized by adopting and implementing or extending the self-service strategy. This varies greatly in each company and must be looked at very carefully. Each company is at various stages of growth and maturity and one size does not fit all. Here are some of the ways you can approach this step and complete the ROI section of the business case:

▶ Harvest transactional data from your current HR system and determine how many of the transactions that you are targeting for self-service occur on a monthly basis.

▶ If applicable, further breakdown the transaction metrics by determining the source and connecting them to a larger process. For example, you could use the number of position changes average per month and connect them to the number of transfers and promotions initiated by managers per month versus the ones created as part of a reorganization, reduction in force, or an organization maintenance.

▶ Attempt to determine the total cost per transaction by looking at all the labor and waste involved in the process surrounding the transaction. This usually involves taking loaded labor rates and dividing the number of transactions that are completed on an average month. This does not need to be scientific, because only a portion of this cost can be avoided using self-service anyway.

▶ Clearly identify waste in the process. This is sometimes difficult, but when you closely review a process you will find that some portion is either redundant or requires too many handoffs to complete. You should target any unnecessary approvals or stops in the process that don't add value.

▶ Focus on data accuracy and issues that result with data entry off of forms being submitted to HR or the service center. Transactions that result in input error require significantly more time to correct and will alter the total cost per transaction because it engages more people than are normally required to enter and complete the transaction.

▶ Quantify the mailing and printing of materials that can be avoided by making the information available online. This can range from remuneration and compensation statements to benefits enrollment forms and plan books that are usually sent to employees to decide which benefits plans they can elect.

▶ Quantify the workload that HR and HR service centers need to perform to support existing transactions and contrast it to the reduced workload or time savings after self-service is introduced. You have several options at this point to either highlight reduced headcount in those areas or increased capacity for strategic work.

The preceding bullet points provide a good starting point and can help structure your business case to highlight all of the areas that can return value to the business. This is by no means an exhaustive list of areas to look at but can get you thinking of how to approach your business case.

In contrast to these points, you will need to focus on the costs associated to supporting your self-service platform by taking into consideration software licensing, hardware, support, and increase technical resources. These items will reduce your ROI but, if included, will provide a balanced view of the benefits that can be realized when implementing self-service.

Assess the Project Parameters

Once you have defined what you are going to deliver and the potential return on investment, you must move to estimate the cost of implementation. This will provide a further basis for the ROI because you can include the one-time cost for the project implementation. When assessing the project, you may want to consider sending out a Request for Proposal (RFP) to get competitive quotes from leading vendors. At this point, you should have a clear idea of what you want to implement as well as the benefits you wish to receive by implementing this project. Vendors will also be able to validate your assumptions and help you think through issues that you may have missed.

It is important to provide a detailed breakdown of the project costs when delivering them as part of a business case. We recommend that you include the following summarized costs with the details available in an appendix.

▸ Total internal and external budget needed to complete the project. (This can further be broken out in phases like requirements, design, development, etc.)

▸ Total hardware and software budget.

▸ Total training required for new technology.

▸ Total budget required for expenses such as travel and lodging. (This can be significant depending upon the size of the project and the number of out-of-town consultants.)

This section of the business case should also contain the project timeline with high level project milestones and a resource breakdown with the types of resources and associated costs.

Determine Whether to Pursue the Project

This section of the business case is dependent on how your company approaches business cases. What we have typically done at the end of the business case is list the key benefits and the lost opportunities of not pursuing the project. We have also laid out the ROI showing how fast the value can be realized after the project has been implemented. At a minimum, we recommend that you include the base criteria for making the decision and what would happen if the project was rejected.

3.3   Summary

In this chapter, we covered a range of value propositions that can be adapted and added to your business case as you develop it. When putting your business case together, it is important to think holistically and think in concrete terms of time and cost savings that can be realized by implementing ESS and MSS. Your business case should also be viewed as a living document that gets updated throughout the project as decisions around scope and processes are made. It is critical that the impact of those decisions be reflected and metrics refined so that the planned efficiencies can be measured effectively and accurately.

In the next chapter, we will discuss some of the foundational components of ESS and MSS needed to get you started in the right direction for a successful implementation.

A few concepts play an integral part of the self-service solution within the SAP system. These concepts, including the definition of manager (including the "chief"), the importance of a healthy and up-to-date organizational structure, and workflow, all have a crucial impact on self-service implementations. In this chapter, we will explore these concepts in detail and explain why they are fundamental to your self-service functionality in the SAP system.

4 The Foundation of Employee Self-Service (ESS) and Manager Self-Service (MSS)

There are several fundamental components to any self-service implementation. Whether you are rolling out MSS for 300 managers at a midsize company or to 3,000 managers at a global Fortune 100 firm, the basic principles are the same. This chapter discusses some of the most important aspects of setting up the underlying structure for self-service. We will first look at the employee side (components within Personnel Administration) and then look into the ever-important organizational structure within Organizational Management (OM), which serves as the "backbone" for the MSS solution. Discussion of the "chief" manager, position and vacancy management, as well as workflow will also provide insight on how to ready your SAP environment for your self-service deployment.

4.1 Personnel Administration

One of the base requirements for ESS and MSS (and most other functionality in SAP HCM) is the Personnel Administration (PA) component. PA is where the core Human Resources (HR) infotypes are stored (all of which are connected to an employee's personnel number). Infotype 0000 ("Actions"), for example, stores an employee's HR actions (e.g., the hiring, transfer, leave of absence information, including effective date and reason code) whereas Infotype 0006 ("Address") stores an employee's various addresses (mailing, home, etc.). Clean and up-to-date employee master data is a critical part of rolling out functionality to your company because it provides the baseline, core HR data with which to work.

In this section, we will discuss the elements from the PA side of the system that form an integral part to support ESS and MSS. Without an employee and user master record, self-service is not possible.

4.1.1 The Employee

Every employee in your company is hired and tracked within PA. As with other components, such as Payroll, Time, and Benefits, PA supports OM and the self-service platform in general. In fact, most of the services available in ESS update the PA component. (A lengthy discussion on the available ESS services is covered in Chapter 6, "Functionality Available in Employee Self-Service.")

The personnel number within PA exists as an integrated object within OM — identified as object type P. Each personnel number is tied to one (and only one) user (the concept of a user is described shortly). The user tells the portal and self-service application which connected personnel number should be updated when an employee is updating data online.

4.1.2 The User

A user is created for every personnel number. This user name (for example, GHANSON) is attached to an employee's personnel file. In order for any employee to utilize self-service functionality (whether it be an employee or manager), an Infotype 0105 "Communication," subtype 0001 "System user name (SY-UNAME)" needs to be created and assigned the appropriate security. Figure 4.1 shows this assignment of user name GHANSON to personnel number 10 effective on 01/14/2005.

By associating a user to a personnel number, the portal can recognize who that user is once they are logged in (Figure 4.2). This diagram illustrates how objects in OM support the portal to render the appropriate information on the various iViews. The portal can easily determine the user's position and organizational unit using the standard relationships.

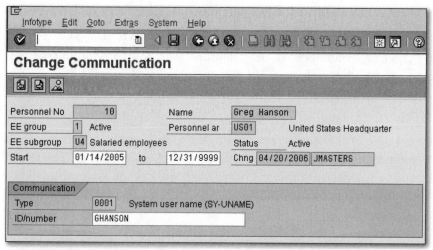

Figure 4.1 System User Name (SY-UNAME) for Employee Greg Hanson

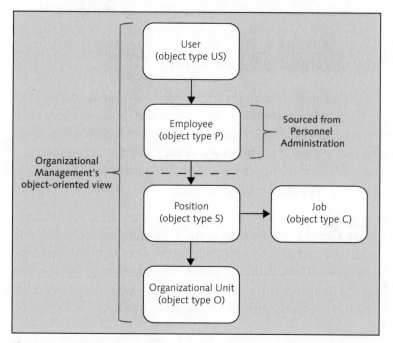

Figure 4.2 User, Employee, Position, Job, and Organizational Unit Objects and Their Relationships Placed Within the Context of Personnel Administration and OM

The user exists as an integrated object within OM — identified as object type US.

In our previous example, the user logged in (GHANSON) is associated with an employee (personnel number 10, Greg Hanson), who holds a position (and job) within an organization unit. Because the portal and ESS or MSS applications "know" this information, many iViews within the portal can act with a lot more intelligence.

Another example of this intelligence is with the identification of manager. Each user whose personnel number holds a position that is denoted as "chief" can immediately be recognized within the portal framework as a manager. This allows for dynamic, robust functionality on the portal — all based on standard SAP master data in the backend.

> **Note**
>
> A detailed discussion on the user (US) object and the various security roles needed to support ESS and MSS will be discussed in Chapter 9, "Authorization Management."

4.2 A Healthy Organizational Structure

One of the first items that should be on your list before implementing MSS is an evaluation of how "healthy" your organizational structure is. Although most companies do maintain an organizational structure today within the OM component, many are not doing the best job in supporting a hierarchy that is truly representative of HR. For example, what HR needs from their structure is not what Finance needs; it may not be what Procurement needs either.

Also, we have seen many organizations struggle to keep the organizational structure current. Even large organizations with a shared services model (either outsourced or insourced) have had difficulty maintaining the organizational hierarchy. New hires, transfers, promotions, reorganizations, reductions in workforce, and terminations all bring a tremendous amount of volatility to a company's organizational structure, and it is extremely difficult to keep it up to date.

4.2.1 Organizational Structure Basics

Before we gauge your preparedness for MSS given your current organizational structure environment, let's quickly review some basics around organizational maintenance. This will help ground us and help us move forward with ESS and MSS.

For MSS to function, a minimum requirement is to have implemented the OM component. OM is one of two "core" SAP ERP HCM components (the other being PA). Many clients are accustomed to maintaining their own organizational structure for employee tracking, organizational charting, and other purposes within this component. The structure may also support existing processes in other areas, such as Time and Expense approvals (for Finance), and workflow for approvals (for Procurement).

Organizational units are usually more granular than typical "departments." Take Finance for example. You would never have just one organizational unit to represent all of Finance. In fact, at a minimum, an organizational unit should be created for each one of your managers (the topic of manager is discussed later in this chapter). Each organizational unit will have one, and only one, "parent" organizational unit. Each organizational unit can have one or many "children" organizational units. These relationships form an organizational hierarchy that, for some large corporations, can be quite big. Global companies with operations in different countries end up having hundreds — even thousands — of organizational units.

In Figure 4.3, part of the organizational structure is displayed. A fictitious company, called ABC Global Corporation, is identified by the root organizational unit. Subordinate organizations have been tied to this parent organizational unit via the standard OM relationship 002. This relationship is used to connect all organizational units within the hierarchy.

By creating this structure, the "backbone" of MSS functionality is established. Organizational units allow managers to view the organization in a structured format (allowing a manager to see their full span-of-control — either "direct reports" or "direct and indirect" reports). The organizational structure also enables certain functionality in areas such as compensation management (by allowing budget units to be created based on the organization structure), performance management (by allowing appraisals to be created en masse using the organizational structure), as well as authorization management (by allowing structural authorization to use the organization structure for filtering purposes).

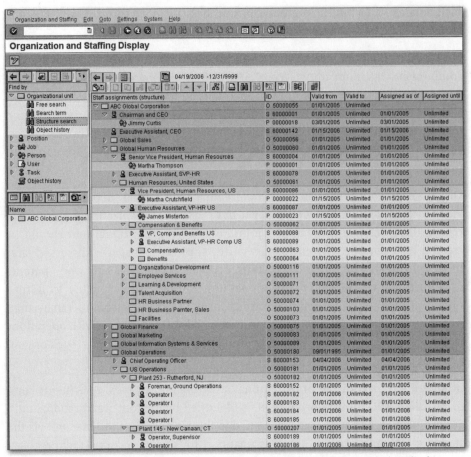

Figure 4.3 Example of an Organization Structure with Managers Identified with the "Chief" Relationship

4.2.2 Determining the Readiness of Your Organizational Structure

For the purposes of this book, we will assume that your company has already implemented OM and has been maintaining the organizational structure for a number of years. But, there are a few questions to ask yourself before you build your MSS functionality on top of your existing structure. These questions are meant to gauge your readiness. It is always better to step back for a moment and understand your existing design and habits before layering more complexity on top. So let's take a look at some questions and considerations.

Question #1: Has the "chief" manager relationship been implemented yet in your system?

Considerations: Without this critical relationship (relationship 012 between a manager's position and the organizational(s) unit they manage), out-of-the box MSS will not work. Although it is possible to deliver MSS functionality using other relationships to describe a manager in the system (e.g., the 002 "Reports To" relationship), you will not be able to leverage most of the standard MSS iViews in the business package if you do not use the chief relationship. We consider it a mandatory requirement for your system if you want to implement and sustain MSS. Put simply, the chief manager relationship is SAP software's way of identifying managers within the organizational hierarchy and your company should be following this business practice.

Question #2: Has the "chief" manager relationship been implemented consistently in your system?

Considerations: A consistent definition of the chief manager must be agreed and adhered to enterprise-wide. The consistency behind the use of this relationship is in large part a function of your organization's definition of a manager, and the definition of a manager is explored in detail later in this chapter. It is one of the more complex issues at its core, although from the outside, identifying a manager in the organization seems fairly straightforward.

Question #3: Does your structure represent an HR organizational structure or another structure, for example, Finance's cost center hierarchy?

Considerations: Some companies have set up their HR organizational structure incompletely or incorrectly. By this, we mean a structure that is not HR-centric. For example, several companies have created their organizational structure based on a cost center hierarchy or based principally by geography when, in reality, the organizational structure should be representative of an HR reporting hierarchy.

Tip

If your organizational structure is not set up to best support the HR function, this might be a good time to evaluate the feasibility of revamping your structure to support HR in addition to MSS. Of course, this must be done with extreme caution because you might have existing processes using the structure (for example, existing workflow processes).

Question #4: Has your organizational hierarchy been broken down to the lowest level possible?

Considerations: Some organizations have not provided the granularity needed to fully utilize the HR functionality inherent in MSS. Some organizational structures are broken down to only the director or senior manager level. Although this may be sufficient for processes that involve higher level staff (succession planning and workforce planning, for example), processes such as performance management, compensation management, leave request management, and personnel change requests are more and more frequently expected to be initiated by the manager "closest" to the employee. If this is the case, be sure that your organizational structure has the granularity it needs to support the processes you plan to support on the portal. This will most likely mean the creation of additional organizational units as well as additional chief relationship assignments.

Question #5: How up-to-date do you keep your organizational structure?

Considerations: Whether your company has a centralized HR function, shared services organization, or a decentralized structure, the organizational hierarchy is always changing due to employee movement and unexpected organizational events, such as reorganizations and reductions in workforce. As stated earlier, new hires, transfers, and terminations are just some of the ways your structure seems ever-changing. For large companies, literally hundreds of these actions are occurring every day. It is therefore easy to see how the structure can become stale if proper procedures are not instituted. Defined business procedures should be implemented and measured against. And metrics on transaction errors as well as speed of processing should be analyzed in order to understand how the HR structure can be more effectively managed.

We hope that these questions and considerations have given you some perspective on how ready your organizational structure is to support MSS. Depending on your current practices, MSS capability could be an easy transition for your service delivery. However, most customers have opportunities to improve their HR practices with respect to OM maintenance. In many respects, implementing MSS will expose your OM practices to your line management, which will, in the long run, improve quality of service and data accuracy.

4.3   Definition of Manager

For many organizations, defining a manager seems like a straightforward task, but it can quickly become complicated if your company places varying responsibilities on the different layers of management. Ask yourself this question: Are the same managers who are evaluating employees' performance (via performance appraisals) also involved in succession planning? If the answers is no, you are not alone because most firms permit succession management activities to a higher level of management. This is a classic example of the different layers of management. Line management versus middle management versus senior management — different managers such as these groups are typically responsible for different activities, with varying degrees of sensitive data.

If your company operates on a global scale, it is also likely that one country's definition of manager is different from another. For example, countries in Europe may be impacted by European Union regulations that may or may not correspond to an equivalent requirement in the United States or Canada. The level of "disclosure" for employee information may vary from country to country depending on each country's cultural and legal requirements. Data privacy laws in Europe may prohibit your managers from seeing information regarding their employees. HIPAA laws in the United States forbid managers from seeing benefits-related information on employees. Cultural factors play a role at a global level as well (and not just regulatory statutes). For example, salary and grade information in China is often not disclosed even within management circles compared with other countries in Asia and certainly around the globe.

Another question that must be considered is: What types of employees are being managed by the manager? In other words, is the manager managing salaried employees, hourly nonpay scaled employees, or hourly employees on a pay scale (i.e., step progression)? This will most likely mean very different levels of responsibility. Those employees on a union agreement, for example, will be managed differently through MSS, in part, based on the stipulated bargaining unit agreement. For example, because their base pay is based on a contractual agreement, the manager will most likely not have discretion on their merit increase. The union agreement may or may not allow managers to evaluate these employees via performance management. Especially challenging are those cases where a manager has a mix of bargaining unit and non-bargaining unit employees. In these cases, additional configurations or enhancements will most likely be needed in order to satisfy business requirements.

Now that we know some of the complexities behind the definition of a manager, let's review some of the standard definitions.

4.3.1 The "Chief" Manager

Within SAP ERP HCM, the "chief" relationship to define a manager drives MSS on the portal. Without this demarcation, managers would not be able to use any of the standard iViews within the MSS Business Packages. The concept of a "chief" manager is invaluable to a discussion concerning MSS.

From a system perspective, a chief manager is defined as an employee within your company who holds a position that has A 012 "Managers" relationship to one or more organizational units that he manages. In Table 4.1, the "top down" and "bottom up" OM relationships for the "chief" designation are listed. This is the standard configuration in the SAP system and should not be altered.

Object	Object Type Text	A/B	Relationship	Relationship Name	Related Object Type
O	Organizational unit	B (top down)	012	Is managed by...	S
S	Position	A (bottom up)	012	Manages...	O

Table 4.1 Standard OM Relationship A/B 012 Used to Define"Chiefs" in the Organizational Structure

To understand how to effectively use these relationships, it is important to understand the concept of time constraints. Time constraints determine how often infotype records can exist at one time (or if they are permitted to be valid at all times). The system uses these indicators as a way to retain data integrity. Every infotype has a time constraint configured, but it is not recommended that you change them. Table 4.2 describes the standard time constraints in the system.

SAP ERP HCM delivers the following time constraints for the chief manager A/B 012 relationship.

Time constraint	Time constraint text	Time constraint description
0	May only be present once	This time constraint allows a maximum of one infotype record of the same type for the same object at the same time.
1	Without gaps	This time constraint allows a maximum of one infotype record of the same type for the same object at the same time. No gaps in time can exist between records.
2	With gaps	This time constraint allows a maximum of one infotype record of the same type for the same object at the same time. Gaps in time can exist between records.
3	Unlimited	This time constraint allows for several infotype records of the same type for the same object at the same time. Gaps in time can exist between records.

Table 4.2 Standard Time Constraints in SAP ERP HCM

For the organizational unit object (O), the B 012 relationship "Is managed by" has a time constraint equal to 2. This means that only one position can manage an organizational unit at one time, but gaps can exist between the infotype records. In other words, there may be a period of time where there is not a chief identified for that organizational unit. This makes sense in situations where a manager leaves the company without a replacement, or for those organizational units that (for any number of reasons) simply do not have a chief assigned.

For the position object (S), the A 012 relationship "manages" has a time constraint equal to 3. This means that a manager's position can be a "chief" for just one or multiple organizational units. Managers having a span-of-control in different parts of the organization are becoming more and more frequent as functions, such as supply chain, procurement, and legal become more and more global. Typically, though, one manager has responsibility for one top-level organizational unit only (indicated by the "chief" relationship).

Although it is possible through configuration to change the time constraints of these relationships, it is not recommended to do so. From a business perspective you may have cases where HR feels that two managers "own" the same organizational unit, but it is not a Best Practice to represent this in the system. Defined business rules should be established to permit only one manager to be chief of an organizational unit (and, therefore, of an employee as well). There may indeed be instances where other types of managers need to be tracked in the system. For example, a company with a highly matrixed organization may need to enhance the system through the use of custom objects or relationships to satisfy their business requirements (see the upcoming discussion on "other" managers).

Each "chief" manager could have both direct and indirect reports. It is expected that a chief will at least have one direct report (i.e., those lowest level chiefs) unless a position is presently vacant. Those managers higher in the organization will have both direct and indirect reports. As an example, a supervisor on the ground at a factory might have only direct reports while a Chief Financial Officer (CFO) will most certainly have both direct and indirect reports.

> **Note**
>
> The term "span-of-control" describes the full breadth of responsibility for a manager, (i.e., their full list of direct and indirect reports). In several MSS processes, such as compensation management, managers may be responsible for managing and approving their full "span-of-control" in addition to their planning responsibilities for their direct reports. Traditionally, the more vast a manager's "span-of-control," the more varied and critical the manager's job responsibilities are.

From an OM context, it is important to define what a direct report is. On the surface, it seems like it would be fairly easy to define. However, placed within the context of the SAP organizational structure, a more detailed explanation is needed.

A direct report can fall into one of the following three categories:

1. An employee who holds a position in an organizational unit that the manager managers;

2. An employee who themselves hold a chief position in a subordinate organizational unit;

3. An employee who holds a position in a subordinate organizational unit that does not itself have a chief position assigned. This employee, therefore, inherits the chief assignment.

In Figure 4.4, a portion of an organizational structure is represented as viewed from Transaction PPOSE. In this example, both Barbara Thompson and Martha Crutchfield are chief managers within this part of the organizational structure. (In the SAP system, positions in red color indicate that these positions are chiefs for the organizational unit). Kyle Johnson and Martha Crutchfield are direct reports to Barbara Thompson. James Miserton is an indirect of Barbara Thompson; his chief manager is Martha Crutchfield.

Global Human Resources	O	50000060	01/01/2005	Unlimited	01/01/2005	Unlimited
Senior Vice President, Human Resources	S	60000004	01/01/2005	Unlimited	01/01/2005	Unlimited
Barbara Thompson	P	00000001	01/01/2005	Unlimited	01/01/2005	Unlimited
Executive Assistant, SVP-HR	S	60000078	01/01/2005	Unlimited	01/01/2005	Unlimited
Kyle Johnson	P	00000021	01/15/2005	Unlimited	01/15/2005	Unlimited
Human Resources, United States	O	50000061	01/01/2005	Unlimited	01/01/2005	Unlimited
Vice President, Human Resources, US	S	60000086	01/01/2005	Unlimited	01/01/2005	Unlimited
Martha Crutchfield	P	00000022	01/15/2005	Unlimited	01/15/2005	Unlimited
Executive Assistant, VP-HR US	S	60000087	01/01/2005	Unlimited	01/01/2005	Unlimited
James Misterton	P	00000023	01/15/2005	Unlimited	01/15/2005	Unlimited

Figure 4.4 Example Snippet of an Organization Structure, Viewed From Transaction PPOSE, Showing Direct and Indirect Reports to Chief Managers

Some questions companies ask related to the chief manager are: *Where should chief managers sit in the organizational structure? In the same organizational unit they manage or in the organizational unit above? Can the chief sit in a completely different part of the organizational structure from which they manage?*

The answer to all of the above questions is *yes*. The placement of the chief position can either be in the organizational unit in which they manage or in the superior organizational unit to the one they manage. In most companies, we have seen the chief sit in the same organizational unit in which they manage. Occasionally (and more frequently for Executives and for cross-functional or cross-geographical management), a chief can sit in an entirely different section of the organization structure from which they manage. For example, a global Vice President (VP) of Supply Chain may need to be a chief for several top level organizations. The exact placement of this chief would most likely depend on who this VP reports to. If this VP reported to the Chief Operating Officer (COO), for example, this VP would need to be identified as a direct report based on the criteria laid out earlier in the chapter.

> **Note**
>
> In the older versions of SAP software, the manager relationship was defined by the A/B 002 "Reports To" relationship. This relationship has since been replaced by the chief A/B 012 "Managers" relationship.
>
> The standard MSS iViews will not work with the S-S reporting relationships. Additional configuration within the Object and Data Provider (OADP) Framework is possible if you wanted to leverage the iViews, but it is not recommended as you would be going off strategy. It is recommended that if you are currently using S-S reporting relationships, that you switch your reporting relationships to the chief relationship concepts in order to prepare your organization for current and future MSS functionality from SAP software.
>
> S-S relationships require extra maintenance because they need to be maintained one-for-one at the position level. The chief relationship, by contrast, is maintained only once at the organizational unit level and therefore reduces your overall maintenance effort.

In addition to the chief manager, other managers frequently need to be identified either for reporting or for transactional needs. These types of managers are discussed next.

4.3.2 Other Managers

Many companies need to identify a variety of managers to support their business requirements. The chief manager designation is, in most cases, not enough to capture the entirety of the management at a company. Typically, the chief manager represents the "lowest level" manager, but other managers are usually needed to support other processes. Some popular "other managers" include the following:

- dotted-line manager
- dual-line manager
- functional manager
- legal manager
- operational manager
- headcount-approval manager
- budgeting manager
- compensation-approval manager
- succession-planning manager

This is just a sampling of the variety of managers an organization can have. Let's take the dotted-line manager as an example. A dotted-line manager — a manager who may have functional responsibility for an employee — may need to provide feedback and input during the performance management and compensation management processes. In this case, the dotted-line manager may need to be represented in HCM as a custom relationship. This is quite common. Using the OADP, discussed in Chapter 8, "Advanced Concepts in Employee and Manager Self-Service," custom views can be created to allow different managers access to information about their indirect reports.

4.4   Position and Vacancy Management

Another important fundamental component for the successful rollout of MSS is position management. Position management is defined as the administration of SAP positions (object type S) in order to effectively track object history, vacancies, and employee transactions (such as new hires, position changes, and terminations). Positions are one of the central constructs in all of SAP HR — positions connect many meaningful parts of HR together including employee, job, organizational unit, qualifications, and even cost centers. Figure 4.5 shows a pictorial description of how central the position is in SAP HCM. In this figure, the position is shown as a black chair integrated with the job, organizational unit, and other objects.

Typically, each employee holds one position. In some cases, an employee can hold multiple positions (in the case of a job share or in the event of a backfill, for example), but it is not common in most companies. Every position will be tied to one job (object type C). The job holds important information, such as the salary structure information (including salary/pay grade) on its Infotype 1005 "Planned Compensation." This information (and much more) can be defaulted from the job when an employee is hired into that position.

Each position can either be vacant or filled. Vacancy information is stored on Infotype 1007 in OM. Figure 4.6 shows a position, "Sales Support Assistant," whose vacancy is indicated as "Open." By flagging this position as vacant, several HR processes can be supported. For example, online Personnel Change Request (PCR) Adobe forms for E-Recruiting that may require knowledge of the vacancies within a manager's span-of-control can be implemented. Transfers, both within and outside a manager's span-of-control, can be implemented through PCRs as well as if vacancies are maintained consistently.

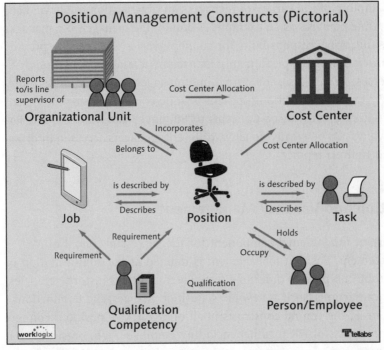

Figure 4.5 The Position Object (Represented as a Black Chair) in Context with Other Objects and Relationships in OM

Caution!

A position with a vacancy status of "Open" on its Infotype 1007 does not necessarily mean that the position has no holder (i.e., has no employee assigned). Rather, an "Open" headcount can mean that the system will identify this in headcount reports and in other process areas (such as E-Recruiting) as a position that should be considered vacant now or in the future. This way, a position that is currently held (but that is known to be vacant in the future) can be requisitioned for within E-Recruiting.

If business procedures are established for positions and vacancies, HR processes can become enabled on the SAP Portal by the standard iViews available within the MSS Business Package. Several standard iViews track vacancy and position holder information. If this data is not properly and consistently maintained, you will not be able to benefit from the standard functionality available on the portal.

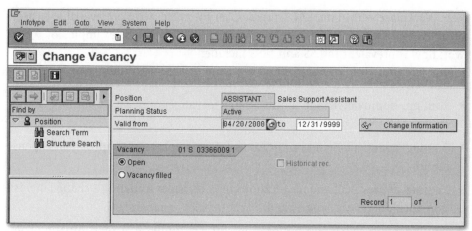

Figure 4.6 OM Infotype 1007 "Vacancy"

> **Note**
>
> Some clients engage in a "claiming process" before going live with MSS. This process may include a claiming procedure, where managers "claim" their direct reports to HR or a project team. Typically, HR Managers or HR Generalists in the field provide assistance with this process because they know the management and organization better than anyone else.
>
> You might be surprised by how many managers cannot identify their own direct reports. This process also brings awareness to the manager's responsibilities that could prompt a wake-up call to those managers who do not understand the full requirements of being a leader of others.
>
> The real advantage of doing this exercise is that you are able to clean up your organizational hierarchy before rolling out any functionality to managers. Imagine rolling out compensation management and having managers see salaries for employees that don't even report to them. For some customers, there may be merit in doing this extra effort to confirm the structure.
>
> More detailed information on positions, vacancies, and the "chief" relationship can be found in Sylvia Chaudoir's book, *Mastering SAP ERP HCM Organizational Management* (Galileo Press/SAP PRESS; 2008).

4.5 Workflow

This section serves as an introduction to SAP workflow. Chapter 8 will explore workflow in greater detail. Without workflow, many ESS and MSS processes could not exist. The same workflow-enabled processes that are supported by the Business Workplace within the SAP Graphic User Interface (GUI) are available to users on the SAP Portal via the Universal Worklist (UWL). A few examples of where workflow is prevalent in ESS and MSS include:

▶ Routing, approval(s), and notifications for an employee requesting leave;

▶ Routing, approval(s), and notifications for an employee submitting a time sheet;

▶ Routing, approval(s), and notifications for an employee submitting an expense report;

▶ Routing, approval(s), and notifications for a manager initiating a change in position, including pay changes; and

▶ Routing, approval(s), and notifications for a planning manager initiating compensation adjustments for a merit increase.

In addition to handling the routing and approvals, workflow controls the notifications behind the process. By notifications, we mean work items and emails. For example, if HR needs to be notified after an employee updates his bank details, a workflow can be triggered to send an email or send a work item notification to a group box. So, when would you send a work item versus an email?

Typically, you would send a work item if there is something actionable for the recipient to do. In this example, if HR is needed to validate the employee's bank information, then the workflow should be generating a work item so progress can be tracked and monitored. Once the HR resource completes the activity, the workflow would continue to its next approval or until the process ends.

However, if there is nothing actionable and the participant in the process has only to be informed, an email (sent to the corporate Outlook, Lotus Notes, etc.) may be a better option, because it's questionable how often a user will check their portal inbox for work items or notifications.

4.5.1 Workflow Basics

Workflows are based on workflow templates defined in the system. Many workflow templates (object type WS) are provided out of the box. These templates are frequently copied into the customer's name space and enhanced based on your company's specific business requirements. It is actually quite common for customers to enhance the standard workflows, because SAP software could never deliver something that could be used 100% by all companies. Custom workflows can be created from scratch as well, but are less common.

Note

Detailed information on workflow can be found in Alan Rickayzen's book, *Practical Workflow for SAP: Effective Business Processes Using SAP's WebFlow Engine* (Galileo Press/SAP PRESS; 2002).

One of the most robust aspects of workflow is that every step in the workflow history is logged. A full audit trail is recorded throughout the entire lifetime of the workflow. All users involved in the routing and approval process are monitored as well. Within each workflow, actions by users (identified as agents) are documented in the system. In Figure 4.7, the full audit log trail of a custom workflow for delegation is recorded with a history of all users who have been involved in the process up until this part of the process. Workflow logs offer robust functionality to track down exactly who touched what and when.

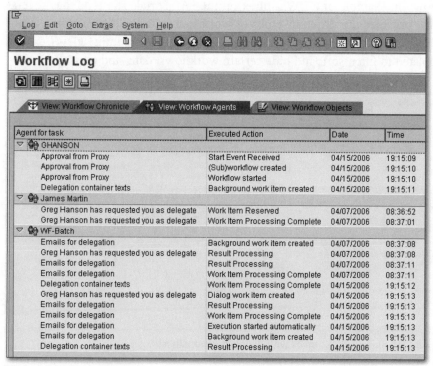

Figure 4.7 View of Workflow Agents within a Workflow Log

Now that we have the basics of workflow, let's look at the portal inbox functionality, the UWL.

4.5.2 UWL

The UWL is the central repository for all inbox activity on the SAP Portal. The workflow-enabled actions during an approval process (for example, the approval of an expense report) are routed through to this iView. This iView provides a similar view of work items on the portal as Transaction SBWP (Business Workplace) provides in the SAP GUI. Through portal configuration, you can determine if you want only some work items to appear in the UWL.

The UWL enables a process to become web enabled. Work items can be created and routed based on business rules. A work item, for example, may be needed to request an "approve" or "reject" decision or allow the user to click into another transaction to follow up with an open item for comments. Much of the user experience on the UWL is driven by configuration in the portal via XML files. Figure 4.8 shows an example of a UWL inbox on the SAP Portal. The UWL has several tabs that organize the different types of work items (Tasks, Alerts, Notification, Tracking, etc.). Additional tabs can be created and the columns' views can be manipulated to filter, sort, and hide certain workflows, data, and messages.

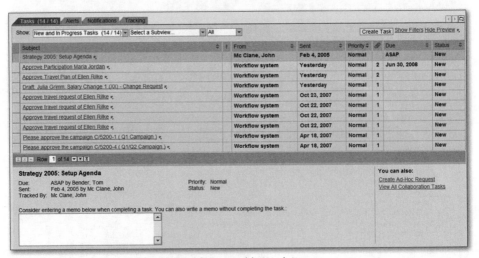

Figure 4.8 Example of a UWL Inbox with Actionable Work Items

One of the most important points is that workflow cannot function without an organizational structure. Approval routing is based on set business rules. For example, the approval for a leave request for three days of bereavement versus the approval for one year of unpaid leave will most likely need a different set of approvals. Based on your company's business rules, the workflow can easily use role resolution to route the request accordingly. In the example above, the request for bereavement may only need a direct manager (i.e., chief manager) approval whereas the unpaid leave may need two or three levels of management approval as well as HR approval. As you can see, without a healthy organizational structure and a consistent business process for position maintenance, workflow routing within self-service would be impossible.

4.6   Summary

In this chapter, we reviewed some of the baseline components for enabling ESS and MSS functionality. First, we discussed the basics of the PA component. In order for self-service to be viable, both an employee and user master record must exist with sufficient data and authorizations. Second, a robust organizational structure is needed in order to provide the foundation on which to build MSS transactions. Without a solid organizational hierarchy, the system will not know how to render the organizational hierarchy. Third, the *chief* relationship is paramount to the identification of managers within the company. The chief manager relationship enables viewing and transacting on direct and indirect reports using standard MSS iViews within the portal. Although alternatives do exist to identify other types of managers within your system, it is advisable to utilize the chief relationship wherever possible in order for you to take full advantage of standard MSS functionality. Finally, the organizational structure and chief relationship support the robust workflow capabilities. Workflow is used to support many processes and services, including leave requests, personnel change requests, and performance management. Workflows can be used to send out actionable work items or email notifications.

In the next chapter, "ESS and MSS Installation and Setup," we dive into the technical installation and setup of the application.

A successful Employee Self-Service (ESS) and Manager Self-Service (MSS) installation and setup is an important piece to get your implementation started on the right foot. In this chapter, we discuss the steps needed to deploy and configure the employee and manager business packages within your SAP Self-Service environment.

5 ESS and MSS Installation and Setup

The installation of ESS and MSS is composed of several steps and components. The components that need to be installed and configured will depend on your implementation and the applications that you want to leverage.

In this chapter we will discuss the installation process and the dependencies that are needed, including portal and SAP backend settings. We will also highlight the compatible versions that need to be matched during installation.

5.1 Terminology

SAP software has introduced many new technologies in the latest versions of the backend system, SAP NetWeaver Portal and Web Dynpro applications. The following list of terminology will provide you with a high-level understanding of the various components and systems related to installing and configuring self-service applications.

▶ **System Landscape Directory (SLD)** is the central information provider in a system landscape. The SLD acts like a directory or registry that holds information about all of the components that are installed in the system and their versions. The SLD also contains information about all of the installed systems in the landscape, making it easier to refer to components in your landscape.

▶ **Business Package:** The business package is a collection of portal objects (components in your portal, such as iViews, Worksets, Pages, etc.), and applications, roles and base configurations that you can install to get specific functionality within your SAP NetWeaver Portal. Business packages are grouped into business roles and typically contain self-service applications or iViews that expose applications and content that caters to that role.

- **Single Sign-On** (SSO) allows you to configure the system so that users log in to the portal once and, depending on authorizations, can navigate to other parts of the system and use the same portal credentials to get access without requiring additional logins

- **Java Connector (JCO)** provides front-end applications within the portal the ability the connect to SAP backend functionality. JCO is also used for nonportal applications

- **Adobe Document Services (ADS)** is an advanced technology offered by Adobe and integrated into the SAP system. ADS allows for the generation of Acrobat forms that merge SAP data and user input in a powerful form-based solution. ADS generates a PDF for users with the ability to gather user input and perform document and field-level validation.

5.2   ESS Installation

In order to implement ESS functionality, you must first download and install the Business Package for ESS from the online SAP Developer Network (SDN) community. The content is sourced from the SAP Content Portfolio *https://www.sdn.sap.com/irj/sdn/contentportfolio*. Figure 5.1 shows the SAP Portal Content Portfolio with a listing of all business packages that can be downloaded and imported into your own portal.

Welcome to the SAP Portal Content Portfolio

Portal & Collaboration SDN Page // Product Availability Matrix for Portal Content

The Portal Content Portfolio is your location for downloading predefined, packaged portal content to speed up your portal implementation. This business content consists of iViews bundled into hundreds of role-specific business packages based on solutions from SAP. You can browse the portfolio according to user roles. By then clicking a title in the resulting list of packages, you receive additional details about that package. To download portal content, click on the Download link for the respective list entry. Please note that SAP Se required for this.

If you encounter an error page after Service Marketplace login, please check with your account manager if you have the license(s) required for the respective business package.

Portal content developed by partners is available via the Partner Directory.

Most newly developed Business Packages are now downloadable and installable via SAP Solution Manager. They are therefore not listed in the Portal Content Portfolio here on SDN.

Categories: **Business Packages for Every User** | Business Packages for Managers | Business Packages for Specialists

Download	Title	Release	Availability
🔽	Business Package for Common Parts (mySAP ERP)	1.0	Unrestricted Shipment
🔽	Business Package for Design Collaboration	60.1	Unrestricted Shipment
🔽	Business Package for DMS Connector for KM	1.0	Unrestricted Shipment
🔽	Business Package for Employee Self-Service (mySAP ERP 2004)	60.2	Unrestricted Shipment
🔽	Business Package for Employee Self-Service (mySAP ERP)	1.0	Unrestricted Shipment
🔽	Business Package for Employee Self-Service 4.6C - 4.7	50.4	Unrestricted Shipment
🔽	Business Package for Learning	50.2	Unrestricted Shipment
🔽	Business Package for Learning	1.0	Unrestricted Shipment
🔽	Business Package for Project Portfolio Management and Design Collaboration	4.0 SP4	Unrestricted Shipment
🔽	Business Package for Project Self-Service (mySAP ERP)	1.0	Unrestricted Shipment
🔽	Business Package for Projects	50.3.1	Unrestricted Shipment
🔽	Business Package for SAP Higher Education and Research	1.0	Restricted Shipment
🔽	Business Package for SAP xApp Resource and Portfolio Management	2.0 SP7	Unrestricted Shipment

Figure 5.1   SAP Portal Content Portfolio, Showing Category Business Packages for Every User

Within the SAP Portal Content Portfolio, select the category Business Packages for Every User (if not already set). Depending on your portal and SAP backend versions, you will need to install one of the following ESS business packages.

Table 5.1 lists the released ESS business packages available for download. Each business package is listed in the table with its version, compatible ERP Central Component (ECC) backend release, and compatible portal release.

Business Package Name	Version	ECC Backend Release	Portal Release
Business Package for ESS (mySAP ERP)	1.0	ECC 6.0	SAP NetWeaver 7.0 (2004s) (SP Stack 05 and higher)
Business Package for ESS (mySAP ERP 2004)	60.2	ECC 5.0	SAP NetWeaver '04 (SP Stack '03 and higher), SAP NetWeaver 7.0 (2004s) (SP Stack '04 and higher)
Business Package for ESS 4.6C - 4.7	50.4	4.6C and Enterprise 4.7	Enterprise Portal 5.0 (SP 5 and higher), Enterprise Portal 6.0 (SP 0 and higher)

Table 5.1 Available ESS Business Packages

To download any one of these business packages, click on the Download icon next to the business package's name. Once selected, the system will ask you for your service marketplace ID. After validating your user name and password, the software component application (SCA) files relevant to the implementation can be found via the path: BP ERPO5 ESS 1.0. • BP ERPO5 ESS 1.0 • #OS INDEPENDENT • DOWNLOADS (see Figure 5.2).

After all of the files have been added to your download basket, you can download these objects onto your server for installation. You can reference SAP Note 761266 (Self-Service Patches).

Internet Transaction Server (ITS) — an important technology that served as the foundation for SAP software's earlier ESS functionality — has been moved into the SAP NetWeaver stack. Therefore, no standalone ITS functionality is supported. Rather, an "Integrated ITS" is available for those customers who still need an environment to utilize ITS-based transactions. SAP Note 709038 discusses the

Integrated ITS. Note 870126 (ITS-based ESS services in SAP ERP2005) explains the strategy for moving from ITS-based transactions to Web Dynpro applications.

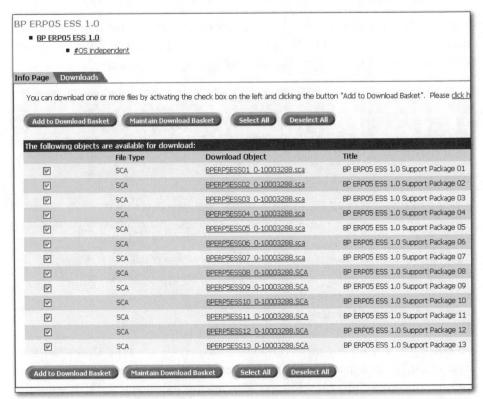

Figure 5.2   Downloading SCA Files from the SAP Portal Content Portfolio

> **Note**
>
> As of SAP ERP 2004, most services within the business packages have been converted to Web Dynpro for Java technology. Other useful technology SAP Notes include Note 870126 (ITS-based ESS services in mySAP ERP 2005), Note 952692 (Transfer of SAP MSS functions to mySAP ERP 2005), and Note 953254 (Transfer of ERP processes (HCM) into new functions).

This concludes the installation and setup of components within the ESS business package. Now let's discuss how to set up MSS.

5.3 MSS Installation

As with ESS, the installation procedures for MSS follow the same procedures.

Within the SAP Portal Content Portfolio (see Figure 5.3), select the suitable category Business Package for Managers. This contains a list of business packages. Depending on your Portal and SAP backend versions, you will need to install one of the following ESS business packages.

Figure 5.3 SAP Portal Content Portfolio, Showing Category Business Packages for Managers

Table 5.2 lists the released ESS business packages available for download. Each business package is listed in the table with its version, compatible ECC backend release, and compatible portal release.

Business Package Name	Version	ECC Backend Release	Portal Release
Business Package for MSS (mySAP ERP)	1.0	ECC 6.0	SAP NetWeaver 7.0 (2004s) (SP Stack '05 and higher)
Business Package for MSS (mySAP ERP 2004)	60.1.2	ECC 5.0	SAP NetWeaver '04 (SP Stack '03 and higher), SAP NetWeaver 7.0 (2004s) (SP Stack '04 and higher)
Business Package for MSS	60.1.20	4.0B, 4.5A, 4.5B, 4.6A, 4.6B, 4.6C, 4.7, or ECC 5.0	Enterprise Portal 5.0 (SP 5 and higher), Enterprise Portal 6.0 (SP 0 and higher)

Table 5.2 Available MSS Business Packages

To download a business package, click on the Download icon to the left of the business package's name. Once selected, the system will ask you for your service marketplace ID. After validating your user name and password, the SCA files relevant for the implementation can be found via the path: BP MSS (ERP 2004) 60.1. • BP ERP05 ESS 1.0 • #OS INDEPENDENT • DOWNLOADS.

In addition to a business package, the Business Package for Common Parts (mySAP Enterprise Resource Planning (ERP)) must be implemented if the Business Package for MSS (mySAP ERP) is implemented (i.e., if you are running ERP 2005). This business package, containing "common parts," consists of iViews, worksets, and pages that are used in several roles in SAP ERP 2005.

5.4 Configuring Connections

Once you have uploaded the business packages and Web Dynpro applications for ESS and MSS, you need to configure the appropriate connections for the applications to interact with the backend SAP ECC system.

5.4.1 Setting Up the JCo Connections

Web Dynpro applications use SAP JCo to connect to the SAP ECC system. You will need to configure your JCo connections using the Content Administrator for Web Dynpro Applications.

To get access to the Web Dynpro Content Administrator, you will need to log in to the portal using an administrator ID. Once you have logged into the portal, select the Content Administration tab and then select the Web Dynpro option in the second-level navigation. Figure 5.4 shows the content administrator screen. Content Administrator for Web Dynpro allows you to see all of your Web Dynpro applications and configure your JCo connections.

Select the Maintain JCo Destinations button to bring up the screen that contains your JCo destinations. If you don't see any destinations listed, then cancel and select Create JCo Destinations. Figure 5.5 shows the screen that appears when you select Maintain JCo Destinations.

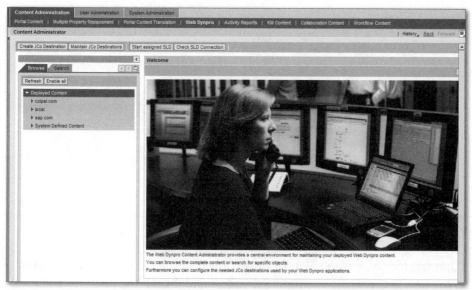

Figure 5.4 Content Administrator Central Configuration Environment for Web Dynpro Applications

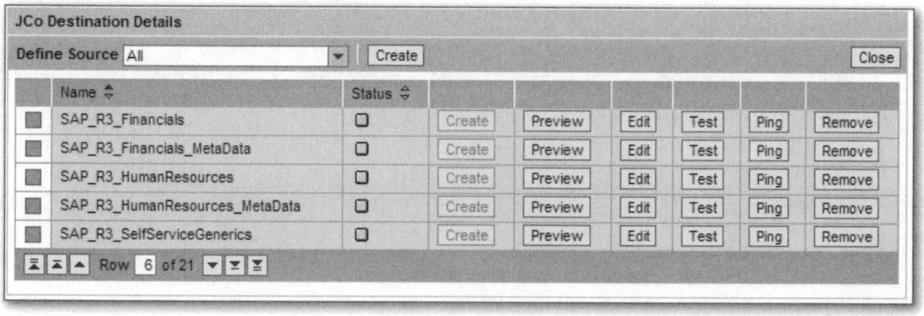

JCo Destination Details

Define Source All | Create | Close

	Name	Status						
	SAP_R3_Financials		Create	Preview	Edit	Test	Ping	Remove
	SAP_R3_Financials_MetaData		Create	Preview	Edit	Test	Ping	Remove
	SAP_R3_HumanResources		Create	Preview	Edit	Test	Ping	Remove
	SAP_R3_HumanResources_MetaData		Create	Preview	Edit	Test	Ping	Remove
	SAP_R3_SelfServiceGenerics		Create	Preview	Edit	Test	Ping	Remove

Row 6 of 21

Figure 5.5 Destinations That Have Been Configured in the Web Dynpro Content Administrator

JCo destinations need to be created for both applications and metadata. Any destination that is determined as required and has not been created will show up with a red status, which indicates it needs to be created.

Let's configure the SAP_R3_HumanResources destination. To configure the destination, you select the Edit or Create button and complete the wizard process. Figure 5.6 shows the first step in the wizard.

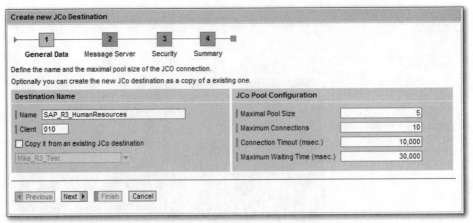

Figure 5.6 General Data for the JCo Connection Creation

Complete the name of the destination and the respective client that it will point to in the SAP ECC system. Additionally, you should discuss the pool size and maximum connections with your Basis administrator before configuring these settings in production. These settings need to be based on the results of performance tests, the size of the hardware, and the number of users that will use these applications concurrently.

In the next step, you need to configure the Message Server for your SAP ECC system. Figure 5.7 shows the second step in the wizard.

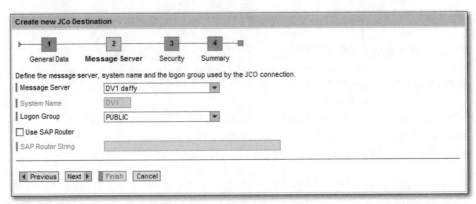

Figure 5.7 Message Server Configuration for the JCo Destination

In step 2, you need to provide the corresponding message server and logon group that were configured in SAP ECC. Select next.

The last step in the configuration is the security. You will use the Used Method equal to User / Password (see Figure 5.8) when configuring an application destination you will set the Used Method to Ticket.

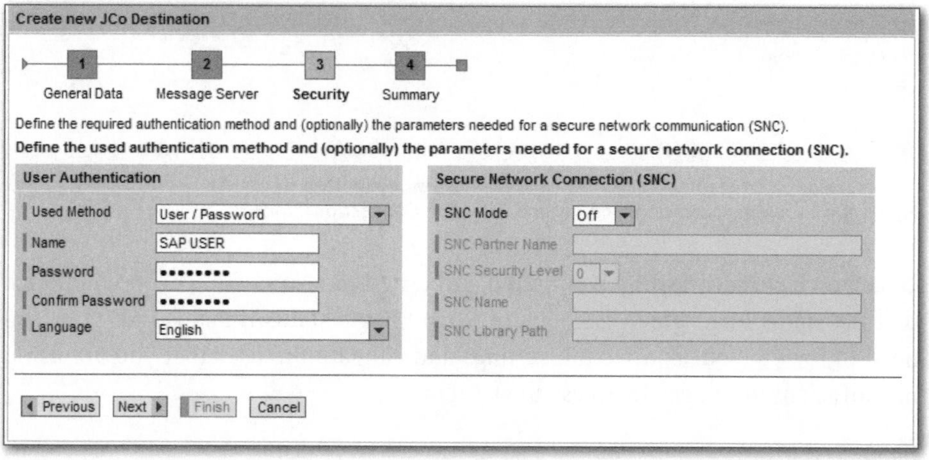

Figure 5.8 Security Configuration for the JCo Destination

Also, when creating a destination for metadata, change the destination name to SAP_R3_HumanResources_MetaData. This will eliminate any confusion in your system when you are determining which connection is used for what purpose.

When creating the different connections for application data versus metadata, you will need to select the correct data type. Figure 5.9 shows the wizard for creating a new connection. If you are creating a destination connection for metadata then you need to select the Dictionary Meta Data connection type. If you are creating a destination connection for applications, then you need to select the Application Data connection type.

Notice that we selected a different authentication security mechanism for each connection type. The reason for this is that the metadata calls happen independent of the application data calls and once the metadata is retrieved, it is cached for later use. Metadata is also not user dependant and does not need to be associated with the user that is using the application.

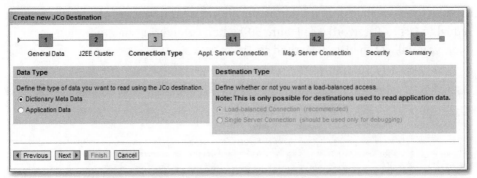

Figure 5.9 Creating New Connections and Selecting Connection Type

Once you have successfully configured and tested the connections you will notice that the status turns green (see Figure 5.10). If the status remains red, then you need to review your connection settings and validate the user that you are using has sufficient privileges to access the system.

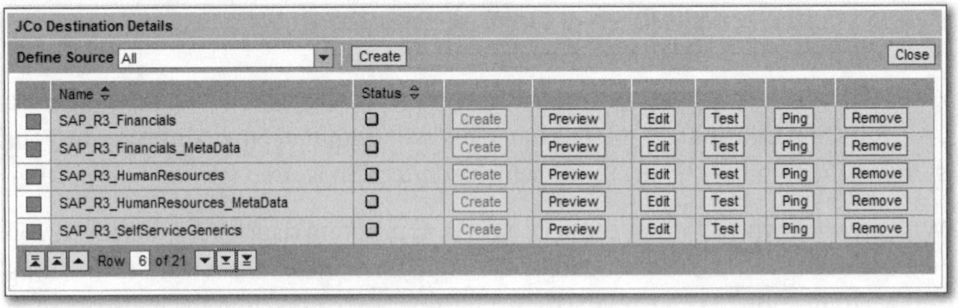

Figure 5.10 Destinations Configured Correctly

Depending on which applications you will be using, you need to configure the following destinations:

▶ SAP_R3_HumanResources

▶ SAP_R3_HumanResources_MetaData

▶ SAP_R3_Financials

▶ SAP_R3_Financials_MetaData

▶ SAP_R3_Travel

- SAP_R3_Travel_MetaData
- SAP_Web Dynpro_XSS

5.4.2 Configuring the System Connections in SAP NetWeaver Portal

To complete the connection setup, you will need to set up system landscape connections in the SAP Portal. You will need to log in to the portal with the appropriate administrator access and navigate to System Administration and then select System Configuration. You will see the System Landscape section in the portal. You must browse to your connection or create one in the appropriate folder. Common practice is to create a folder called Landscape Connections.

Once you have created your folder, right-click on the folder and select New System (from the template). You will be presented with a list of templates to choose from. Select the one that is appropriate to your step and click on Next. Provide System Name, ID, and prefix for your connection. Figure 5.11 shows the list of templates that will be presented when selecting New (from the template).

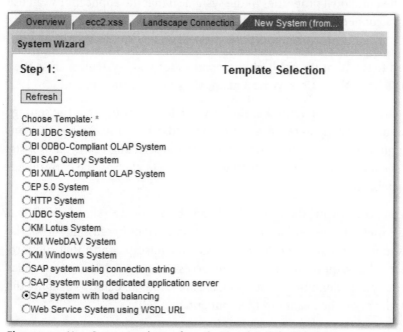

Figure 5.11 New System Landscape from the Template Selection Screen

Once you have created the system, you will need to configure the properties. Right-click on the system and select Open Object as shown in Figure 5.12.

Figure 5.12 Open System to Configure Properties

You can set the individual properties in the system so that the applications can use the settings to connect to the corresponding connection. Figure 5.13 shows the SAP ECC connection settings set under the property category Connector.

You will need to set all of the applicable properties for your system, such as Web Application Server (WAS), User Management, User Administration, and ITS.

Once a system has been configured, it can be validated to ensure that the settings are correct and connecting to the systems in the landscape. You can test the connection by right-clicking on the system landscape and selecting Connection Tests. Figure 5.13 shows the option in the menu when you right-click on the corresponding system landscape.

The final step in configuring the system landscape is to provide a set of aliases that can be used to refer to the connections. This is important because it allows the applications to use a set alias and have one system landscape entry that supports all applications that require the same system access. Figure 5.14 shows the alias settings in the system definition. You can navigate to this screen by changing the Display dropdown on the header of the Configuration tab.

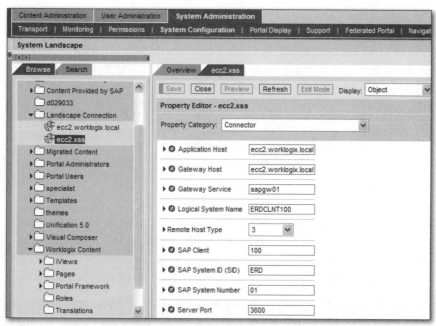

Figure 5.13 Property Configuration of the System Landscape

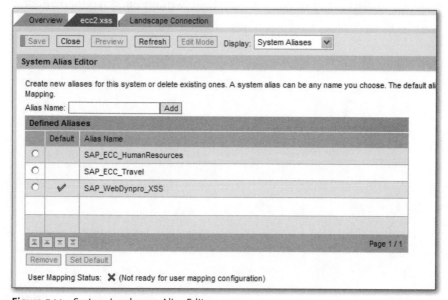

Figure 5.14 System Landscape Alias Editor

Once the connections are in place you can start to work with your self-service applications and confirm they are working. Additionally, you may need to configure SSO between your SAP Portal and backend systems. SAP software has created help content specifically for configuring SSO between the SAP Portal and the corresponding backend systems.

Refer to the following for detailed steps in configuring SSO: *http://help.sap.com/ saphelp_nw70/helpdata/EN/89/6eb8deaf2f11d5993700508b6b8b11/frameset.htm.*

5.5 Summary

The process for installing ESS and MSS is fairly straightforward once you get the software from the SAP Service Marketplace and apply all of the software components into the system. Depending on your specific requirements, you will need to install and configure Adobe Document Services and other specific components.

Remember to match your system releases with the software you are downloading and to try and move to the latest versions of the applications and business packages.

Let's move on to discuss the standard functionality within Employee Self-Service.

Employee Self-Service (ESS) has been around for more than a decade, but over the past few years SAP software's solution has evolved to become one of the leading platforms for allowing employees to view and update their own data. This chapter explores the functionality available in the latest release of SAP ERP HCM — both from the portal and backend perspective.

6 Functionality Available in Employee Self-Service

Whether it's entering time, requesting leave, accessing pay statements, enrolling in benefits, or simply updating an address, ESS empowers employees in the organization. Providing employees an online mechanism to update and view their HR data has become the norm with most companies today. With the ERP Central Component (ECC) 6.0 release, the SAP system has provided its farthest reach into the self-service area for the employee. A new suite of services is provided — delivered via the SAP NetWeaver platform. This new technology platform has created quite a buzz in the industry, as its open standards and more robust development environment have convinced customers that self-service is viable and here to stay. SAP software has also placed a heavier focus on user experience — an area in which many clients feel SAP has not delivered in the past. Look-and-feel and usability are more critical in the self-service space, as these online applications have farther reach within organizations. Some applications, such as Performance Management, may be used by all employees within the company.

In this chapter, we will review the basics of SAP's ESS functionality. We will cover the out-of-the-box roles, worksets, iViews, and overall self-service framework. We will focus our attention on select iViews, as covering every iView in detail within the business package would not be within the scope of this book.

6.1   Application Components for ESS

Each iView within ESS is associated with an application component. This application component defines the associated support area within the SAP system — an important item when logging customer messages or searching for SAP Notes. The application component for ESS is Cross-Application (CA-ESS) and Personnel Administration (PA-ESS). CA is used because some of the services in ESS span across different SAP software components. PA is associated to services supporting infotypes within the Personnel Administration component, such as IT0002 (Personal Data), IT0006 (Address), IT0009 (Bank Details), and IT0021 (Family Data).

> **Note**
>
> There are many "cross-application" uses of ESS — several of which are outside the HCM component. For example, using procurement functionality within ESS, employees can create and manage goods and services they have purchased through the portal. (As a prerequisite for procurement, you must have implemented the SAP Supplier Relationship Management (SRM) component). Within the Cross-Application Timesheet (CATS) component, work orders, purchase orders, and WBS elements can be associated to recorded time entries on an employee's time sheet. Equipment monitoring is another ESS service whose core functionality does not exist in HR.

PA-ESS is further broken down into PA-ESS-DE for Germany-relevant transactions, PA-ESS-US for US-relevant transactions, and PA-ESS-OCY for transactions related to all other countries. Also, PA-ESS-XX (for "Common Parts") is general to all countries while PA-ESS-XX-CE is reserved for Concurrent Employment–related transactions.

CA-ESS is further broken down into ITS-based technology and Web Dynpro technology. CA-ESS-ITS (ESS ITS) and CA-ESS-WD (ESS Web Dynpro) are the two sub-application components available. Functionality within the CA-ESS-ITS will not be discussed here, because our focus will be on the latest Web Dynpro technology, which is represented as CA-ESS-WD. This application component supports both Web Dynpro for Java and Web Dynpro for ABAP.

It is important to note that although the majority of the business package for ESS is based on Web Dynpro for Java, the latest Web Dynpro applications are being built on the Web Dynpro for ABAP technology. (For example, the latest in Travel Management uses the Web Dynpro for ABAP technology even though there is similar technology supported using Web Dynpro for Java.) Despite this being SAP software's technology direction, Web Dynpro for Java is still SAP software's technology solution for most applications within the latest business package and is supported like any other standard application.

In the following section, we will discuss how services within ESS are rendered on the SAP NetWeaver Portal. Using SAP software's standard Homepage Framework, page layout and navigation for ESS services are streamlined as configurable items within the Implementation Guide (IMG).

6.2 ESS Homepage Framework

The Homepage Framework provides the foundation for navigation, look-and-feel, and overall user experience for ESS. Its components exist as configuration activities within the IMG to provide more flexibility and reduced maintenance. The configuration for the Homepage Framework can be accessed a few ways for ESS applications via the path: PERSONNEL MANAGEMENT • EMPLOYEE SELF-SERVICE • GENERAL SETTINGS • HOMEPAGE FOR SELF-SERVICES OR VIA CROSS-APPLICATION COMPONENTS • HOMEPAGE FRAMEWORK. In each of these IMG sections, the following components of the Homepage Framework are configured:

- Area Group Pages
- Area Pages
- Subareas
- Services
- Resources

We will review each component of the framework and provide example configuration entries when applicable. Each element is a building block of the framework and, like many other configurations, dependencies exist.

As discussed, the framework provides the ability to integrate services into the portal. The logical grouping of services (whether they be transactional or non-transactional in nature) allow you to construct an experience for the end user — all using configuration in the IMG. What does this mean from a project and support perspective? It means that the self-service platform in the SAP system can be supported using more functional resources and less technical and portal resources because the navigation is based on standard configuration entries and not through portal configuration or development, such as Java.

Let's get started in our review of the framework. We will first start with the area group page.

6.2.1 Area Group Page

An area group page is essentially the homepage or landing page of an ESS "Area." An area group page contains a pictogram (i.e., a graphic in either .JPG or .GIF format), header, short description, and (optionally) a "Quick Links" section. It provides the linking to area pages (discussed next). Figure 6.1 shows the standard area group page.

Figure 6.1 Standard Area Group Page

> **Note**
>
> Quick Links can be placed inside both area group pages and area groups. They provide users with a shortcut to the most popular services. For example, if timesheets are one of the more frequently used applications within your company, a Quick Link, perhaps labelled "Submit Your Time," could be placed on your area group page. When clicked, the timesheet would be launched directly (bypassing the area page).

Figure 6.2 shows area group SAPDEFAULTESS_ERP2005, which is the default area group for the landing page within the latest business package for ESS.

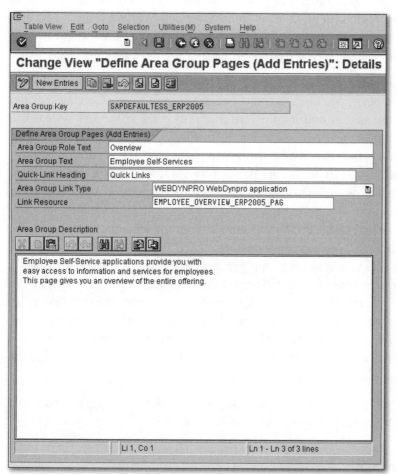

Figure 6.2 Area Group Page SAPDEFAULTESS_ERP2005 Tied to Link Resource EMPLOYEE_ OVERVIEW_ERP2005_PAG and Other Key Data

Area group pages can be changed in view V_T7XSSSERARGBC in Transaction SM30 or by following the IMG path: CROSS-APPLICATION COMPONENTS • HOMEPAGE FRAMEWORK • HEADERS AND AREA GROUP PAGES • DEFINE AREA GROUP PAGES • DEFINE AREA GROUP PAGES (CHANGE ENTRIES). Standard settings can be manually overwritten by choosing the same key SAPDEFAULTESS_ERP2005 (in this example) and providing different information. The system will know to replace the standard configuration entries with your customer-specific information. For example, the area group description could be changed to read something more relevant to your organization. The area group role text could also be changed from "Overview" to "Welcome." This area group text provides the heading of the page and tab on the portal. Users will see this text in the second-level navigation when they log in and click on ESS.

In addition to changing the existing area group page via the override feature explained previously, you can also create new area group pages. You may consider doing this if you are customizing the layout of the portal, as the SAP system will most likely keep a consistent, simplified user experience for their out-of-the-box configuration. In order to add new area group pages, add a new entry in view V_ T7XSSSERARGB. You can do this via Transaction SM30 or through the IMG path: CROSS-APPLICATION COMPONENTS • HOMEPAGE FRAMEWORK • HEADERS AND AREA GROUP PAGES • DEFINE AREA GROUP PAGES • DEFINE AREA GROUP PAGES (ADD ENTRIES). Adding a new area group page may be needed if, for example, your implementation had multiple employee portal roles. For example, you might have different services available for hourly employees versus salaried employees. Conceivably, you could also cater a different user experience for executives versus nonexecutives. (The concept of an "executive dashboard" is becoming more commonplace within the industry). After an analysis of your business requirements, the need for additional "landing pages" should become clear to you. Do you have subsidiaries within company that need a totally different user experience? If you have union or bargaining unit employees, do they need a different set of services?

Next, we discuss an area page. The area page links within an area group page and is another fundamental component in the framework.

6.2.2 Area Page

An area page contains services that are related to each other. The Personal Information area page, for example, contains services such as address, bank information, family members/dependents, and personal data. Employees access area pages from an area group page. You can either accept the standard layout or modify the area page based on your business requirements.

The area page for Personal Information (defined in the SAP configuration as EMPLOYEE_PERSINFO_ERP2005), for example, defines the area page for the Personal Information section of the site (see Figure 6.3 for how it appears on the portal). This area page contains the text of the area, the picture resource (in this case, EMPLOYEE_PERSINFO_PIC), an area description (summary), and area description (long text) among other information. The area description (long text) is what is shown on the right of the page, while the area group description (summary) is what is on the higher level area group page as a blurb of what is contained on the area page.

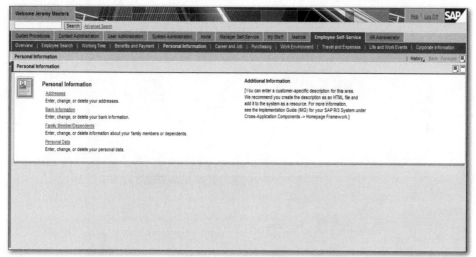

Figure 6.3 Standard Area Page Personal Information

Changing an Area Page

Area pages can be changed in view V_T7XSSSERARBC via Transaction SM30 or by following the IMG path: Cross-Application Components • Homepage • Framework • Areas • Define Areas • Define Areas (Change Entries). Standard settings can be manually overwritten by choosing the same key EMPLOYEE_PERSINFO_ERP2005 (in this example, see Figure 6.4) and providing a different configuration. For example, the summary or long-text area description could be changed to something more relevant to your organization. Perhaps you would like to add helpdesk numbers to your HRIS or Information Technology (IT) organization, or maybe provide links to frequently asked questions about the service.

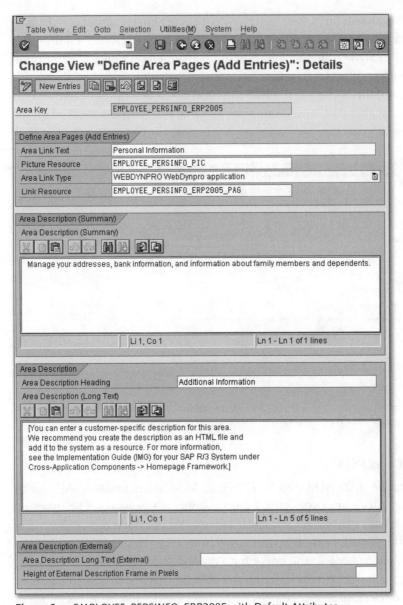

Figure 6.4 EMPLOYEE_PERSINFO_ERP2005 with Default Attributes

Hiding an Area Page

You will most likely want to remove certain area pages from the standard configuration. If you want to hide any area pages, you should never delete the entries from the area group page or area page tables. Rather, you should enter a "0" in the position field next to the appropriate field in view V_T7XSSSERARGC in Transaction SM30 or by following the IMG path: CROSS-APPLICATION COMPONENTS • HOMEPAGE FRAMEWORK • AREAS • ASSIGN AREAS TO AREA GROUP PAGES • ASSIGN AREAS TO AREA GROUP PAGES (ADD AND CHANGE ENTRIES). This way, if you ever want to integrate the page back into your framework in the future, you can do so by simply assigning a new value in the Position field.

Creating a Custom Area Page

You may need to create new area pages if the standard pages do not fully meet your business requirements. If you need to create custom area pages, you will need to perform activities in both the SAP Portal and the SAP backend system. These activities are outlined next.

In the SAP Portal, perform the following tasks. You will need to work closely with your portal team to complete these tasks as they involve creating portal objects. Implement the following changes:

1. Create a custom workset in your customer name space that will define your custom area.

2. Create at least two pages for this workset — one that defines the menu and one that contains the services.

3. Create two iViews, both of type SAP Web Dynpro iView. One iView will need to call the XSSMenuArea application. The parameter sap.xss.menuarea on the iView must contain the area key you define in the "Define Area" IMG activity. For example, the application parameters for your custom iView might be something like: sap.xss.menuarea=Z_EMPLOYEE_SEARCH &sap.xss.menuargrp=SAPDEFAULTESS_ERP2005, where Z_EMPLOYEE_SEARCH is the custom area page you have defined in the IMG and SAPDEFAULTESS_ERP2005 is the standard area group page you want to embed the custom area page within.

In the SAP backend, you must perform the following tasks:

1. Define Resource for Area Page. A resource must be defined for your area pages. A custom employee search resource for an area page could be named Z_EMPLOY-

EE_SEARCH_ PAG, for example. You do this through the IMG path: CROSS-APPLICATION COMPONENTS • HOMEPAGE FRAMEWORK • RESOURCES • DEFINE RESOURCES • DEFINE RESOURCES (ADD ENTRIES). Resources will be discussed in more detail later in the chapter.

2. Define Resource for Pictogram. Including a pictogram for your area page is optional. A custom resource for the pictogram could be named Z_EMPLOYEE_SEARCH_PIC, for example. Be sure to specify the image file in the field "Object Name."

3. Define Area. A custom area needs to be created. The custom area page could be named Z_EMPLOYEE_SEARCH. You can do this through the IMG path: CROSS-APPLICATION COMPONENTS • HOMEPAGE FRAMEWORK • AREAS • DEFINE AREAS • DEFINE AREAS (ADD ENTRIES).

4. Assign Area to Area Page Group. After creating your Custom Area, you can assign it to a Standard or Custom Area group page. You can do this through the IMG path: CROSS-APPLICATION COMPONENTS • HOMEPAGE FRAMEWORK • AREAS • ASSIGN AREAS TO AREA GROUP PAGES • ASSIGN AREAS TO AREA GROUP PAGES (ADD AND CHANGE ENTRIES). In our example, custom area page Z_EMPLOYEE_SEARCH would be assigned to standard area group page SAPDEFAULTESS_ERP2005.

Following these steps should allow you to incorporate a custom area page within your portal's Homepage Framework. This also provides lots of flexibility with how your employees experience the portal.

In addition to area pages, subareas are another way to delineate the services available through ESS.

6.2.3 Subareas

Using a subarea, you can split an area into two or more sections. For example, the area page EMPLOYEE_BENEFITPAY_ERP2005 is composed of subareas EMPLOYEE_BENEFITPAY_SUBBENEFITS_2005 and EMPLOYEE_BENEFITPAY_SUBPAYMENT_2005. Subarea EMPLOYEE_BENEFITPAY_SUBBENEFITS_2005 is in position 1 while Subarea EMPLOYEE_BENEFITPAY_SUBPAYMENT_2005 is in position 2, meaning the Benefits subarea will appear on top of the Pay subarea on the area page. Figure 6.5 shows area pages with their respective subareas and their position IDs.

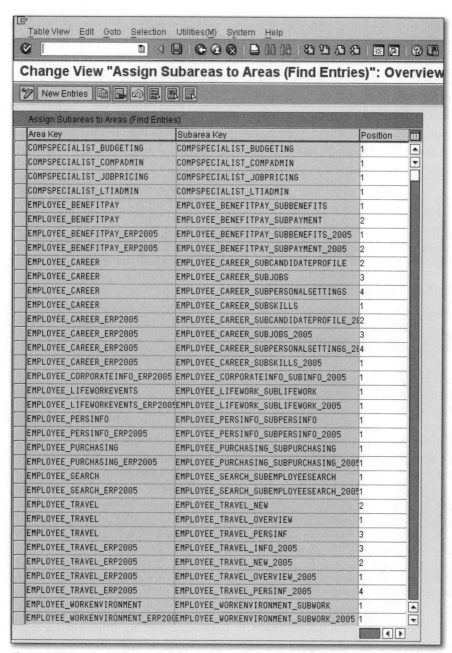

Table View   Edit   Goto   Selection   Utilities(M)   System   Help

Change View "Assign Subareas to Areas (Find Entries)": Overview

New Entries

Assign Subareas to Areas (Find Entries)

Area Key	Subarea Key	Position
COMPSPECIALIST_BUDGETING	COMPSPECIALIST_BUDGETING	1
COMPSPECIALIST_COMPADMIN	COMPSPECIALIST_COMPADMIN	1
COMPSPECIALIST_JOBPRICING	COMPSPECIALIST_JOBPRICING	1
COMPSPECIALIST_LTIADMIN	COMPSPECIALIST_LTIADMIN	1
EMPLOYEE_BENEFITPAY	EMPLOYEE_BENEFITPAY_SUBBENEFITS	1
EMPLOYEE_BENEFITPAY	EMPLOYEE_BENEFITPAY_SUBPAYMENT	2
EMPLOYEE_BENEFITPAY_ERP2005	EMPLOYEE_BENEFITPAY_SUBBENEFITS_2005	1
EMPLOYEE_BENEFITPAY_ERP2005	EMPLOYEE_BENEFITPAY_SUBPAYMENT_2005	2
EMPLOYEE_CAREER	EMPLOYEE_CAREER_SUBCANDIDATEPROFILE	2
EMPLOYEE_CAREER	EMPLOYEE_CAREER_SUBJOBS	3
EMPLOYEE_CAREER	EMPLOYEE_CAREER_SUBPERSONALSETTINGS	4
EMPLOYEE_CAREER	EMPLOYEE_CAREER_SUBSKILLS	1
EMPLOYEE_CAREER_ERP2005	EMPLOYEE_CAREER_SUBCANDIDATEPROFILE_2005	2
EMPLOYEE_CAREER_ERP2005	EMPLOYEE_CAREER_SUBJOBS_2005	3
EMPLOYEE_CAREER_ERP2005	EMPLOYEE_CAREER_SUBPERSONALSETTINGS_2005	4
EMPLOYEE_CAREER_ERP2005	EMPLOYEE_CAREER_SUBSKILLS_2005	1
EMPLOYEE_CORPORATEINFO_ERP2005	EMPLOYEE_CORPORATEINFO_SUBINFO_2005	1
EMPLOYEE_LIFEWORKEVENTS	EMPLOYEE_LIFEWORK_SUBLIFEWORK	1
EMPLOYEE_LIFEWORKEVENTS_ERP2005	EMPLOYEE_LIFEWORK_SUBLIFEWORK_2005	1
EMPLOYEE_PERSINFO	EMPLOYEE_PERSINFO_SUBPERSINFO	1
EMPLOYEE_PERSINFO_ERP2005	EMPLOYEE_PERSINFO_SUBPERSINFO_2005	1
EMPLOYEE_PURCHASING	EMPLOYEE_PURCHASING_SUBPURCHASING	1
EMPLOYEE_PURCHASING_ERP2005	EMPLOYEE_PURCHASING_SUBPURCHASING_2005	1
EMPLOYEE_SEARCH	EMPLOYEE_SEARCH_SUBEMPLOYEESEARCH	1
EMPLOYEE_SEARCH_ERP2005	EMPLOYEE_SEARCH_SUBEMPLOYEESEARCH_2005	1
EMPLOYEE_TRAVEL	EMPLOYEE_TRAVEL_NEW	2
EMPLOYEE_TRAVEL	EMPLOYEE_TRAVEL_OVERVIEW	1
EMPLOYEE_TRAVEL	EMPLOYEE_TRAVEL_PERSINF	3
EMPLOYEE_TRAVEL_ERP2005	EMPLOYEE_TRAVEL_INFO_2005	3
EMPLOYEE_TRAVEL_ERP2005	EMPLOYEE_TRAVEL_NEW_2005	2
EMPLOYEE_TRAVEL_ERP2005	EMPLOYEE_TRAVEL_OVERVIEW_2005	1
EMPLOYEE_TRAVEL_ERP2005	EMPLOYEE_TRAVEL_PERSINF_2005	4
EMPLOYEE_WORKENVIRONMENT	EMPLOYEE_WORKENVIRONMENT_SUBWORK	1
EMPLOYEE_WORKENVIRONMENT_ERP2005	EMPLOYEE_WORKENVIRONMENT_SUBWORK_2005	1

Figure 6.5 Standard Area Page to Subarea Mapping Configuration Table

Subareas provide a way to group services together logically. Within the Personal Information subarea (EMPLOYEE_PERSINFO_SUBPERSINFO_2005), for example, services for address (EMPLOYEE_PERSINFO_ADDRESS05), bank information (EMPLOYEE_PERSINFO_BANK05), family data (EMPLOYEE_PERSINFO_FAM-MEMBER05), and personal information (EMPLOYEE_PERSINFO_PERSDATA05), are listed along with a position ID (which positions them from top to bottom of the screen). These associations are made in the configuration via IMG path: CROSS-APPLICATION COMPONENTS • HOMEPAGE FRAMEWORK • SERVICES • ASSIGN SERVICES TO SUBAREAS • ASSIGN SERVICES TO SUBAREAS (ADD AND CHANGE ENTRIES).

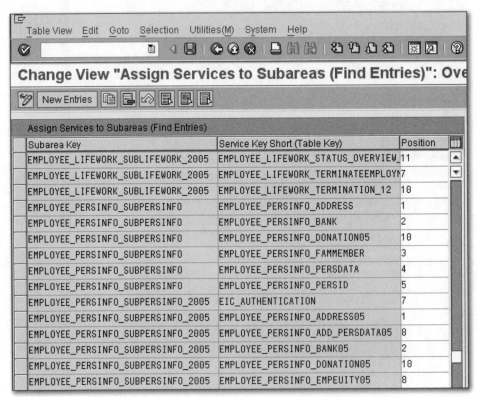

Figure 6.6 Standard Services to Subarea Mapping Configuration Table

Figure 6.6 shows the mapping of subareas to services. The position operates in the same fashion as the other areas within the Homepage Framework configuration:

the links to the services on the screen are listed from top to bottom based on position number, meaning that a service with a position ID of 1 would appear above a service with a position ID of 2.

So far, we have discussed how to configure area group pages, area pages, and subareas. This provides the navigation and layout for the employee. Ultimately though, it is in the contents of the service where the user will transact or view. Let's discuss what services are and how they are configured.

6.2.4 Services

Services drive all transactions and content in ESS. A service is associated with one of several different kinds of "service types." (Service types are described in Table 6.1, covered later.) A service is also associated to an area page via a subarea. For each service, a hyperlink and a short description appear on the area page. This provides the user with access to that service as well as basic information on what the service does.

Defining a Service

Services are defined in view V_T7XSSSERSRV. You can access this view in Transaction SM30 or by following the IMG path: Cross-Application Components • Homepage Framework • Services • Define Services • Define Services (Add Entries) to add new services. For changing services, you must configure activity Cross-Application Components • Homepage Framework • Services • Define Services • Define Services (Change Entries). The "Add Entries" and "Change Entries" delineation is consistent with the rest of the Homepage Framework configuration. If you want to leverage the existing service but override part of the standard configuration, you can provide your customer-specific information by "changing" entries. "Adding entries" means you have defined a brand new service without reference to an SAP standard service.

An example service EMPLOYEE_PERSINFO_BANK05, seen in Figure 6.7, has a service type of Web Dynpro (Web Dynpro Java application). This means that the service is linked to a Web Dynpro for Java application.

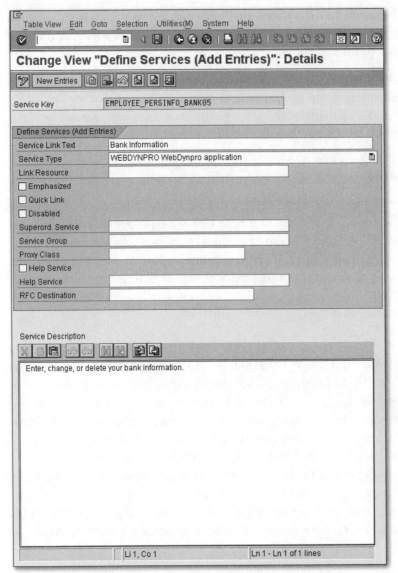

Figure 6.7 Bank Information Service EMPLOYEE_PERSINFO_BANK05

The Homepage Framework supports the following service types: BSP, ITS, POR-TALPAGE, URL, or Web Dynpro. Table 6.1 lists all service types as well as a short definition, directory path (if relevant), and any object name requirements.

Service Type	Service Type Description	Directory Path	Object Name
BSP	Service built with Business Server Page (BSP)	No Entry	BSP Application/BSP Page
ITS	ITS-based Service	No Entry	ITS Application
PORTALPAGE	A call to a Portal page (in the Portal Content Directory)	No Entry	No Entry
URL	Direct URL launched in a separate window	You can either enter the relevant parts of the URL in the Directory Path and Object Name fields or enter an absolute URL in the URL of PCD Page field.	
Web Dynpro	Web Dynpro Java application	Vendor/ DC-Name	Web Dynpro Application
WDABAP	Web Dynpro ABAP Application	No Entry	No Entry

Table 6.1   Available Service Types and Expected Configuration Values

Let's look at an example of a widely used service for employees. Within ESS, the "Record Working Time" functionality allows employees to submit their timesheets via the standard CATS functionality. The standard service EMPLOYEE_WORKTIME_ RECORDWORKTIME05, as seen in Figure 6.8, is used to link to this application.

The service type for this service is identified as a Web Dynpro Java application, meaning the underlying technology used is Web Dynpro for Java. The "Link Resource" is defined as EMPLOYEE_RECORDWORKTIME_SERVICE05 for the Record Working Time application. A "link resource" (or simply "resource") provides the specifics of the application (including object name, directory path, URL, etc.). Resources are discussed in more detail later in this chapter. Every service must be assigned to a resource, either explicitly or indirectly via the configuration. The distinction is based on whether or not the application is country specific or not.

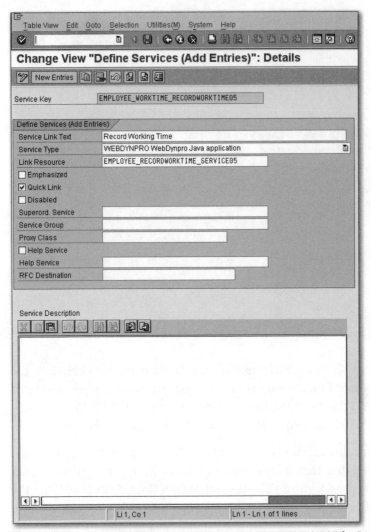

Figure 6.8 Service EMPLOYEE_WORKTIME_RECORDWORKTIME05 for Recording Working Time Using the CATS Application

Let's look at an example with a service that is country specific. Services that are country specific are configured differently. Service EMPLOYEE_PERSINFO_ BANK05, for example, does not have an explicit reference to a resource link. See Figure 6.9. In order to assign resources for country-specific services, you must link each service to a resource defined in view V_T7XSSSERSRVCG, found in the IMG via path: CROSS-APPLICATION COMPONENTS • HOMEPAGE FRAMEWORK • SERVICES • DEFINE COUNTRY-SPECIFIC SERVICES • DEFINE COUNTRY-SPECIFIC SERVICES.

Using this method, you only have to define a service once in view V_T7XSSS-ERSRV, regardless of whether or not it is country specific. You would only configure view V_T7XSSSERSRVCG to assign resources to a service if there were country variations. For example, service EMPLOYEE_PERSINFO_BANK05 is linked to resource EMPLOYEE_BANK_US_SERVICE05 for country grouping 10 (United States) but uses service EMPLOYEE_BANK_VE_SERVICE05 for country grouping 17 (Venezuela's bank information service).

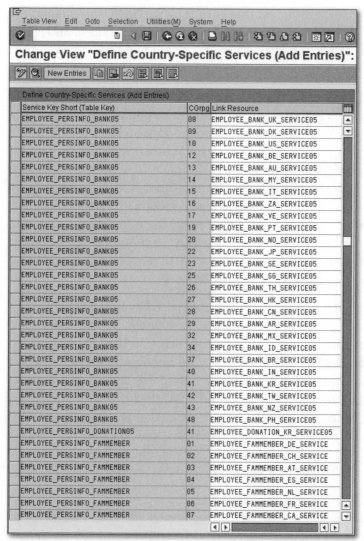

Figure 6.9 Service EMPLOYEE_PERSINFO_BANK05 Linked to Several Country-specific Resources

There is other configuration on the service that you may want to use within your implementation. For example, if the "Emphasized" checkbox is checked, attention can be drawn to the service link – the ❶ icon is placed to the left of the link. You can do this, for example, if benefits enrollment is ending soon and you want employees to be aware of the need to complete their enrollment.

As mentioned previously, the "Quick Link" checkbox would be checked if you need the service link to be available on the area group page.

If the "Disabled" checkbox is checked, the link for the service is rendered (for display purposes), but the user cannot access the hyperlink. The service name appears in grey text instead of a blue hyperlink. You may want to do this if you want to restrict users from accessing functionality but not remove the access point from the portal.

You can also logically group services together. You can do so via superordinate services as well as service groups. Although not as popular, these groupings can provide a further breakdown of the area page and subarea. For example, a service group called *Additional Travel Information* could contain three services: Corporate Travel Policy, Visa Information, and Travel Risk and Threat Advisory. Like a subarea for the area page, the service group allows a logical grouping of services. The definition of service groups is performed in the configuration by following the IMG path: CROSS-APPLICATION COMPONENTS • HOMEPAGE FRAMEWORK • SERVICES • DEFINE SERVICE GROUPS. The actual assignment of the service group to the service is performed in the service configuration itself (view V_T7XSSSERSRV).

A very powerful part of the ESS framework is the *proxy class concept*. A service that contains a proxy class allows you to influence the behavior of the service using your own customer-specific programming. To do this, you need to create a class that implements the IF_XSS_SER_PROXY_SERVICE interface. In the standard system, proxy class CL_PAYSLIP_PROXY_SERVICE is used within the standard service for pay check statements, EMPLOYEE_BENEFITPAY_PAYCHECK05. This proxy class can influence when this service is visible or hidden to the employee. This may be important during or after payroll processing time, because you may not want an employee viewing his pay stub during certain time periods. Functionality such as this can be affected using a proxy class.

A service can also be defined as a help service. Service EIC_SERVICE_REQUEST, for example, is defined as a help service (via the Help Service checkbox and, therefore, appears in the drop down for Help Service). Help services typically accompany transactional services to provide assistance with the completion of the transaction. When an employee clicks on this link, he can fill out an Adobe form and send the request to the Employee Interaction Center (EIC).

In addition, a Remote Function Call (RFC) destination is provided in the event that the service is found on another logical system. Providing the logical system name can enable you to access services residing in other environments.

> **Tip**
>
> If you have a country-specific service that should only be available for one country, you can configure this using views V_T7XSSSERSRV and V_T7XSSSERSRVCG. The trick is to define the service in V_T7XSSSERSRV without explicitly naming a resource. In view V_T7XSSSERSRVCG, only assign the resource to the country that you want to make the service available to. For example, if your company does business in the United States, Mexico, and Venezuela, you could make the service only available in the United States and Venezuela (but not Mexico) by defining the resources in V_T7XSSSERSRVCG but not defining any resource for Mexico.

Integrating Your Custom Service

If you need to integrate a new service into the Homepage Framework, you will need to follow the next procedure. You might need to integrate a service if, for example, you have created a new custom application (i.e., a Web Dynpro for Java or Web Dynpro for ABAP application). Perform these four steps to integrate a new custom service into your landscape:

1. *Define Server* (optional). Defining a server for a resource is an optional step. Resource servers are defined in detail later in the chapter.

2. *Define Resource.* A resource must be defined for your custom application. You do this through the IMG path: CROSS-APPLICATION COMPONENTS • HOMEPAGE FRAMEWORK • RESOURCES •DEFINE RESOURCES •DEFINE RESOURCES (ADD ENTRIES). Resources will be discussed in more detail later in the chapter.

3. *Define Service.* The custom service will need to be created. Be sure to include references to your link resource and identify the correct service type (Web Dynpro for Java, BSP, etc.).

4. *Assign Service to a Subarea.* As mentioned previously, your services can only be included in the framework by assigning it to a subarea. The subarea is included within an area page housed within your portal layout.

Removing Services

As with area pages, you can remove (hide) services within your Homepage Framework using standard configuration. To do this, enter "0" in the position field next to the appropriate service in view V_T7XSSSERSARC in Transaction SM30 or by following the IMG path: CROSS-APPLICATION COMPONENTS • HOMEPAGE FRAMEWORK • SERVICES • ASSIGN SERVICES TO SUBAREAS • ASSIGN SERVICES TO SUBAREAS (ADD AND CHANGE ENTRIES). This way, if you ever want to integrate the service back into your framework in the future, you can do so by simply assigning a new value in the position field.

Confirmation Screen Links

At the end of all standard ESS transactions, a confirmation screen appears. The SAP system provides a standard way of offering the choices on the screen by changing the configuration in view V_T7XSSSERLNK in Transaction SM30, or by following the IMG path CROSS-APPLICATION COMPONENTS • HOMEPAGE FRAMEWORK • SUBAREAS • DEFINE LINKS ON CONFIRMATION PAGE. Figure 6.10 shows the confirmation screen links for the standard service EMPLOYEE_PERSINFO_US_BANK.

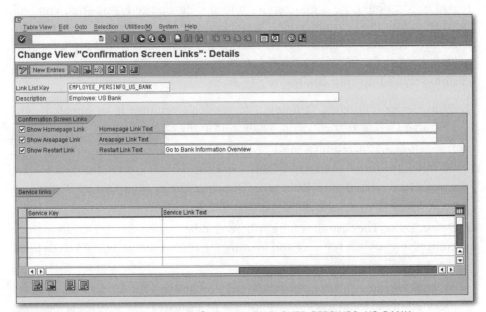

Figure 6.10 Confirmation Screen Links for Service EMPLOYEE_PERSINFO_US_BANK

You have the option to show the link back to the homepage, an area page, or to restart the service. You can also override the default text by entering content in the textbox next to the Homepage Link Text, Area page Text Link Text, or Restart Link Text. Also, additional service links can be included by providing the appropriate service and link text in the area entitled *Service links* found at the bottom of the screen.

Figure 6.11 shows what the confirmation screen looks like on the SAP Portal. The links appear after the question "What do you want to do next?". Options "Go to Bank Information Overview," "Go to Personal Information Overview," and "Go to Employee Self-Services Homepage" will take the user back to the service, the area page, or homepage, respectively. Additional configured service links would appear below these links.

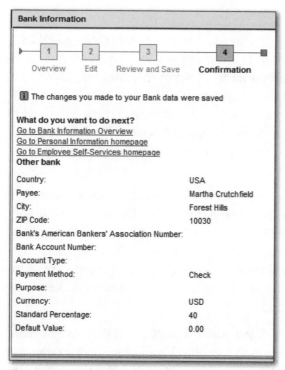

Figure 6.11 Confirmation Page for Bank Information Service

Now that we have reviewed services, including their definition and how they can be catered to handle country-specific scenarios via standard configuration, let's move on to *resources,* which are equally important because they provide further technical details behind a service.

6.2.5 Resources

A resource is another basic building block within the SAP ESS solution. Resources can be transactional and non-transactional assets. Each component of ESS at its lowest level is a resource. Resources are also reusable. Once defined, resources can be used anywhere in the portal. Resources are referenced by a service.

A resource is defined in the IMG by following the path: CROSS-APPLICATION COMPONENTS • HOMEPAGE FRAMEWORK • RESOURCES • DEFINE RESOURCES • DEFINE RESOURCES (ADD ENTRIES) to define new resources, and path: CROSS-APPLICATION COMPONENTS • HOMEPAGE FRAMEWORK • RESOURCES • DEFINE RESOURCES • DEFINE RESOURCES (CHANGE ENTRIES) to change existing resources.

As an example, Figure 6.12 displays the standard resource EMPLOYEE_ADDRESS_ US_SERVICE05 (US Address Service). This resource is a Web Dynpro-based application and has *sap.com/ess~us~* address for its Directory Path and Per_Address_US for its Object Name. The URL of the Portal Content Directly (PCD) Page is specified as *ROLES://portal_content/com.sap.pct/every_user/com.sap.pct.erp.ess.bp_folder/ com.sap.pct.erp.ess.roles/com.sap.pct.erp.ess.employee_self_service/com.sap.pct.erp.ess. employee_self_service/com.sap.pct.erp.ess.area_personal_information/persinfo_us/com. sap.pct.erp.ess.add.*

The resource tells the system the exact application to call when rendering the service (that has called the resource). Whether it is Web Dynpro for Java, Web Dynpro for ABAP, Business Server Page (BSP), ITS, or portal link, these resources serve as the key indicator for the application to render a specific technical application. All portal components (regardless of the technology used) require a resource assigned to them in order to render within the Homepage Framework. Resources provide this fundamental layer to ESS.

In addition to the directory path, object name, and PCD location, one or more URL parameters can be passed on to the technical application. For example, a BSP resource EMPLOYEE_CANDIDATE_PROFILE_SERVICE05 contains parameters passed to E-Recruiting BspClient=XXX&rcfLogAppl=PROFILE_BUILDER where XXX is the client where the E-Recruiting profile builder resides. Another example is for the Web Dynpro for ABAP iView within the HCM Processes and Form functionality. This iView contains URL parameters as INITIATOR_ROLE=HRASRB&PERNR_MEM_ID=MSS01 within the MSS_HCM_HRAS_START_PROCESSES resource. These parameters are passed to this application during initialization.

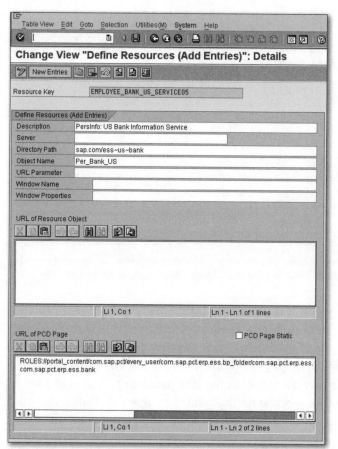

Figure 6.12 Resource for US Bank EMPLOYEE_BANK_US_SERVICE05

Resource Server

A resource can reference a server, if needed. A resource server provides you with the ability to create a relative link (URL, file share, etc.) that can be referenced again and again within the configuration. For example, server BENEFITSDOCS is shown in Figure 6.13. At runtime, this server constructs the URL *https://servername:8080/*

benefits/documentation. This server is then made available for the resource as a starting point.

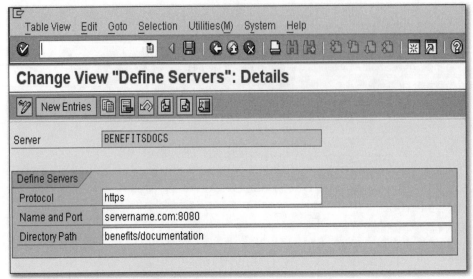

Figure 6.13 Server BENEFITSDOCS Defined with Protocol, Name, Port, and Directory Path

As an example, let's say you want to store documentation on benefit plans for your ESS benefits application. To house this documentation, the URL *https://server-name:8080/benefits/documentation/hsa/hsa_plan_overview.doc* could be constructed in a custom service by specifying BENEFITSDOCS as the server, "hsa" as the Directory Path, and "hsa_plan_overview.doc" as the URL parameter. This service would dynamically render the URL at portal runtime and the link would launch the Word document regarding your HSA plan. Figure 6.14 shows this configuration.

The resource server is one of those items often overlooked, yet it can save you a lot of time if used correctly. The resource server is an excellent example of a reusable component that can speed up your configuration time and help reduce maintenance of the system.

So this wraps up the coverage of the major components of the Homepage Framework. Area group pages, area pages, subareas, resources, and resources all play an integral role in the layout of the functionality for the employee on the SAP Portal. Let's move on to discuss the core components of ESS — the standard functionality available in SAP software's latest release.

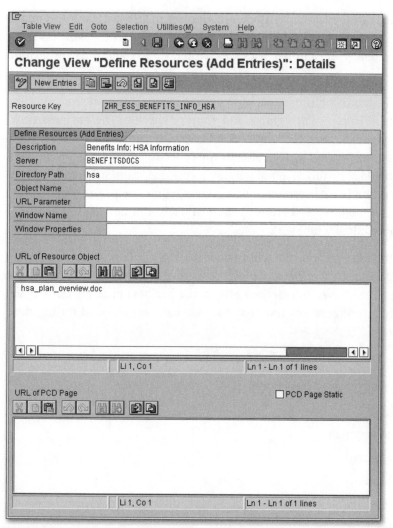

Figure 6.14 Resource ZHR_ESS_BENEFITS_INFO_HSA Defined with Server BENEFITSDOC, Directory Path "hsa", and Resource Object URL "hsa_plan_overview.doc"

6.3   Business Package for ESS

Now that you understand the Homepage Framework including its configuration, let's discuss the standard functionality available within the ESS business package. The business package provided by the SAP system contains prepackaged iViews that you can copy into your own customer namespace to kick-start your ESS implementation. To review where and how to download and import the business package in your system, you can refer back to Chapter 5, "ESS and MSS Installation and Setup."

Out of the box, the ESS business package delivers 1 role, 10 worksets, and over 300 pages and iViews — both global and country specific. The business package provides one role, called "Employee Self-Service" (technical name *com.sap.pct. erp.ess.employee_self_service*), which contains the collection of worksets, pages, and iViews. You should copy this role into your own customer namespace and manipulate your customized role based on your business requirements. It would be rare to use the out-of-the-box role because you most likely will not want to use all of the functionality initially (or ever).

Throughout the next section, we will review the ESS application catalog within the business package by workset and highlight particular applications. We will not be reviewing all employee transactions within the business package, but we will focus on certain configuration and "gotchas" we have experienced during their implementation.

The following lists the out-of-the-box worksets:

▶ Employee Search (or Address Book)
▶ Working Time
▶ Benefits and Payment
▶ Personal Information
▶ Career and Job
▶ Procurement
▶ Work Environment
▶ Life and Work Events
▶ Corporate Information

The services available within each of these worksets will be discussed in detail throughout the rest of this chapter. Feel free to browse ahead to find those applications most relevant to your particular implementation. A typical ESS implementation would not involve the deployment of all of these iViews, so just focus on the items most pertinent to your organization.

> **Note**
>
> Procurement functionality within ESS will not be discussed in this book, but for more information on procurement (and Supplier Relationship Management in general), you can read SAP PRESS's book *Enhancing Supplier Relationship Management Using SAP SRM* by Sachin Sethi.
>
> Also, the Work Environment workset, which provides employees with the ability to request an equipment repair or loss, will not be discussed. The Equipment Overview service can be found through this URL: *http://help.sap.com/erp2005_ehp_02/helpdata/ en/59/b37d40d04e5537e10000000a1550b0/frameset.htm*.

6.3.1 Employee Search (Address Book)

The Employee Search workset (whose technical name is *com.sap.pct.erp.ess.area_ employee_search*) contains functionality for the employee to search for and view other employee's basic organizational data as well as change some of their own basic HR data, such as office number and office room number.

The Employee Search workset is sometimes referred to as the "Address Book" workset within the SAP software documentation because it contains address-type information. The workset contains the following iViews:

▶ Who's Who

▶ Organizational Chart

▶ Change Own Data

Each of these iViews will be discussed next, along with their technical data provided in a tabular format.

▶ The *runtime technology* indicates the type of technology used to build the application.

▶ The *technical name of iView* is the name used within the Portal content directory to identify the application. All standard iViews provided by the SAP system will contain "com.sap" as its prefix. Custom iViews purchased or created by other vendors should contain the technical name in its own name space (e.g., a Worklogix iView for compensation statements could be called com.worklogix. comp.statements).

- The *technical name of the Wed Dynpro Application* is the name referenced within the Web Dynpro console. The first two parts of this name references the directory path (e.g., "sap.com/ess~wiw" in the "Who's Who" iView) and the last part references the object name (e.g., WhoIsWhoApplication).

- Release information and compatibility are defined in the *Available as of* and *Data Source* sections. This is where information on SAP NetWeaver 2004 versus SAP NetWeaver 2005, as well as ECC 5.0 versus ECC 6.0 is clarified. With certain iView, RFCs are provided for reference.

- *Software Component* identifies the SAP software component. All iViews are part of the HR Extension Set (EA-HR) component on either the 5.0 or 6.0 version.

- *Support* identifies the application component for the iView. This is important for support purposes, because this is used when searching for SAP Notes as well as logging customer messages to the SAP system.

- *Supported Languages* lists all of the languages that the iView can support. For the most part, multi-language is never an issue with these services because the SAP system designs everything in multi-language.

Let's now discuss the functionality within the Employee Search workset, starting with the Who's Who iView.

The Who's Who service allows employees to search for other employees in the organization using simple and advanced search criteria. The standard simple search criteria is last name and first name and the advanced search criteria includes elements such as organization unit, position, and system user. The technical data for the Who's Who iView is shown in Table 6.2.

Who's Who iView

The selection and output of this service is based on a standard SAP infoset and query. Infoset /SAPQUERY/HR_XX_PA_ESS is used as the basis for the Who's Who iView. Most data from IT0000 (Actions), IT0001 (Organizational Assignment), IT0002 (Personal Data), IT0032 (Internal Data), and IT0105 (Communication Data) is made available for query and output. It is up to you to determine which elements should be made available for selection as well as output.

Who's Who	
Runtime Technology	Web Dynpro Java iView
Technical Name of iView	com.sap.pct.erp.ess.whoiswho
Technical Name of Web Dynpro Application	sap.com/ess~wiw/WhoIsWhoApplication
Service Key	EMPLOYEE_SEARCH_WHOSWHO05
Available as of	SAP NetWeaver 2004
Data Source	SAP ECC 5.0 or above
Software Component	EA-HR
Support	PA-ESS-XX
Support Languages	All languages supported by the SAP system

Table 6.2 Technical Data for Who's Who iView

It is important to know that Employment Status is controlled outside the query tool in system Table T77S0. The value in group "ESS," semantic abbreviation "STAT2," determines whether active, inactive, retired, and terminated employees show up in the queries. In Figure 6.15, the value "13" means that both inactive (STAT2=1) and active (STAT2=3) employees will appear in the result list. You may need to create this entry in your system if it does not already exist in Table T77S0.

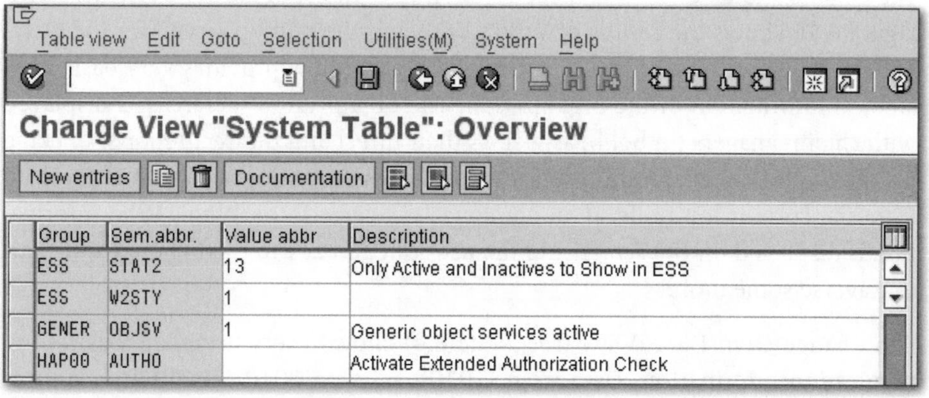

Figure 6.15 Group ESS, Semantic Abbreviation STAT2, in System Table T77S0

The Who's Who iView also integrates with the Organizational Chart and the Change Own Data iViews, both of which are discussed next (see Table 6.3). There are several instances where iViews can interconnect. Parameters can be passed from one iView to another via URL parameters or eventing.

Organizational Chart iView

Organizational Chart	
Runtime Technology	Web Dynpro Java iView
Technical Name of iView	com.sap.pct.erp.ess.orgchart
Technical Name of Web Dynpro Application	sap.com/ess~org/Orgchart
Service Key	EMPLOYEE_SEARCH_ORGCHART05
Available as of	SAP NetWeaver 2004s
Data Source	SAP ECC 5.0 or above
Software Component	EA-HR
Support	PA-ESS-XX
Support Languages	All languages supported by the SAP system

Table 6.3 Technical Data for the Organizational Chart iView

The Organizational Chart is launched from the result list of the Who's Who search. Figure 6.16 shows the results of Who's Who and the pop-up screen for the Organizational Chart iView. The Organizational Chart iView provides very basic hierarchical information of the organization. The organization hierarchy is displayed with chief managers (in bold), as well as their direct and indirect reports. Clicking on the Superior Level button will refresh the organizational chart one level up from the current top node. If an employee is selected, the Who's Who information is displayed on the screen and the user can go back to the organization chart to traverse some more.

The Change Own Data iView (see Table 6.4) allows users to update basic communication information. Data from IT0105 subtype 0010 (Email) and subtype 0020 (Work number), as well as building number, room number, and license plate number from IT0032 (Internal Data) can be updated in addition to the employee's company photo.

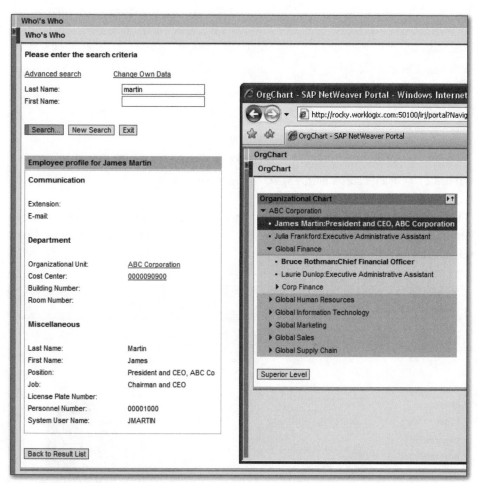

Figure 6.16 Organizational Chart iView Launched From the Results of Who's Who

Change Own Data iView

Change Own Data	
Runtime Technology	Web Dynpro Java iView
Technical Name of iView	com.sap.pct.erp.ess.changeowndata
Technical Name of Web Dynpro Application	sap.com/ess~cod/ChangeOwnDataApplication

Table 6.4 Technical Data for the Change Own Data iView

Change Own Data	
Service Key	EMPLOYEE_SEARCH_CHANGEOWNDATA05
Available as of	SAP NetWeaver 2004
Data Source	SAP ECC 5.0 or above
Software Component	EA-HR
Support	PA-ESS-XX
Support Languages	All languages supported by the SAP system

Table 6.4 Technical Data for the Change Own Data iView (Cont.)

Please note that SAP ArchiveLink must be set up in order for you to use the photo upload and store functionality. Figure 6.17 shows an example of the Change Own Data iView.

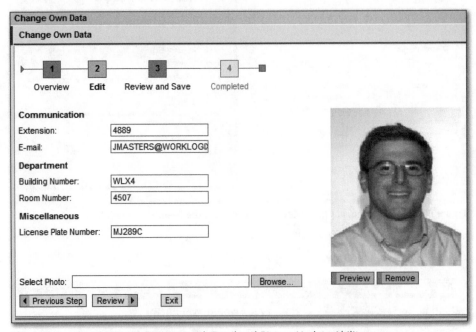

Figure 6.17 Change Own Data iView with Email and Picture Update Ability

The Change Own Data iView is also integrated within the Who's Who iView (an option for Change Own Data is available on the simple and advanced search). It also exists as a standalone service within the Employee Search area page.

6.3.2 Working Time

The Working Time workset (whose technical name is *com.sap.pct.erp.ess.area_ working_time*) contains functionality for the employee to request leave, view time accounts, record working time, and view/print a time statement. The workset contains the following iViews:

- ▶ Leave Request
- ▶ Time Accounts
- ▶ CATS /Record Working Time
- ▶ Clock-In/Clock-Out Corrections
- ▶ Time Statement

Each of these iViews will be discussed next, along with their technical data provided in a tabular format.

> **Note**
>
> There are several services available in ESS for Effort Reporting – functionality pertinent to the US Public Sector. We will not be covering this functionality. More information on the US-specific services for Effort Reporting can be found online at: *http://help.sap.com/ erp2005_ehp_02/helpdata/en/42/f1494ff8501aa2e10000000a422035/frameset.htm*.

The Leave Request iView is one of the most popular components within ESS (*see* Figure 6.18 for a screenshot). This application allows employees to request and track their leave requests, such as vacation, illness, bereavement, and any other configured leave.

Additional functionality includes allowing the employee to see their coworkers' planned absences via the Team Calendar, an overview of their Time Accounts (i.e., quotas for absences and attendances), as well as an overview of their leave. Table 6.5 lists the technical data for the Leave Request iView.

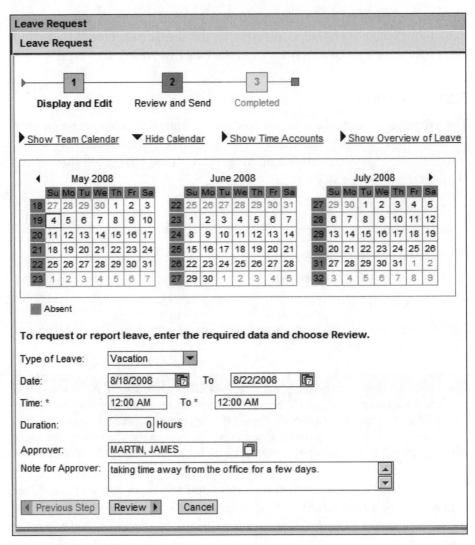

Figure 6.18 Leave Request iView

Leave Request iView

Employees can be grouped into Rule Groups. Feature WEBMO is available to chunk out employees into the appropriate rule group based on employee group, employee subgroup, personnel area, personnel subarea, etc.

Leave Request	
Runtime Technology	Web Dynpro Java iView
Technical Name of iView	com.sap.pct.erp.ess.leaverequest
Technical Name of Web Dynpro Application	sap.com/ess~lea/LeaveRequest
Service Key	EMPLOYEE_WORKTIME_LEAVEREQUEST05
Available as of	SAP NetWeaver 2004s
Data Source	SAP ECC 5.0 and higher
	RFC function components called:
	PT_ARQ_ACCOUNTS_GET
	PT_ARQ_CUSTOMIZING_GET
	PT_ARQ_EECALE_GET
	PT_ARQ_REQLIST_GET
	PT_ARQ_REQUEST_CHECK
	PT_ARQ_REQUEST_EXECUTE
	PT_ARQ_REQUEST_PREPARE
	PT_ARQ_SEARCH_NEXT_PROCESSOR
	PT_ARQ_TEAMCALE_GET
Software Component	EA-HR 500 and higher
Support	PT_RC_UI_XS
Support Languages	All languages supported by the SAP system

Table 6.5 Technical Data for the Leave Request iView

Leave request configuration is performed in the IMG under the path: Personnel Management • Employee Self-Service • Service-Specific Settings • Working Time • Leave Request.

The Time Accounts iView allows employees to check their past, current, and future leave entitlements (see Table 6.6 for the technical data).

Time Accounts iView

Time Accounts	
Runtime Technology	Web Dynpro Java iView
Technical Name of iView	com.sap.pct.erp.ess.quotaoverview
Technical Name of Web Dynpro Application	sap.com/ess~quotas/QuotaOverview
Service Key	EMPLOYEE_WORKTIME_QUOTAOVERVIEW05
Available as of	SAP NetWeaver 2004s
Data Source	SAP ECC 6.00 and higher RFC function components called: PT_ARQ_ACCOUNTS_GET
Software Component	EA-HR 600 and higher
Support	PT_RC_UI_XS
Support Languages	All languages supported by the SAP system

Table 6.6 Technical Data for the Time Accounts iView

A dropdown called Entitlement Type is available for filter if the employee wants to view information only on that particular entitlement type (vacation, sick days, etc.). Figure 6.19 shows the Time Accounts iView vacation quota of 80 hours with a balance of 20 hours.

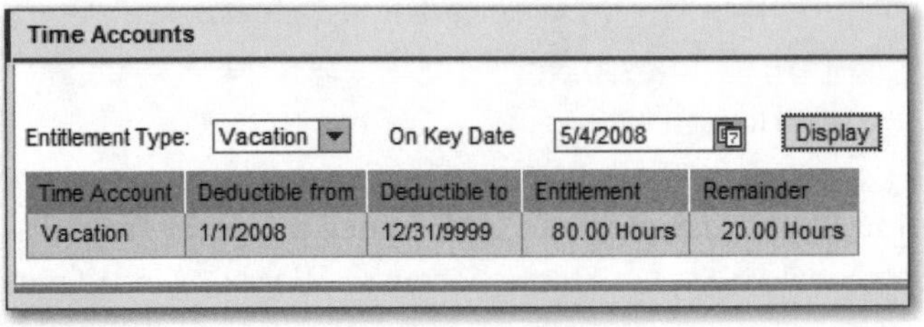

Figure 6.19 Time Accounts iView Listing Entitlement and Remainder Hours

The Record Working Time, or CATS, application is a popular functionality (and covering all of its configurations is certainly outside the scope of this book). CATS configuration for the employee timesheet is performed in the IMG under the path: PERSONNEL MANAGEMENT • EMPLOYEE SELF-SERVICE • SERVICE-SPECIFIC SETTINGS • WORKING

TIME • RECORD WORKING TIME • RECORD WORKING TIME. In this section of the IMG, you configure the data entry profiles for CATS, the fields used in the timesheet, and the allowed attendances and absences. Figure 6.20 shows an example of a simple time sheet and Table 6.7 lists the technical data.

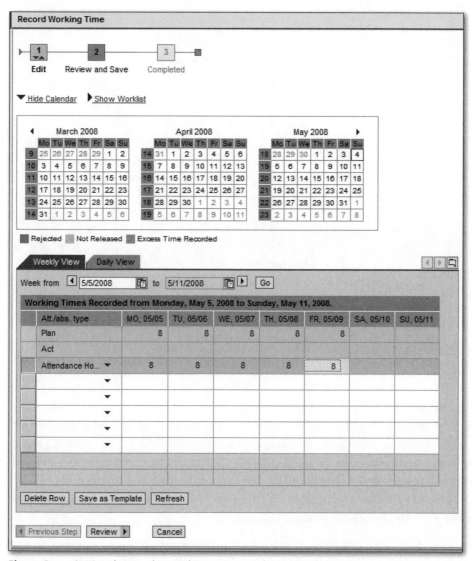

Figure 6.20 CATS with Attendance/Absence Type and Weekly Working Hours

CATS/Record Working Time iView

CATS/Record Working Time	
Runtime Technology	Web Dynpro Java iView
Technical Name of iView	com.sap.pct.erp.ess.recordworktime
	com.sap.pct.erp.ess.releaseworktime
Technical Name of Web Dynpro Application	sap.com/ess~cat/CatDataRecord
	sap.com/ess~cat/CatDataRelease
Available as of	SAP NetWeaver 7.0
Service Key	EMPLOYEE_WORKTIME_PROXYWORKTIME
	EMPLOYEE_WORKTIME_RECORDWORKTIME
	EMPLOYEE_WORKTIME_RECORDWORKTIME_TARGT
	EMPLOYEE_WORKTIME_RECORDWORKTIME_CMPL
	EMPLOYEE_WORKTIME_RECORDWORKTIME_REJ
	EMPLOYEE_WORKTIME_RELEASEWORKTIME
	EMPLOYEE_WORKTIME_RELEASEWORKTIME_DIS
Data Source	SAP ECC 6.00 and higher
	RFC function components called:
	HRXSS_CAT_WD
Software Component	EA-HR 500 and higher
Support	CA-TS-IA-XS
Languages Available	All languages supported by the SAP system

Table 6.7 Technical Data for the CATS/Record Working Time iView

Data entry profiles, assigned to the user via user profile parameter ID "CVR," allow you to manage employees' CATS experiences, such as general settings, time settings, approval, worklists, and data entry validations. Figure 6.21 shows an example of a custom data entry profile named ZHR_WLX. Data entry profiles are configured in the IMG under the path: PERSONNEL MANAGEMENT • EMPLOYEE SELF-SERVICE • SERVICE-SPECIFIC SETTINGS • WORKING TIME • RECORD WORKING TIME • RECORD WORKING TIME • SET UP DATA ENTRY PROFILES.

Under IMG path: PERSONNEL MANAGEMENT • EMPLOYEE SELF-SERVICE • SERVICE-SPECIFIC SETTINGS• WORKING TIME • RECORD WORKING TIME • RECORD WORKING TIME • DEFINE

Field Selection, the timesheet appearance is defined, including what elements are required, display only, and hidden.

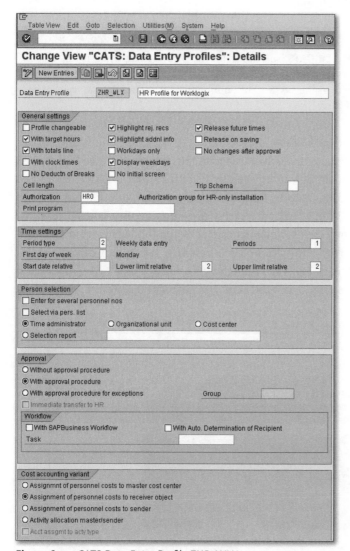

Figure 6.21 CATS Data Entry Profile ZHR_WLX

IMG activity via the path: Personnel Management • Employee Self-Service • Service-Specific Settings • Working Time • Record Working Time • Record Working Time • Select Allowed Absence Types allows you to filter out any attendance or absence type that you do not want available to employees. There may be certain absence or attendances, such as "Disability," that you want to restrict access to and manage within your HR department only.

> **Note**
>
> For an in-depth reference on CATS, see the SAP PRESS book *Integrating CATS, second edition* by Martin Gillet, or *Configuring and Using CATS* by Manuel Gallardo. These books cover many aspects of the CATS solution in depth, including data entry profiles, authorizations, and reporting.

The Clock-In/Out Corrections iView allows employees to enter, view, and correct clock-in and clock-out time entries that are erroneous or missing (see Figure 6.22 and Table 6.8). This application can be used by itself for supporting a clock-in and clock-out scenario. (In other words, employees can use the functionality to both log a clock-in and clock-out.) In some cases, the functionality is used to allow employees to review/correct any clock-ins or clock-outs that occur from an external time-recording device from various time vendors. At a plant or factory, for example, an employee may inadvertently clock-in but not clock-out, or clock-in twice. This iView allows employees the ability to correct these errors.

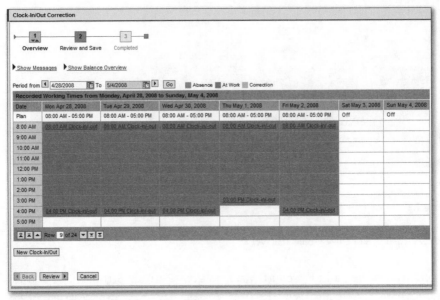

Figure 6.22 Clock-In/Out Correction iView

Clock-In/Out Corrections iView

Clock-In/Out Corrections	
Runtime Technology	Web Dynpro Java iView
Technical Name of iView	com.sap.pct.erp.ess.timecorrection
Technical Name of Web Dynpro Application	sap.com/ess~wtcor/WTimeCor
Service Key	EMPLOYEE_WORKTIME_TIMECORRECTION05
Available as of	SAP NetWeaver 2004s
Data Source	SAP ECC 5.0 and higher
	RFC function components called:
	PTCOR_SEARCH_NEXT_PROCESSOR
	PTCOR_UIA_CUSTOMIZING_GET
	PTCOR_UIA_EVALMESSAGES
	PTCOR_UIA_FORM_ACCEPT
	PTCOR_UIA_FORM_DELEGATE
	PTCOR_UIA_FORM_PREPARE
	PTCOR_UIA_TIME_ACCOUNTS
	PTCOR_UIA_WEEKLY_CALENDAR
Software Component	EA-HR 500 and higher
Support	PT_RC_UI_XS
Support Languages	All languages supported by the SAP system

Table 6.8 Technical Data for the Clock-In/Out Corrections iView

There is quite a bit of functionality in this area, including an entire workflow-enabled process. The workflow is controlled based on settings in the system table PTREQ_STATUS_TRA (Status Transitions). The table specifies which document status changes and events trigger, continue, and terminate the workflow. Class Interface CL_PT_REQ_WF_ATTRIBS controls the processing of the workflow and can be enhanced by Business Add-In (BAdI) PT_GEN_REQ (Control Processing Processes for Web Applications). For more detailed information on the workflow for clock-ins and clock-outs, visit SAP Help at *http://help.sap.com/erp2005_ehp_02/helpdata/ en/10/dd7941a933010de10000000a1550b0/frameset.htm.*

There are several standard programs that support the clock-in and clock-out functionality. For example, report RPTCORTMAIL can be run after time evaluation runs to alert employees that they have made incorrect time entries. Other reports include:

Reports for Control Processing
▶ RPTCORTMAIL (Clock-In/Out Corrections: Request Correction of Errors)
▶ RPTCOREMAIL (Clock-In/Out Corrections: Emails to Involved Persons)
▶ RPTCORPOST (Clock-In/Out Corrections: Post)
▶ RPTCORSTOPWF (Clock-In/Out Corrections: End Open Processes)
▶ RPTCORLIST (Clock-In/Out Corrections: Check Corrections
▶ RPTCORERR (Clock-In/Out Corrections: Process Errors in Entries)
▶ RPTCORAPP (Clock-In/Out Corrections: Approve Documents)

Reports for Testing Customizing Settings
▶ RPTREQWEBMO (Determine Rule Group)
▶ RPTREQAPPRCHK (Determine Approver)

Reports for Displaying and Maintaining the Database
▶ RPTCORDBVIEW (Display Clock-In/Out Corrections (Database)
▶ RPTCORDBDEL (Clock-In/Out Corrections: Delete Obsolete Documents)

Test Programs
▶ RPTCORUIATEST (Test Report for the UIA Interface for Clock-In/Out Corrections)
▶ RPTCORAPTEST (Test Report for the UIA Area Page for Clock-In/Out Corrections)

IMG activities under the path: PERSONNEL MANAGEMENT • EMPLOYEE SELF-SERVICE • SERVICE-SPECIFIC SETTINGS • WORKING TIME • CLOCK-IN/OUT CORRECTIONS allow you to configure settings for clock-in/clock-out corrections.

An example Time Statement is found in Figure 6.23 and the technical data in Table 6.9. This form shows vacation balance for an employee. The time statement can be used regardless of whether or not you use Time Evaluation. It can be made complex or simple.

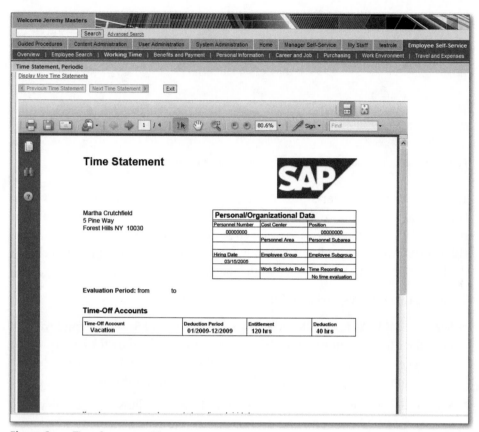

Figure 6.23 Time Statement iView

Time Statement iViews

Time Statements	
Runtime Technology	Web Dynpro Java iView
Technical Name of iView	com.sap.pct.erp.ess.timestatement/ com.sap.pct.erp.ess.timestatementper
Technical Name of Web Dynpro Application	sap.com/ess~tim/Timestatement/ sap.com/ess~tim/TimeStatementPer
Service Key	EMPLOYEE_WORKTIME_TIMESTATEMENT05/ EMPLOYEE_WORKTIME_TIMSTATEMENTPER05

Table 6.9 Technical Data for the Time Statement iViews

Time Statements	
Available as of	SAP NetWeaver 2004s
Data Source	SAP ECC 5.0 and higher
Software Component	EA-HR
Support	PT-RC-UI-XS
Support Languages	All languages supported by the SAP system

Table 6.9 Technical Data for the Time Statement iViews (Cont.)

The Time Statement iViews provide employees access to their time data via HR Forms statements. Feature HRFOR should be configured to point to the right time statement. Time statements are developed in the HR Forms Workplace, Transaction HRFORMS. You will need to work with your ABAP development team to change the layout (including logo) as well as the data that is getting pulled in.

There are two services available for Time Statements:

- Service EMPLOYEE_WORKTIME_TIMESTATEMENTPER allows employees to view their time statements for the periods already defined by the company. The employee can select the desired period in the service. A table is displayed providing an overview of the time evaluation results within this period.

- Service EMPLOYEE_WORKTIME_TIMESTATEMENT allows the employee to specify a desired start and end date to display the time statement. Employees can use this service to display their time statements for any period they wish.

Two ESS applications within this workset, Change Working Time and Status Overview of Processes in Working Time, are part of the HR Administrative Services (PA-AS) functionality and will not be covered in this book. These services are only available in Enhancement Package 2 for SAP ERP 6.0.

6.3.3 Benefits and Payment

The Benefits and Payment workset (whose technical name is *com.sap.pct.erp.ess. area_benefits_payment*) contains functionality for the employee to view and elect benefits, display and print salary statements as well as total compensation statements. The workset contains the following iViews:

- Enrollment
- Participation Overview

▶ Salary Statement

▶ Total Compensation Statement

Each of these iViews will be discussed next, along with their technical data provided in table format.

In addition to these four iViews, there are several country-specific iViews within the Benefits and Payment workset. We will not be covering these country-specific iViews, but a list is provided below along with the country it's released for:

▶ Deferred Compensation (Germany)

▶ Tax Withholding W4 (United States)

▶ Superannuation (Australia)

▶ Flexible Benefits Enrollment (Great Britain)

▶ Flexible Benefits Participation (Great Britain)

▶ Flexible Benefits Print Form (Great Britain)

▶ Singapore Income Tax IR8A (Singapore)

▶ Singapore Income Tax IR8S (Singapore)

Enrollment iView

Enrollment	
Runtime Technology	Web Dynpro Java iView
Technical Name of iView	com.sap.pct.erp.ess.enrollment
Technical Name of Web Dynpro Application	sap.com/ess~ben/BenefitsApplication
Service Key	EMPLOYEE_BENEFITPAY_OPEN_ENROLLMENT05
	EMPLOYEE_BENEFITPAY_GENERIC_ENROLLMENT05
Available as of:	SAP NetWeaver 2004s
Data Source	SAP ECC 6.0 or above
Software Component	EA-HR
Support	PA-BN-ES
Support Languages	All languages supported by the SAP system

Table 6.10   Technical Data for the Enrollment iView

Like CATS and Leave Request, benefits enrollment is another popular service within ESS. Using the benefits enrollment service, employees can elect benefits during annual (open) enrollment as well as throughout the year via life events (birth, marriage, etc.). One of the prerequisites to this iView is the Benefits component.

The iView is organized in three main steps: Plan Selection, Enrollment Review, and Confirmation. During Plan Selection (step 1), the employee can add, edit, or remove benefits plans, identify dependents and beneficiaries per plan, as well as understand the costs associated to each plan. Figure 6.24 shows a screen shot of an employee during this step. If the Review Enrollment button is clicked, the employee is then presented with a summary of all benefit plans they have selected during the Enrollment Review (step 2). Additional edits on plan selection can be performed at this stage. If submitted, a confirmation page is reached that displays all benefits plans they are enrolled in (step 3).

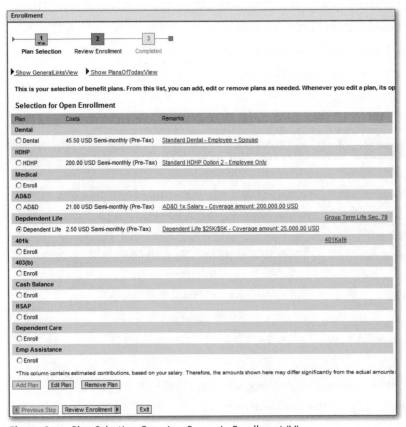

Figure 6.24 Plan Selection Overview Screen in Enrollment iView

See Table 6.11 for the technical data overview.

Participation Overview iView

Participation Overview	
Runtime Technology	Web Dynpro Java iView
Technical Name of iView	com.sap.pct.erp.ess.enrollment
Technical Name of Web Dynpro Application	sap.com/ess~ben/BenefitsApplication
Service Key	EMPLOYEE_BENEFITPAY_OPEN_ENROLLMENT05
	EMPLOYEE_BENEFITPAY_GENERIC_ENROLLMENT05
Available as of:	SAP NetWeaver 2004s
Data Source	SAP ECC 6.0 or above
Software Component	EA-HR
Support	PA-BN-ES
Support Languages	All languages supported by the SAP system

Table 6.11 Technical Data for the Participation Overview iView

The Participation Overview iView allows an employee to view a list of plans in which they are currently enrolled in based on a key date. Information on each plan's cost, coverage, and participation period, as well as data on their dependents and beneficiaries is displayed for the employee. Figure 6.25 shows an example of a user displaying an overview of their enrollment based on a key date of 5/5/2009. Note that the information on each plan is not displayed on one screen; rather, the user needs to click on each plan to display details on the particular benefits plan.

One of the prerequisites to this iView is the Benefits component.

If you run payroll within the SAP system, the Salary Statement iView allows you to provide pay statements to your employees. Using this service, employees can view, print, and download one or more pay statements for a selected period. The pay statement is an Adobe form either created in the HR Forms Workplace in Transaction HRFORMS or via the Forms Editor in Transaction PE51.

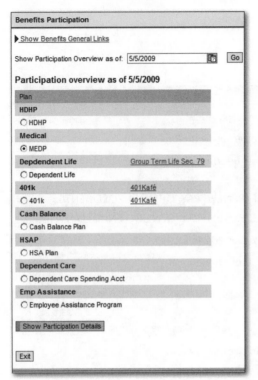

Figure 6.25 Participation Overview Based on Key Date 5/5/2009

Figure 6.26 shows the pay statement with the overview screen. The overview screen provides the employee with the high-level numbers (gross, net, etc.). The dropdown selection allows the employee to select previous pay statements. A push-button is provided to print the statement as well. Many of these settings can be changed via enhancements performed by implementing BAdI XSS_REM_INTERFACE.

The BAdI XSS_REM_INTERFACE allows you to control the output of the salary statements to employees. Class CL_DEF_IM_XSS_REM_INTERFACE is the default implementation and can be overridden based on your own business needs via BAdI XSS_REM_INTERFACE. The BAdI contains six methods that provide flexibility on how and when the statement is rendered to an employee. Each method is explained as follows:

▸ Using method PROVIDE_FILTERED_RGDIR, you can restrict the list of available salary statements based on your customer-specific logic. The default delay in providing salary statements to employees is three days.

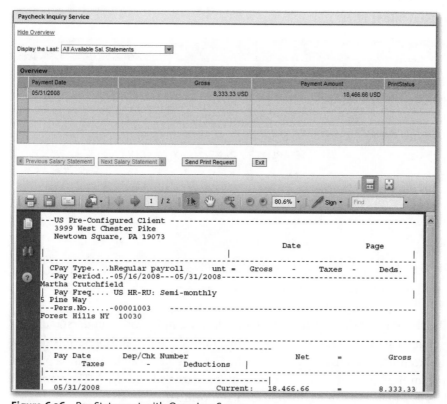

Figure 6.26 Pay Statement with Overview Screen

▶ Method DEFINE_PRINTBUTTON_STATUS determines whether the "Send Print Request" push button for the salary statement is active and visible for the employee.

▶ You can influence the selection of salary statements via method PROVIDE_DROPDOWN_ENTRIES.

▶ You can define the layout of the overview table for the salary statements via method PROVIDE_OVERVIEWTAB_FIELDCAT.

▶ Method PROVIDE_OVERVIEWTAB_LINE allows you to determine the contents of the overview table.

▶ Method PROVIDE_SRVDESCRIPTION allows you to manipulate the description of the pay statement within the area page.

See Table 6.12 for the technical data overview.

Salary Statement iView

Salary Statement	
Runtime Technology	Web Dynpro Java iView
Technical Name of iView	com.sap.pct.erp.ess.paycheck_service
Technical Name of Web Dynpro Application	sap.com/ess~rem/PaySlip2
Service Key	EMPLOYEE_BENEFITPAY_PAYCHECK05
Available as of	SAP ERP 6.0
Data Source	SAP ECC 5.0 or above
Software Component	EA-HR
Support	PY-XX-FO-ESS
Support Languages	All languages supported by the SAP system

Table 6.12 Technical Data for the Salary Statement iView

The Total Compensation Statement iView allows employees to understand their total compensation with the company, including benefits and prerequisite data (see the technical data listed in Table 6.13). The statement can be run for a particular span of time (i.e., the employee can enter a start and end date). The statement renders as a PDF and can be downloaded and printed.

Total Compensation Statement iView

Total Compensation Statement	
Runtime Technology	Web Dynpro Java iView
Technical Name of iView	com.sap.pct.erp.ess.totalcomp
Technical Name of Web Dynpro Application	sap.com/ess~com/Tcs
Service Key	EMPLOYEE_BENEFITPAY_TOTALCOMP05
Available as of	SAP ERP 6.0
Data Source	SAP ECC 6.0 or above
Software Component	EA-HR
Support	PY-XX-FO-ESS
Support Languages	All languages supported by the SAP system

Table 6.13 Technical Data for the Total Compensation Statement iView

IMG activities under the path: PERSONNEL MANAGEMENT • ENTERPRISE COMPENSATION MANAGEMENT • COMPENSATION STATEMENTS are available for configuration. The configuration allows for categories and subcategories to be created for the statement. These categories and subcategories form the structure, content, and calculations of the statement. For example, the standard category PAY (Payment) has two subcategories SLR (Salary) and BNS (Bonus) where base pay and bonus information can be organized, respectively. Wage types are then associated per category via IMG activity path: PERSONNEL MANAGEMENT • ENTERPRISE COMPENSATION MANAGEMENT • COMPENSATION STATEMENTS • SELECT WAGE TYPES FOR 'PAY' CATEGORY (see Figure 6.27). Wages types are identified by country grouping with a start and end date as well as an "arithmetic symbol" indicating whether the wage should be added or subtracted from the total.

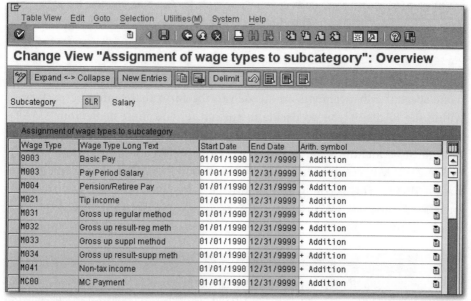

Figure 6.27 Total Compensation Statement IMG Activity "Select Wage Types for 'Pay' Category"

The total compensation statement (SMARTFORM HR_CMP_TCS) can be manipulated via BAdIs. The following is a list of 10 BAdIs available to enhance the output of the Total Compensation Statement. Many of these BAdIs provide a way of manipulating the data within the subcategories (Table 6.14).

Total Compensation Statement BAdIs available	
HRCMP00TCS0001	Read TCS Data for SAP-defined Subcategory (PAY)
HRCMP00TCS0002	Read TCS Data for Customer-defined Subcategory (PAY)
HRCMP00TCS0003	Read TCS Data for SAP-defined Subcategory (CMP)
HRCMP00TCS0004	Read TCS-Data for Customer-defined Subcategory (CMP)
HRCMP00TCS0005	Read Person's TCS Data for Customer-defined Category
HRCMP00TCS0006	Authorization Check for Total Compensation Statement
HRPDV00TCS0001	Read Data for SAP Subcategory (PDV)
HRPDV00TCS0002	Read Data for Customer-specific Subcategory (PD)
HRBEN00PAY0013	Customer Enhancements for SAP Benefits Plan Category
HRBEN00TCS0001	Customer Enhancement for Customer-specific Benefits Categories

Table 6.14 Available Total Compensation Statement BAdIs

The standard SMARTFORM HR_CMP_TCS can also be copied into your custom name space if enhancements are needed to the form that cannot be performed within the BAdIs. If you do decide to customize, you must name your SMART-FORM 10 characters at most because the custom total compensation statement form must be identified in system Table T7SS0. In Figure 6.28, custom SMART-FORM ZHRCMP_TCS is seen configured in Group PCOMP and Semantic Abbreviation SFTCS. This is configured via IMG activity path: PERSONNEL MANAGEMENT • ENTERPRISE COMPENSATION MANAGEMENT •COMPENSATION STATEMENTS • DETERMINE STANDARD FORMS FOR TOTAL COMPENSATION STATEMENT.

> **Note**
>
> The Compensation Review Statement (CRS) is not the same as the Total Compensation Statement. The CRS is the statement used in the Enterprise Compensation Management (ECM) component for rendering merit and bonus letters, for example. BAdI HRECM00_CRS is available to enhance this statement.

Three ESS applications within this workset, Membership Fees Sports Club, Company Loan, and Status Overview of Processes in Benefits and Payment are part of the HR Administrative Services (PA-AS) functionality and will not be covered in this book. These services are only available as part of Enhancement Package 2 for SAP ERP 6.0.

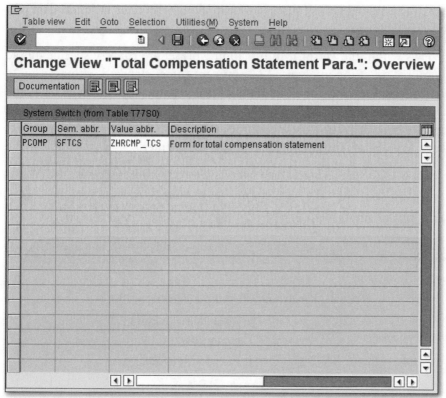

Figure 6.28 Entry for Custom SMARTFORM ZHRCMP_TCS, configured in Group PCOMP and Semantic Abbreviation SFTCS

6.3.4 Personal Information

The Personal Information workset (whose technical name is *com.sap.pct.erp.ess. area_personal_information*) contains functionality for the employee to view and update their personal information, including Infotypes 0002 (Personal Data), 0006 (Address), 0009 (Bank Information), and 0021 (Family Data). The workset contains the following iViews:

- Address
- Personal Data
- Bank Information
- Family Data

Each of these iViews will be discussed next, along with their technical data provided in table format.

All iViews within the Personal Information workset are country specific due to the local nature of the infotypes. SAP software comes standard with a set of 34 country-specific services for each address, bank information, personal data, and family data infotype. For those countries not included, the SAP system provides an approach for delivering these countries not included in the standard business package. We will cover this approach later in the chapter.

See Table 6.15 for the technical data overview for the Address iView.

Address iView

Address	
Runtime Technology	Web Dynpro Java iView
Technical Name of iView	com.sap.pct.erp.ess.address
Technical Name of Web Dynpro Application	sap.com/ess~**~addr/Per_Address_** where ** = country code
Service Key	EMPLOYEE_PERSINFO_ADDRESS05
Available as of	SAP NetWeaver 2004s
Data Source	SAP ECC 5.0 or above
Software Component	EA-HR
Support	See Table 6.16
Support Languages	English and languages for country-specific versions

Table 6.15 Technical Data for the Address iView

The Address iView provides employees with the ability to view and update their different address records in ESS. Address information is stored on Infotype 0006. The following address types are available as seen in Figure 6.30:

- ▶ Permanent Residence (subtype 1)
- ▶ Emergency Address (subtype 4)
- ▶ Mailing Address (subtype 5)

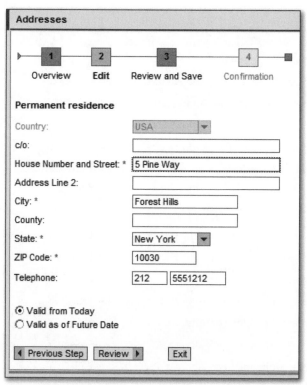

Figure 6.29 Address iView Edit Screen

Table 6.16 lists the country-specific services for address functionality in ESS.

Country	Country-Specific Service	Support Component
Argentina	sap.com/ess~ar~addr/Per_Address_AR	PA-ESS-OCY
Australia	sap.com/ess~au~addr/Per_Address_AU	PA-ESS-OCY
Belgium	sap.com/ess~be~addr/Per_Address_BE	PA-ESS-OCY
Brazil	sap.com/ess~br~addr/Per_Address_BR	PA-ESS-OCY
China	sap.com/ess~cn~addr/Per_Address_CN	PA-ESS-OCY
Denmark	sap.com/ess~dk~addr/Per_Address_DK	PA-ESS-OCY
Germany	sap.com/ess~de~addr/Per_Address_DE	PA-ESS-DE
Finland	sap.com/ess~fi~addr/Per_Address_FI	PA-ESS-OCY

Table 6.16 List of All Country-specific Address Services by Country with Their Support Component

Country	Country-Specific Service	Support Component
France	sap.com/ess~fr~addr/Per_Address_FR	PA-ESS-OCY
United Kingdom	sap.com/ess~uk~addr/Per_Address_UK	PA-ESS-OCY
Hong Kong	sap.com/ess~hk~addr/Per_Address_HK	PA-ESS-OCY
India	sap.com/ess~in~addr/Per_Address_IN	PA-ESS-OCY
Indonesia	sap.com/ess~id~addr/Per_Address_ID	PA-ESS-OCY
Italy	sap.com/ess~it~addr/Per_Address_IT	PA-ESS-OCY
Japan	sap.com/ess~jp~addr/Per_Address_JP	PA-ESS-OCY
Canada	sap.com/ess~ca~addr/Per_Address_CA	PA-ESS-OCY
Malaysia	sap.com/ess~my~addr/Per_Address_MY	PA-ESS-OCY
Mexico	sap.com/ess~mx~addr/Per_Address_MX	PA-ESS-OCY
New Zealand	sap.com/ess~nz~addr/Per_Address_NZ	PA-ESS-OCY
The Netherlands	sap.com/ess~nl~addr/Per_Address_NL	PA-ESS-OCY
Norway	sap.com/ess~no~addr/Per_Address_NO	PA-ESS-OCY
Austria	sap.com/ess~at~addr/Per_Address_AT	PA-ESS-OCY
Philippines	sap.com/ess~ph~addr/Per_Address_PH	PA-ESS-OCY
Portugal	sap.com/ess~pt~addr/Per_Address_PT	PA-ESS-OCY
Sweden	sap.com/ess~se~addr/Per_Address_SE	PA-ESS-OCY
Switzerland	sap.com/ess~ch~addr/Per_Address_CH	PA-ESS-OCY
Singapore	sap.com/ess~sg~addr/Per_Address_SG	PA-ESS-OCY
Spain	sap.com/ess~es~addr/Per_Address_ES	PA-ESS-OCY
South Africa	sap.com/ess~za~addr/Per_Address_ZA	PA-ESS-OCY
South Korea	sap.com/ess~kr~addr/Per_Address_KR	PA-ESS-OCY
Taiwan	sap.com/ess~tw~addr/Per_Address_TW	PA-ESS-OCY
Thailand	sap.com/ess~th~addr/Per_Address_TH	PA-ESS-OCY
USA	sap.com/ess~us~addr/Per_Address_US	PA-ESS-US
Venezuela	sap.com/ess~ve~addr/Per_Address_VE	PA-ESS-OCY

Table 6.16 List of All Country-specific Address Services by Country with Their Support Component (Cont.)

See Table 6.17 for the technical data overview of the Bank Information iView.

Bank Information iView

Bank Information	
Runtime Technology	Web Dynpro Java iView
Technical Name of iView	com.sap.pct.erp.ess.bank
Technical Name of Web Dynpro Application	sap.com/ess~**~bank/Per_Bank_** where ** = country code (see table)
Service Key	EMPLOYEE_PERSINFO_BANK05
Available as of	SAP NetWeaver 2004
Data Source	SAP ECC 5.0 or above
Software Component	EA-HR
Support	See Table 6.18
Support Languages	English and languages for country-specific versions

Table 6.17 Technical Data for the Bank Information iView

The Bank Information iView provides employees with the ability to view and update their bank information in ESS. Bank Information is stored in Infotype 0009. The following bank types are available (Figure 6.30):

- Main Bank (subtype 0)
- Travel Expenses (subtype 2)
- Other Bank (subtype 1)

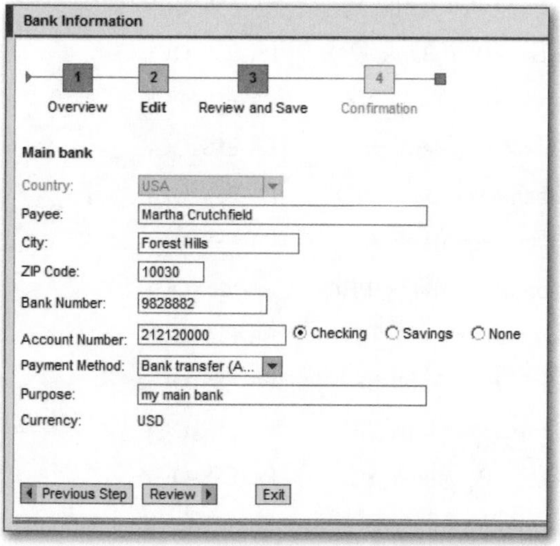

Figure 6.30 Bank Information Edit Screen

Table 6.18 lists the country-specific services for Bank Information functionality in ESS.

Country	Country-Specific Service	Support Component
Argentina	sap.com/ess~ar~bank/Per_Bank_AR	PA-ESS-OCY
Australia	sap.com/ess~au~bank/Per_Bank_AU	PA-ESS-OCY
Belgium	sap.com/ess~be~bank/Per_Bank_BE	PA-ESS-OCY
Brazil	sap.com/ess~br~bank/Per_Bank_BR	PA-ESS-OCY
China	sap.com/ess~cn~bank/Per_Bank_CN	PA-ESS-OCY
Denmark	sap.com/ess~dk~bank/Per_Bank_DK	PA-ESS-OCY
Germany	sap.com/ess~de~bank/Per_Bank_DE	PA-ESS-DE
Finland	sap.com/ess~fi~bank/Per_Bank_FI	PA-ESS-OCY
France	sap.com/ess~fr~bank/Per_Bank_FR	PA-ESS-OCY
United Kingdom	sap.com/ess~uk~bank/Per_Bank_UK	PA-ESS-OCY
Hong Kong	sap.com/ess~hk~bank/Per_Bank_HK	PA-ESS-OCY
India	sap.com/ess~in~bank/Per_Bank_IN	PA-ESS-OCY
Indonesia	sap.com/ess~id~bank/Per_Bank_ID	PA-ESS-OCY
Italy	sap.com/ess~it~bank/Per_Bank_IT	PA-ESS-OCY
Japan	sap.com/ess~jp~bank/Per_Bank_JP	PA-ESS-OCY
Canada	sap.com/ess~ca~bank/Per_Bank_CA	PA-ESS-OCY
Malaysia	sap.com/ess~my~bank/Per_Bank_MY	PA-ESS-OCY
Mexico	sap.com/ess~mx~bank/Per_Bank_MX	PA-ESS-OCY
New Zealand	sap.com/ess~nz~bank/Per_Bank_NZ	PA-ESS-OCY
The Netherlands	sap.com/ess~nl~bank/Per_Bank_NL	PA-ESS-OCY
Norway	sap.com/ess~no~bank/Per_Bank_NO	PA-ESS-OCY
Austria	sap.com/ess~at~bank/Per_Bank_AT	PA-ESS-OCY
Philippines	sap.com/ess~ph~bank/Per_Bank_PH	PA-ESS-OCY
Portugal	sap.com/ess~pt~bank/Per_Bank_PT	PA-ESS-OCY
Sweden	sap.com/ess~se~bank/Per_Bank_SE	PA-ESS-OCY
Switzerland	sap.com/ess~ch~bank/Per_Bank_CH	PA-ESS-OCY
Singapore	sap.com/ess~sg~bank/Per_Bank_SG	PA-ESS-OCY

Table 6.18   List of All Country-specific Bank Information Services By Country with Their Support Component

Country	Country-Specific Service	Support Component
Spain	sap.com/ess~es~bank/Per_Bank_ES	PA-ESS-OCY
South Africa	sap.com/ess~za~bank/Per_Bank_ZA	PA-ESS-OCY
South Korea	sap.com/ess~kr~bank/Per_Bank_KR	PA-ESS-OCY
Taiwan	sap.com/ess~tw~bank/Per_Bank_TW	PA-ESS-OCY
Thailand	sap.com/ess~th~bank/Per_Bank_TH	PA-ESS-OCY
USA	sap.com/ess~us~bank/Per_Bank_US	PA-ESS-US
Venezuela	sap.com/ess~ve~bank/Per_Bank_VE	PA-ESS-OCY

Table 6.18 List of All Country-specific Bank Information Services By Country with Their Support Component (Cont.)

Table 6.19 lists the technical data overview for the Personal Data iView.

Personal Data iView

Personal Data	
Runtime Technology	Web Dynpro Java iView
Technical Name of iView	com.sap.pct.erp.ess.pdata
Technical Name of Web Dynpro Application	sap.com/ess~**~pdata/Per_Personal_** where ** = country code
Service Key	EMPLOYEE_PERSINFO_PERSDATA05
Available as of	SAP NetWeaver 2004
Data Source	SAP ECC 5.0 or above
Software Component	EA-HR
Support	See Table 6.20
Support Languages	English and languages for country-specific versions

Table 6.19 Technical Data for the Personal Data iView

The Personal Data iView provides employees with the ability to view and update their personal information in ESS. Data, such as name, nickname, nationality, and title are available for viewing and updating. Personal Data information is stored on Infotype 0002 (Figure 6.31).

Figure 6.31 Personal Data iView Edit Screen

Table 6.20 lists the country-specific services for personal data functionality in ESS.

Country	Country-Specific Service	Support Component
Argentina	sap.com/ess~ar~pdata/Per_Personal_AR	PA-ESS-OCY
Australia	sap.com/ess~au~pdata/Per_Personal_AU	PA-ESS-OCY
Belgium	sap.com/ess~be~pdata/Per_Personal_BE	PA-ESS-OCY
Brazil	sap.com/ess~br~pdata/Per_Personal_BR	PA-ESS-OCY
China	sap.com/ess~cn~pdata/Per_Personal_CN	PA-ESS-OCY
Denmark	sap.com/ess~dk~pdata/Per_Personal_DK	PA-ESS-OCY

Table 6.20 List of All Country-Specific Personal Data Services by Country with Their Support Component

Country	Country-Specific Service	Support Component
Germany	sap.com/ess~de~pdata/Per_Personal_DE	PA-ESS-DE
Finland	sap.com/ess~fi~pdata/Per_Personal_FI	PA-ESS-OCY
France	sap.com/ess~fr~pdata/Per_Personal_FR	PA-ESS-OCY
United Kingdom	sap.com/ess~uk~pdata/Per_Personal_UK	PA-ESS-OCY
Hong Kong/China	sap.com/ess~hk~pdata/Per_Personal_HK	PA-ESS-OCY
India	sap.com/ess~in~pdata/Per_Personal_IN	PA-ESS-OCY
Indonesia	sap.com/ess~id~pdata/Per_Personal_ID	PA-ESS-OCY
Italy	sap.com/ess~it~pdata/Per_Personal_IT	PA-ESS-OCY
Japan	sap.com/ess~jp~pdata/Per_Personal_JP	PA-ESS-OCY
Canada	sap.com/ess~ca~pdata/Per_Personal_CA	PA-ESS-OCY
Malaysia	sap.com/ess~my~pdata/Per_Personal_MY	PA-ESS-OCY
Mexico	sap.com/ess~mx~pdata/Per_Personal_MX	PA-ESS-OCY
New Zealand	sap.com/ess~nz~pdata/Per_Personal_NZ	PA-ESS-OCY
The Netherlands	sap.com/ess~nl~pdata/Per_Personal_NL	PA-ESS-OCY
Norway	sap.com/ess~no~pdata/Per_Personal_NO	PA-ESS-OCY
Austria	sap.com/ess~at~pdata/Per_Personal_AT	PA-ESS-OCY
Philippines	sap.com/ess~ph~pdata/Per_Personal_PH	PA-ESS-OCY
Portugal	sap.com/ess~pt~pdata/Per_Personal_PT	PA-ESS-OCY
Sweden	sap.com/ess~se~pdata/Per_Personal_SE	PA-ESS-OCY
Switzerland	sap.com/ess~ch~pdata/Per_Personal_CH	PA-ESS-OCY
Singapore	sap.com/ess~sg~pdata/Per_Personal_SG	PA-ESS-OCY
Spain	sap.com/ess~es~pdata/Per_Personal_ES	PA-ESS-OCY
South Africa	sap.com/ess~za~pdata/Per_Personal_ZA	PA-ESS-OCY
South Korea	sap.com/ess~kr~pdata/Per_Personal_KR	PA-ESS-OCY
Taiwan	sap.com/ess~tw~pdata/Per_Personal_TW	PA-ESS-OCY
Thailand	sap.com/ess~th~pdata/Per_Personal_TH	PA-ESS-OCY
USA	sap.com/ess~us~pdata/Per_Personal_US	PA-ESS-US
Venezuela	sap.com/ess~ve~pdata/Per_Personal_VE	PA-ESS-OCY

Table 6.20 List of All Country-Specific Personal Data Services by Country with Their Support Component (Cont.)

Table 6.21 lists the technical data overview for the Family Member/Dependents iView.

Family Member/Dependents iView

Family Member/Dependents	
Runtime Technology	Web Dynpro Java iView
Technical Name of iView	com.sap.pct.erp.ess.fam
Technical Name of Web Dynpro Application	sap.com/ess~**~fam/Per_Family_** where ** = country code
Service Key	EMPLOYEE_PERSINFO_FAMMEMBER05
Available as of	SAP NetWeaver 2004
Data Source	SAP ECC 5.0 or above
Software Component	EA-HR
Support	See Table 6.22
Support Languages	English and languages for country-specific versions

Table 6.21 Technical Data for the Family Members/Dependents iView

The Family Members/Dependent Data iView provides employees the ability to view and update information regarding their family members and dependents via ESS. Family Members/Dependent information is stored on Infotype 0021 (Figure 6.32).

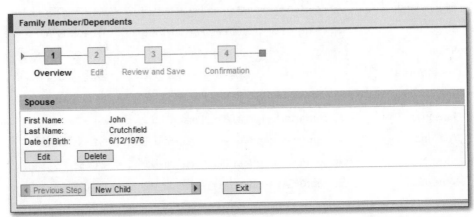

Figure 6.32 Family Member/Dependents Overview Screen

Table 6.22 lists the country-specific services for personal data functionality in ESS.

Country	Country-Specific Service	Support Component
Argentina	sap.com/ess~ar~fam/Per_Family_AR	PA-ESS-OCY
Australia	sap.com/ess~au~fam/Per_Family_AU	PA-ESS-OCY
Belgium	sap.com/ess~be~fam/Per_Family_BE	PA-ESS-OCY
Brazil	sap.com/ess~br~fam/Per_Family_BR	PA-ESS-OCY
China	sap.com/ess~cn~fam/Per_Family_CN	PA-ESS-OCY
Denmark	sap.com/ess~dk~fam/Per_Family_DK	PA-ESS-OCY
Germany	sap.com/ess~de~fam/Per_Family_DE	PA-ESS-DE
Finland	sap.com/ess~fi~fam/Per_Family_FI	PA-ESS-OCY
France	sap.com/ess~fr~fam/Per_Family_FR	PA-ESS-OCY
United Kingdom	sap.com/ess~uk~fam/Per_Family_UK	PA-ESS-OCY
Hong Kong	sap.com/ess~hk~fam/Per_Family_HK	PA-ESS-OCY
India	sap.com/ess~in~fam/Per_Family_IN	PA-ESS-OCY
Indonesia	sap.com/ess~id~fam/Per_Family_ID	PA-ESS-OCY
Italy	sap.com/ess~it~fam/Per_Family_IT	PA-ESS-OCY
Japan	sap.com/ess~jp~fam/Per_Family_JP	PA-ESS-OCY
Canada	sap.com/ess~ca~fam/Per_Family_CA	PA-ESS-OCY
Malaysia	sap.com/ess~my~fam/Per_Family_MY	PA-ESS-OCY
Mexico	sap.com/ess~mx~fam/Per_Family_MX	PA-ESS-OCY
New Zealand	sap.com/ess~nz~fam/Per_Family_NZ	PA-ESS-OCY
The Netherlands	sap.com/ess~nl~fam/Per_Family_NL	PA-ESS-OCY
Norway	sap.com/ess~no~fam/Per_Family_NO	PA-ESS-OCY
Austria	sap.com/ess~at~fam/Per_Family_AT	PA-ESS-OCY
Philippines	sap.com/ess~ph~fam/Per_Family_PH	PA-ESS-OCY
Portugal	sap.com/ess~pt~fam/Per_Family_PT	PA-ESS-OCY
Sweden	sap.com/ess~se~fam/Per_Family_SE	PA-ESS-OCY
Switzerland	sap.com/ess~ch~fam/Per_Family_CH	PA-ESS-OCY
Singapore	sap.com/ess~sg~fam/Per_Family_SG	PA-ESS-OCY

Table 6.22 List of All Country-Specific Family Member/Dependents Services by Country with Their Support Component

Country	Country-Specific Service	Support Component
Spain	sap.com/ess~es~fam/Per_Family_ES	PA-ESS-OCY
South Africa	sap.com/ess~za~fam/Per_Family_ZA	PA-ESS-OCY
South Korea	sap.com/ess~kr~fam/Per_Family_KR	PA-ESS-OCY
Taiwan	sap.com/ess~tw~fam/Per_Family_TW	PA-ESS-OCY
Thailand	sap.com/ess~th~fam/Per_Family_TH	PA-ESS-OCY
USA	sap.com/ess~us~fam/Per_Family_US	PA-ESS-US
Venezuela	sap.com/ess~ve~fam/Per_Family_VE	PA-ESS-OCY

Table 6.22 List of All Country-Specific Family Member/Dependents Services by Country with Their Support Component (Cont.)

Let's take a closer look at one of the more important configuration activities within the ESS functionality. Activating subtypes and assignment application use cases are discussed next.

Defining Active Subtypes and Application Case

For all services within the Personal Information area, you will need to configure (by country) permitted subtypes and use cases. You can define which subtypes are to be active for each infotype and which can be changed by employees. Furthermore, you can define the use case for each infotype or subtype. Defining active subtypes and use cases are configured in view V_T7XSSPERSUBTYP or in the IMG by following the path: PERSONNEL MANAGEMENT • EMPLOYEE SELF-SERVICE • SERVICE-SPECIFIC SETTINGS • OWN DATA • DEFINE ACTIVE SUBTYPES AND APPLICATION CASE (see Figure 6.33).

By defining a use case, you control which type of data records your employees are permitted to create. Only use cases A1 to A6 and B1 to B5 are available. The first character of the key is the validity indicator. Use cases beginning with *A* indicate that a record can be created specifying the valid start or end date. This means that multiple records can exist. By default, ESS scenarios will allow you to specify the start date as either today's date or a future date. If you wish to enable ESS scenarios to accept a start date in the past, BAdI HRXSS_PER_BEGDA can be implemented. (We will discuss this later in the chapter.)

Use cases beginning with *B* indicate that a record can be created without specifying the valid start or end date. This means that multiple records cannot exist. If future records exist, they will not be displayed to an employee in ESS.

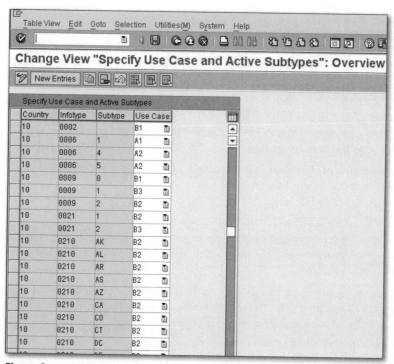

Figure 6.33 Active Subtypes and Use Case by Country Grouping, Infotype, and Subtype

Table 6.23 lists the use case, use case description, and an example scenario.

Use Case	Use Case Description	Example Scenario
B1	One infotype record must exist at all times for the employee. Once a record for an infotype/subtype is available, the "New <infotype/subtype>" button will not be available on the overview screen.	Personal Data
B2	Once a record for an infotype/subtype is available, the "New <infotype/subtype>" button will not be available on the overview screen.	Family Member/ Dependent (e.g., Spouse)
B3	The "New <infotype/subtype>" button will always be available on the overview screen. This use case is applicable for both time constraint 2 with object identification permitted and time constraint 3.	Family Member/ Dependent (e.g., Child)

Table 6.23 Use Case, Description, and Scenario

Use Case	Use Case Description	Example Scenario
B4	A variant of B1. In addition to the behavior of B1, the "New <infotype/subtype>" button will always be available on the overview screen.	Permanent address
B5	A variant of B2. In addition to the behavior of B2, the "New <infotype/subtype>" button will always be available on the overview screen.	Mailing address
A1	One infotype record must exist at all times for the employee. Once a record for an infotype/subtype is available, the "New <infotype/subtype>" button will not be available on the overview screen.	Personal Data
A2	Once a record for an infotype/subtype is available, the "New <infotype/subtype>" button will not be available on the overview screen.	Family Member/ Dependent (e.g., Spouse)
A3	Multiple infotype records of the same entity cannot exist at the same time. The "New <infotype/subtype>" button will always be available on the overview screen. This use case can only be if the time constraint of the infotype/subtype is 2 and if object identification is permitted.	Family Member/ Dependent (e.g., Child)
A4	A variant of A1, the difference to A1 being the "New <infotype/subtype>" button will always be available on the overview screen.	Permanent address
A5	A variant of A2, the difference to A2 being the "New <infotype/subtype>" button will always be available on the overview screen.	Mailing address
A6	Multiple infotype records of the same type may exist for an employee at the same time the "New <infotype/subtype>" button will always be available on the overview screen. This use case can only be used if the time constraint of the infotype/subtype is 3.	Other Bank

Table 6.23 Use Case, Description, and Scenario

Creating Services for Other Countries

You may need to create services for other countries. For example, no services exist for Uruguay. However, the functionality in the services for Argentina may be very similar to that needed in Uruguay. In this case, you can leverage the delivered services for Argentina by following a few steps.

1. **Assign Screen Structure to Infotype Versions**

   Identify the country-specific application that is best suited to be copied and adapted as your new country-specific application. Note in particular whether the screen structure and user interface suit your requirements and whether you can adapt the screen structure to your application logic.

   In this step, you specify the screen structure for your country-specific application. The name of the structure is listed in the V_T588IT_SCREEN view. This view contains the country-specific structures. Copy the name and the type of the required structure.

2. **Define Active Subtypes and Use Case**

   Active subtypes and use cases for the new country must be configured in V_T7XSSPERSUBTYP or in the IMG by following the path: PERSONNEL MANAGEMENT • EMPLOYEE SELF-SERVICE • SERVICE-SPECIFIC SETTINGS • OWN DATA • DEFINE ACTIVE SUBTYPES AND APPLICATION CASE.

3. **Define Country-Specific Applications**

   You then define your country-specific application using the functions of the Homepage Framework. Enter the service key and the resource of your application.

Changing the Default Start Date

Using BAdI HRXSS_PER_BEGDA, you can specify a default start date for any of the iViews within the Personal Information workset (e.g., address, personal data, bank details, family members/dependents, etc.). The standard functionality uses the system date (current date) as the default date when updating records. You can overwrite this setting with customer logic by implementing BAdI Method DEFAULT_DATE, which can import country grouping (MOLGA), personnel number (PERNR), infotype (INFTY), and subtype (SUBTY) to change the begin date (BEGDA).

Changing the Default Subtype

You can also change subtypes using custom logic. BAdI HRXSS_PER_SUBTYPE has Method MODIFY_SUBTYPES, which can import country grouping (MOLGA), personnel number (PERNR), infotype (INFTY), and the begin date (BEGDA) to change the standard subtype (SUBTY).

Other Available iViews

In addition to these iViews, there are two iViews that are only relevant if you have implemented the Employee Interaction Center (EIC). These EIC-specific iViews include:

▶ Authentication for EIC (updates EIC Infotype 0816)

▶ EIC Request (sends Adobe forms to EIC)

There are also three country-specific iViews within the Personal Information workset. These include the following:

▶ Personal IDs (for Singapore, Malaysia, Hong Kong, Taiwan, Indonesia, and Thailand)

▶ Payment Summary (for Australia)

▶ Employment Equity (for Canada)

Three delivered ESS applications within this workset — Change of Address (US), Display Personnel File, and Status Overview of Processes in Personal Information — are part of the HR Administrative Services (PA-AS) functionality and will not be covered in this book. These services are only available as part of Enhancement Package 2 for SAP ERP 6.0.

6.3.5 Career and Job

The Career and Job workset (whose technical name is *com.sap.pct.erp.ess.area_career_job*) contains functionality for the employee to view and update career-related information, such as their resume, skills, and job aspirations. Most of the iViews contained in this workset are contingent on you also implementing E-Recruiting. With SAP E-Recruiting, employees can view and update their candidate profile, search for internal jobs, and view their applications online. The Skills Profile iView is the only iView that does not rely on E-Recruiting data. The workset contains the following iViews:

▶ Skills Profile

▶ Candidate Profile (E-Recruiting)

▶ Data Overview (E-Recruiting)

▶ Profile Release (E-Recruiting)

▶ Apply Directly (E-Recruiting)

▶ Search for Jobs (E-Recruiting)

▶ Favorites (E-Recruiting)

▶ Applications (E-Recruiting)

▶ Personal Settings (E-Recruiting)

The E-Recruiting iViews all call Business Server Pages (BSPs) in the E-Recruiting system (assuming you have implemented E-Recruiting). Depending on your technical landscape, these iViews might be pointing to BSP applications that reside on another SAP system (where E-Recruiting is installed). Regardless of where E-Recruiting is deployed in your environment, these iViews are seamlessly integrated into the Homepage Framework by providing Single Sign-On (SSO) (from the Portal to the BSP applications). However, E-Recruiting and its ESS functions are not covered in this book, but for all of the details, you can read SAP PRESS, *E-Recruiting with SAP ERP HCM* by Ben Hayes. In this section, only the Skills iView will be discussed.

Table 6.24 lists the technical data overview for the Skills Profile iView.

Skills Profile iView

Skills	
Runtime Technology	Web Dynpro Java iView
Technical Name of iView	com.sap.pct.erp.ess.skills
Technical Name of Web Dynpro Application	sap.com/ess~skl/SkillsApplication
Service Key	EMPLOYEE_CAREER_SKILLSPROFILE05
Available as of	SAP NetWeaver 2004
Data Source	SAP ECC 5.0 or above
Software Component	EA-HR
Support	PA-ESS-XX
Support Languages	All languages supported by the SAP system

Table 6.24 Technical Data for the Skills Profile iView

The skills profile provides employees with the ability to view and update skills information, such as certifications, languages, and mobility preferences. Figure 6.34 shows the profile overview screen, listing the employee's skills, required proficiency (if any), and existing proficiency. The required proficiency would be populated only if skills were maintained at the position or job level.

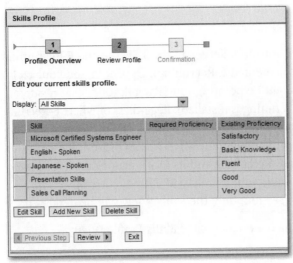

Figure 6.34 Skills Profile

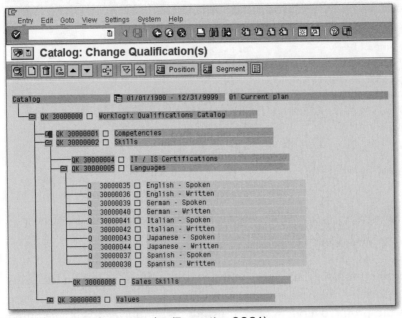

Figure 6.35 Qualification Catalog (Transaction OOQA)

A prerequisite for the Skills Profile is that a qualification catalog must be built for the organization. Figure 6.35 shows the qualification catalog via Transaction OOQA. Qualification groups (object type QK) and qualifications (object types Q) should be constructed in such a way as to show what skills are important to the organization. Also, you will most likely want to restrict which qualifications an employee can add to his own profile.

Figure 6.36 shows system Table T7SS0 with the root (top) qualification group identified as the value for group QUALI and semantic abbreviation ESSST.

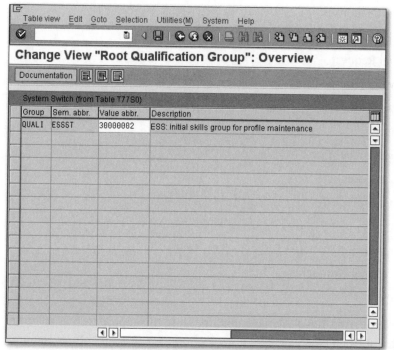

Figure 6.36 Root Qualification Group Identified in System Table T7SS0, Group QUALI, Semantic Abbreviation ESSST

This top node is the qualification group in your qualification catalog that contains the skills you want to expose on the portal for the employee. In our example, the qualifications catalog shows qualification group 30000002, entitled *Skills*, which itself contains qualification groups IT/IS Certifications, Languages, and Sales Skills. In this case, employees would only be able to edit qualifications in these qualification groups and not, for example, their own competencies.

6.3.6 Trips and Expenses

The technical name of the Trips and Expenses workset is *com.sap.pct.erp.ess.area_travel_expenses*. As of SAP ECC 6.0, Enhancement Package 2, you can activate the Travel Management business function (FIN_TRAVEL_1). If you do not activate this business function, you will need to continue to use the Web Dynpro Java-based applications. If you activate this business function, the Web Dynpro ABAP-based applications replace the Web Dynpro Java-based applications.

The Trips and Expenses workset contains the following iViews:

- My Trips and Expenses
- My Travel Profile
- Create Travel Request
- Delete Travel Request
- Create Travel Plan
- Route Planning
- Cancel/Delete Travel Plan
- Create Expense Report
- Delete Expense Report
- Display Forms
- Personalization
- Unlock Personnel Number
- My Employees

We will not be covering Travel Management, because this topic deserves an entire book to itself. But, Travel Management is a very popular component to implement. It also has an offline component to it that is great for a mobile workforce, such as companies with large sales teams.

6.3.7 Life and Work Events

The technical name of the Life and Work Event workset is *com.sap.pct.erp.ess.area_life_work*. The Life and Work Events workset contains the following iViews:

- ▶ My First Days

- ▶ Benefits

- ▶ Change in Employment Status

- ▶ Terminate Employment

- ▶ Birth/Adoption

- ▶ Marriage

- ▶ Divorce

These iViews are viewed as "samples," because the new Life and Work Events functionality is entirely based on guided procedures. The old ITS-based Life and Work Events are not available in the latest release.

Guided Procedures is a framework for modeling and managing workflows using simple and user-friendly tools. It is part of the Composite Application Framework (CAF). It forms the basis of the new "Life and Work Events" functionality in the latest business package, because it allows you to build and support employee life and career events via a checklist-like procedure. Guided Procedures will be discussed in more detail in Chapter 8, "Advanced Concepts in Employee and Manager Self-Service."

The iViews in Tables 6.25-6.31 represent example processes.

My First Days iView

My First Days	
Runtime Technology	Web Dynpro Java iView
Technical Name of iView	com.sap.pct.erp.ess.lwe_myfirstdays
Technical Name of Web Dynpro Application	sap.com/caf~eu~gp~ui~inst/AInstantiation
Service Key	EMPLOYEE_LIFEWORK_FIRSTDAYS
Available as of	SAP NetWeaver 2004s
Data Source	SAP ECC 6.0 or above
Software Component	EA-HR
Support	CA-ESS-WD
Support Languages	English (US specific)

Table 6.25 Technical Data for the My First Days iView

Benefits iView

Benefits	
Runtime Technology	Web Dynpro Java iView
Technical Name of iView	com.sap.pct.erp.ess.lwe_benefits
Technical Name of Web Dynpro Application	sap.com/caf~eu~gp~ui~inst/AInstantiation
Service Key	EMPLOYEE_LIFEWORK_BENEFITS
Available as of	SAP NetWeaver 2004s
Data Source	SAP ECC 6.0 or above
Software Component	EA-HR
Support	CA-ESS-WD
Support Languages	English (US specific)

Table 6.26 Technical Data for the Benefits iView

Change in Employment Status iView

Change in Employment Status	
Runtime Technology	Web Dynpro Java iView
Technical Name of iView	com.sap.pct.erp.ess.lwe_changeemploymentstatus
Technical Name of Web Dynpro Application	sap.com/caf~eu~gp~ui~inst/AInstantiation
Service Key	EMPLOYEE_LIFEWORK_CHANGESTATUS
Available as of	SAP NetWeaver 2004s
Data Source	SAP ECC 6.0 or above
Software Component	EA-HR
Support	CA-ESS-WD
Support Languages	English (US specific)

Table 6.27 Technical Data for the Change in Employment Status iView

Terminate Employment iView

Terminate Employment	
Runtime Technology	Web Dynpro Java iView
Technical Name of iView	com.sap.pct.erp.ess.lwe_terminateemployment
Technical Name of Web Dynpro Application	sap.com/caf~eu~gp~ui~inst/AInstantiation
Service Key	EMPLOYEE_LIFEWORK_TERMINATEEMPLOYMENT
Available as of	SAP NetWeaver 2004s
Data Source	SAP ECC 6.0 or above
Software Component	EA-HR
Support	CA-ESS-WD
Support Languages	English (US specific)

Table 6.28 Technical Data for the Change in Employment Status iView

Birth/Adoption iView

Birth/Adoption	
Runtime Technology	Web Dynpro Java iView
Technical Name of iView	com.sap.pct.erp.ess.lwe_birthadoption
Technical Name of Web Dynpro Application	sap.com/caf~eu~gp~ui~inst/AInstantiation
Service Key	EMPLOYEE_LIFEWORK_BIRTH
Available as of	SAP NetWeaver 2004s
Data Source	SAP ECC 6.0 or above
Software Component	EA-HR
Support	CA-ESS-WD
Support Languages	English (US specific)

Table 6.29 Technical Data for the Birth/Adoption iView

Marriage iView

Marriage	
Runtime Technology	Web Dynpro Java iView
Technical Name of iView	com.sap.pct.erp.ess.lwe_marriage
Technical Name of Web Dynpro Application	sap.com/caf~eu~gp~ui~inst/AInstantiation
Service Key	EMPLOYEE_LIFEWORK_MARRIAGE
Available as of	SAP NetWeaver 2004s
Data Source	SAP ECC 6.0 or above
Software Component	EA-HR
Support	CA-ESS-WD
Support Languages	English (US specific)

Table 6.30 Technical Data for the Marriage iView

Divorce iView

Divorce	
Runtime Technology	Web Dynpro Java iView
Technical Name of iView	com.sap.pct.erp.ess.lwe_divorce
Technical Name of Web Dynpro Application	sap.com/caf~eu~gp~ui~inst/AInstantiation
Service Key	EMPLOYEE_LIFEWORK_DIVORCE
Available as of	SAP NetWeaver 2004s
Data Source	SAP ECC 6.0 or above
Software Component	EA-HR
Support	CA-ESS-WD
Support Languages	English (US specific)

Table 6.31 Technical Data for the Divorce iView

> **Note:**
> Four ESS applications within this workset, Maternity Leave (Germany), Birth of a Child (US and Germany), Terminate Employment (US and Germany), and Status Overview of Processes in Life and Work Events, are part of the HR Administrative Services (PA-AS) functionality and will not be covered in this book. These services are only available as part of Enhancement Package 2 for SAP ERP 6.0.

6.3.8 Corporate Information

The technical name of the Corporate Information workset is *com.sap.pct.erp.ess. area_corporate_info*. The Corporate Information workset contains one iView called Code of Business Conduct, which is based on Adobe Form technology. In order to use this iView, you need to have implemented Adobe Document Services. Also, you need to have enough Adobe form licenses. Speak to your SAP software contact if you have questions about licensing, because each company and contract are unique.

Table 6.32 provides the technical data for the Code of Business iView.

Code of Business Conduct iView

Code of Business Conduct	
Runtime Technology	Web Dynpro Java iView
Technical Name of iView	com.sap.pct.erp.ess.codeofconductapplication
Technical Name of Web Dynpro Application	sap.com/ess~essforms/CodeOfConductApplication
Service Key	EMPLOYEE_CORPORATE_CONDUCT05
Available as of	SAP NetWeaver 2004s
Data Origin	SAP ECC 6.0 or above
Software Component	EA-HR
Support	PA-ESS-XX
Support Languages	All languages supported by the SAP system

Table 6.32 Technical Data for the Code of Business Conduct iView

6.4   Summary

In this chapter, we reviewed the core functionality of ESS — from the Homepage Framework architecture to the standard services available by workset within the business package for ESS.

As you can see, with the SAP system you can deliver ESS within the SAP Portal out of the box. The advantages afforded to us via the new SAP NetWeaver technology — coupled with the flexibility of the Homepage Framework — have placed SAP's ESS solution in a favorable position. Its rich, configurable platform allows you to effectively deliver real-time HR transactions and information to your company's most precious asset — its employees.

In the next chapter, we will cover the core functionality within MSS. You will see many parallels between the MSS and ESS functionality (including the Homepage Framework), but there are some nuances that are important to clarify.

Manager Self-Service (MSS) provides line management with access to their employee's real-time data and a foundation on which to deliver key operational activities, such as workforce planning, performance management, and compensation management. This chapter explores the MSS functionality available in SAP's latest business package for MSS, including Best Practices for its implementation.

7 Functionality Available in Manager Self-Service

Although MSS has existed in Human Resources (HR) service delivery models since the late 1990s, its usage and efficiencies have only recently taken root within the industry. In recent years, SAP has invested a tremendous amount of time and energy in improving and broadening the scope of services offered via the SAP Portal for managers. MSS functionality has made major improvements since the first SAP Enterprise Portal (version 5.0). The offerings and improved look-and-feel of the latest SAP Portal (SAP NetWeaver version 7.0 2004s) have empowered HR and Information Technology (IT) decision-makers to implement self-service for managers more quickly and at a faster adoption rate. The offering has also expanded from a global perspective, as more services are offered in different countries. The portal also supports the following 30 languages: English, French, German, Italian, Portuguese, Spanish, Arabic, Bulgarian, Chinese (simplified), Chinese (traditional), Croatian, Czech, Danish, Dutch, Finnish, Greek, Hebrew, Hungarian, Japanese, Korean, Norwegian, Polish, Romanian, Russian, Serbian, Slovenian, Slovakian, Swedish, Thai, and Turkish.

In this chapter, we will review the basics of the MSS functionality. We will examine the delivered roles, worksets, and iViews contained within the business package. And, as we did with Employee Self-Service (ESS), we will focus our attention on a select group of iViews that we feel offer customers the most value. Technical details on the backend and portal configuration are provided as well.

7.1 Application Component for MSS

Each iView within MSS is associated with an application component for categorization and support purposes. The application component is used both in searching for SAP Notes and when creating SAP Customer Messages. The application component for MSS is EP-PCT-MGR-HR for HR-related components within the business package and EP-PCT-MGR-CO for the Finance-related ones. Additional components are available for function-specific iViews, such as CA-TS-IA-XS for the Cross-Application Timesheet (CATS), PT_RC_UI_XS for Leave Requests, and EP-PCT-PLM-PSS for Project Systems functionality.

> **Note**
>
> For an inventory of SAP Notes related to MSS in ERP2005, refer to SAP Note 903319. This is the composite SAP Note that contains all SAP Notes relevant for the latest release of MSS.

7.2 What We Will Cover

The focus of this chapter will be on the HR functionality availability within the business package for MSS — application component EP-PCT-MGR-HR. Worksets, pages, and iViews within this component are all HR-related MSS transactions whether it be for Personnel Change Requests, Compensation Management, or Timesheet approvals. We will not be covering Finance-related functionality within the business package for MSS — application component EP-PCT-MGR-CO.

The HR functionality to be reviewed in this chapter focuses on the iViews within the following worksets. A workset is a set of pre-delivered pages and iViews available in the standard delivery. It contains pages and iViews that contain transactional services, such as compensation planning and employee search.

▶ Work Overview Workset, contains the Universal Worklist (UWL) functionality and iViews on time and attendance functionality.

▶ Team Workset, contains most of the HR-related functionality for managers, including the functionality for leave management, performance management, compensation management, recruitment, and more. iViews within this workset will be the majority of our discussion in this chapter.

▶ Planning Workset, contains links to compensation planning and compensation approval iViews.

▶ Reports Workset, contains report-related iViews, including the generic iViews for table and list.

We will also cover some iViews not included in a standard workset, such as the suite of organizational unit-based and position-based iViews for managers. These iViews provide managers with an inventory of organizational information within their span-of-control.

iViews included within the Budget and Projects Worksets will not be covered. The Budget Workset contains financial data, such as information on the manager's profit centers, cost centers, and internal orders, while the Projects Workset contains services from the Business Package for Project Self-Service (mySAP ERP) such as project services, plan consumption, budget, and resource availability. The intent of this chapter is to explain MSS from an HR perspective.

In addition, Business Intelligence (BI) iViews will not be discussed. For more information on BI, reference *HR Reporting with SAP* by Hans-Jürgen Figaj, Richard Haßmann, and Anja Junold from SAP PRESS.

Tip

All business packages, including the Business Package for MSS (mySAP ERP) (Release 1.0), can be downloaded from the SAP Developer's Network (SDN) content portfolio at *https://www.sdn.sap.com/irj/sdn/contentportfolio* under the category Business Packages for Managers. A Service Marketplace user name and password is required to log in and download.

Throughout the chapter, references will be made to the Object and Data Provider (OADP) and UWL functionality. In Chapter 8, "Advanced Concepts in ESS and MSS," we will discuss these topics in detail, as they play a crucial role in the delivery of many MSS solutions.

Before we review the functionality within MSS, let's first discuss the home page framework for MSS.

7.3 MSS Home Page Framework

As with ESS, the home page framework provides the foundation for navigation, look-and-feel, and overall user experience for MSS. The configuration for the home page framework for MSS components can be accessed from the Implementation Guide (IMG) via the path: Cross-Application Components • Homepage Framework. Because ESS and MSS share the same configuration activities, the steps should be familiar to you. Configuration is needed for area group pages, area pages, subareas, services, and resources within the home page framework.

> **Important**
>
> In the standard delivery of the MSS, the home page framework is not used. However, the SAP system does provide many of the standard elements of the framework, including area group pages, area pages, subareas, and services for you to incorporate into your own custom version.

Let's first discuss the area group page.

7.3.1 Area Group Page

As with ESS, the area group page is used as the landing page for managers when they enter self-service. Area group page SAPDEFAULTMSS is the delivered area group page for MSS. Area group pages can be added in view V_T7XSSSERARGB via Transaction SM30 or by following the IMG path: Cross-Application Components • Homepage Framework • Headers and Area Group Pages • Define Area Group Pages • Define Area Group Pages (Add Entries).

Area group pages can be changed in view V_T7XSSSERARGC via Transaction SM30 or by following the IMG path: Cross-Application Components • Homepage Framework • Headers and Area Group Pages • Define Area Group Pages • Define Area Group Pages (Change Entries).

Figure 7.1 shows the default area group page SAPDEFAULTMSS with reference to link resource MSS_HCM_AREAGROUP_OVERVIEW_PAG. An area group description is available to provide end users with an introduction to the MSS launch page.

As in ESS, the area group page is straightforward. Let's move on to discuss area pages and the available standard within the home page framework.

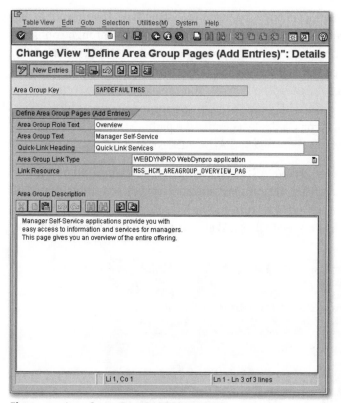

Figure 7.1 Area Group Page SAPDEFAULTMSS

7.3.2 Area Pages

SAP software provides six delivered area pages within the home page framework for MSS. All area pages pertinent for MSS begin with the prefix MSS. The following area pages are available:

- MSS_HCM_AREA_ATTENDANCE
- MSS_HCM_AREA_HEADCOUNT
- MSS_HCM_AREA_PERSONNELCHANGEREQUEST
- MSS_HCM_AREA_RECRUITING
- MSS_HCM_AREA_RELATEDACTIVITY
- MSS_HCM_AREA_REPORTING

Area pages provide the high-level entry points to MSS functions. If you want to add or change the area pages for your implementation, you can do so through configuration. To add additional area pages, you must configure in view V_T7XSSSERARB or via the IMG under the path: CROSS-APPLICATION COMPONENTS • HOMEPAGE FRAMEWORK • AREAS • DEFINE AREAS • DEFINE AREAS (ADD ENTRIES). You can also override configuration of the standard delivered areas with your customer-specific requirements by configuring view V_T7XSSSERARBC or via the IMG under the path: CROSS-APPLICATION COMPONENTS • HOMEPAGE FRAMEWORK • AREAS • DEFINE AREAS • DEFINE AREAS (CHANGE ENTRIES).

Figure 7.2 shows area MSS_HCM_AREA_RECRUITING for recruitment applications. As with area pages in ESS, the long text and summary descriptions should be configured per your requirements. Picture and link resources should be populated and area link type should be specified as a Web Dynpro for Java application.

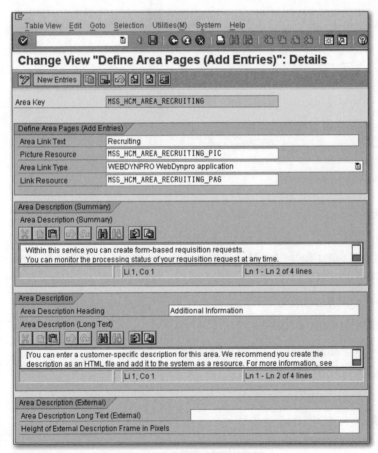

Figure 7.2 Area Page MSS_HCM_AREA_RECRUITING

You can also import and export text from a local file by using the Load Local File and Save as Local File options located above the free text boxes. This is helpful if you have a lot of text to include in the description fields of the area summary or heading.

Next, let's discuss subareas and how they can be incorporated into these area pages within your MSS framework.

7.3.3 Subareas

With subareas, you can divide an area page into unique sections. The SAP system provides the following standard eight subareas within the home page framework for MSS. These include:

- MSS_HCM_ATTENDANCE
- MSS_HCM_HEADCOUNT
- MSS_HCM_PCR
- MSS_HCM_RC_CANDIDATEASSESSMENTS
- MSS_HCM_RC_REQUEST
- MSS_HCM_REPORTING
- MSS_HCM_SUB_RELATEDACTIVITY_ESS
- MSS_HCM_SUB_RELATEDACTIVITY_PCR

Subareas are associated to area pages and allow you to assign services relevant to MSS functions. There may also be reasons to add or change the subarea pages for your implementation based on your unique requirements.

Figure 7.3 shows the subareas available. To add additional subarea pages, you must configure in view V_T7XSSSERSARB or via the IMG under the path: CROSS-APPLICATION COMPONENTS • HOMEPAGE FRAMEWORK • SUBAREAS • DEFINE SUBAREAS • DEFINE SUBAREAS (ADD ENTRIES). You can also override configuration of the standard delivered areas by configuring view V_T7XSSSERSARBC or via the IMG under the path: CROSS-APPLICATION COMPONENTS • HOMEPAGE FRAMEWORK • SUBAREAS • DEFINE SUBAREAS • DEFINE SUBAREAS (CHANGE ENTRIES).

All that is configured here is the text of the subarea. The text can be up to 80 characters long.

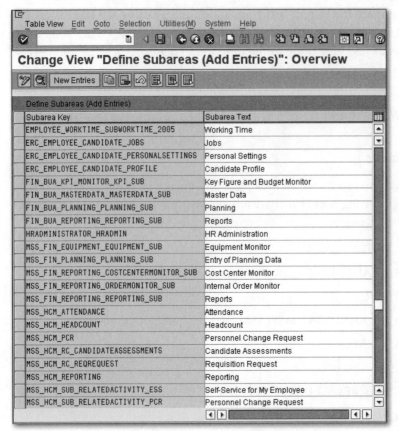

Figure 7.3 Subarea Definition, Including Two Delivered Subareas for Recruitment: MSS_HCM_ RC_REQREQUEST and MSS_HCM_RC_CANDIDATEASSESSMENTS

► Each of these subareas are then assigned to an area page. The assignment of subareas to areas is performed in view V_T7XSSSERAR or in the IMG under the path: CROSS-APPLICATION COMPONENTS • HOMEPAGE FRAMEWORK • SUBAREAS • ASSIGN SUBAREAS TO AREAS (ADD AND CHANGE ENTRIES).

► In Figure 7.4, area MSS_HCM_AREA_RECRUITING is comprised of subareas MSS_HCM_RC_REQREQUEST (in position 1) and MSS_HCM_RC_CANDI-DATEASSESSMENTS (in position 2). This indicates that the requisition request subarea will be positioned above the candidate assessments subarea within the recruitment area page of MSS. The position is used to "stack" the subareas, from top to bottom based on numerical order.

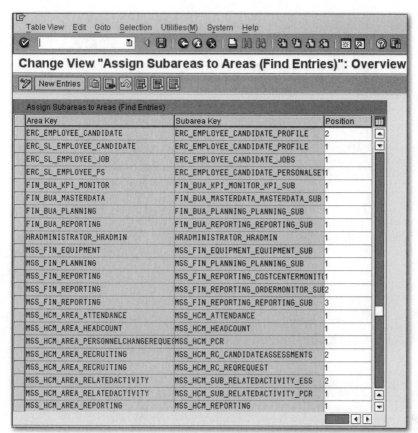

Figure 7.4 Assign Subareas to Areas Showing Subareas MSS_HCM_RC_REQREQUEST and MSS_HCM_RC_CANDIDATEASSESSMENTS Assigned to Area MSS_HCM_AREA_RECRUITING

Once you have configured your area group page, area pages, and associated subareas, it is time to configure the services you want to provide managers with on those pages.

7.3.4 Services

The MSS home page framework also includes several delivered services. Most manager services begin with the prefix MSS_HCM. MSS_HCM_RECRUITING_NEWREQ_REQUEST, for example, is a service that allows managers to create requisitions using Adobe Forms. Figure 7.5 shows this service with its Link Resource MSS_HCM_SERV_RECRUITING_NEW_REQ.

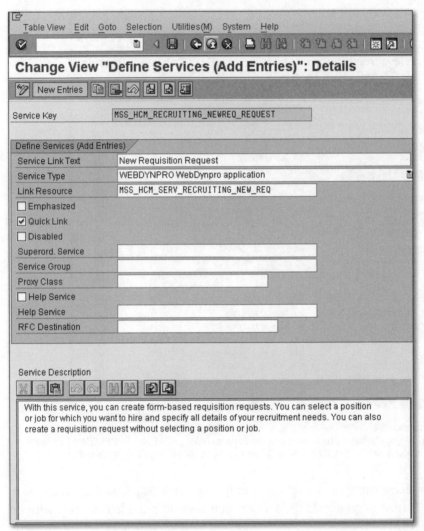

Figure 7.5 Service MSS_HCM_RECRUITING_NEWREQ_REQUEST

Service configuration is identical to what we covered within ESS. The same functionality is available. For example, a service can be disabled or "emphasized." A service description is also available to provide the user with additional information on the functionality.

The proxy class can also be a helpful mechanism within MSS. A custom proxy class can be created to only render a link based on some type of manager's data.

For example, a custom proxy class could be created to determine if a service link should only appear on an area page depending on the salary grade of the logged-on manager. This is helpful because it can reduce the number of portal pages needed to support your processes. A service ordinarily only granted to a manager via a portal role could now be granted dynamically via logic within a proxy class. A link to the Compensation Approval iView, for instance, may require only making it available if the manager is executive level (i.e., if their salary grade is over 20).

Every service points to a resource, which is discussed next.

7.3.5 Resources

Delivered resources for MSS are also included within the home page framework. Resource MSS_HCM_SERV_RECRUITING_NEW_REQ — a resource that defines functionality to allow managers to create requisition requests — is an example of this. This resource supports the service MSS_HCM_RECRUITING_NEWREQ_REQUEST previously discussed. This resource is configured in view V_T7XSSSERRES or in the IMG under the path: CROSS-APPLICATION COMPONENTS • HOMEPAGE FRAMEWORK • RESOURCES • DEFINE RESOURCES • DEFINE RESOURCES (ADD ENTRIES).

Figure 7.6 shows the details of resource MSS_HCM_SERV_RECRUITING_NEW_REQ. The resource references the Web Dynpro for Java application via a directory path (sap.com/mss~rec~req) and object name (RequisitionCreation). A URL parameter is also identified: sap.xss.req.crt.viewid1=RECPOS&sap.xss.req.crt.viewid2=RECJOB&sap.xss.req.crt.viewgr3=REC_OVERVIEW2&sap.xss.req.crt.cachelifetime=0&sap.xss.req.crt.visiblerows=11. This string will be passed to the iView at runtime. These parameters influence how the iView is rendered. In this example, information on views and view groups within the OADP, a caching setting, and the number of visible rows will be specified in the URL during the resource's call to the backend Web Dynpro for Java application.

As we have seen, defining a home page framework for MSS follows the exact same procedures as ESS. Although the standard business package for MSS does not utilize the home page framework, it may make sense to leverage the framework across both ESS and MSS platforms.

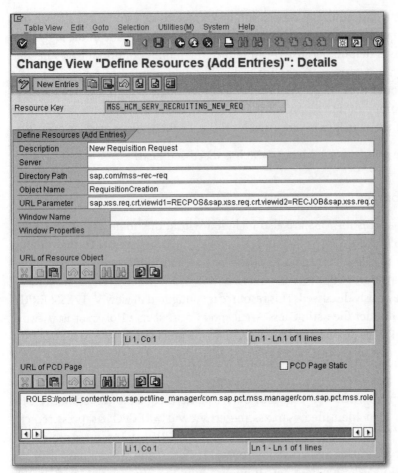

Figure 7.6 Resource MSS_HCM_SERV_RECRUITING_NEW_REQ for New Requisition Request within Recruitment

7.4 Business Package for MSS

The business package provides one role called MSS with the technical name *com.sap.pct.erp.mss.manager_self_service*. This role contains a collection of worksets, pages, and iViews. It is recommended that you copy this role into your own customer name space and manipulate your customized role based on your business requirements. It would be rare to use the out-of-the-box role as you most likely will not want to use all of the functionality included in the role. The business package is a way for the SAP system to deliver the functionality in an organized and logical format.

> **Note**
>
> One of the prerequisites to use MSS is to have deployed the Business Package for Common Parts (mySAP ERP). This role (with technical name *com.sap.pct.erp.common.erp_common*) contains technical prerequisites for MSS including internal service requests (ISRs), launchpad, and general navigation functionality. It can be downloaded from the SDN content portfolio at *https://www.sdn.sap.com/irj/sdn/contentportfolio* under the category Business Packages for Every User. A Service Marketplace user name and password is required to log in and download.

We will review each functional area (working time, recruitment, talent management, etc.) within the MSS business package and highlight particular applications and their functionality. Where relevant, the backend SAP configuration and portal iView configuration will be discussed as well. The majority of the MSS iViews are "plug-and-play" — meaning that most work out of the box without much, if any, configuration assuming that the backend component is implemented. Other iViews require more pre-work or technical prerequisites. The Business Server Page (BSP) iViews for Performance Management, for example, need to be created and placed on a page before they can be accessed by an employee or manager.

The standard MSS role contains six worksets. The following is a list of the worksets with their technical names:

► Work Overview (com.sap.pct.erp.mss.work_overview)
► Team Workset (com.sap.pct.erp.mss.team)
► Budget Workset (com.sap.pct.erp.mss.budget) [not covered in this book]
► Project Workset (com.sap.pct.erp.mss.projects) [not covered in this book]
► Planning Workset (com.sap.pct.erp.mss.planning)
► Reports Workset (com.sap.pct.erp.mss.reports)

These worksets contain a mix of services relevant to HR, Finance, and Project Systems functionality. Some iViews are based on NetWeaver BI and will not be functional unless you have a BI system, so our focus will remain on the HCM functionality available within these worksets.

Instead of looking at the various services by workset, we have broken down functionality by functional area. We believe this is the best way of presenting the information due to the volume of iViews available within the business package. Reviewing the applications by function will also provide you with a more holistic understanding of how all of the components interrelate.

We will start with one of the most popular functional areas — Time Management.

7.4.1 Working Time

The Working Time iViews allow managers to track the time and attendance data for their direct and indirect reports. With this functionality, managers can understand more information on the absences and attendances taken by their employees. Visibility into leave requests, time accounts, and reasons for absences empower managers to plan their workforce more effectively.

The following iViews related to Working Time are available within the MSS business package:

- Attendance Overview
- Team Calendar
- Absence Days
- Reminder of Dates

Each of these is discussed next.

> **Note**
>
> There are several services available for Effort Reporting — functionality pertinent only to the U.S. Public Sector. We will not be covering this functionality. However, information can be found online at: *http://help.sap.com/saphelp_erp2005vp/helpdata/en/42/ f159a9f8501aa2e10000000a422035/frameset.htm*.

Attendance Overview iView

Table 7.1 provides the technical data for the Attendance Overview iView.

The Attendance Overview iView displays the attendance status (Absent, At Work, etc.) of the manager's direct and indirect reports for the current day. Clicking the status link will provide a pop-up box with details on each employees' absence or attendance. A Show Details button is available to display more information on the absences if required by the manager. The detailed information includes the employees' absence times and the names of employees who are at work. Information for absences and attendances are sourced from Infotype 2001 (Absences) and Infotype 2002 (Attendances) as well as any requested leave from the Leave Request application (if implemented).

Attendance Overview	
Runtime Technology	Java/Web Dynpro
Technical Name of iView	com.sap.pct.erp.mss.attendanceoverview
Technical Name of Web Dynpro Application	sap.com/mss~ato/AttendanceOverviewApp
Available as of	SAP NetWeaver 2004s
Data Origin	SAP ECC 6.0 and higher
	Remote Function Call (RFC) function component called:
	PT_ARQ_AVAIL_OVERVIEW
Software Component	EA-HR
Support	EP-PCT-MGR-HR

Table 7.1 Technical Data for the Attendance Overview iView

Figure 7.7 shows a manager with two direct reports, both of whom are absent.

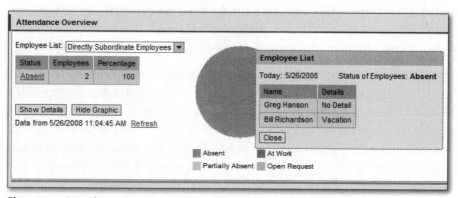

Figure 7.7 Attendance Overview iView with Detail on Absent Employees

The Employee List dropdown box is based on the configuration-defined view V_ PTREQ_TEAM or in the IMG under the path: Integration with Other mySAP.com

COMPONENTS • BUSINESS PACKAGES/FUNCTIONAL PACKAGES • MANAGER SELF-SERVICE (MYSAP ERP) • WORKING TIME • ATTENDANCE OVERVIEW • SELECT EMPLOYEES.

Figure 7.8 shows the table view that associates a mode to a view group. In the case of the Attendance Overview iView, mode O Attendance Overview is linked to organizational view MSS_LAV_EE. Organizational view MSS_LAV_EE is defined in the OADP framework. Organizational views are discussed in detail in the next chapter. This view returns all directly reporting employees to the manager. The manager can also switch to view all of his reports via the dropdown selection.

Table View	Edit	Goto	Selection	Utilities(M)	System	Help

Change View "Select Employees": Overview

Expand <-> Collapse	New Entries	Delimit

Select Employees

Rule Group	Name of Rule Group	Start Date	End Date	Mode	View/Grp.	Group of Organiza	Group
00000001	SAP Standard	01/01/1800	12/31/9999	A Approval Mode	V View Grp	MSS_LEA_EE	
00000001	SAP Standard	01/01/1800	12/31/9999	C CATS Approval	V View Grp	MSS_LCA_EE	
00000001	SAP Standard	01/01/1800	12/31/9999	O Attendance Overview	V View Grp	MSS_LAV_EE	
00000001	SAP Standard	01/01/1800	12/31/9999	R Request Mode	V View Grp	ESS_LEA_EE	
00000001	SAP Standard	01/01/1800	12/31/9999	T Team View Mode	V View Grp	MSS_LTV_EE	

Figure 7.8 Organizational Views Definition for Each Mode and Rule Group within Working Time iViews

You can also identify employees by "rules groups." A rule group is an eight-digit number defined across all time-management applications on the portal. Rule groups are configured in the IMG under the path: INTEGRATION WITH OTHER MYSAP.COM COMPONENTS • BUSINESS PACKAGES/FUNCTIONAL PACKAGES • MANAGER SELF-SERVICE (MYSAP ERP) • WORKING TIME • ATTENDANCE OVERVIEW • CREATE RULE GROUPS • CREATE RULE GROUPS.

Feature WEBMO is used to assign employees to rule groups. In Figure 7.9, feature WEBMO is assigning different rule groups based on cost center. You can use many fields to determine an employee's rule group, including employee group, employee subgroup, personnel area, and personnel subarea. Feature WEBMO is configured in the IMG under the path: INTEGRATION WITH OTHER MYSAP.COM COMPONENTS • BUSINESS PACKAGES/FUNCTIONAL PACKAGES • MANAGER SELF-SERVICE (MYSAP ERP) • WORKING TIME • ATTENDANCE OVERVIEW • CREATE RULE GROUPS • ADJUST WEBMO FEATURE.

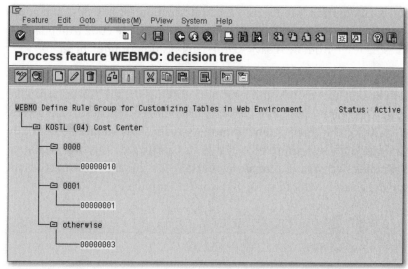

Figure 7.9 Feature WEBMO — Assignment of Rule Groups to Employees

Team Calendar iView

Table 7.2 provides the technical data for the Team Calendar iView.

Team Calendar	
Runtime Technology	Java/Web Dynpro
Technical Name of iView	com.sap.pct.erp.mss.teamcalendar
Technical Name of Web Dynpro Application	sap.com/ess~lea/TeamView
Available as of	SAP NetWeaver 2004s
Data Origin	SAP ECC 5.0 and higher RFC function component called: PT_ARQ_TEAMCALE_GET
Software Component	EA-HR
Support	EP-PCT-MGR-HR

Table 7.2 Technical Data for the Team Calendar iView

The Team Calendar iView allows managers to quickly view absence and attendance information for their direct and indirect reports. Clicking on the actual absence/attendance for an employee will expose more information on the leave, including the type, the dates, and total duration (see Figure 7.10). Information for absences and atten-dances are sourced from Infotype 2001 (Absences) and Infotype 2002 (Attendances) and any requested leave from the Leave Request application (if implemented).

Within the iViews, managers can select a date in the past or the future by select-ing a combination of the month and year and clicking on the Go button. Like the Attendance Overview iView, the OADP is driven off of entries in table view V_PTREQ_TEAM (for the Team Calendar, mode T Team View should be used). By default, organizational view group MSS_LTV_EE is configured. This organizational view group contains two organizational views: MSS_LTV_EE_DIR for Directly Sub-ordinate Employees and MSS_LTV_EE_ALL for All Employees.

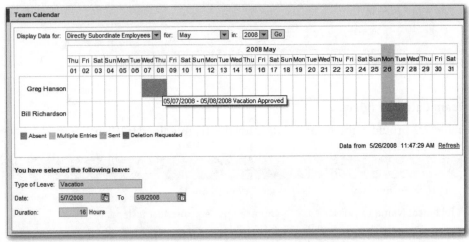

Figure 7.10   Team Calendar iView with Additional Information Selected

As with the Attendance Overview iView, rule groups and OADP views should be configured based on your requirements. All configurations for the Team Calendar are performed in the IMG under the path: INTEGRATION WITH OTHER MYSAP.COM COM-PONENTS • BUSINESS PACKAGES/FUNCTIONAL PACKAGES • MANAGER SELF-SERVICE (MYSAP ERP) • TEAM CALENDAR.

You can restrict which absence and attendance types are viewable in the iView through the standard configuration. To filter these absences/attendances by rule group, you can perform the necessary configuration in the IMG under the path: INTEGRATION WITH OTHER MYSAP.COM COMPONENTS • BUSINESS PACKAGES/FUNCTIONAL PACK-AGES • MANAGER SELF-SERVICE (MYSAP ERP) • WORKING TIME • TEAM CALENDAR • SPECIFY ABSENCES TO BE DISPLAYED.

You can also adjust the layout (colors, legend, etc.) of the Team Calendar iView by implementing enhancement spot PT_ABS_REQ. Methods SET_CALENDAR_COLOR, SET_CALENDAR_LEGEND_COLORS, and TEAM_CALE_ENRICHMENT are available to enhance the application. The number of rows and cache settings can be set in the IMG under the path: INTEGRATION WITH OTHER MYSAP.COM COMPONENTS • BUSINESS PACKAGES/FUNCTIONAL PACKAGES • MANAGER SELF-SERVICE (MYSAP ERP) • WORKING TIME • TEAM CALENDAR • DEFINE LAYOUT OF TEAM CALENDAR. You can specify defaults on how leaves are displayed and from and until when in the IMG under the path: INTEGRATION WITH OTHER MYSAP.COM COMPONENTS • BUSINESS PACKAGES/FUNCTIONAL PACKAGES • MANAGER SELF-SERVICE (MYSAP ERP) • WORKING TIME • TEAM CALENDAR • SPECIFY COLOR DISPLAY OF ABSENCES.

> **Note**
>
> If the calendar within the Team Calendar iView does not render properly, this may mean you have not properly installed or configured the Internet Graphics Server (IGS). IGS is part of the installation and deployment of MSS. More information can be found at *http://help.sap.com/saphelp_erp2005vp/helpdata/en/17/86c039c7811f11e10000000a114084/frameset.htm* and within the business package installation guides.

Absence Days iView

Table 7.3 provides the technical data for the Absence Days iView.

Absence Days	
Runtime Technology	Java/Web Dynpro
Technical Name of iView	com.sap.pct.erp.mss.generalinfo_absencedays
Technical Name of Web Dynpro Application	sap.com/mss~eepro/GeneralInformation
Available as of	SAP NetWeaver 2004s
Data Source	SAP ECC 6.0 and higher
	RFC function component called:
	HRWPC_RFC_EP_READ_ABSENCEDAYS
Software Component	EA-HR
Support	EP-PCT-MGR-HR

Table 7.3 Technical Data for the Absence Days iView

The Absence Days iView is not a standalone iView. The iView functions after the manager selects the employees within the Employee Search iView. This Employee Search iView serves as the "master iView" and the Absence Days iView is dependent on the employee selection from this iView.

The Absence Days iView displays all of an employee's absence types from IT2001 (Absences). If you only want to display certain absence types to the manager, enhancement HRWPCABS (Filtering Absence Records) can be implemented to restrict certain absence types from appearing on the iView. This enhancement can be created via user exit functionality available in Transaction CMOD. Alternatively, you can use iView parameter Absence Type (ABSENCE_TYPE) to filter absence types. Work with your portal content administration to add the list of absences you want to filter.

Note

Program RPTARQUIATEST can be used to test time management iViews from the SAP backend. This program (originally an SAP internal program) is used to simulate the time applications leave request (both display and create), time accounts, attendance overview, and the team calendar. The calendar tab has no function.

Reminder of Dates iView

Table 7.4 provides the technical data for the Reminder of Dates iView.

Reminder of Dates	
Runtime Technology	Java/Web Dynpro
Technical Name iView	com.sap.pct.erp.mss.reminderofdates
Technical Name Web Dynpro application	sap.com/mss~rod/ReminderOfDatesApp
Available from Portal (release)	SAP NetWeaver 2004s
Data Source	RFC function component called: HRMSS_RFC_RD_DATES_GETLIST
Software Component	EA-HR 600 and above
Support	EP-PCT-MGR-HR

Table 7.4 Technical Data for the Reminder of Dates iView

The Reminder of Dates iView displays the tasks for a manager's employees based on the IT0019 (Monitoring of Tasks) data. By default, all employees are shown to the manager (as the preconfigured object selection is MSS_ROD_SEL1) but this can be changed to another object selection via the OADP configuration. The iView shows a month view and the user can scroll left and right to see past and future dates as well. Both the event and the name of the employee have links.

The General Data iView is launched when the user clicks on the employee's name. A Monitoring of Tasks iView — containing task name, task status, date, and reminder date — is launched when clicking on the Event.

Figure 7.11 shows the iView with two employees, Greg Hanson and Bill Richardson, who have four dates — two reminders and two tasks. (An asterisk next to the date indicates a reminder for a task.)

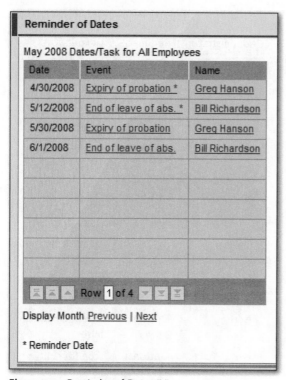

Figure 7.11 Reminder of Dates iView

There are several iView properties that are configurable, including the evaluation period, the task types that should be visible to the user, and sensitive information such as status, age, and birthdays. Table 7.5 lists the properties of the Reminder of Dates iView, along with who maintains them (the user or a portal administrator) and any default values.

Description (GUI)	Property	Maintained By	Type of Entry	Allowed Entries
Anniversaries to be displayed (yearly ranges)	ANNIVERSARY_RANGES	User	Required	Default = 10,20,25
Service Key of the application to display employee's detailed information	EE_DETAIL_COMPONENT	Administrator	Required	Default = MSS_ROD_TRGT_GENERALDATA
Service Key of the application to display employee's monitoring of tasks information	EE_MONTASK_COMPONENT	Administrator	Required	Default = MSS_ROD_TRGT_MOT
Object selection ID (key) for the object and data provider	OBJSEL	Administrator	Required	Default = MSS_ROD_SEL1
Number of rows displayed per page	ROWS	User	Optional	Default = 0 (Values of 0 or less will display all available records
Display age	SHOW_AGE	Administrator	Required	True (default) or false
Display anniversaries	SHOW_ANNIVERSARY	User	Optional	True (default) or false
Display birthdays	SHOW_BIRTHDAY	User	Optional	True (default) or false

Table 7.5 iView Properties for Reminder of Dates

Description (GUI)	Property	Maintained By	Type of Entry	Allowed Entries
Display task data from IT0019	SHOW_MONTASK	User	Optional	True (default) or false
Employment status for anniversary	STATUS_ANNIVERSARY	Administrator	Optional	Allowed employment status key for anniversary list from Infotype 0000
Employment status for birthday	STATUS_BIRTHDAY	Administrator	Optional	Allowed employment status key for birthdays from Infotype 0000
Employment status for monitoring of tasks	STATUS_MONTASK	Administrator	Optional	Allowed employment status key for monitoring of tasks from Infotype 0000
Task types (key) for monitoring of tasks	TASKTYPES	Administrator	Optional	Input field for task types from IT0019 that are to be displayed
Display reminder date	SHOW_REMINDERDATE	User	Optional	True (default) or false

Table 7.5 iView Properties for Reminder of Dates (Cont.)

This concludes our review of the Working Time functional area. The four available iViews — Attendance Overview, Team Calendar, Absence Days, and Reminder of Dates — empower managers to plan their workforce more efficiently because absence and attendance data is at their fingertips.

7.4.2 Employee Information

The functionality related to the Employee Information functional area allows managers to view general employment and work-related data for their direct and indirect reports. Basic employee data, such as name, and organizational and company information, are available for display. The following iViews related to general employee information are available within the business package:

▶ Employee Search (master iView)

▶ General Data

▶ Personal Data

▶ Monitoring of Tasks

▶ Company Property

▶ Photo

▶ Archived Documents

Each of these is discussed next.

Employee Search

Table 7.6 provides the technical data for the Employee Search iView.

Employee Search	
Runtime Technology	Java/Web Dynpro
Technical Names of iViews	com.sap.pct.erp.mss.employeesearch_geinfo
	com.sap.pct.erp.mss.employeesearch_coinfo
	com.sap.pct.erp.mss.teamviewer_persdev
Technical Names of Web Dynpro Applications	sap.com/mss~eepro/GeneralInformation
	sap.com/mss~eepro/CompensationInformation
	sap.com/mss~eepro/PersonnelDevelopment
Available From	SAP NetWeaver 2004s
Data Source	SAP ECC 6.0 or above
	RFC function components called: function components of the function group HRWPC_OADP_UI
Software Component	EA-HR 600 and above
Support	EP-PCT-MGR-HR

Table 7.6 Technical Data for the Employee Search iView

Figure 7.12 shows the Employee Search iView. The Employee Search iView is a "master" iView because it is used to launch other iViews. It is the replacement for the TeamViewer iView in previous versions of SAP MSS. The Employee Search can be found on three pages within the MSS business package: the General Information page (technical name *com.sap.pct.erp.mss.general_information*), the Compensation Information page (technical name *com.sap.pct.erp.mss.compensation_information*) and the Personnel Development page (technical name *com.sap.pct.erp.mss. personnel_development*). In all cases, the Employee Search functionality is the same — it's the content of the page that is different.

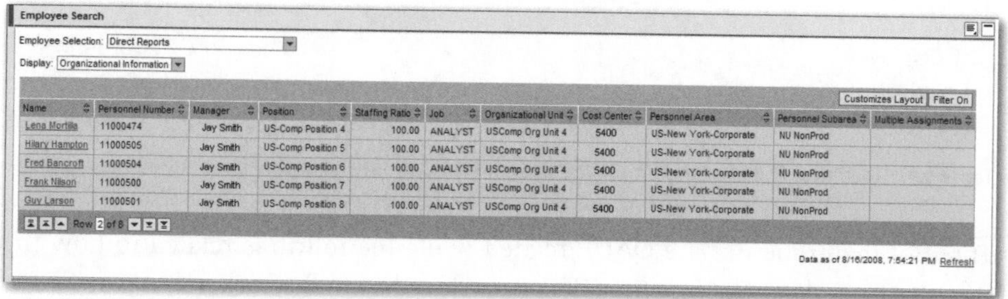

Figure 7.12 Employee Search iView

The iView is driven entirely off of the OADP framework. OADP is a robust mechanism for allowing managers to search for, view, and transact on employees within their span-of-control. We will cover OADP in detail in the next chapter.

Table 7.7 lists the properties of the Employee Search iView, along with who maintains them (the user or a portal administrator) and the allowed entries.

Description (GUI)	Property	Maintained By	Type of Entry	Allowed Entries
Group organizational structure views	sap.xss.tmv. orgviewgroup	Administrator	Optional	Organizational structure view group, for example, MSS_TMV_EE, stored in Customizing
Individual organizational structure view	sap.xss.tmv. orgview	Administrator	Optional	Organizational structure view, for example, MSS_TMV_EE_DIR, stored in Customizing

Table 7.7 Technical Data for the Employee Search iView

Description (GUI)	Property	Maintained By	Type of Entry	Allowed Entries
Cache lifetime, in days	sap.xss.tmv.cachemaxage	Administrator	Mandatory	−1, 0 and all natural numbers
Organizational structure views with list display in navigation area	sap.xss.tmv.navlistorgviews	Administrator	Optional	Organizational structure view, for example, MSS_TMV_EE_ORG1, stored in Customizing

Table 7.7 Technical Data for the Employee Search iView (Cont.)

Three of the properties are OADP related while the fourth is related to how the iViews caches data. The first time data is retrieved from the backend, it is stored in a cache from which it can be accessed efficiently. Property *sap.xss.tmv.cachemaxage* defines the number of days that the cache remains valid before it is discarded and the data is read again from the backend. To turn the cache off, use a value of −1. To turn it on, use a value of 0 or greater. The user can reset the cache at anytime by clicking on the Refresh link. We recommend that you use the cache due to system performance reasons.

General Data iView

The General Data iView provides basic employee information to the manager, including:

▶ the building and office information from IT0032 Internal Data

▶ the telephone number from IT0032 Internal Data or from IT0105 Communication, subtype 0020

▶ the email address from IT0105 Communication, subtype 0010

▶ position data from IT0001 Organizational Assignment; and,

▶ salary data from IT0008 Basic Pay

Table 7.8 provides the technical data for the General Data iView.

General Data	
Runtime Technology	Java/Web Dynpro
Technical Names of iViews	com.sap.pct.erp.mss.generalinfo_generaldata
	com.sap.pct.erp.mss.compensationinfo_generaldata
	com.sap.pct.erp.mss.personneldev_generaldata
	com.sap.pct.erp.mss.compensationprofiles_generaldata
Technical Names of Web Dynpro Applications	sap.com/mss~eepro~GeneralInformation
	sap.com/mss~eepro~CompensationInformation
	sap.com/mss~eepro~PersonnelDevelopment
	sap.com/mss~eepro~compensationprofiles~CompensationProfiles
Available From	SAP NetWeaver 2004s
Data Source	SAP ECC 6.0 and higher
	RFC function component called: HRMSS_RFC_EP_READ_GENERALDATA
Software Component	EA-HR
Support	EP-PCT-MGR-HR

Table 7.8 Technical Data for the General Data iView

The General Data iView cannot be used by itself. This iView is rendered based on the selection from the Employee Search iView, the Compensation Management Profile, and from the Holders iView within the Position Profile.

There are two available links within the General Data iView (see Figure 7.13). The link Organizational Assignments beside the Organizational Assignments header links out to the Organizational Assignments iView (technical name *sap.com/mss~e epro~organizationalassignments*). In this iView, the manager can see a full position history, including the manager and his contact information (email, phone, etc.).

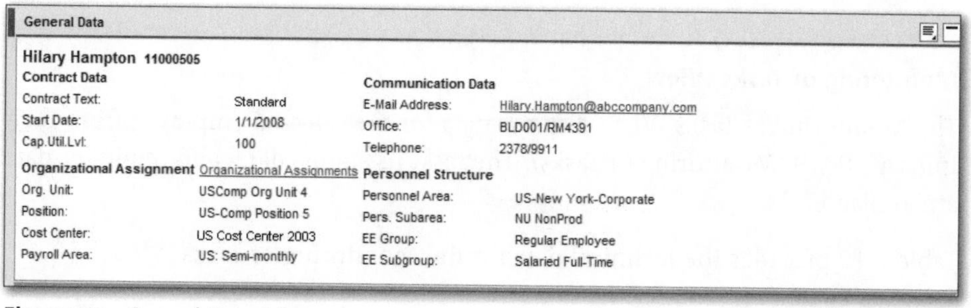

Figure 7.13 General Data iView

Personal Data iView

The Personal Data iView shows the employee's birth-date, marital status, and home address. In some countries, this information may be regarded as sensitive so be cautious when deploying.

Table 7.9 provides the technical data for the Personal Data iView.

Personal Data	
Runtime Technology	Java/Web Dynpro
Technical Name iView	com.sap.pct.erp.mss.generalinfo_personaldata
Technical Name Web Dynpro application	sap.com/mss~eepro/GeneralInformation
Available for Portal (Release)	SAP NetWeaver 2004s
Data Source	SAP ECC 6.0 or higher RFC function component called: HRMSS_RFC_EP_READ_PERSONALDATA
Software Component	EA-HR 600 and above
Support	EP-PCT-MGR-HR

Table 7.9 Technical Data for the Personal Data iView

Personal Data iView is seen in Figure 7.14

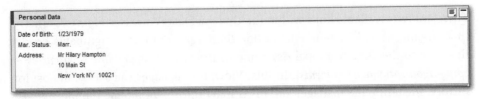

Figure 7.14 Personal Data iView

Monitoring of Tasks iView

The Monitoring of Tasks iView displays data for the selected employee from their Infotype 0019 (Monitoring of Tasks). The task, its status, date, and reminder date are available.

Table 7.10 provides the technical data for the Monitoring of Tasks iView.

Monitoring of Tasks	
Runtime Technology	Java/Web Dynpro
Technical Name iView	com.sap.pct.erp.mss.generalinfo_monitoringtasks
	com.sap.pct.erp.mss.monitoring_of_tasks
Technical Name Web Dynpro application	sap.com/mss~eepro/GeneralInformation
	sap.com/mss~eepro~monitoringoftasks~ MonitoringofTasksApp
Available for Portal (Release)	SAP NetWeaver 2004s
Data Source	SAP ECC 6.0 or higher
	RFC function component called:
	HRMSS_RFC_MONTASK_GETLIST
Software Component	EA-HR 600 and above
Support	EP-PCT-MGR-HR

Table 7.10 Technical Data for the Monitoring of Tasks iView

Two configurable properties are available for the iView in the portal: Month Future and Month Past indicate how many months in the future and how many months in the past the iView should retrieve data for. The default is six for both settings, meaning that a full year's worth of data (the previous six months through the next six months) are returned to the iView. The Monitoring of Tasks iView is seen in Figure 7.15.

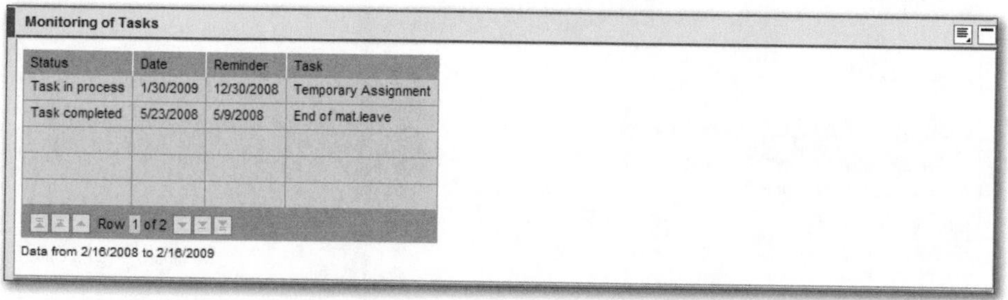

Figure 7.15 Monitoring of Tasks iView

Company Property iView

The Company Property iView retrieves data from Infotype 0040 (Objects on Loan). Each object is listed with its number and unit. Any comments on the company asset are shown in a text area below the table if the user clicks on its link.

Table 7.11 provides the technical data for the Company Property iView.

Company Property	
Runtime Technology	Java/Web Dynpro
Technical Name iView	com.sap.pct.erp.mss.generalinfo_companyproperties
Technical Name Web Dynpro application	sap.com/mss~eepro/GeneralInformation
Available for Portal (Release)	SAP NetWeaver 2004s
Data Source	SAP ECC 6.0 or higher RFC function component called: HRMSS_RFC_EE_GET_ASSETS
Software Component	EA-HR 600 and above
Support	EP-PCT-MGR-HR

Table 7.11 Technical Data for the Company Property iView

An example of the company property is shown in Figure 7.16. This employee has two company assests on loan — a computer and a car.

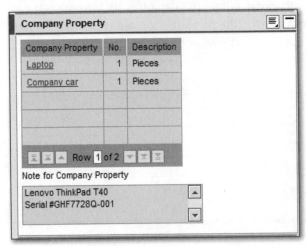

Figure 7.16 Company Property iView

Photo iView

To use the Photo iView, you must be using the SAP ArchiveLink component. If ArchiveLink is active and implemented in your system, be sure to configure table

T77S0 in SM30 for entry GRPID=ADMIN, SEMID=PHOTO. The system needs to know what object type is being used in HR from the archive. The default value is HRICOLFOTO. For more information on SAP Archivelink, visit *http://service.sap. com/archivelink* (a service marketplace user name and password is required).

Table 7.12 provides the technical data for the Photo iView.

Photo	
Runtime Technology	Java/Web Dynpro
Technical Name iViews	com.sap.pct.erp.mss.generalinfo_photo
	com.sap.pct.erp.mss.compensationinfo_photo
	com.sap.pct.erp.mss.personneldev_photo
	com.sap.pct.erp.mss.compensationprofiles_photo
Technical Name Web Dynpro applications	sap.com/mss~eepro/GeneralInformation
	sap.com/mss~eepro/CompensationInformation
	sap.com/mss~eepro/PersonnelDevelopment
	sap.com/mss~eepro~compensationprofiles/ CompensationProfile
Available for Portal (Release)	SAP NetWeaver 2004s
Data Source	SAP ECC 6.0 or higher
	RFC function component called:
	HRMSS_RFC_EP_READ_PHOTO_URI
Software component	EA-HR 600 and above
Support	EP-PCT-MGR-HR

Table 7.12 Technical Data for the Photo iView

Table 7.13 lists the properties of the Photo iView, along with who maintains them (the user or a portal administrator) and the allowed entries.

Description (GUI)	Property	Maintained By	Type of Entry	Allowed Entries
Determines if photo of employee or applicant	ImageClass	Administrator	Required	Employee (default) or Applicant
Width of photo	ImageWidth	Administrator	Required	Default = 120px
Height of photo	ImageHeight	Administrator	Required	Default = 160px

Table 7.13 Technical Data for the Photo iView

193

An example of an employee photo is shown in Figure 7.17.

Figure 7.17   Photo iView

Archived Documents iView

The Archived Documents iView needs the SAP ArchiveLink component installed in your system. For more information on SAP Archivelink, visit *http://service.sap.com/ archivelink* (a service marketplace user name and password is required).

Table 7.14 provides the technical data for the Archived Documents iView.

Archived Documents	
Runtime Technology	Java/Web Dynpro
Technical Name of iView	com.sap.pct.erp.mss.generalinfo_archiveddocs
Technical Name of Web Dynpro Application	sap.com/mss~eepro~GeneralInformation
Available From	SAP NetWeaver 2004s
Data Source	SAP ECC 6.0 and higher
	RFC function component called: HRMSS_RFC_EP_READ_ARCHIVEDDOC
Software Components	EA-HR
Support	EP-PCT-MGR-HR

Table 7.14   Technical Data for the Archived Documents iView

Table 7.15 lists the properties of the Archived Documents iView, along with who maintains them (the user or a portal administrator) and the allowed entries

Description (GUI)	Property	Maintained By	Type of Entry	Allowed Entries
Archiving class (specifies whether data for an employee or applicant is displayed)	com.sap.xss.hr.eeprofile. archiveddocuments. ArchiveClass	Administrator	Mandatory	Employee, Applicant
Document types to display	com.sap.xss.hr.eeprofile. archiveddocuments. DocTypeFilter	Administrator	Optional	List of document types separated by a comma (,) No entry = all document types
Selection period	com.sap.xss.hr.eeprofile. archiveddocuments. YearPast	Administrator	Mandatory	Number of years in the past, such as 99

Table 7.15 Properties for the Archived Documents iView

> **Note**
>
> If you want to integrate your own iView, follow the steps in SAP Note 1112733 (MSS Employee Profile: Integrating other iViews). The Note describes the process for integrating custom iViews into a profile. Your custom iView will need to accept a parameter string. Special consideration is also needed if you have created your custom iView via Web Dynpro for ABAP programming. The SAP Note discusses the workaround needed in this case.

This concludes our review of the Employee Information functional area. We have seen how six iViews — General Data, Personal Data, Monitoring of Tasks,

Company Property, Photo, and Archived Documents and their "master" iView Employee Search — provide managers with important HR data for employees within their span-of-control.

Next, let's discuss the MSS iViews available within Personnel Management.

7.4.3 Personnel Development (Competencies, Performance Management, and Training)

There are several services available for managers to aid them in the personnel development of their staff. Whether it is through training, development planning, or performance management, empowering managers to grow their staff professionally is an extremely valuable tool for morale, retention, and overall employee productivity. The following iViews related to personnel development are available within the MSS business package:

- Qualifications
- Maintain Position Requirements
- Appraisals
- Profile Match-Up and Required Training
- Training Activities
- Training Event Details

Each of these is discussed below.

Qualifications iView

The qualifications iView shows the employee's qualifications and associated proficiency levels (see Figure 7.18). If Personnel Administration (PA)/Personnel Development (PD) integration is turned on, the employee's qualifications are sourced from PD (via the A 032 Fulfills relationship from the employee (P) to the qualification (Q) objects). If PA/PD integration is not activated, the qualifications on the employee's Infotype 0024 (Qualifications) within the PA database are returned.

Table 7.16 provides the technical data for the Qualifications iView.

Qualifications	
Runtime Technology	Java/Web Dynpro
Technical Name iView	com.sap.pct.erp.mss.personneldev_ qualifications
Technical Name Web Dynpro application	sap.com/mss~eepro/ PersonnelDevelopment
Available for Portal (Release)	SAP NetWeaver 2004s
Data Source	SAP ECC 6.0 or higher RFC function component called: HRMSS_RFC_EP_READ_SKILLS
Software Component	EA-HR 600 and above
Support	EP-PCT-MGR-HR

Table 7.16 Technical Data for the Qualifications iView

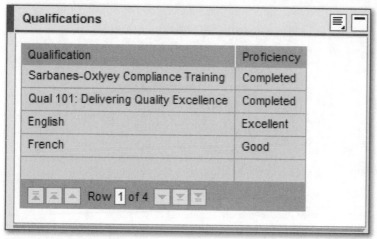

Figure 7.18 Qualifications iView

Position Requirements iView

The next iView, Position Requirements, allows managers to maintain the "requirements" of a position. In other words, a manager using this iView can select qualification levels for each of the positions within their span-of-control (see Figure 7.19). Table 7.17 provides the technical data for the Position Requirements iView.

Position Requirements	
Type of Application	Java/Web Dynpro
Technical Name of iView	com.sap.pct.erp.mss.position_requirements
Technical Name of Web Dynpro Application	sap.com/mss~prq/PosReqApp
Available as of	SAP NetWeaver 2004s
Data Source	SAP ECC 6.0 or above
	RFC function components called:
	XSS_PRQ_APPLY_POS_REQ
	XSS_PRQ_CB_REQINHO
	XSS_PRQ_REQNO
	XSS_PRQ_DELETE_POS_REQ
	XSS_PRQ_DEQUEUE_POSITION
	XSS_PRQ_GET_CONF_DATA
	XSS_PRQ_GET_QUALI_CATALOG
	XSS_PRQ_GET_REQ_DETAILS
	XSS_PRQ_REQ_OVERVIEW
	XSS_PRQ_INTIALIZE_DATA
	XSS_PRQ_RESET_POSITION
	XSS_PRQ_SAVE_POS_REQ
	XSS_PRQ_SEARCH_QUALI
Software Component	EA-HR
Support	EP-PCT-MGR-HR

Table 7.17 Technical Data for the Maintain Position Requirements iView

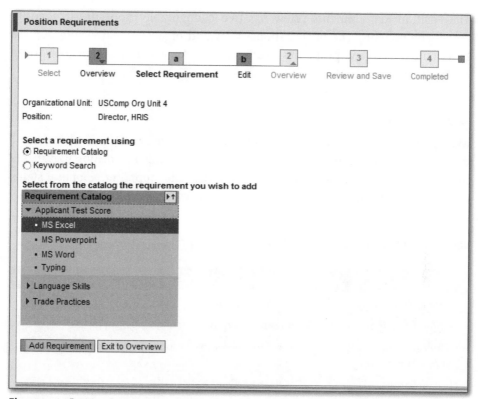

Figure 7.19 Position Requirements iView

Table 7.18 lists the properties of the Position Requirements iView, along with who maintains them (the user or a portal administrator) and the allowed entries.

Description (GUI)	Property	Maintained By	Type of Entry	Allowed Entries
Organizational-structure-view group	orgviewgroup	Administrator	Mandatory	MSS_PRQ_POS
Organizational structure view	orgview	Administrator	Mandatory	MSS_PRQ_POS

Table 7.18 Properties for the Position Requirements iView

The Position Requirements iView has two configurable properties to identify OADP components. The organizational view and organizational view group are two mandatory iView properties needed in the iView configuration that drives the dropdown selection.

Appraisals iView

Managers can gain access to the performance management appraisals for their direct and indirect reports using this iView. The following information is available in the iView: appraisal document name, validity date, appraiser, appraisal status and substatus, value, and result. The value and result columns indicate the final appraisal rating.

Table 7.19 provides the technical data for the Appraisals iView.

Appraisals	
Runtime Technology	Java/Web Dynpro
Technical Name of iView	com.sap.pct.erp.mss.personneldev_appraisals
Technical Name of Web Dynpro Application	sap.com/mss~eepro~PersonnelDevelopment
Available as of	SAP NetWeaver 2004s
Data Source	SAP ECC 6.0 and higher RFC function component called: HRMSS_RFC_EP_READ_APRRAISALS
Software Component	EA-HR
Support	EP-PCT-MGR-HR

Table 7.19 Technical Data for the Appraisals iView

Table 7.20 lists the properties of the Appraisals iView, along with who maintains them (the user or a portal administrator) and the allowed entries.

In the forms property, if no entry has been entered, all appraisal documents are displayed. If more than one template is specified, each template number (i.e., the VA element) must be separated by a comma (e.g., 50027358, 50023741). In Figure 7.20, a listing of two appraisals is shown for an employee.

Description (GUI)	Property	Maintained By	Type of Entry	Example Entry	Allowed Entries
Selection period in the future	eepro. appraisals. yearsfuture	End user	Mandatory	99	Natural numbers from 0 through 99
Selection period in the past	eepro. appraisals. yearspast	End user	Mandatory	5	Natural numbers from 0 through 99
Forms (Templates)	eepro. appraisals. templates	Administrator	Optional	50027358, 50023741	Object key of appraisal templates
Status	eepro. appraisals.status	Administrator	Mandatory	135 (for all documents with status 1, 3, and 5)	Figures from 1 through 9
Results display	eppro. appraisals. showresults	Administrator	Mandatory	Yes	Possible values are yes (standard) or no

Table 7.20 Properties for the Appraisal iView

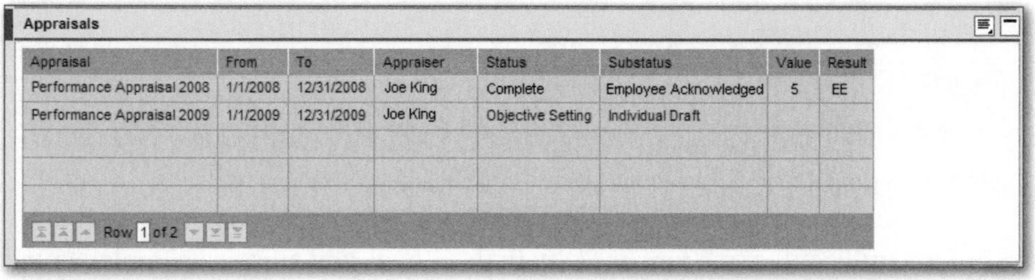

Figure 7.20 Appraisal iView

Profile Match-Up and Required Training iView

Table 7.21 provides the technical data for the Profile Match-Up and Required Training iView.

Profile Match-Up and Required Training	
Runtime Technology	Java/Web Dynpro
Technical Name iView	com.sap.pct.erp.mss.personneldev_profilematchup
Technical Name Web Dynpro application	sap.com/mss~eepro/PersonnelDevelopment
Available from Portal (release)	SAP NetWeaver 2004s
Data Source	SAP ECC 6.0 or higher
	RFC function components called:
	HRMSS_PMU_QUALIF_MANDATORY
	HRMSS_PMU_GET_QUALIF_NAME
	HRMSS_PMU_QUALIF_CURRENT
	HRMSS_PMU_QUALIF_REQUIRED
	HRMSS_PMU_QUALIF_STATUS
	HRMSS_PMU_MAN_BEGDA_ENDDA
	HRMSS_PMU_GET_MAN_DEL_METHOD
	HRMSS_PMU_GET_REC_DEL_METHOD
	HRMSS_PMU_MAN_BEGDA_ENDDA
	HRMSS_PMU_GET_MAN_COURSE_FEE
	HRMSS_PMU_GET_REC_COURSE_FEE
	HRMSS_PMU_GET_REC_TRAIN_IMPQ
	HRMSS_PMU_GET_MAN_TRAIN_NAME
	HRMSS_PMU_GET_REC_TRAIN_NAME
Technical Component(s)	SAP Learning Solution 6.00
Software Component	EA-HR 600 and above

Table 7.21 Technical Data for the Profile Match-up and Required Training iView

In order to utilize all of the functionality in this iView, you must have implemented the SAP Learning Solution (LSO). Without the LSO component, the Recommended Training Courses and the General Mandatory Training Courses' functionality will not work. This iView is launched from selections made in the Employee Search iView.

Training Activities iView

The Training Activities iView displays training activities that have been booked for or attended by employees within the manager's span-of-control.

Table 7.22 provides the technical data for the Training Activities iView.

Training Activities	
Runtime Technology	Java/Web Dynpro
Technical Name of iView	com.sap.pct.erp.mss.personneldev_trainingactivities
Technical Name of Web Dynpro Application	sap.com/mss~eepro~PersonnelDevelopment
Available From	SAP NetWeaver 2004s
Data Source	SAP ECC 6.0 and higher
	RFC function component called: HRMSS_RFC_EP_READ_EVENTS
Software Component	EA-HR
Support	EP-PCT-MGR-HR

Table 7.22   Technical Data for the Training Activities iView

Table 7.23 lists the properties of the Training Activities iView, along with who maintains them (the user or a portal administrator) and the allowed entries.

Description (GUI)	Property	Maintained By	Type of Entry	Allowed Entries
Years in future (data selection period for iView)	com.sap.xss. hr.eeprofile. businessevents. BEYearsFuture	End user	Mandatory	0-99
Years in past (data selection period for iView)	com.sap.xss. hr.eeprofile. businessevents. BEYearsPast	End user	Mandatory	0-99

Table 7.23   Properties for the Training Activities iView

Training Event Details iView

Managers can add details to a training activity, including its description, its objective, and prerequisites with the Training Event Details iView.

Table 7.23 provides the technical data for the Training Event Details iView.

Training Event Details	
Runtime Technology	Java/Web Dynpro
Technical Name of iView	com.sap.pct.erp.mss.trainingeventsdetails
Technical Name of Web Dynpro Application	sap.com/mss~eepro~businesseventdetails~TrainingEventsDetails
Available as of	SAP NetWeaver 2004s
Data Source	SAP ECC 6.0 and higher
	RFC function component called: HRMSS_RFC_EP_READ_EVENTDETAILS
Software Component	EA-HR
Support	EP-PCT-MGR-HR

Table 7.24 Technical Data for the Training Event Details iView

This concludes our review of the Talent Management functional area. We have reviewed six iViews — Qualifications, Maintain Position Requirements, Appraisals, Profile Match-Up and Required Training, Training Activities, and Training Event Details — which provide managers functionality to track the development of their employees.

Next, let's discuss the MSS iViews available within compensation management.

7.4.4 Compensation Management

The iViews supporting Enterprise Compensation Management (ECM) allow managers to make informed compensation decisions for their employees. There is heavy integration with performance management and organizational management. The two iViews — Compensation Planning and Compensation Approval — are at the heart of the compensation process. The other iViews within this functional area are there to support the manager's decision-making. The following iViews related to Compensation Management are available within the business package:

- Compensation Planning
- Compensation Approval
- Compensation Guidelines
- Compensation Eligibility
- Compensation Adjustments
- Long-term Incentives
- Salary Data
- Salary Survey Data
- Salary Development

Each of these is discussed next.

Compensation Planning iView

The Compensation Planning iView is at the crux of the ECM process. Managers use the iView to plan and submit their recommendations for high-level management review. During the planning process, managers can plan and save their recommendations without submitting to higher level management. The status on these saved records stays in the In Planning status during this time. When the manager submits their recommendations to a higher level manager, the statuses are set to Submitted. At this point, only those higher level managers can review the submittals using the Compensation Approval iView.

All forms of compensation — merit, bonuses, and stock — can be planned for using the online functionality.

Table 7.25 provides the technical data for the Compensation Planning iView.

Compensation Planning	
Runtime Technology	Java/Web Dynpro
Technical Name iView	com.sap.pct.erp.mss.compensation_planning
Available from	SAP NetWeaver 2004s

Table 7.25 Technical Data for the Compensation Planning iView

Compensation Planning	
Data Source	RFC function components called:
	HRWPC_RFC_CP_CURRENCY_GETLIST
	HR_ECM_UI_GET_POSS_COMP_REVS
	HR_ECM_UI_GET_PROC_PREP_DATA
	HR_ECM_UI_HANDLE_PROCESS
	HR_ECM_UI_READ_PROCESS_NOTE
	HR_ECM_UI_WRITE_PROCESS_NOTE
	HR_ECM_UI_SET_SELECTED_CPLAN
Software Component	EA-HR 600 and above
Support	EP-PCT-MGR-HR

Table 7.25 Technical Data for the Compensation Planning iView (Cont.)

Figure 7.21 shows a manager planning for two employees. Warning and error messages are visible at the top of the screen in plain sight for the manager while he plans. Messages related to budgeting, guidelines, salary ranges, among others, can be presented to the manager so that proper procedures and controls are adhered to.

Other helpful utilities available to the manager in the planning worksheet include notes functionality, graphical comparisons of planned recommendations, and filtering/sorting capabilities. For those multinational companies implementing ECM, all currencies are supported and can be displayed in the employee's local currency or converted "on the fly" to a common currency for analytical purposes.

The property settings available with the Compensation Planning iView are too numerous to mention in this book. A full list of settings, including the descriptions and allowed entries, can be found at *http://help.sap.com/saphelp_erp60_sp/helpdata/ en/ff/c5d98c226848ebae8e7c2ce106db67/frameset.htm*.

Compensation Approval iView

The Compensation Approval iView is used in conjunction with the Compensation Planning iView. Higher level managers use this iView to review recommendations submitted by lower level managers. The approval manager can either approve or reject the recommendation. If approved, the status on the compensation recommendation is set to Approved and can no longer be changed (from the portal). If rejected, the status on the compensation recommendation is set to Rejected. A lower level manager can then resubmit a revised recommendation for another review from the approver.

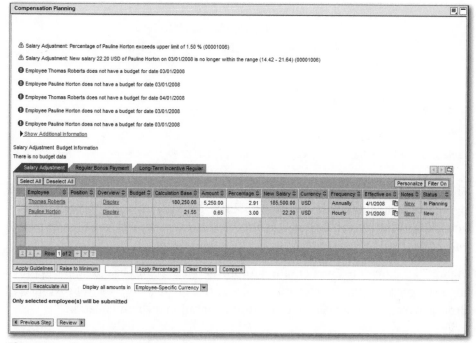

Figure 7.21 Compensation Planning iView

Table 7.26 provides the technical data for the Compensation Approval iView.

Compensation Approval	
Runtime Technology	Web Dynpro iView
Technical Name	com.sap.pct.erp.mss.compensation_approval
Available from	SAP NetWeaver 2004s

Table 7.26 Technical Data for the Compensation Approval iView

Compensation Approval	
Data Source	SAP ERP 2005
	RFC function components called:
	HRWPC_RFC_CP_CURRENCY_GETLIST
	HR_ECM_UI_GET_POSS_COMP_REVS
	HR_ECM_UI_GET_PROC_PREP_DATA
	HR_ECM_UI_HANDLE_PROCESS
	HR_ECM_UI_READ_PROCESS_NOTE
	HR_ECM_UI_WRITE_PROCESS_NOTE
	HR_ECM_UI_SET_SELECTED_CPLAN
Software Component	EA-HR 600 and above
Support	EP-PCT-MGR-HR

Table 7.26 Technical Data for the Compensation Approval iView (Cont.)

The property settings available with the Compensation Approval iView are too numerous to mention in this book. A full list of settings, including the descriptions and allowed entries, can be found at *http://help.sap.com/saphelp_erp60_sp/helpdata/ en/42/b94453c4121d64e10000000a1553f6/frameset.htm*.

Figure 7.22 shows the Compensation Approval iView. In this example, the approving manager is responsible for the review of two employees. The Approve/Reject drop down option is available for each compensation recommendation.

Compensation Guidelines iView

The Compensation Guidelines iView can show what guidelines apply to an employee and each compensation plan. Information that can be displayed includes the compensation area, guideline criteria, guideline key date, guideline variant, and guideline grouping.

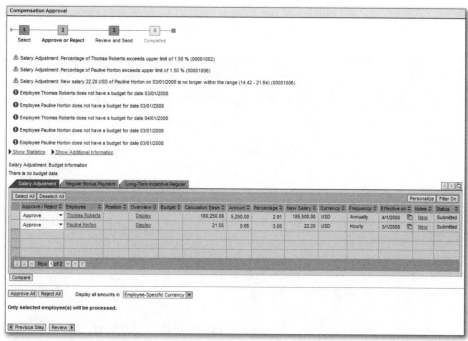

Figure 7.22 Compensation Approval iView

Table 7.27 provides the technical data for the Compensation Guidelines iView.

Compensation Guidelines	
Runtime Technology	Java/Web Dynpro
Technical Name iView	com.sap.pct.erp.mss.compensationprofiles_ compensationguidelines
Technical Name Web Dynpro Application	sap.com/mss~eepro~compensationprofiles
Available from Portal (release)	SAP NetWeaver 2004s
Data origin	SAP ECC 6.0 and higher
	RFC function components called: HRMSS_ECM_UI_VIEW_GUIDELINE
Software Component	EA-HR 600 and higher
Support	EP-PCT-MGR-HR

Table 7.27 Technical Data for the Compensation Guidelines iView

Table 7.28 lists the properties of the Compensation Guidelines iView, along with who maintains them (the user or a portal administrator) and the allowed entries.

Description (GUI)	Property	Maintained By	Type of Entry	Allowed Entries
Display Compensation Area	com.sap.xss.hr.eeprofile. compensationguidelines. DisplayCompensationArea	Administrator	Required	True or false. Default = true
Display Guideline Key Date	com.sap.xss.hr.eeprofile. compensationguidelines. DisplayGuidelineKeyDate	Administrator	Required	True or false. Default = true
Display Guideline Variant	com.sap.xss.hr.eeprofile. compensationguidelines. DisplayGuidelineVariant	Administrator	Required	True or false. Default = true
Display Guideline Grouping	com.sap.xss.hr.eeprofile. compensationguidelines. DisplayGuidelineGrouping	Administrator	Required	True or false. Default = true
Display Guideline Criteria	com.sap.xss.hr.eeprofile. compensationguidelines. DisplayGuidelineCriteria	Administrator	Required	True or false. Default = true

Table 7.28 Properties for the Compensation Guidelines iView

Compensation Eligibility iView

The Compensation Eligibility iView displays an employee's eligibility for a compensation plan and the criteria the employee does or does not meet. For each eligibility criterion, the iView displays whether the employee is eligible together with the required eligibility value and the employee's actual value.

Table 7.29 provides the technical data for the Compensation Eligibility iView.

Compensation Eligibility	
Runtime Technology	Java/Web Dynpro
Technical Name iView	com.sap.pct.erp.mss.compensationprofiles_compensationeligibility
Technical Name Web Dynpro application	sap.com/mss~eepro~compensationprofiles/CompensationProfile
Available from:	SAP Netweaver 2004s
Data Source	SAP ECC 6.0 or higher
	RFC function components called: HR_ECM_UI_VIEW_ELIG_DATA
Software Component	EA-HR 600 and above
Support	EP-PCT-MGR-HR

Table 7.29 Technical Data for the Compensation Eligibility iView

Table 7.30 lists the properties of the Compensation Eligibility iView, along with who maintains them (the user or a portal administrator) and the allowed entries.

Description (GUI)	Property	Maintained By	Type of Entry	Allowed Entries
Display Compensation Area	DisplayCompensationArea	Administrator	Optional	True (default) or false
Display Eligibility Key Date	DisplayEligibilityKeyDate	Administrator	Optional	True (default) or false
Display Eligibility Variant	DisplayEligibilityVariant	Administrator	Optional	True (default) or false
Display Eligibility Grouping	DisplayEligibilityGrouping	Administrator	Optional	True (default) or false
Display Eligibility Criteria	DisplayEligibilityCriteria	Administrator	Optional	True (default) or false

Table 7.30 Properties for the Compensation Eligibility iView

Compensation Adjustments iView

The Compensation Adjustment iView displays compensation adjustments from Infotype 0759 (Compensation Process) during a given period for the employees under the manager's span-of-control. All compensation adjustments are listed in tabular format with the effective date, calculation base, amount, percentage, and status.

Table 7.31 provides the technical data for the Compensation Adjustments iView.

Compensation Adjustments	
Runtime Technology	Java/Web Dynpro
Technical Name iView	com.sap.pct.erp.mss.compensationinfo_ compensationadjustments
	com.sap.pct.erp.mss.compensationprofiles_ compensationadjustments
Technical Name Web Dynpro application	sap.com/mss~eepro/CompensationInformation
	sap.com/mss~eepro~compensationprofiles/ CompensationProfile
Available for Portal (Release)	SAP NetWeaver 2004s
Data Source	SAP ECC 6.0 or higher
	RFC function component called:
	HR_ECM_UI_VIEW_PROCESS_DATA
Software Component	EA-HR 600 and above
Support	EP-PCT-MGR-HR

Table 7.31 Technical Data for the Compensation Adjustments iView

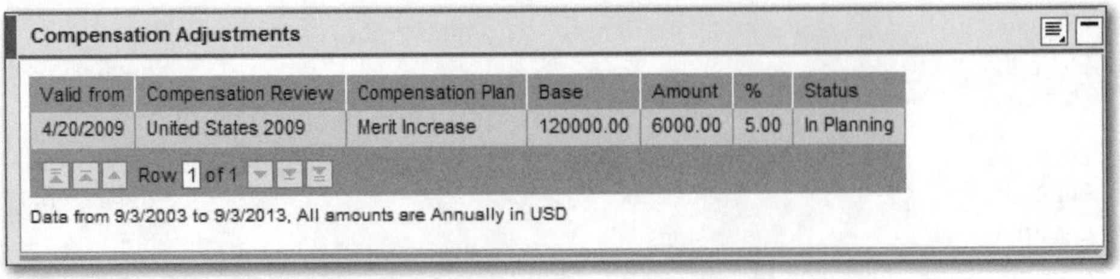

Figure 7.23 Compensation Adjustments iView

Figure 7.23 shows the Compensation Adjustments iView with one adjustment for a 2009 Merit Increase. The meritable base pay on which the adjustment was calculated from is displayed in the field Base. The merit increase and percentage are specified in addition to the status.

Long-Term Incentives iView

The Long-term Incentives iView allows the manager to view the long-term incentive data from Infotype 0761 (LTI Granting) and Infotype 0762 (LTI Exercising) for employees in his span-of-control.

Table 7.32 provides the technical data for the Long-term Incentives iView.

Long-term Incentives	
Runtime Technology	Java/Web Dynpro
Technical Name iViews	com.sap.pct.erp.mss.compensationinfo_longtermincentives
	com.sap.pct.erp.mss.compensationprofiles_longtermincentives
Technical Name Web Dynpro applications	sap.com/mss~eepro/CompensationInformation
	sap.com/mss~eepro~compensationprofiles/CompensationProfile
Available for Portal (Release)	SAP NetWeaver 2004s
Data Source	SAP ECC 6.0 or higher
	RFC function component called:
	HR_ECM_UI_VIEW_LTI_DATA
Software Component	EA-HR 600 and above
Support	EP-PCT-MGR-HR

Table 7.32 Technical Data for the Long-term Incentives iView

Salary Data iView

The Salary Data iView allows the manager to view the salary of each of his employees compared to the compa-ratio and the percentage position in the salary range.

Table 7.33 provides the technical data for the Salary Data iView.

Salary Data	
Runtime Technology	Java/Web Dynpro
Technical Name iView	com.sap.pct.erp.mss.compensationinfo_salarydata
	com.sap.pct.erp.mss.compensationprofiles_salarydata
Technical Name Web Dynpro application	sap.com/mss~eepro/CompensationInformation
	sap.com/mss~eepro~compensationprofiles/ CompensationProfile
Available for Portal (Release)	SAP NetWeaver 2004s
Data Source	SAP ECC 6.0 or higher.
	RFC function component called:
	HR_ECM_UI_VIEW_SALARY_DATA
Software component	EA-HR 600 and above
Support	EP-PCT-MGR-HR

Table 7.33 Technical Data for the Salary Data iView

Table 7.34 lists the properties of the Salary Data iView, along with who maintains them (the user or a portal administrator) and the allowed entries.

Description (GUI)	Property	Maintained By	Type of Entry	Allowed Entries
Currency in which amounts are displayed	Currency	Administrator	Required	Three-character currency abbreviation from SAP Table TCURC. For example, USD, EUR, GBP, etc.
Time unit for displaying amounts	Frequency	Administrator	Required	01 = Monthly; 02 = Semimonthly; 03 = Weekly, 04; = Bi-weekly; 05 = Every four weeks; 06 = Annually; 07 = Quarterly; 08 = Half-yearly; 99 = Hourly

Table 7.34 Properties for the Salary Data iView

Description (GUI)	Property	Maintained By	Type of Entry	Allowed Entries
Display compa ratio to reference salary	DisplayCompa Ratio	Administrator	Required	True (Default) or False
Display position within salary range	DisplayPercentIn Range	Administrator	Required	True (Default) or False. (* see below)
Display chart	DisplayChart	User	Required	True (Default) or False
Display values in chart	DisplayChart Values	User	Required	True (Default) or False

Table 7.34 Properties for the Salary Data iView (Cont.)

Salary Development iView

The Salary Development iView lets the manager view salary development data for employees within this span-of-control. The data is displayed for a given period and can be grouped by compensation type (annualized salary, short-term incentives, and long-term incentives). The iView can determine annual values based on payroll results and payroll-related Infotype records, such as Basic Pay (0008), Recurring Payments and Deductions (0014), and Additional Payments (0015).

Table 7.35 provides the technical data for the Salary Development iView.

Salary Development	
Runtime Technology	Java/Web Dynpro
Technical Name iViews	com.sap.pct.erp.mss.compensationinfo_salarysurvey
	com.sap.pct.erp.mss.compensationprofiles_ salarysurveydata
Technical Name Web Dynpro applications	sap.com/mss~eepro/CompensationInformation
	sap.com/mss~eepro~compensationprofiles/ CompensationProfile
Available for Portal (Release)	SAP NetWeaver 2004s

Table 7.35 Technical Data for the Salary Development iView

Salary Development	
Data Source	SAP ECC 6.0 or higher
	RFC function components called:
	HR_ECM_UI_VIEW_JPR_EE_DATA
	HR_ECM_UI_VIEW_JPR_SURVEY_DATA
Software Component	EA-HR 600 and above
Support	EP-PCT-MGR-HR

Table 7.35 Technical Data for the Salary Development iView (Cont.)

Enhancement HRWPCEP1 can be implemented to adapt the periods used for determining the annual salary based on your unique business requirements. This user exit must be implemented using Transaction CMOD.

This concludes our review of the Compensation Management functional area. We have reviewed nine iViews including Compensation Planning, Compensation Approval, Compensation Guidelines, Compensation Eligibility, Compensation Adjustments, Long-term Incentives, Salary Data, Salary Survey Data, and Salary Development. These iViews provide managers with access to key performance and compensation-related data. By doing so, managers can make better-informed decisions so that talent is rewarded and retained within the organization.

Next, let's discuss the MSS iViews available within personnel administration.

7.4.5 Personnel Administration

Within the Personnel Administration functional area, a few options are available. Recent enhancements (starting with ERP 2005, Enhancement Package 2) include HCM Processes and Forms, which has become SAP's preferred direction for online change requests. SAP has created advanced options to use Adobe Interactive Forms using the HR Administrative Services component (PA-AS). HCM Processes and Forms is described in great detail in SAP Note 952693 (MSS: Interactive forms and HCM processes and forms). HCM Processes and Forms is beyond the scope of this book. More information on HCM Processes and Forms can be found on the SAP Service Marketplace.

The following iViews related to personnel administration are available within the business package:

▶ Start Processes (HCM Processes and Forms)

▶ Personnel Change Request

▶ Personnel Change Request: Direct Launch

▶ Status Overview of Personnel Change Requests

Each of these is discussed next.

Start Processes iView

Managers can use the Start Processes iView to request an administrative change for an employee. This iView is used exclusively with the new HCM Processes and Form functionality. A Personnel Change Request cannot be triggered from this iView.

Table 7.36 provides the technical data for the Start Processes iView.

Start Processes (HCM Process and Forms)	
Runtime Technology	Java/Web Dynpro
Technical Name of iView	com.sap.pct.erp.mss.pcrasr
Technical Name of Web Dynpro Application	sap.com/pa~asr~procst~StartProcessForManager
Available From	SAP NetWeaver 2004s
Data Source	SAP ECC 6.0 or above
	RFC function components called:
	HR_ASR_SELECT_PROCESSES
	HR_ASR_CHECK_PROCESS
	ISR_LAUNCHPAD_SCENARIO_CHECK
Software Component	EA-HR
Support	EP-PCT-MGR-HR

Table 7.36 Technical Data for the Start Processes iView

Table 7.37 lists the properties of the Start Processes iView, along with who maintains them (the user or a portal administrator) and the allowed entries.

Description (GUI)	Property	Maintained By	Type of Entry	Allowed Entries
Lifetime of cache	sap.mss.hras. cachemaxage	Administrator	Mandatory	Number of days (standard setting: 1)
Group of organizational structure views	sap.mss.hras. orgviewgroup	Administrator	Optional	Organizational structure view groups of OADP defined in Customizing (standard setting: MSS_TMV_EE)
Organizational structure view	sap.mss.hras. orgview	Administrator	Optional	Organizational structure views of OADP defined in Customizing (standard setting: no organizational structure view)
Organizational structure views with list display in navigation area	sap.mss.hras. navlistorgviews	Administrator	Optional	Organizational structure views of OADP defined in Customizing (standard setting: MSS_TMV_EE_ ORG1)
Service ID	sap.mss.hras. serviceid	Administrator	Mandatory	Service key defined in Customizing (standard setting: MSS_HCM_ HRAS_CALL_ASR_ PROCESS)

Table 7.37 Properties for the Start Processes iView

Figure 7.24 shows Step 1 of the Start Processes iView where the manager has the ability to search for and select any employee within his control. Selection can be based on criteria such as personnel subarea, employee group, employee subgroup, etc. Once submitted, workflow will route the request for the necessary approvals and then onto the SAP system for auto-update or to an HR processor for a manual update.

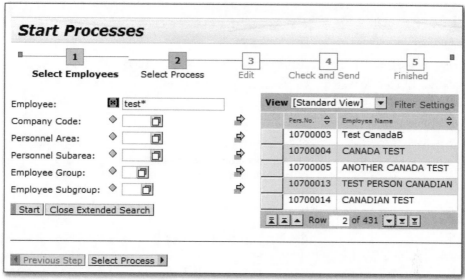

Figure 7.24 Start Processes iView

Whether or not you automate the update is oftentimes a big debate for customers. Customers must weigh the pros and cons with this important decision, as it has important impacts on service delivery. If automation is chosen for some scenarios, the error handling of the process must be ironed out well ahead of implementation.

Now, let's discuss Personnel Change Requests (PCRs) and their place within MSS.

PCR iView

PCRs allow managers to request updates to their employees' HR data using Adobe Interactive Forms technology. This is not part of the HCM Process and Forms functionality. After a manager has submitted a PCR, a workflow approval process can be initiated. Once all approvals are obtained, the request is routed to an HR processor so that the action can be processed on the backend. Unlike HCM Processes and Form, there is no standard auto update feature with PCRs. (The topic of workflow, approvals, and routing is discussed in detail in the next chapter.)

Table 7.38 provides the technical data for the PCR iView.

PCR	
Runtime Technology	Java/Web Dynpro
Technical Name of iView	com.sap.pct.erp.mss.pcrapplication
Technical Name of Web Dynpro Application	sap.com/mss~pcr/PcrApplication
Available as of	SAP NetWeaver 2004
Data Source	SAP ECC 5.0 or above RFC function components called: HRWPC_PCR_ACTIONS HRWPC_PCR_CF HRWPC_PCR_CF_ERP HRWPC_PCR_EG_ACTIONS HRWPC_PCR_EG_UTILITIES HRWPC_PCR_PA_ACTIONS HRWPC_PCR_PA_UTILITIES HRWPC_PCR_PD_ACTIONS HRWPC_PCR_PD_UTILITIES HRWPC_PCR_PM_ACTIONS HRWPC_PCR_PM_UTILITIES HRWPC_PCR_PS_ACTIONS HRWPC_PCR_PS_UTILITIES HRWPC_PCR_RFC HRWPC_PCR_ROLES HRWPC_PCR_SD_UTILITIES HRWPC_PCR_SE_ACTIONS HRWPC_PCR_SE_UTILITIES HRWPC_PCR_SP_ACTIONS HRWPC_PCR_SP_UTILITIES HRWPC_PCR_TD_ACTIONS HRWPC_PCR_TD_UTILITIES HRWPC_PCR_TR_ACTIONS HRWPC_PCR_TR_UTILITIES HRWPC_PCR_UTILITIES HRWPC_PCR_VIEWS HRWPC_PCR_WT_ACTIONS HRWPC_PCR_WT_UTILITIES
Software Component	EA-HR
Support	EP-PCT-MGR-HR

Table 7.38 Technical Data for the PCR iView

SAP software delivers the following 11 scenarios. Each scenario is listed with four-character code.

▶ Change Employee Group and Subgroup (SPEG)

▶ Change Personnel Area and Subarea (SPPA)

▶ Change Working Time (SPWT)

▶ Request Special Payment (SPSP)

▶ Request Promotion (SPPM)

▶ Change Position (SPPS)

▶ Request Transfer (SPTR)

▶ Request Separation (SPSE)

▶ Change Position (Enhanced) (SPPD)

▶ Request Transfer (Enhanced) (SPTD)

▶ Request Separation (Enhanced) (SPSD)

Figures 7.25 and 7.26 show the first two steps in the PCR request process. In Figure 7.25, the manager searches for the employee he will transact on. In Figure 7.26, the manager then selects the suitable form/process (Change Position, Request Transfer, etc.) on which he will submit the request for.

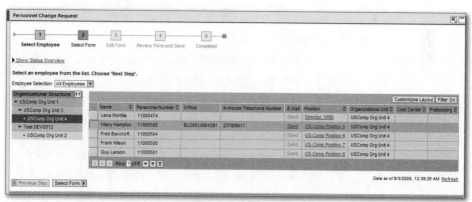

Figure 7.25 Personnel Change Request iView — Select Employees

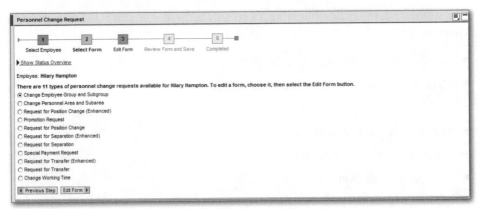

Figure 7.26 Personnel Change Request iView — Select Form

Personnel Change Requests: Direct Launch iView

The Direct Launch iView for PCRs offers the same functionality as the PCR iView but with a slight twist. Because the Direct Launch iView is placed on a page with the Employee Search capability, the manager does not have to search for the employee to start a process. Rather, the manager simply selects the link of the change request they desire for that employee.

Table 7.39 provides the technical data for the PCRs: Direct Launch iView.

PCRs: Direct Launch	
Runtime Technology	Java/Web Dynpro
Technical Names of iViews	com.sap.pct.erp.mss.relatedactivity_pcrdirectlaunch_speg
	com.sap.pct.erp.mss.relatedactivity_pcrdirectlaunch_sppa
	com.sap.pct.erp.mss.relatedactivity_pcrdirectlaunch_spwt
	com.sap.pct.erp.mss.relatedactivity_pcrdirectlaunch_spsp
	com.sap.pct.erp.mss.relatedactivity_pcrdirectlaunch_sppm
	com.sap.pct.erp.mss.relatedactivity_pcrdirectlaunch_spps
	com.sap.pct.erp.mss.relatedactivity_pcrdirectlaunch_sptr
	com.sap.pct.erp.mss.relatedactivity_pcrdirectlaunch_spse
	com.sap.pct.erp.mss.relatedactivity_pcrdirectlaunch_sppd
	com.sap.pct.erp.mss.relatedactivity_pcrdirectlaunch_sptd
	com.sap.pct.erp.mss.relatedactivity_pcrdirectlaunch_spsd
	com.sap.pct.erp.mss.pcrdirectlaunch

Table 7.39 Technical Data for the PCRs: Direct Launch iView

PCRs: Direct Launch	
Technical Name of Web Dynpro Application	sap.com/mss~pcr/PcrDirectLaunchApplication
Available From	SAP NetWeaver 2004s
Data Source	SAP ECC 6.0 or above
	RFC components called: same RFCs as in PCR iView
Software Component	EA-HR
Support	EP-PCT-MGR-HR

Table 7.39 Technical Data for the PCRs: Direct Launch iView (Cont.)

Status Overview for Personnel Change Requests

The Status Overview of the PCR iView allows managers to track the status of their personnel change requests after they have been submitted.

Table 7.40 provides the technical data for the Status Overview for the PCRs iView.

Status Overview for PCRs	
Runtime Technology	Java/Web Dynpro
Technical Name of iView	com.sap.pct.erp.mss.pcrstatusoverview
Technical Name of Web Dynpro Application	sap.com/pcui_gp~isr/IsrStatusoverview
Available as of	SAP NetWeaver 2004s
Data Origin	SAP ECC 6.0 or above
	RFC components called: same RFCs as in PCR iView
Software Component	EA-HR
Support	EP-PCT-MGR-HR

Table 7.40 Technical Data for the Status Overview of the PCRs iView

This concludes our review of the Personnel Administration functional area. We have reviewed four iViews, including Start Processes (HCM Processes and Forms), PCR, PCR: Direct Launch, and the Status Overview of PCRs iViews. These iViews provide managers with the ability to request and track changes to their employee's master data. PCRs will still be supported for the short-term, but HCM Processes and Forms will be the technology choice going forward for the SAP system.

Next, let's discuss the MSS iViews available within the recruiting functional area.

7.4.6 Recruiting

MSS also offers recruitment functions, including the ability to request requisitions and assess candidates. To maximize the offerings in this area and integration, SAP's E-Recruiting component should be implemented. The following iViews related to recruiting are available within the business package:

- ▶ Create New Requisition Request
- ▶ Create New Candidate Assessment
- ▶ Requisition Status Overview
- ▶ Candidate Status Overview

Each of these is discussed next.

Create New Requisition Request iView

Table 7.41 provides the technical data for the Create New Requisition Request iView.

Create New Requisition Request	
Runtime Technology	Java/Web Dynpro
Technical Name	com.sap.pct.erp.mss.requisition_creation
Technical Name Web Dynpro Application	sap.com/mss~rec~req/RequisitionCreation
Available from Portal (release)	SAP NetWeaver 2004s
Data origin	SAP ECC 6.0 and higher
	RFC function components called:
Technical Components	SAP E-Recruiting 3.0 or higher
Software component	EA-HR 600 and higher
Support	EP-PCT-MGR-HR

Table 7.41 Technical Data for the Create New Requisition Request iView

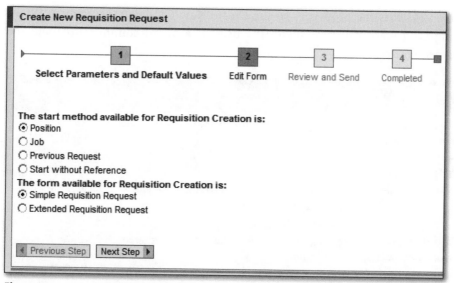

Figure 7.27 Create New Requisition Request iView with Start Method and Form Selection

Create New Candidate Assessment iView

The Create New Candidate Assessment iView allows the manager to view a complete overview of existing candidate assessments, including questionnaires and candidate statuses and requisition information.

Table 7.42 provides the technical data for the Create New Candidate Assessment iView.

Create New Candidate Assessment	
Runtime Technology	Java/Web Dynpro
Technical Name iView	com.sap.pct.erp.mss.candidate_assessment
Technical Name Web Dynpro application	sap.com/mss~rec~cand/CandidateAssessment
Available from Portal (release)	SAP NetWeaver 2004s
Data Source	SAP ECC 6.0 or higher
Software Component	EA-HR 600 and above
	SAP E-Recruiting 3.0 or higher
Support	EP-PCT-MGR-HR

Table 7.42 Technical Data for the Create New Candidate Assessment iView

Table 7.43 lists the properties of the Create New Candidate Assessment iView, along with who maintains them (the user or a portal administrator) and the allowed entries.

Description (GUI)	Property	Maintained By	Type of Entry	Allowed Entries
Organizational Structure View for Select Candidate table	com.sap.xss. hr.rec.cand. orgviewcan	Administrator	Required	Default = MSS_ CAN_SEL_CAN
Lifetime of cache	com.sap.xss. hr.rec.cand. cachemaxage	Administrator	Required	Default = 0
Organizational Structure View for Select Candidate table	com.sap.xss. hr.rec.cand. orgviewreq	Administrator	Required	Default = MSS_ CAN_SEL_REQ

Table 7.43 Properties for the Create New Candidate Assessment iView

Requisition Status Overview iView

The Requisition Status Overview iView allows the manager to determine the status of a submitted requisition request. The manager can display the status on both the Simple Requisition Request and Extended Requisition Request forms.

Table 7.44 provides the technical data for the Requisition Status Overview iView.

Requisition Status Overview	
Runtime Technology	Java/Web Dynpro
Technical Name iView	com.sap.pct.erp.mss.candidate_assessment
Technical Name Web Dynpro application	sap.com/mss~rec~cand/CandidateAssessment
Available from Portal (release)	SAP NetWeaver 2004s
Data Source	SAP ECC 6.0 or higher
Software Component	EA-HR 600 and above
	SAP E-Recruiting 3.0 or higher
Support	EP-PCT-MGR-HR

Table 7.44 Technical Data for the Requisition Status Overview iView

Candidate Status Overview iView

The Candidate Status Overview iView displays the status of candidates that are assigned to a manager's requisition request, and for whom the manager has sent feedback, by means of a questionnaire, to the recruiter.

Table 7.45 provides the technical data for the Candidate Status Overview iView.

Candidate Status Overview	
Runtime Technology	Java/Web Dynpro
Technical Name iView	com.sap.pct.erp.mss.candidate_assessment
Technical Name Web Dynpro application	sap.com/mss~rec~cand/CandidateAssessment
Available from Portal (release)	SAP NetWeaver 2004s
Data Source	SAP ECC 6.0 or higher
Software Component	EA-HR 600 and above SAP E-Recruiting 3.0 or higher
Support	EP-PCT-MGR-HR

Table 7.45 Technical Data for the Candidate Status Overview iView

Table 7.46 lists the properties of the Candidate Status Overview iView, along with who maintains them (the user or a portal administrator) and the allowed entries.

Description (GUI)	Property	Maintained By	Type of Entry	Allowed Entries
Organizational Structure View for Candidate Status Overview Table	com.sap.xss. hr.rec.cand. orgviewstatus	Administrator	required	Default entry = MSS_CAN_SEL_CAP
Cache lifetime (in days)	com.sap.xss. hr.rec.cand. cachemaxage	Administrator	required	Default = 0

Table 7.46 Properties for the Candidate Status Overview iView

7.4.7 Headcount Planning

MSS also has functionality to support workforce planning. The following iViews related to workforce management planning are available within the business package:

- ▶ Headcount Planning
- ▶ Planning Transfer

Each of these is discussed next.

Headcount Planning iView

With the Headcount Planning iView, a manager can plan for the number of positions required for each job within the manager's span-of-control.

Table 7.47 provides the technical data for the Headcount Planning iView.

Headcount Planning	
Runtime Technology	Java/Web Dynpro
Technical Name iView	com.sap.pct.erp.mss.java_sap_com_mss~qtp_com_sap_mss_qtp_applquotaplanning_QuotaPlanning_base
Technical Name Web Dynpro application	sap.com/mss~qtp/QuotaPlanning
Available from Portal (release)	SAP NetWeaver 2004s
Data Source	SAP ECC 6.0 or higher
Software Component	EA-HR 600 and above
Support	EP-PCT-MGR-HR

Table 7.47 Technical Data for the Headcount Planning iView

If you are want to use the Quota Planning iView, the planning type and planning periods must be defined within the configuration. To do that, you must configure IMG activity: PERSONNEL MANAGEMENT • ORGANIZATIONAL MANAGEMENT • INFOTYPE SETTINGS • QUOTA PLANNING • DEFINE PLANNING TYPE AND PERIODS.

Figure 7.28 shows a manager on Step 2 of the process of headcount planning. Planning type (for example, first planning, second planning, etc.) and planning period (for example, weeks, months, quarters, etc.) are specified before the Edit Planning step, which allows the manager to indicate the number of positions per job.

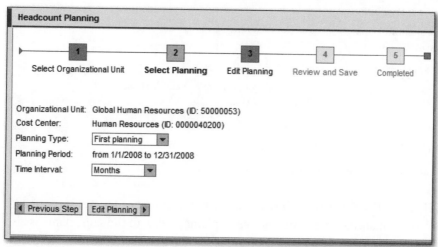

Figure 7.28   Headcount Planning iView with Planning Type and Interval Selected

Planning Transfer iView

With the Planning Transfer iView, a manager can transfer the results from headcount planning for his or her assigned cost centers to Accounting in the form of statistical key figures. The results are taken from the work performed within the Headcount Planning iView. The planning data is posted to the Controlling (CO) component. If your accounting component is in another system, an Application Linking and Enabling (ALE) scenario must be set up to transfer results from your HR system to the your Finance system.

Table 7.48 provides the technical data for the Planning Transfer iView.

Planning Transfer	
Runtime Technology	Java/Web Dynpro
Technical Name iView	com.sap.pct.erp.mss.java_sap_com_mss~qtt_com_sap_mss_qtt_quotatransfer_Headcount_Transfer_base

Table 7.48   Technical Data for the Planning Transfer iView

Planning Transfer	
Technical Name Web Dynpro application	sap.com/mss~qtt/Headcount_Transfer
Available from Portal (release)	SAP NetWeaver 2004s
Data Source	SAP ECC 6.0 or higher RFC function component called: HRXSS_SER_GETMENUDATA
Software Component	EA-HR 600 and above
Support	EP-PCT-MGR-HR

Table 7.48 Technical Data for the Planning Transfer iView (Cont.)

BAdI HRWPC00_HEADCNT2CO is also available to influence the transfer of head-count to the Finance system. An inactive implementation of the same name is also available. Figure 7.29 shows Step 2 of the Planning Transfer iView.

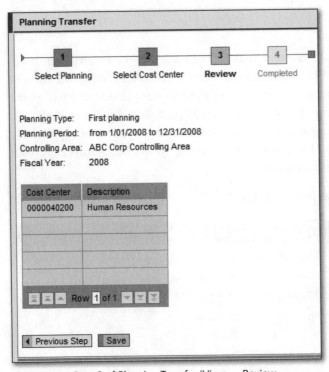

Figure 7.29 Step 2 of Planning Transfer iView — Review

Let's now switch our focus from workforce planning to organizational management.

7.4.8 Organizational Management

The Organizational Management functional area comprises two main functionalities: one on positions via the "position profile" and the other on organizational units via the "organizational unit profile." Both profiles are important as they provide access to organizational management to the manager.

The following iViews related to positions from the position profile are available within the business package:

- Position Search (master iView)
- Position Description
- Cost Distribution
- Working Time
- Employee Group/Subgroup
- Planning Compensation
- Accounting
- Holder
- Requirements
- Vacancy

7.4.9 Position Profile

Out of the box, the position profile iViews can be accessed from the following iViews: Create New Requisition Request, Create New Candidate Assessment, Compensation Planning, Personnel Change Request, and Position Holder from the Organizational Unit Profile.

Let's first discuss the important Position Search iView.

Position Profile — Position Search

The Position Search iView is the "master iView" to the others that follow (just as the Employee Search is the master iView to the employee-related iViews). This means that positions selected within this iView cause the other iViews on the page to refresh with that position's information.

Table 7.49 provides the technical data for the Position Search iView within the Position Profile.

Position Search (Position Profile)	
Runtime Technology	Java/Web Dynpro
Technical Names of iViews	com.sap.pct.erp.mss.posprofile_positionsearch
Technical Names of Web Dynpro Applications	sap.com/mss~ppro/PositionProfileApp
Available From	SAP NetWeaver 2004s
Data Source	SAP ECC 6.0 or above
Software Component	EA-HR 600 and above
Support	EP-PCT-MGR-HR

Table 7.49 Technical Data for the Position Search iView

Table 7.50 lists the properties of the Position Search iView, along with who maintains them (the user or a portal administrator) and the allowed entries.

Description (GUI)	Property	Maintained By	Type of Entry	Allowed Entries
Application group	teamviewer. sap.xss.tmv. applicationgroup	Administrator	Optional	Group of Web Dynpro applications (standard setting: no application group)
Lifetime of cache	teamviewer. sap.xss.tmv. cachemaxage	Administrator	Mandatory	Number of days (standard setting: 1)
Group of organizational structure views	teamviewer. sap.xss.tmv. orgviewgroup	Administrator	Optional	Organizational structure view groups of OADP defined in Customizing (standard setting: MSS_TMV_EE)

Table 7.50 Properties for the Position Search iView

Description (GUI)	Property	Maintained By	Type of Entry	Allowed Entries
Organizational structure view	teamviewer.sap. xss.tmv.orgview	Administrator	Optional	Organizational structure views of OADP defined in Customizing (standard setting: no organizational structure view)
Organizational structure views with list display in navigation area	teamviewer. sap.xss.tmv. navlistorgviews	Administrator	Optional	Organizational structure views of OADP defined in Customizing (standard setting: MSS_TMV_EE_ ORG1)

Table 7.50   Properties for the Position Search iView (Cont.)

Position Profile — Position Description iView

The Position Description iView displays the position description from the Description Infotype (1002) (see Figure 7.30).

Table 7.51 provides the technical data for the Position Description iView within the Position Profile.

Position Description (Position Profile)	
Runtime Technology	Java/Web Dynpro
Technical Name of iView	com.sap.pct.erp.mss.posprofile_description
Technical Name of Web Dynpro Application	sap.com/mss~ppro~PositionProfileApp
Available as of	SAP NetWeaver 2004s
Data Origin	SAP ECC 6.0 or above
	RFC function component called: HRMSS_RFC_RC_ GET_1002_DESCR
Software Component	EA-HR
Support	EP-PCT-MGR-HR

Table 7.51   Technical Data for the Position Description iView

233

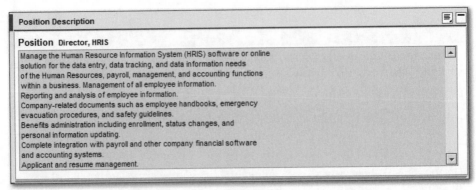

Figure 7.30 Position Description from the Position Profile

Position Profile — Cost Distribution iView

The Cost Distribution iView displays the position's account assignment objects (cost center, work breakdown structure (WBS) element, order) together with the controlling area and percentage from the Cost Distribution Infotype (1018). If no data is stored in the system at the position level, the data for the corresponding organizational unit is displayed.

Table 7.52 provides the technical data for the Cost Distribution iView within the Position Profile.

Cost Distribution (Position Profile)	
Runtime Technology	Java/Web Dynpro
Technical Name of iView	com.sap.pct.erp.mss.posprofile_costdistribution
Technical Name of Web Dynpro Application	sap.com/mss~ppro~PositionProfileApp
Available as of	SAP NetWeaver 2004s
Data Origin	SAP ECC 6.0 or above
	RFC function component called: HRMSS_RFC_PP_COSTDISTRIBUTION
Software Component	EA-HR
Support	EP-PCT-MGR-HR

Table 7.52 Technical Data for the Cost Distribution iView

Position Profile — Working Time iView

The Working Time iView displays the hours per day, hours per week, hours per month, and hours per year from the position's Working Time Infotype (IT1011) (see Figure 7.31). If no data exists at the position level, the working time for the assigned organizational unit is shown.

Table 7.53 provides the technical data for the Working Time iView within the Position Profile.

Working Time (Position Profile)	
Runtime Technology	Java/Web Dynpro
Technical Name of iView	com.sap.pct.erp.mss.posprofile_workingtime
Technical Name of Web Dynpro Application	sap.com/mss~ppro~PositionProfileApp
Available as of	SAP NetWeaver 2004s
Data Origin	SAP ECC 6.0 or above
	RFC function component called: HRMSS_RFC_PP_WORKINGTIME
Software Component	EA-HR
Support	EP-PCT-MGR-HR

Table 7.53 Technical Data for the Working Time iView

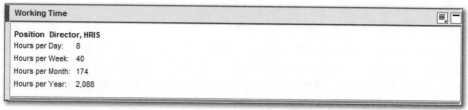

Figure 7.31 Working Time iView within the Position Profile

Position Profile — Employee Group/Subgroup iView

The Employee Group/Subgroup iView displays the employee group and employee subgroup for a position from the Employee Group/Subgroup Infotype (1013) (see Figure 7.32).

Table 7.54 provides the technical data for the Employee Group/Subgroup iView within the Position Profile.

Employee Group/Subgroup (Position Profile)	
Runtime Technology	Java/Web Dynpro
Technical Name of iView	com.sap.pct.erp.mss.posprofile_employeegroup
Technical Name of Web Dynpro Application	sap.com/mss~ppro~PositionProfileApp
Available as of	SAP NetWeaver 2004s
Data Origin	SAP ECC 6.0 or above RFC function component called: HRMSS_RFC_PP_EEGROUP
Software Component	EA-HR
Support	EP-PCT-MGR-HR

Table 7.54   Technical Data for the Employee Group/Subgroup iView

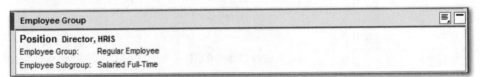

Figure 7.32   Employee Group/Subgroup iView within the Position Profile

Position Profile — Compensation iView

The Compensation iView allows you to display compensation information for a position (or job, if no position data exists) from the Planned Compensation Infotype (1005) (see Figure 7.33). The compensation returned will either be pay grade, pay scale, or direct, depending on what is planned/defaulted at the position or job level.

Table 7.55 provides the technical data for the Compensation iView within the Position Profile.

Compensation (Position Profile)	
Runtime Technology	Java/Web Dynpro
Technical Name of iView	com.sap.pct.erp.mss.posprofile_compensation
Technical Name of Web Dynpro Application	sap.com/mss~ppro~PositionProfileApp
Available as of	SAP NetWeaver 2004s
Data Origin	SAP ECC 6.0 or above RFC function component called: HRMSS_RFC_PP_COMPENSATION
Software Component	EA-HR
Support	EP-PCT-MGR-HR

Table 7.55 Technical Data for the Compensation iView

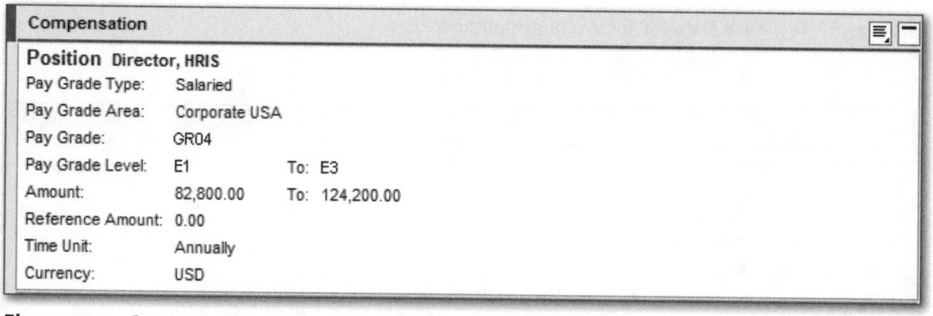

Figure 7.33 Compensation iView within the Position Profiles

Position Profile — Accounting iView

The Accounting iView displays the cost assignment data of a position from the Account Assignment Features Infotype (1008) (see Figure 7.34). This includes Company code, Business area, Personnel area, Personnel subarea, Controlling area, and Cost center.

Table 7.56 provides the technical data for the Accounting iView within the Position Profile.

Accounting (Position Profile)	
Runtime Technology	Java/Web Dynpro
Technical Name of iView	com.sap.pct.erp.mss.posprofile_accounting
Technical Name of Web Dynpro Application	sap.com/mss~ppro~PositionProfileApp
Available as of	SAP NetWeaver 2004s
Data Origin	SAP ECC 6.0 or above RFC function component called: HRMSS_RFC_PP_ACCOUNTING
Software Component	EA-HR
Support	EP-PCT-MGR-HR

Table 7.56 Technical Data for the Accounting iView

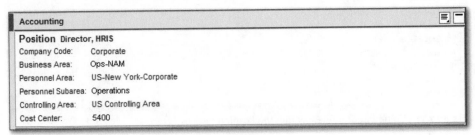

Figure 7.34 Accounting iView within the Position Profile

Position Profile — Holders iView

The Holders iView displays the holder or holders of a position and the relevant staffing percentage and staffing hours (per month) (see Figure 7.35).

Table 7.57 provides the technical data for the Holders iView within the Position Profile.

Holders (Position Profile)	
Runtime Technology	Java/Web Dynpro
Technical Name of iView	com.sap.pct.erp.mss.posprofile_positionholders
Technical Name of Web Dynpro Application	sap.com/mss~ppro~PositionProfileApp
Available as of	SAP NetWeaver 2004s
Data Origin	SAP ECC 6.0 or above
	RFC function component called: HRMSS_RFC_PP_HOLDERS
Software Component	EA-HR
Support	EP-PCT-MGR-HR

Table 7.57 Technical Data for the Holders iView

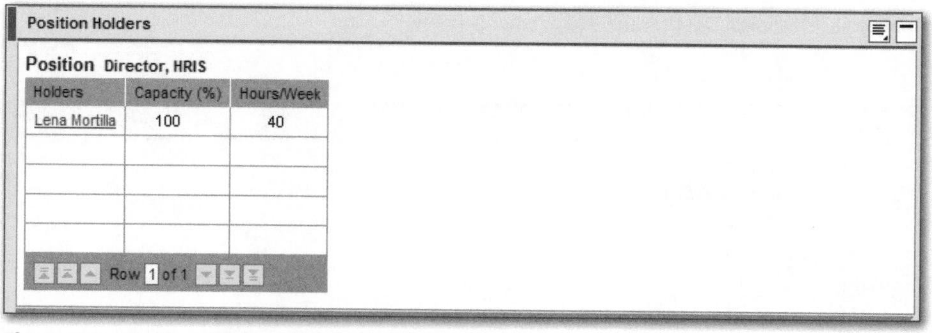

Figure 7.35 Holders iView within the Position Profile

Position Profile — Requirements iView

The Requirements iView displays the requirements for a position and the corresponding job (see Figure 7.36). If data is available for the position and the assigned job, the iView displays data for both. The requirements for positions and jobs are stored in the SAP system in the Relationships Infotype (1001) using the relationship A031 (Required) for object type Q (Qualification).

Table 7.58 provides the technical data for the Requirements iView within the Position Profile.

Requirements (Position Profile)	
Runtime Technology	Java/Web Dynpro
Technical Name of iView	com.sap.pct.erp.mss.posprofile_requirements
Technical Name of Web Dynpro Application	sap.com/mss~ppro~PositionProfileApp
Available as of	SAP NetWeaver 2004s
Data Origin	SAP ECC 6.0 or above RFC function component called: HRMSS_RFC_PP_QUALIFICATION
Software Component	EA-HR
Support	EP-PCT-MGR-HR

Table 7.58 Technical Data for the Requirements iView

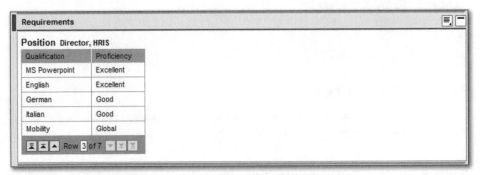

Figure 7.36 Requirements iView within the Position Profile

Position Profile — Vacancy iView

The Vacancy iView displays the vacancy status (i.e., vacant or occupied), approval percentage, and staffing percentage about a position from the Vacancy Infotype (1007) (see Figure 7.37).

Table 7.59 provides the technical data for the Vacancy iView within the Position Profile.

240

Vacancy (Position Profile)	
Runtime Technology	Java/Web Dynpro
Technical Name of iView	com.sap.pct.erp.mss.posprofile_vacancy
Technical Name of Web Dynpro Application	sap.com/mss~ppro~PositionProfileApp
Available as of	SAP NetWeaver 2004s
Data Origin	SAP ECC 6.0 or above
	RFC function component called: HRMSS_RFC_PP_VACANCY
Software Component	EA-HR
Support	EP-PCT-MGR-HR

Table 7.59 Technical Data for the Vacancy iView

Figure 7.37 Vacancy iView within the Position Profile

That concludes the review of the position profile-related iViews. The various iViews within the position profile provide managers with a holistic view of their organization from a headcount perspective. Important statistics on vacancies and compensation-related data on positions within their span-of-control provides more transparency within the organization.

7.4.10 Organizational Unit Profile

Let's change focus now from the position to the organizational unit. Within MSS, there is a suite of iViews based on the organizational unit entity. The following iViews from the organizational unit profile are available within the business package:

▶ Organizational Unit Search (master iView)

▶ Accounting

▶ General Description

- ▶ Working Time
- ▶ Position Holders
- ▶ Cost Distribution
- ▶ Qualifications
- ▶ Qualification Details

Let's first review the organizational unit search iView.

Organizational Unit Profile — Organizational Unit Search iView

Like the Employee Search and Position Search iViews, this Organizational Unit Search iView plays the role of master iView for all other iViews within the profile (see Figure 7.38).

Table 7.60 provides the technical data for the Organizational Unit Search iView within the Organizational Unit Profile.

Organizational Unit Search (Organizational Unit Profile)	
Runtime Technology	Java/Web Dynpro
Technical Name iView	com.sap.pct.erp.mss.orgprofiles_search
Technical Name Web Dynpro application	sap.com/mss~opro/OrganizationalProfile
Available from Portal (Release)	SAP NetWeaver 2004s
Data Source	SAP ECC 6.0 or higher RFC function component called: HRWPC_RFC_GET_VIEWS HRWPC_RFC_GET_COL_CONTENT HRWPC_RFC_GET_COL_INFO HRWPC_RFC_GET_OBJECTS HRWPC_RFC_EXPAND_OBJECT (as of PI 2002.2 for displaying in structure tree)
Software Component	EA-HR 600 and above
Support	EP-PCT-MGR-HR

Table 7.60 Technical Data for the Organizational Search iView

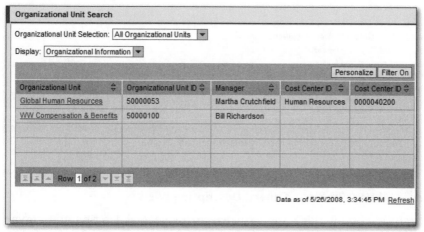

Figure 7.38 Organizational Unit Search iView

Organizational Unit Profile — Accounting iView

The Accounting iView displays the cost assignment data of an organizational unit from the Account Assignment Features Infotype (1008) (see Figure 7.39). This includes Company code, Business area, Personnel area, Personnel subarea, Controlling area, and Cost center.

Table 7.61 provides the technical data for the Accounting iView within the Organizational Unit Profile.

Accounting (Organizational Unit Profile)	
Runtime Technology	Java/Web Dynpro
Technical Name iView	com.sap.pct.erp.mss.java_sap_com_mss~opro_com_sap_xss_hr_oprofile_OrgProfileConfig_accounting
Technical Name Web Dynpro application	sap.com/mss~opro/OrganizationalProfile
Available for Portal (Release)	SAP NetWeaver 2004s
Data Source	SAP ECC 6.0 or higher RFC function component called: HRMSS_RFC_PP_ACCOUNTING
Software component	EA-HR 600 and above
Support	EP-PCT-MGR-HR

Table 7.61 Technical Data for the Accounting iView within the Organizational Unit Profile

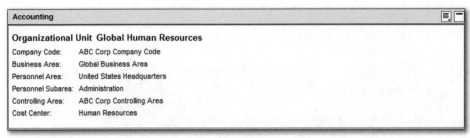

Figure 7.39 Accounting iView within the Organizational Unit Profile

Organizational Unit Profile — General Description iView

The General Description iView shows managers the general description (Infotype 1002, Subtype 0001) for a selected organizational unit (see Figure 7.40).

Table 7.62 provides the technical data for the General Description iView within the Organizational Unit Profile.

General Description (Organizational Unit Profile)	
Runtime Technology	Java/Web Dynpro
Technical Name iView	com.sap.pct.erp.mss.java_sap_com_mss~opro_com_sap_xss_hr_oprofile_OrgProfileConfig_generaldesc
Technical Name Web Dynpro application	sap.com/mss~opro/OrganizationalProfile
Available for Portal (Release)	SAP NetWeaver 2004s
Data Source	SAP ECC 6.0 or higher RFC function component called: HRMSS_RFC_ORG_DESCRIPTION
Software Component	EA-HR 600 and above
Support	EP-PCT-MGR-HR

Table 7.62 Technical Data for the General Description iView within the Organizational Unit Profile

Figure 7.40 General Description iView within the Organizational Unit Profile

Organizational Unit Profile — Working Time iView

The Working Time iView displays the hours per day, hours per week, hours per month, and hours per year from the organizational units' Working Time Infotype (IT1011) (see Figure 7.41).

Table 7.63 provides the technical data for the Working Time iView within the Organizational Unit Profile.

Working Time (Organizational Unit Profile)	
Runtime Technology	Java/Web Dynpro
Technical Name iView	com.sap.pct.erp.mss.java_sap_com_mss~opro_com_sap_xss_hr_oprofile_OrgProfileConfig_workingtime
Technical Name Web Dynpro application	sap.com/mss~opro/OrganizationalProfile
Available for Portal (Release)	SAP NetWeaver 2004s
Data Source	SAP ECC 6.0 or higher
	RFC function component called: HRMSS_RFC_WORKSCHEDULE_GETLIST
Software Component	EA-HR 600 and above
Support	EP-PCT-MGR-HR

Table 7.63 Technical Data for the Working Time iView within the Organizational Unit Profile

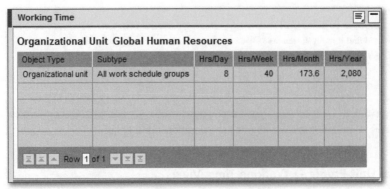

Figure 7.41 Working Time iView within the Organizational Unit Profile

Organizational Unit Profile — Position Holders iView

The Position Holders iView enables a manager to display the relevant positions and position holders for a selected organizational unit (see Figure 7.42).

Table 7.64 provides the technical data for the Position Holders iView within the Organizational Unit Profile.

Position Holders (Organizational Unit Profile)	
Technology	Java/Web Dynpro
Technical Name iView	com.sap.pct.erp.mss.java_sap_com_mss~opro_com_sap_xss_hr_oprofile_OrgProfileConfig_positionholders
Technical Name Web Dynpro application	sap.com/mss~opro/OrganizationalProfile
Available for Portal (Release)	SAP NetWeaver 2004s
Data Source	SAP ECC 6.0 or higher RFC function component called: HRMSS_RFC_STRUCTURE_GET
Software component	EA-HR 600 and above
Support	EP-PCT-MGR-HR

Table 7.64 Technical Data for the Position Holders iView within the Organizational Unit Profile

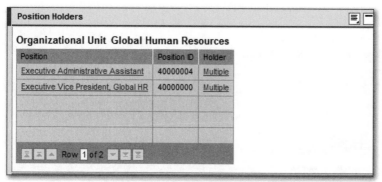

Figure 7.42 Position Holders iView within the Organizational Unit Profile

Organizational Unit Profile — Cost Distribution iView

The Cost Distribution iView displays the organizational unit's account assignment objects (cost center, WBS element, order) together with the controlling area and percentage from the Cost Distribution Infotype (1018) (see Figure 7.43).

Table 7.65 provides the technical data for the Cost Distribution iView within the Organizational Unit Profile.

Cost Distribution (Organizational Unit Profile)	
Runtime Technology	Java/Web Dynpro
Technical Name iView	com.sap.pct.erp.mss.java_sap_com_mss~opro_com_sap_xss_hr_oprofile_OrgProfileConfig_costdistribution
Technical Name Web Dynpro application	sap.com/mss~opro/OrganizationalProfile
Available for Portal (Release)	SAP NetWeaver 2004s
Data Source	SAP ECC 6.0 or higher RFC function component called: HRMSS_RFC_PP_COSTDISTRIBUTION
Software Component	EA-HR 600 and above
Support	EP-PCT-MGR-HR

Table 7.65 Technical Data for the Cost Distribution iView within the Organizational Unit Profile

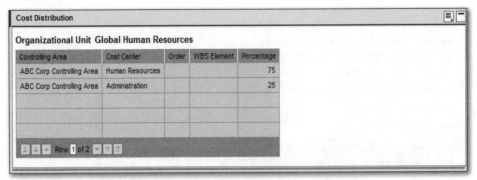

Figure 7.43 Cost Distribution iView within the Organizational Unit Profile

Organizational Unit Profile — Qualifications iView

The Qualifications iView enables managers to display the existing qualifications and the average proficiency of the qualifications for a selected organizational unit (see Figure 7.44).

Table 7.66 provides the technical data for the Qualifications iView within the Organizational Unit Profile.

Qualifications (Organizational Unit Profile)	
Runtime Technology	Java/Web Dynpro
Technical Name iView	com.sap.pct.erp.mss.java_sap_com_mss~opro_com_sap_xss_hr_oprofile_OrgProfileConfig_qualifications
Technical Name Web Dynpro application	sap.com/mss~opro/OrganizationalProfile
Available for Portal (Release)	SAP NetWeaver 2004s
Data Source	SAP ECC 6.0 or higher RFC function component called: HRMSS_RFC_ORG_QUALIFICATION
Software Component	EA-HR 600 and above
Support	EP-PCT-MGR-HR

Table 7.66 Technical Data for the Qualifications iView within the Organizational Unit Profile

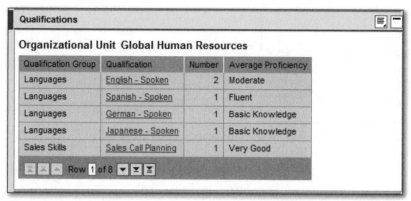

Figure 7.44 Qualifications iView within the Organizational Unit Profile

Organizational Unit Profile — Qualification Details iView

The Qualification Details iView shows the manager the employees in a specific organizational unit who possess a selected qualification (see Figure 7.45).

Table 7.67 provides the technical data for the Qualification Details iView within the Organizational Unit Profile.

Qualification Details (Organizational Unit Profile)	
Runtime Technology	Java/Web Dynpro
Technical Name iView	com.sap.pct.erp.srvconfig.qualificationdetails
Technical Name Web Dynpro application	sap.com/mss~opro/OrganizationalProfile
Available for Portal (Release)	SAP NetWeaver 2004s
Data Source	SAP ECC 6.0 or higher RFC function component called: HRMSS_RFC_QUALIFICATION_STAFF
Software Component	EA-HR 600 and above
Support	EP-PCT-MGR-HR

Table 7.67 Technical Data for the Qualification Details iView within the Organizational Unit Profile

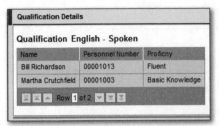

Figure 7.45 Qualification Details iView within the Organizational Unit Profile

This concludes a review of the iViews available within the organizational unit profile. Now, let's discuss options for organizational charting.

7.4.11 Organizational Charting

SAP software provides an interface for organizational charting. SAP HR Organizational Charting Interface (HR OCI) is an SAP-certified interface for external organizational charting applications. Third-party vendors, such as HumanConcepts, Aquire, Nakisa, and Worklogix have developed robust applications that "plug-in" to SAP software's organizational management structure for organizational charting, display, and modeling purposes through the SAP Portal and other platforms. Organizational data extractions — some in batch and others in real time — allow information to stream out of the SAP system and into the organizational charting applications of these vendors for a more user-friendly experience for end users, including managers and executives.

SAP software provides several tools to assist the test and linkages from the SAP system to these third-party applications. The following iViews related to OCI are available within the business package:

- Organizational Chart Link
- Organizational Chart Launcher
- Organizational Chart Tester

Organizational Chart Link iView

This iView displays a list of links that users can use to call the organizational charting application.

Table 7.68 provides the technical data for the Organizational Chart Link iView.

Organizational Chart	
Runtime Technology	Java/Web Dynpro
Technical Name iView	com.sap.pct.erp.mss.oci_link
Technical name Web Dynpro application	sap.com/mss~oci
Available from Portal (release)	SAP NetWeaver 2004s
Data source	SAP ECC 6.0 or higher
Software component	EA-HR 600 and above
Support	EP-PCT-MGR-HR

Table 7.68   Technical Data for the Organizational Chart iView

Organizational Chart Launcher iView

If implementing online data extraction, the Organizational Chart Launcher iView extracts organizational data from the SAP backend and accesses the Organizational Chart Tester iView or the third-party vendor's organizational charting application.

Table 7.69 provides the technical data for the Organizational Chart Launcher iView.

Organizational Chart Launcher	
Runtime Technology	Java/Web Dynpro
Technical Name iView	com.sap.pct.erp.mss.oci_launcher
Technical Name Web Dynpro application	sap.com/mss~oci
Available from Portal (release)	SAP NetWeaver 2004s
Data origin	SAP ECC 6.0 or higher RFC function component called: HRMSS_GET_ORGSTRUCTURE_AS_XML
Software component	EA-HR 600 and above
Support	EP-PCT-MGR-HR

Table 7.69   Technical Data for the Organizational Chart Launcher iView

Organizational Chart Tester iView

The Organizational Chart Tester is a test organizational charting application provided by the SAP system that mimics a third-party vendor's organizational charting application.

Table 7.70 provides the technical data for the Organizational Chart Tester iView.

Organizational Chart Tester	
Runtime Technology	Java/Web Dynpro
Technical Name iView	com.sap.pct.erp.mss.oci_tester
Technical Name Web Dynpro application	sap.com/mss~oci
Available from Portal (release)	SAP NetWeaver 2004s
Data Source	SAP ECC 6.0 or higher
Software component	EA-HR 600 and above
Support	EP-PCT-MGR-HR

Table 7.70 Technical Data for the Organizational Chart Tester iView

We have completed our review of the three organizational charting application iViews. Using these three utilities, you can test and launch any third-party organizational charting products that conform to the HR OCI interface.

Now, let's discuss generic iViews and their use within MSS.

7.5   Generic iViews

If the standard iViews do not meet all of your business requirements, customer-specific iViews, called "generic iViews," can be created that use an InfoSet to retrieve query data from HR infotypes in the SAP backend.

In the standard system, the iViews are displayed on a test page — *com.sap.pct. erp.mss.genericiviewtestpage.* You can use this page to obtain an overview of how the generic iViews can be used. The page is part of the business package for MSS (mySAP ERP) but it is not, however, part of an MSS role. The page also includes the Employee Search iView so that you can select an employee on the test page.

There are two kinds of generic iViews: one for lists or tables. Each will be explained in the following sections.

Generic iView for Lists

A generic iView is used to create customer iViews that display data from HR infotypes in a list format. The list display works better when only one record of data is expected for the selected employee.

Table 7.71 provides the technical data for the Geneic iView for Lists.

Generic iView for Lists	
Runtime Technology	Java/Web Dynpro
Technical Names of Example iViews	com.sap.pct.erp.mss.genericiview_communication com.sap.pct.erp.mss.genericiview_homeaddress
Technical Name of Web Dynpro Application	sap.com/mss~eepro~genericiview~TestGenericIview
Available as of	SAP NetWeaver 2004s
Data Source	SAP ECC 6.0 or above RFC function component called: HRMSS_INFO_GET_USING_QUERY Delivered query examples: MSS_IT0006 MSS_IT0105
Software Component	EA-HR
Support	EP-PCT-MGR-HR

Table 7.71 Technical Data for the Generic iView for Lists

To create a customer-specific generic iView based on an underlying infoset query, reference the procedures noted on SAP Help at *http://help.sap.com/saphelp_erp60_sp/helpdata/en/6c/9358f7d8dc43838e4f1135b9c37adb/frameset.htm*.

Table 7.72 lists the properties of the Generic iView for Lists, along with who maintains them (the user or a portal administrator) and the allowed entries.

Description (GUI)	Property	Maintained By	Type of Entry	Allowed Entries
Work area of query	workSpace	Administrator	Mandatory	
User group for query	userGroup	Administrator	Mandatory	
Name of query	queryName	Administrator	Mandatory	
Name of iView	iViewName	Administrator	Mandatory	
Groupings	groupings	Administrator	Optional	Number of query fields per group, separated by a comma (,), for example, 3,4,5 (= group 1 with three query fields, group 2 with four query fields, and group 3 with five query fields)
A minimum of two and a maximum of four groups are allowed	Title of first group	groupHeader1	Administrator	Optional
Header of first group defined with groupings property	Title of second group	groupHeader2	Administrator	Optional
Header of second group defined with groupings property	Title of third group	groupHeader3	Administrator	Optional

Table 7.72 Properties for the Generic iView for Lists

Description (GUI)	Property	Maintained By	Type of Entry	Allowed Entries
Header of third group defined with groupings property	Title of fourth group	groupHeader4	Administrator	Optional
Header of fourth group defined with groupings property	Number of columns displayed in iView	numberOfIview Columns	Administrator	Mandatory
1, 2, 3, or 4	Sort sequence	orderUpDown	Administrator	Mandatory
true (= from top to bottom/ according to column) or false (= from right to left/ according to rows)	Selection period in the past	yearsPast	End user	Mandatory
Natural numbers from 0 to 99 (default: 0)	Selection period in the future	yearsFuture	End user	Mandatory

Table 7.72 Properties for the Generic iView for Lists (Cont.)

Generic iView for Tables

The concept behind the Generic iView for Tables is the same as the Generic iViews for Lists. However, the output of data is done via a table and not a list.

Table 7.73 provides the technical data for the Generic iView for Tables.

Generic iView for Tables	
Runtime Technology	Java/Web Dynpro
Technical Name of Example iView	com.sap.pct.erp.mss.genericiview_dependents
Technical Name of Web Dynpro Application	sap.com/mss~eepro~genericiview~TestGenericIview
Available as of	SAP NetWeaver 2004s
Data Source	SAP ECC 6.0 or above RFC function component called: HRMSS_INFO_GET_USING_QUERY Delivered query example: MSS_IT0021
Software Component	EA-HR
Support	EP-PCT-MGR-HR

Table 7.73 Technical Data for the Generic iView for Tables

Table 7.74 lists the properties of the Generic iView for Tables, along with who maintains them (the user or a portal administrator) and the allowed entries.

Description (GUI)	Property	Maintained By	Type of Entry	Allowed Entries
Work area of query	workSpace	Administrator	Mandatory	
User group for query	userGroup	Administrator	Mandatory	
Name of query	queryName	Administrator	Mandatory	
Name of iView	iViewName	Administrator	Mandatory	
Selection period in the past	yearsPast	End user	Mandatory	Natural numbers from 0 to 99 (default: 0)
Selection period in the future	yearsFuture	End user	Mandatory	Natural numbers from 0 to 99 (default: 0)

Table 7.74 Properties for the Generic iView for Tables

This concludes our review of generic iViews. As you can see, generic iViews can be created (relatively easily) based on underlying infoset queries. It is an easy way to deliver custom functionality without the need for ABAP programming on the backend.

Finally, let's cover our last area: reporting.

7.6 Reporting

SAP software offers two launchpads within MSS in order to facilitate reporting functionality on the portal.

Launchpad

The Launchpad iView renders links to reporting applications. The following applications can be launched from this iView: SAP BI reports (queries or Web templates), Report Writer Reports, Transactions, URLs, and the manager's desktop application.

Table 7.75 provides the technical data for the Launchpad iView.

Launch Pad	
Runtime Technology	Java/Web Dynpro
Technical name of the iView	com.sap.pct.erp.common.reportlaunchpadpcd
Technical name of the Web Dynpro application	ReportLaunchpadPcdApp (Namespace: sap.com/mss~lpa)
Available as of	SAP NetWeaver 2004s
Data Source	SAP ECC 6.0 and higher
Software Component	SAP_APPL
Support	EP-PCT-FIN-BUA

Table 7.75 Technical Data for the Launchpad iView

LPA (Reporting Launchpad)

The Launchpad and LPA (Reporting Launchpad) iView provide managers access to reports on the SAP Portal.

Table 7.76 provides the technical data for the LPA iView.

LPA	
Runtime Technology	Java/Web Dynpro
Technical Name iView	com.sap.pct.erp.mss.lpareporting
Technical Name Web Dynpro application	sap.com/mss~rpt/LPAReporting
Available from:	SAP NetWeaver 2004s
Data origin	AP ECC 6.0 and above
Technical Components	SAP Manager's Desk Top (MDT)
Software components	EA-HR 600 and above

Table 7.76 Technical Data for the LPA iView

Table 7.77 lists the properties of the LPA iView, along with who maintains them (the user or a portal administrator) and the allowed entries.

Description (GUI)	Property	Maintained By	Type of Entry	Allowed Entries
Scenario	scenario	Administrator	Required	Default = RPT0
View Group	viewgroup	Administrator	Required	Default = MSS_RPT_SELECT
Empty selection forbidden	emptyselection forbidden	Administrator	Optional	Default = true
iView folder	iviewfolder	Administrator	Optional	See SAP Help documentation
BW iView	BW	Administrator	Optional	See SAP Help documentation
CR iView	CR	Administrator	Optional	See SAP Help documentation
IAC iView	IAC	Administrator	Optional	See SAP Help documentation

Table 7.77 Properties for the LPA iView

The technology and usability is improving in the reporting area. A lot of attention is now being paid to BI, as BI is where online analytics will be in the future for many customers. Therefore, it is questionable how many improvements will be made to these reporting iViews over the next few years.

7.7 Summary

In this chapter, we explained the functionality available in MSS by functional area. As you can see, the SAP system offers robust out-of-the-box functionality in its delivery of MSS on the portal. Needless to say, the services offered within this business package are an evolution, but SAP has taken good measure of the path forward. HCM Processes and Forms, for example, offer the next generation of online form requests for employees, managers, and HR Professionals. This area is destined to grow in leaps and bounds from what PCRs ever were.

In the next chapter, we cover some of the more advanced self-service topics, including the OADP, Workflow, the UWL, and delegation and employee checklist functionality via Guided Procedures.

There are several advanced topics within Employee Self-Service (ESS) and Manager Self-Service (MSS) that deserve particular attention due to their overall importance within the solution. This chapter discusses four of these advanced concepts, including the Object and Data Provider (OADP) framework, workflow and the Universal Worklist (UWL), delegation (including substitutions), and Guided Procedures to support process checklists.

8 Advanced Concepts in ESS and MSS

Several topics within ESS and MSS deserve special attention. Most of these concepts are critical to ESS or MSS because they meet some important business requirements within a self-service solution. For example, workflow is frequently needed in many self-service scenarios involving one-up or multilevel approvals. Allowing an employee the ability to request a leave of absence on the portal typically requires workflow to route a work item to a particular approver or set of approvers. Depending on your unique business rules, this workflow is "smart enough" to route to all necessary approvals and update the SAP system directly or route to a Human Resources (HR) processor for a manual update to the SAP system. This scenario is a relatively simple case. Other workflow processes get a lot more complicated.

Other advanced topics, such as SAP's Guided Procedures, will be discussed as well. Guided Procedures serve as company-provided checklists for an employee's work and life events. These procedures allow employees and managers to manage a personal event, such as a birth of a child, or a work event, such as a transfer or promotion, with a task list to complete. This checklist can contain transactional tasks (e.g., providing the ability to enroll/change their own benefits) or more informational tasks (e.g. providing a link to an external website, such as a government site to review important information). Other alternatives to checklists are discussed as well.

The topics of delegation and substitution are also important within the self-service context. More and more, companies are providing tools to assist management with proxy responsibility. Allowing non-managers (e.g., administrative staff) to perform the more mundane tasks needed from management (such as leave approvals and initiating requests for transfers within the organization) is now becoming one of the most common requirements when implementing manager-initiated processes online. Although the SAP system does provide standard workflow substitution, it does not yet provide a comprehensive delegation solution for all components supported by MSS. In this chapter, we will discuss how to enhance your system to deliver full delegation functionality.

The OADP will be discussed first. OADP provides a comprehensive framework for rendering objects (e.g., employees, positions, and organizational units) and information about those objects (e.g., name of employee, position number, cost center of organizational unit) on the portal based on the user's selection (e.g., direct reports, all reports). Much of the OADP is driven off the standard configuration but the latest enhancements to the framework provide additional capabilities with several Business Add-Ins (BAdIs). The OADP is discussed in detail next.

8.1 OADP

We will first provide a quick overview of the OADP to understand its use and importance at a macro level. We later dive into each component of the framework and explain its role in the overall solution.

8.1.1 Overview

The OADP offers a key operational framework for many iViews within the Business Package for MSS. OADP provides the mechanism for managers to search, view, and transact on "objects" within the manager's span-of-control, regardless of whether that view displays organizational units, positions, employees, or a mix of all three. A view can also appear in a tree structure, so that managers can easily navigate objects in a hierarchy (a good example is the organizational structure).

Many iViews are dependent on OADP configuration. Standard OADP configuration allows out-of-the-box iViews to render with preconfigured views. For example, views such as "Directly Reporting Employees" and "All Employees" are included in the standard configuration for the Personnel Change Request (PCR) Selection iView. This option allows managers to use either of these views (and any other configured views later added to this iView) to help initiate a PCR. Examples of other iViews that use the OADP include:

- Compensation Planning (shown in Figure 8.1)
- Compensation Approval
- Performance Management Status Overview
- Employee Search
- Position Search
- Organizational Search
- Cross-Application Timesheet (CATS) Approval
- HCM Processes and Forms

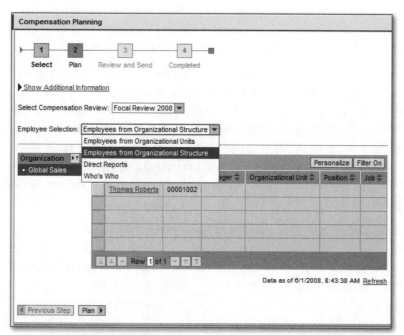

Figure 8.1 Compensation Planning iView with OADP Views for Employee Selection.

As the name states, the OADP is composed of an Object Provider and a Data Provider. The Object Provider is an evaluation of the organizational structure and the underlying organizational unit objects (whether it be organizational units, positions, or employees) that are displayed in a selection screen. The Data Provider is an evaluation of additional data of the displayed objects in a column format. Organizational views support the Object Provider and data views support the Data Provider. Both organizational views and data views provide the core technical components of an OADP framework. They are supported by several other components, including object selections, object selection rules, columns, and column groups. Each of these pieces together allows robust functionality for the manager to search, view, and transact on employees and other objects within their span-of-control.

OADP functionality controls both the selection of data and the actual data rendered on the iView. Most changes to and additions of OADP views can be achieved through the standard configuration. Where the standard configuration cannot achieve business requirements, ABAP development can provide the enhancements needed via BAdIs or custom function components. The bulk of OADP configuration is located within the Implementation Guide (IMG) under the following path: Integration with Other mySAP.com Components • Business Packages/Functional Packages • Manager Self-Service (mySAP ERP) • Object and Data Provider.

Alternatively, Transaction SM30 (Maintain Table Views) is a quick way to see all of the table views related to the OADP framework. Most experienced analysts who are responsible for OADP configuration typically use this transaction. All table views within OADP start with the prefix V_TWPC_*. By putting this string and selecting the dropdown in Transaction SM30, a full list of OADP table views appears. Also, additional configuration is found in cluster table views starting with prefix VC_TWPC_*. These cluster table views can be found in Transaction SM34 (View Cluster Maintenance).

As of ERP 2005, OADP has been enhanced with several new features, including employee search, enhanced caching, a more intuitive "look-and-feel," and improved "eventing" capabilities. For customers using the earlier OADP functionality, a standard migration program is provided by SAP software. We will highlight any new OADP functionality within ERP 2005 so that customers using earlier versions can understand the impacts when upgrading.

Note

As of ERP 2005, the Employee Search iView has replaced the previous TeamViewer iView within the MSS Business Package. The Employee Search iView is found on the Employee Profile, Position Profile, and Organizational Unit Profile pages. The concept of "eventing" is the same as the previous TeamViewer functionality. For example, an employee who has been selected from the "sender" Employee Search iView will influence the appropriate data in the other "receiver" iViews on that same portal page (i.e., personal data, address, emergency contacts, qualifications, etc.). Eventing continues to be an important construct within the new ESS/MSS framework.

Let's now take a more detailed look into the OADP framework's components and its associated configuration. We will first review the concept of an organizational view group, the highest level within the OADP configuration.

8.1.2 Organizational View Groups

As its name indicates, an organizational view group contains a grouping of organizational views. Organizational views — which form the basis for the Object Provider part of OADP — are discussed in detail next. Organizational view groups are configured in the IMG under the path: INTEGRATION WITH OTHER MYSAP.COM COMPONENTS • BUSINESS PACKAGES/FUNCTIONAL PACKAGES • MANAGER SELF-SERVICE (MYSAP ERP) • OBJECT AND DATA PROVIDER • ORGANIZATIONAL STRUCTURE VIEWS • GROUP ORGANIZATIONAL STRUCTURE VIEWS or via Transaction SM34 in view cluster VC_TWPC_ORGVWGRP.

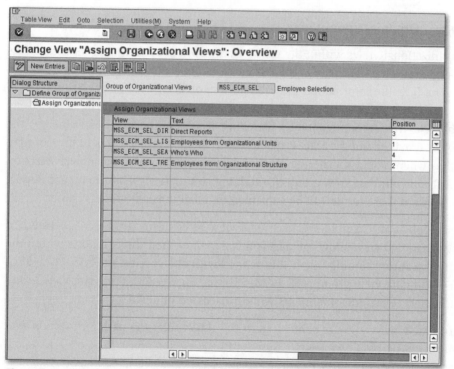

Figure 8.2 Organizational View Group MSS_ECM_SEL with Four Views

Organizational view group MSS_ECM_SEL is the standard organizational view group for the Compensation Planning iView. Figure 8.2 shows the configuration for the assignment of views MSS_ECM_SEL_DIR (Direct Reports), MSS_ECM_SEL_LIS (Employees from Organizational Units), MSS_ECM_SEL_SEA (Who's Who), and MSS_ECM_SEL_TRE (Employees from Organizational Structure) to the organizational view group MSS_ECM_SEL (Employee Selection). Next to each view is a column for Position, which indicates the order of views available in the dropdown of the iView.

Other standard view groups are used in over ten different MSS iViews, including the Performance Management Status Overview iView (MSS_HAP_STATUS), the CATS approval iView (MSS_LCA_EE), as well as the Employee Profile (MSS_TMV_EE), Position Profile (TDS_PRQ_POS), and Organizational Profile (MSS_TMV_ORG).

Let's now turn our attention to an important configuration element within the OADP – organizational views.

8.1.3 Organizational Views

Organizational views within the OADP framework provide managers with access to organizational objects (i.e., organizational units, positions, and employees) and its data (i.e., the information describing these objects, such as a position's name, an employee's manager) within their span-of-control. Data can be accessed via table lists, tree structures, or by searching. The organizational view merges the Object Provider and the Data Provider components together. It is in this configuration where you associate the object selection (containing your object selection rules) and your data view groups (containing your data views) to an organizational view. All of these terms will be explained in detail throughout the chapter.

Let's look at an example organizational view MSS_ECM_SEL_DIR. This standard organizational view allows managers to view all of their direct reports within the Compensation Planning iView. It is defined with object selection MSS_ECM_SEL_OB1 and data view group MSS_ECM_SEL (see Figure 8.3). (The data view group and object selection components will be discussed in detail.)

Organizational views are configured in the IMG under the path: INTEGRATION WITH OTHER MYSAP.COM COMPONENTS • BUSINESS PACKAGES/FUNCTIONAL PACKAGES • MANAGER SELF-SERVICE (MYSAP ERP) • OBJECT AND DATA PROVIDER • ORGANIZATIONAL STRUCTURE VIEWS • DEFINE ORGANIZATIONAL STRUCTURE VIEWS or via Transaction SM30 in table view V_TWPC_ORGVW. In this activity, you identify the core "backbone" of the view, which includes both the selection of objects and what data for these objects should be available for display.

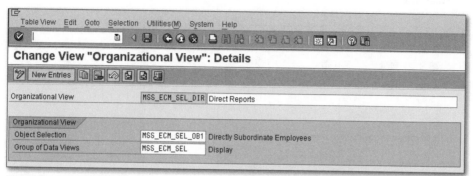

Figure 8.3 Organization View MSS_ECM_SEL_DIR with Object Selection MSS_ECM_SEL_OB1 and Data View Group MSS_ECM_SEL

Let's look at some possibilities of organizational views. Within the organizational view group for the Compensation Planning iView, for example, the following views are available. Each view is accompanied with a short description of its use.

▶ Directly Subordinate Employees (view MSS_ECM_SEL_DIR) — This standard view uses object selection MSS_ECM_SEL_OB1 (Directly Subordinate Employees) and data view group MSS_ECM_SEL (Display). The view allows a manager to see all of their direct reports.

▶ Employees from Organizational Units (view MSS_ECM_SEL_LIS) — This standard view uses object selection MSS_ECM_SEL_OB2 (Object Selection SAP_MANG, ORGEH_T, O-P) and the data view group MSS_ECM_SEL (Display). The view allows a manager to see all organizational units under his span-of-control in a tabular list. The manager can select one or more organizational units for selection.

▶ Employee Search (sometimes referred to as Who's Who) (view MSS_ECM_SEL_SEA) — This standard view uses object selection MSS_ECM_SEL_OB3 (Employee Selection) and the data view group MSS_ECM_SEL (Display). The view allows a manager to conduct both a basic and advanced search for employees within their span-of-control. Figure 8.4 shows the Employee Search view with the advanced search functionality.

▶ Employees from Organizational Structure (view MSS_ECM_SEL_TRE) — This standard view uses object selection MSS_ECM_SEL_OB4 (Obj.Sel.Tree Str. SAP_

MANG, ORGEH_T, O-P) and data view group MSS_ECM_SEL (Display). This standard allows a manager to view his organizational span-of-control via a tree structure.

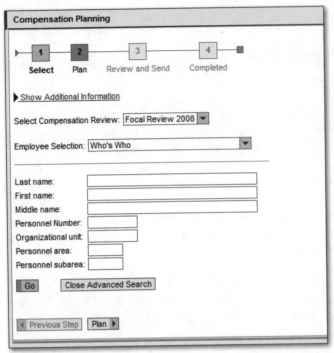

Figure 8.4 Employee Selection Option "Employee Search," (or Who's Who) within the Compensation Planning iView

> **Note**
>
> The Employee Search functionality (e.g., used in organizational view MSS_ECM_SEL_ SEA) is one of the newest features within the enhanced OADP framework (available as of ERP 2005). In addition to the basic and advanced search capabilities, the new OADP framework allows for the flexibility to influence additional searching using "selection IDs" and "parameter groups." These are discussed in detail later in this chapter.

Organizational views are one of the most important components of the configuration as they assist the manager with perspective on how to view or transact on the data. Whether it be via an organizational structure, a listing of direct reports, or through a complex search, data returned from these views allow the manager to more effectively use the MSS functionality. It is important that you review these views with your business users to ensure that managers can understand how to navigate between the various selections.

These organizational views are comprised of so-called "object selections." These object selections (and the embedded object selection rules within them) define the Object Provider part of the OADP framework. Next, we will discuss object selection rules and their importance in defining the underlying structure of the organizational view.

8.1.4 Object Selection Rules

An object selection rule is comprised of either an evaluation path or a function module for determining objects. An evaluation path is a configurable entity that dynamically determines which object types and relationship(s) are to be returned based on a starting object node or nodes. A function module is a snippet of ABAP code that can be called from the OADP framework to programmically return data based on customer-specific logic. In either case, the object selection rule provides the instructions to the system to retrieve the raw data for the iView.

Object selection rules are used to construct an object selection (which we will discuss next). Within the Compensation Planning iView, object selection rule MSS_ECM_SEL_RU1 is used (see the configuration of this rule in Figure 8.5). Object selection rules are configured in the IMG path: INTEGRATION WITH OTHER MYSAP.COM COMPONENTS • BUSINESS PACKAGES/FUNCTIONAL PACKAGES • MANAGER SELF-SERVICE (MYSAP ERP) • OBJECT AND DATA PROVIDER • OBJECT PROVIDER • DEFINE RULES FOR OBJECT SELECTION or via Transaction SM34 in view cluster VC_TWPC_OBJSELRULE.

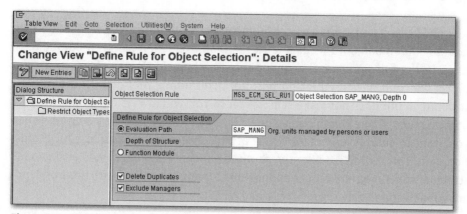

Figure 8.5 Object Selection Rule MSS_ECM_SEL_RU1 with Evaluation Path SAP_MANG

This object selection rule uses standard evaluation path SAP_MANG (Org. units managed by persons or users) to determine all organizational units that are managed by the chief manager (i.e., the user logged in). Figure 8.6 shows the definition of evaluation path SAP_MANG. Evaluation paths are configured in Transaction OOAW. Based on the user logged in, the evaluation path determines the user's employee record (via the 208 "Is identical to" relationship). From this employee object (P), the position object (S) is found via the 008 "Holder" relationship. Once this position is found, the system attempts to find all organizational units (O) where this position is identified as being the "chief." This is done by evaluating the relationship (012 "Manages") from the position to the organizational unit. This process is repeated until all organizational units are returned. (If the user is a chief manager of more than one high-level organizational unit, he might manage more than one top-level organizational unit.) The object selection rule returns these organizational unit(s) to the object selection.

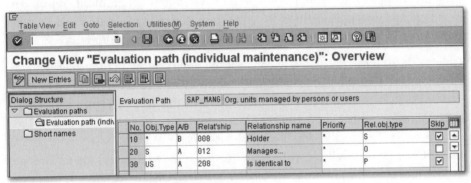

Figure 8.6 Standard Evaluation Path SAP_MANG

As previously stated, an object selection rule must either use an evaluation path or a function module for its data retrieval. If an evaluation path is used, the technical depth of the structure can be indicated in the field "Depth of Structure." For object selection rules used for purposes of determining root objects, indicating a structure depth does not make sense because you will always only want the root object(s) (i.e., where depth equals one). However, there may be occasions when you want to control how many levels of objects get returned from your evaluation path. This setting specifies the depth to which the system should evaluate the structure containing the organizational units. If left blank, no restrictions of depth are applied and the structure is returned in full.

Two flags, "Delete Duplicates" and "Exclude Managers," are available for selection as well. If an object (e.g., a person) is assigned more than once to a structure, the system would normally display this object twice. However, when the "Delete Duplicates" checkbox is selected, the system automatically removes any duplicate objects from being retrieved in the result set. In most cases, it makes sense to select this option, as you would not want to present the manager with duplicates of the same object (e.g., person) in an iView.

We know that a manager is also assigned to an organizational unit that he is responsible for. He would ordinarily see himself in the result set of the evaluation path. To prevent this from occurring, the "Exclude Managers" checkbox should be selected. This flag excludes the user logged in (i.e., the manager) and any other manager assigned to the same organizational unit as the logged-on manager. The default implementation uses function HRWPC_OADP_EXCLUDE_MANAGER for this restriction. Method EXCLUDE_MANAGER within BAdI HRWPC_EXCL_MAN-AGERS can be implemented to change the result set of the object selection rule. Figure 8.7 shows BAdI HRWPC_EXCL_MANAGERS.

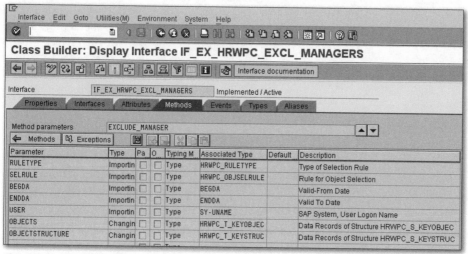

Figure 8.7 Method EXCLUDE_MANAGER in BAdI HRWPC_EXCL_MANAGERS

There are four object selection rules used within the standard views supporting the Compensation Planning and Compensation Approval iViews. Tables 8.1 lists these four views with their description, evaluation path used, and the description of the evaluation path. This should give you a good idea of what is possible in the configuration (there are over 70 object selection rules in the standard system).

Object Selection Rule	Object Selection Rule Description	Evaluation Path Used	Evaluation Path Description
MSS_ECM_SEL_RU1	Object Selection SAP_MANG, Depth 0	SAP_MANG (Org. units managed by persons or users)	US-P-S-O = used to determine the start object (org unit) for the second evaluation path
MSS_ECM_SEL_RU2	Object Selection ORGEH_T Struct. Depth 50	ORGEH_T (Organizational structure with all underlying objects/teams (003))	O-O, Depth of 5
MSS_ECM_SEL_RU3	Object Selection MSSDIREC, Struc. Depth 0	MSSDIREC (Manager Under Manager for MSS)	O-O-S-P-US = includes the Relationship B900 between O-S and O-O. B900 is a relationship that includes a program. This program selects employees of the root org unit, selects managers of subordinated org units, and selects employees of subordinated org units without manager position.
MSS_ECM_SEL_RU4	Object Sel.Tree Struc. ORGEH_T, Depth 50	ORGEH_T	O-O, Depth of 5 (as a tree structure)

Table 8.1 Object Selection Rules Used within Object Selections for Compensation Planning and Approval iViews

OADP uses three "types" of evaluation paths to select objects. The first evaluation path determines the organizational units the user (manager) is responsible for (e.g., SAP_MANG). These organizational units are then used as root objects for the second evaluation. Starting with the root object found by the first evaluation path (e.g., the manager's organizational unit(s)), the system uses a second evaluation path to select all objects along the structure and displays the relevant object types for navigation. Once an object is selected for navigation, these objects are used as a root object for the third evaluation path, to determine the objects to be shown in the data views. Data views are discussed later in the chapter. In summary, an object selection rule can support a selection of root objects, the selection of navigation objects, and the selection of target objects.

As an alternative to an evaluation path, a custom function module can be created to determine the objects instead. You can use function module HRWPC_PATH-ROOTS as a model for your custom function component (see Figure 8.8). The OADP framework expects a certain interface, so modeling off this standard function module will speed up implementation time. SAP user name, start date, and end date are mandatory import parameters to the function. Based on a supplied user name, the system could perform customer-specific logic to return a result set based on the manager logged in. This would be used in lieu of the evaluation path.

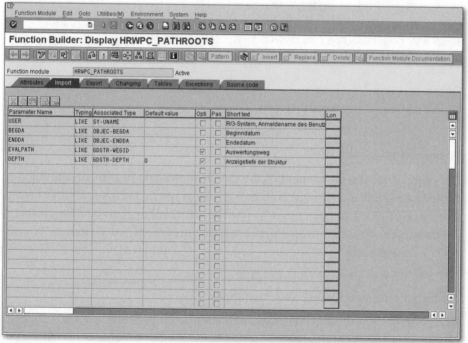

Figure 8.8 Import Parameters of Standard Function Component HRWPC_PATHROOTS

For each object selection rule, the "Restrict Object Types" folder needs to be configured. Each object selection rule should have the appropriate object type(s) identified according to which objects should be displayed in the organizational view. If no object types are configured, all objects returned from the evaluation path or function module will be retrieved. Figure 8.9 shows standard object selection rule MSS_ECM_SEL_RU4 with object type O (organizational unit) identified as its restricted object. This means that only organizational unit objects will be returned regardless of the objects that are returned from the evaluation path or function module.

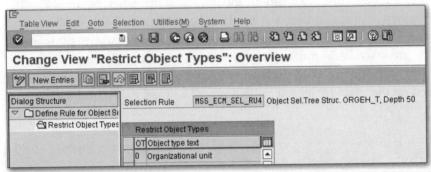

Figure 8.9 Object Selection Rule MSS_ECM_SEL_RU4 Identified with Restricted Object Type O (Organizational Unit)

Object selections comprise up to three object selection rules (or an object search). Object selections are explained next.

8.1.5 Object Selections

The object selection component of the OADP allows you to provide a method of retrieving organizational objects in one of two ways: 1) via a set of object selection rules, or 2) via an object search. The approach will depend on how you want the data to be accessed (via organizational structures or via a user search). We will cover each separately.

Object Selection via Object Selection Rules

Using the first method — via object selection rules — Rules for Root Objects, Navigation Objects, and Targets Objects are specified (see Figure 8.10). At a minimum, a rule must be provided for at least the Rule for Root Objects and the Rule for Target Objects. The Rule for Root Objects is used to determine the root (or "top node") object in the evaluation. For example, object selection rule MSS_ECM_SEL_RU1 (Object Selection SAP_MANG, Depth 0) within object selection MSS_ECM_SEL_OB1 (Directly Subordinate Employees) retrieves all organizational units that are managed by the chief. The organizational units returned from object selection rule MSS_ECM_SEL_RU1 are considered the "root objects" of the object selection rule for the object selection.

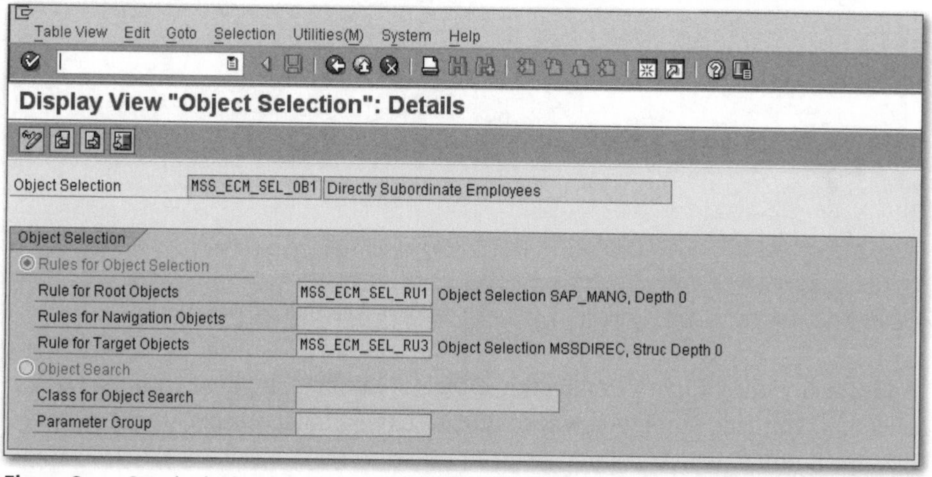

Figure 8.10 Standard Object Selection MSS_ECM_SEL_OB1, Which Includes Rule for Root Objects MSS_ECM_SEL_RU1 and Rule for Target Objects MSS_ECM_SEL_RU3.

Meanwhile, object selection rule MSS_ECM_SEL_RU3 (Object Selection MSSDIREC, Struc Depth 0) is defined as the Rule for Target Objects. This object selection rule returns all employees who are considered direct reports to the manager based on the starting organizational unit. In other words, all organizational units identified as "root objects" (from the MSS_ECM_SEL_RU1 object selection rule) are used to retrieve the manager's directly reporting employees as target objects.

Object selection rules MSS_ECM_SEL_RU1 and MSS_ECM_SEL_RU3 are used to build object selection MSS_ECM_SEL_OB1. MSS_ECM_SEL_OB1 is the object selection used in organizational view MSS_ECM_SEL_DIR (Directly Reporting Employees). Any iView (e.g., Compensation Planning) using this organizational view will render the direct reports of the manager. In Figure 8.11, the manager only has two direct reports.

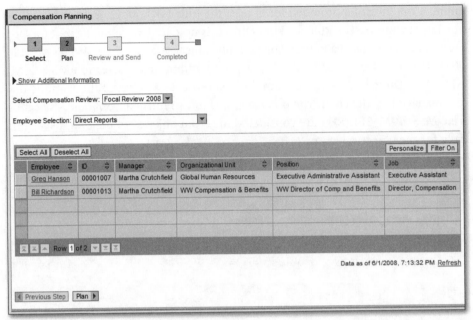

Figure 8.11 Compensation Planning iView with Employee Selection as Direct Reports

Additionally, the "Rule for Navigation Objects" can be populated within an object selection. This rule provides a way to utilize "navigational objects" (typically organizational units) to restrict the view of so-called "target objects." A classic example is object selection MSS_ECM_SEL_OB2, which allows a manager to select any one of the organizational units within his span-of-control. After the "root" organizational units are retrieved using the object selection rule MSS_ECM_SEL_RU1 for the "Rule for Root Objects," all organizational units from these starting points are listed in a table for selection by the manager via the "Rule for Navigational Objects." Once selected, the "Rule for Target Objects" (defined as MSS_ECM_SEL_RU3) lists all of the employees in the selected organizational unit(s). Figure 8.12 shows object selection MSS_ECM_SEL_OB2.

Object selections are configured in the IMG under the path: Integration with Other mySAP.com Components • Business Packages/Functional Packages • Manager Self-Service (mySAP ERP) • Object and Data Provider • Object Provider • Define Object Selections or via Transaction SM30 in table view V_TWPC_OBJSEL.

BAdI HRWPC_MOD_NAVOBJECTS is available to manipulate the text of navigational objects for users. For example, you may want the chief manager's name to appear beside the organizational unit's name within the hierarchy of the organizational structure. (Oftentimes, managers do not know the names of the organizational units they lead, but do know the manager's name.) By implementing such logic within this BAdI, the iView will display the manager's name next to each organizational unit, thus improving the manager's overall user experience. Figure 8.13 shows the parameters within Method GET_TEXTS of BAdI HRWPC_MOD_NAVOBJECTS. Implementing logic within this method will allow you to influence the text on navigational objects.

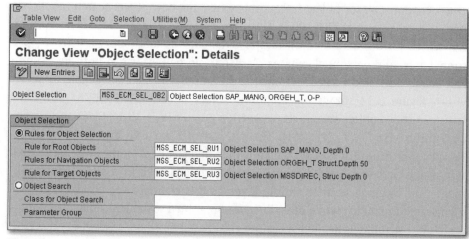

Figure 8.12 Standard Object Selection MSS_ECM_SEL_OB2

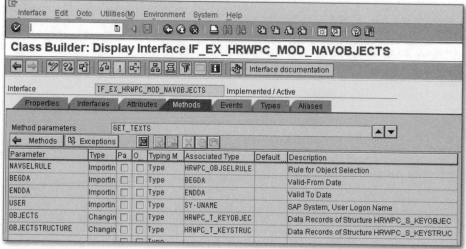

Figure 8.13 Method GET_TEXTS within BAdI HRWPC_MOD_NAVOBJECTS

In most scenarios, you will use an object selection based on an object selection rule. Object selection rules allow flexibility in defining how object rules can support organizational views within the OADP framework. You may, however, need the ability for a manager to search. The object search functionality is discussed next.

Object Selection via Object Search

The second option for object selection is to use the new object search functionality (it is available as of ERP 2005). With the object search functionality, managers can search for objects based on master data, such as first name, last name, personnel area, and personnel subarea. A search can be performed both in a simple and advanced fashion (the difference is the number of fields available to search with). Figure 8.14 shows the standard object selection MSS_ECM_SEL_OB3, which includes object search class CL_HRWPC_SEARCH_VIA_SELID and parameter group MSS_TMV_EE_SRCH. The selection ID is based on search class CL_HRWPC_SEARCH_VIA_SELID, which is included standard in the system. Because this search class was created generically, you do not need to create a new implementation. Some customers simply leverage this standard search class for their own search capability, while others need more robust searching capability. If more searching capability is needed, a custom class based on standard class CL_HRWPC_SEARCH_VIA_SELID should be developed.

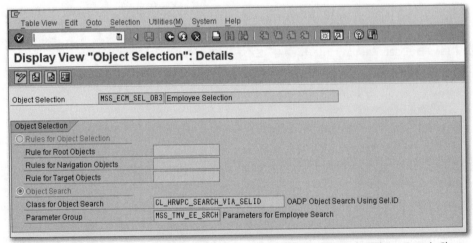

Figure 8.14 Standard Object Selection MSS_ECM_SEL_OB3, Which Includes Object Search Class CL_HRWPC_SEARCH_VIA_SELID and Parameter Group MSS_TMV_EE_SRCH

If the class requires parameters (as standard class CL_HRWPC_SEARCH_VIA_SELID does), a parameter group must exist that contains these parameters. The search class must be able to evaluate the pairs of parameters and parameter values that are assigned to the parameter group. For example, parameter group MSS_TMV_ EE_SRCH (used within object selection MSS_ECM_SEL_OB3) contains parameter value MSS_TMV_ADV_SEARCH for the advanced search parameter (ADVANCED_ SEARCH_SELID) and parameter value MSS_TMV_SIM_SEARCH for the simple search parameter (SIMPLE_SEARCH_SELID). Parameter values are needed in order to tell the iView which selection IDs should be used for which searches (e.g., simple versus advanced). Each parameter within the parameter group is assigned a parameter value. Figure 8.15 shows the configuration of parameters with a parameter value.

> **Note**
>
> Custom parameter groups can be configured in the IMG under the following path: INTE-GRATION WITH OTHER MYSAP.COM COMPONENTS • BUSINESS PACKAGES/FUNC-TIONAL PACKAGES • MANAGER SELF-SERVICE (MYSAP ERP) • OBJECT AND DATA PROVIDER • OBJECT PROVIDER • GROUP PARAMETERS FOR OBJECT SEARCH or via Transaction SM34 in table view cluster VC_TWPC_PARAMGRP. You will want to configure a new parameter group in your own customer name space if the standard configuration does not satisfy all your requirements.

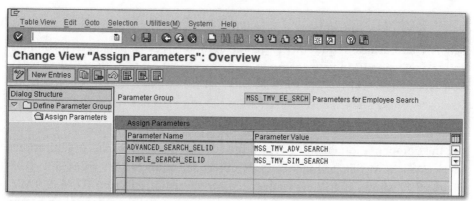

Figure 8.15 Parameter Group MSS_TMV_EE_SRCH with Parameter Values MSS_TMV_ADV_ SEARCH and MSS_TMV_SIM_SEARCH for Advanced and Simple Search, Respectively.

Figure 8.16 shows the configuration for parameter value (or selection ID) MSS_TMV_ADV_SEARCH. For this selection ID, seven fields (Personnel Number from IT0000; Organizational Unit, Personnel Area, and Personnel Subarea from IT0001; and First Name, Last Name, and Middle Name from IT0002) are available for search.

Parameter value (or selection ID) MSS_TMV_SIM_SEARCH (not pictured) allows for only four fields to be searchable: Personnel Number from IT0000 and First Name, Last Name, and Middle Name from IT0002.

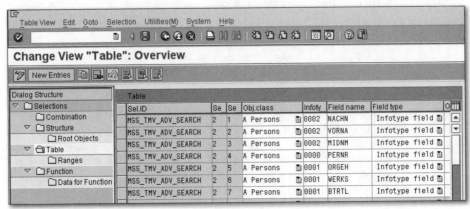

Figure 8.16 Table Values for Selection ID MSS_TMV_ADV_SEARCH

You may need to add additional search parameters if the standard values do not satisfy your business requirements. To add additional search parameters, you must create a selection ID in your customer name space that contains the relevant fields. You create selection IDs via IMG activity path: PERSONNEL MANAGEMENT • HUMAN RESOURCES INFORMATION SYSTEM • SELECTION IDS • DEFINE SELECTION IDs or via Transaction SM34 table view cluster HR_SELECTIONS.

On the Compensation Planning iView, the advanced search for this organizational view (MSS_ECM_SEL_SE) identifies its object selection as MSS_ECM_SEL_OB3. Figure 8.17 shows the iView's advanced search using selection ID MSS_TMV_ADV_SEARCH. Searches can be conducted with the fields personnel area, personnel subarea, and organizational unit, in addition to first name, last name, and personnel number.

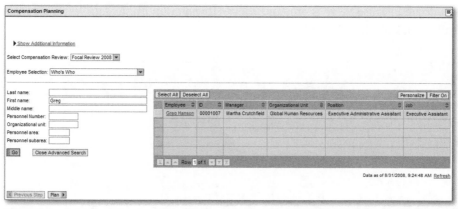

Figure 8.17 Advanced Search within the Compensation Planning iView Using Selection ID MSS_ TMV_ADV_SEARCH

Note

For more information on the search functionality availability within the OADP framework, see SAP Note 1106196 (Configuration of search in OADP). Attached to the Note is an example implementation of a custom search class as reference. You can leverage this code for your own implementation if needed.

We have now seen how robust the new object search functionality is. Simple and advanced searching can be achieved for object selection and applied to an organizational view. The object selection is one importance piece of an organizational view. The other piece contains the data side, including data view groups and data views. Let's discuss data view groups first.

8.1.6 Data View Groups

As organizational view groups group organizational views, data view groups group data views. Data view groups are configured in the IMG under the path: Integration with Other mySAP.com Components • Business Packages / Functional Packages • Manager Self-Service (mySAP ERP) • Object and Data Provider • Data Provider • Group Data Views or via Transaction SM34 in view cluster VC_TWPC_DATAVWGRP.

Data view group MSS_ECM_SEL is the standard data view group for the Compensation Planning iView. In Figure 8.18, data view group MSS_ECM_SEL is pictured with one data view, called MSS_ECM_SEL_ORG (Organizational Information). Next to the view is the Position column, which indicates which order the view should appear in the dropdown box of the iView. In this case, there will be no dropdown because there is only one view. However, multiple data views are now available (as of ERP 2005).

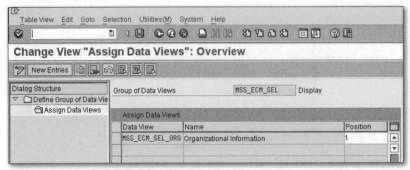

Figure 8.18 Data View Group MSS_ECM_SEL

Let's now talk about data views and their importance within the overall OADP framework.

8.1.7 Data Views

Data views contain the reference to column groups. The column group, discussed next, contains all of the columns that will return the data within the data view. If the standard data views do not meet your business needs, you can create a new one in your customer name space. To create a new data view, you can configure one under the IMG path: INTEGRATION WITH OTHER MYSAP.COM COMPONENTS • BUSINESS PACKAGES / FUNCTIONAL PACKAGES • MANAGER SELF-SERVICE (MYSAP ERP) • OBJECT AND DATA PROVIDER • DATA PROVIDER • DEFINE DATA VIEWS or via Transaction SM30 in table view V_TWPC_DATAVW. Data view MSS_ECM_SEL_ORG is seen in Figure 8.19.

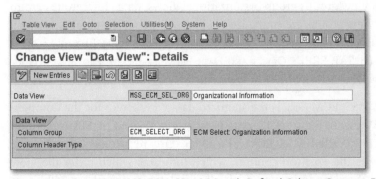

Figure 8.19 Data View MSS_ECM_SEL_ORG with Defined Column Group as ECM_SELECT_ORG.

Data views also contain a field for column header type. Column headers and column header types are explained shortly. Let's first discuss column groups.

8.1.8 Column Groups

Column groups allow you to group columns together and influence the behavior of those columns within that column group. All columns need to be put into a column group in order to be included in a data view. If the standard column groups do not meet your business needs, you can create a new one in your customer name space. To create a new column group, the configuration is performed within the IMG under the path: INTEGRATION WITH OTHER MYSAP.COM COMPONENTS • BUSINESS PACKAGES/FUNCTIONAL PACKAGES • MANAGER SELF-SERVICE (MYSAP ERP) • OBJECT AND DATA PROVIDER • DATA PROVIDER • DEFINE COLUMN GROUPS • CREATE CUSTOMER-SPECIFIC COLUMN GROUPS or via Transaction SM30 in table view V_TWPC_ARRAYTP.

You can view the standard entries for the assignment of columns to column groups (provided by SAP) under the IMG path: INTEGRATION WITH OTHER MYSAP.COM COMPONENTS • BUSINESS PACKAGES/FUNCTIONAL PACKAGES • MANAGER SELF-SERVICE (MYSAP ERP) • OBJECT AND DATA PROVIDER • DATA PROVIDER • DEFINE COLUMN GROUPS • CHECK STANDARD ASSIGNMENT OF COLUMN TO COLUMN GROUP or via Transaction SM30 in table view V_TWPC_ACOL. Although entries in this table are editable, we recommend that you do not change anything in this table.

Any new entries (for your new column group) or any entries that you wish to override from the SAP system (if you are going to use one the standard column groups with changes to the mapping or ordering to columns) can be configured under the IMG path: INTEGRATION WITH OTHER MYSAP.COM COMPONENTS • BUSINESS PACKAGES/FUNCTIONAL PACKAGES • MANAGER SELF-SERVICE (MYSAP ERP) • OBJECT AND DATA PROVIDER • DATA PROVIDER • DEFINE COLUMN GROUPS • CHECK STANDARD ASSIGNMENT OF COLUMN TO COLUMN GROUP or via Transaction SM30 in table view V_TWPC_ACOL_C.

Within this configuration, you perform the following steps.

▶ Map each column to the column group.

▶ Define the "position" of each column within the column group. The position of the column within the column group defines the sequence order (from left to right) of the columns shown in the iView.

▶ Set visibility attributes including "Visible," "Do Not Display," and "Invisible." If "Visible" is checked, the column can never be hidden by the user. If "Do Not

Display" is checked, the column is not displayed at all to the user. If "Invisible" is checked, the column is initially invisible but can be unhidden by the user.

▶ Define a coherence relationship between individual columns (optional). Coherence between two or more columns should exist if each column should be displayed only if all other columns are populated. An example would be two columns, such as start date and end date. In this case, it may only make sense to display both columns if both are populated with data. Coherence relationships can be configured under the IMG path: INTEGRATION WITH OTHER MYSAP.COM COMPONENTS • BUSINESS PACKAGES/FUNCTIONAL PACKAGES • MANAGER SELF-SERVICE (MYSAP ERP) • OBJECT AND DATA PROVIDER • DATA PROVIDER • DEFINE COHERENCE RELATIONSHIPS or via Transaction SM30 in table view V_TWPC_FRIEND.

▶ You can also set column groups to be hierarchical in nature. This means you can include or embed one column group within another, thus making it a reusable entity. Hierarchical relationships can be configured under the IMG path: INTEGRATION WITH OTHER MYSAP.COM COMPONENTS • BUSINESS PACKAGES/FUNCTIONAL PACKAGES • MANAGER SELF-SERVICE (MYSAP ERP) • OBJECT AND DATA PROVIDER • DATA PROVIDER • DEFINE HIERARCHICAL COLUMN GROUPS or via Transaction SM30 in table view V_TWPC_HIERATP_C. (The SAP standard table for hierarchical relationships is V_TWPC_HIERATP but it does not have any delivered entries, so it has not been covered here.) We have not seen this functionality implemented on many projects.

As you can see, column groups do more than just contain columns — they provide additional information on how the columns should be rendered within that column group. This means you can reuse the same columns in different column groups in different ways based on the context of where it is used in the iViews. Let's now talk about columns.

8.1.9   Columns

Just as object selection rules form the foundation of the Object Provider portion of the OADP framework, columns provide the core functionality inherent within the Data Provider. Each column represents one entity of data and typically brings back one field from one infotype record. Typically, a column is associated with a function module that returns this data. There are a few exceptions to this, though. A column can be populated dynamically "on the fly" based on logic in global memory (e.g., the amount field on the Compensation Planning iView based on what the user enters into the percentage field). Most columns, however, are based solely on the logic found within the assigned function components.

Columns are configured under the IMG path: INTEGRATION WITH OTHER MYSAP.COM COMPONENTS • BUSINESS PACKAGES/FUNCTIONAL PACKAGES • MANAGER SELF-SERVICE (MYSAP ERP) • OBJECT AND DATA PROVIDER • DATA PROVIDER • DEFINE COLUMNS or via Transaction SM30 in table view V_TWPC_COL_ERP. (Please note that this table view has replaced the old column table view V_TWPC_COL, although the underlying table is the same). See Figure 8.20 for a view of the table.

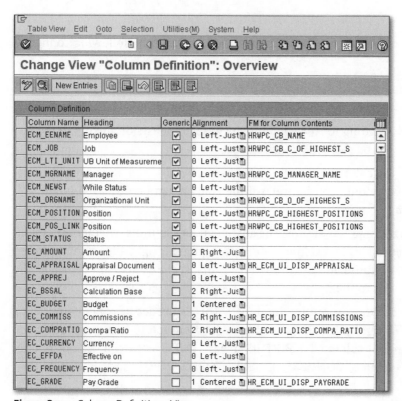

Figure 8.20 Column Definitions View

Double-clicking into one of these columns provides you with the details behind each column. Figure 8.21 shows the detail behind standard column EC_GRADE.

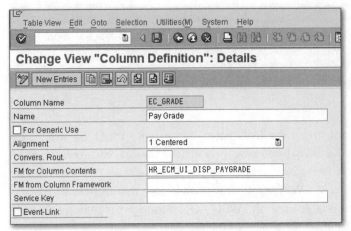

Figure 8.21 Detail of Column EC_GRADE, Including Function Component HR_ECM_UI_DISP_PAYGRADE

If you want to create a new column, you must perform the following configuration steps:

▶ Create a new entry for a custom column. The column name must start with either a Z or Y (i.e., it should be within your customer name space).

▶ Identify the heading for the column. The header appears on the top of the column. It should be clear and concise.

▶ Indicate if the column is For Generic Use (optional). This flag is for informational purposes only and indicates if the column can be displayed in any column group.

▶ Specify an alignment indicator. The alignment flag controls whether the system formats the entries in a column with left alignment, right alignment, centered alignment, or automatically. If no entry is made, the system always aligns the column entries to the right.

▶ Identify a conversion routine (optional). This is needed if contents retrieved from the backend (via ABAP) need manipulation before being output on the iView. Standard column TO_BIRTHDAY has TOBEG as its conversion routine. Function modules CONVERSION_EXIT_TOBEG_INPUT and CONVERSION_

EXIT_TOBEG_OUTPUT are used as the mechanism to perform this conversion before and after the field is rendered on the iView.

▶ Specify a Function Module for Column Content. Most custom columns will need a custom function module. This function module is required to retrieve data from the SAP backend.

▶ Specify a Function Module for Content from Column Framework. If you want to reuse a function module that you have previously created for the Column Framework of the Personnel Management component, enter the function module in this field. This is the column configuration used within the manager's desktop functionality as well as several Organizational Management (OM) views. You can find the relevant function modules in the configuration under the IMG path: GLOBAL SETTINGS IN PERSONNEL MANAGEMENT • COLUMN FRAMEWORK • DEFINE YOUR OWN COLUMNS/CHANGE COLUMN GROUP TEXT • DEFINE YOUR OWN COLUMN • COLUMN GROUP DEFINITION or via Transaction SM30 in table view V_TWPC_COL_ERP (view T77COL).

▶ Identify a Service link (optional). You can hyperlink to a different iView or page containing additional information relevant to the content within that column. For example, standard column ECM_EENAME points to standard service key MSS_ECM_TRGT_COMPENSATION_PROFILES. This service points to a standard resource MSS_HCM_SERV_COMPENSATION_PROFILES, which launches the Employee Profile Compensation page found in the portal under *portal_content/com.sap.pct/line_manager/com.sap.pct.erp.mss.bp_folder/com.sap.pct.erp.mss.pages/com.sap.pct.erp.mss.hcm/com.sap.pct.erp.mss.compensation_profile*.

You specify a unique column header depending on the context or on the object being displayed in the column. If you want to define a header depending on the context or displayed object, you must first define a header type for the column header. You can define a new column header type in the IMG under the path: INTEGRATION WITH OTHER MYSAP.COM COMPONENTS • BUSINESS PACKAGES/FUNCTIONAL PACKAGES • MANAGER SELF-SERVICE (MYSAP ERP) • OBJECT AND DATA PROVIDER • DATA PROVIDER • REDEFINE COLUMN HEADERS • CREATE CUSTOMER-SPECIFIC HEADER TYPES.

Once you have created a new column header type, you can then assign a context-dependent header to the header type. You can view the standard entries for the column headers for standard header types (provided by the software) under the IMG path: INTEGRATION WITH OTHER MYSAP.COM COMPONENTS • BUSINESS PACKAGES/FUNCTIONAL PACKAGES • MANAGER SELF-SERVICE (MYSAP ERP) • OBJECT AND DATA PROVIDER • DATA

Provider • Redefine Column Headers • Check Column Headers for Standard Header Types or via Transaction SM30 in table view V_TWPC_COLHEAD. Although entries in this table are editable, we recommend that you do not change anything in this table.

Any new entries (for your column header type) or any entries that you wish to override from the SAP system (if you are going to use one the standard header types with any existing or new columns) can be configured under the IMG path: Integration with Other mySAP.com Components • Business Packages/Functional Packages • Manager Self-Service (mySAP ERP) • Object and Data Provider • Data Provider • Redefine Column Headers • Create or Change Column Headers or via Transaction SM30 in table view V_TWPC_COLHEAD_C.

A good example of the use of a column header type is MSS_TMV_EE for standard column ORG_OBJID_2 (See Figure 8.22). In this example, the column header text is Personnel Number and not ID, which is the name of the column defined in the column definition table. This way, the same column can be used many times and simply retitled so as to maximize its reusability.

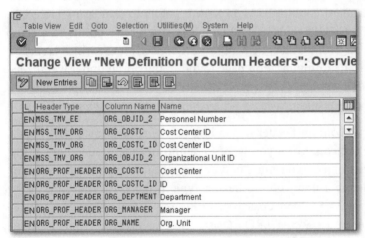

L.	Header Type	Column Name	Name
EN	MSS_TMV_EE	ORG_OBJID_2	Personnel Number
EN	MSS_TMV_ORG	ORG_COSTC	Cost Center ID
EN	MSS_TMV_ORG	ORG_COSTC_ID	Cost Center ID
EN	MSS_TMV_ORG	ORG_OBJID_2	Organizational Unit ID
EN	ORG_PROF_HEADER	ORG_COSTC	Cost Center
EN	ORG_PROF_HEADER	ORG_COSTC_ID	ID
EN	ORG_PROF_HEADER	ORG_DEPTMENT	Department
EN	ORG_PROF_HEADER	ORG_MANAGER	Manager
EN	ORG_PROF_HEADER	ORG_NAME	Org. Unit

Figure 8.22 Header Type MSS_TMV_EE for Column ORG_OBJID_2

This concludes our detailed review of the OADP framework. Let's take a step back and review some of the core concepts within the functionality.

8.1.10   OADP Overview

The OADP framework is complex. With terminology like organizational views, organizational view groups, data views, and data view groups, you are bound to get a bit confused at first. However, with practice, you will soon see how all of the pieces fit together. It is important to understand the dependencies and linkages between the table views. Order of configuration is important, so be sure to understand which configuration elements need to be done before others. You will soon get the hang of it and become comfortable with the functionality.

Figure 8.23 shows an overview of the OADP constructs, accompanied by the technical name of the table view or table view cluster. Here you can see how the organizational view is comprised of an object selection and a data view group. The object selection tells us what root, navigation, and target objects should be displayed on the iView based on the configuration or development identified in the object selection rules. The data view group contains one or more data views. These data views provide additional information on the objects returned from the object selection in the form of columns, organized by column groups.

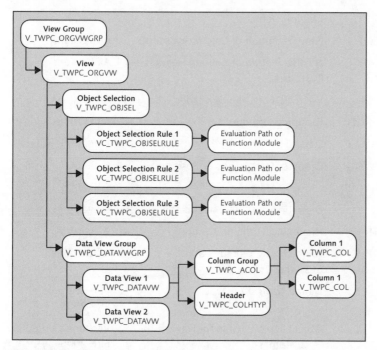

Figure 8.23   OADP Hierarchy with Dependencies, Including Table Views and Table View Clusters

Let's review the inventory of table views and table view clusters available within the OADP framework.

8.1.11 OADP Table View and Table View Cluster Inventory

Table 8.2 lists all of the table views available in the OADP framework (new and old). Each table view is accompanied by its name and its release applicability. Remember that all OADP table views begin with the prefix V_TWPC_*.

Table View	Table View Name	Release Applicability
V_TWPC_ACOL	Put Columns Together in a Column Group	All versions
V_TWPC_ACOL_C	Put Columns Together in a Column Group — Customer	All versions
V_TWPC_ARRAYTP	Definition of Column Groups	All versions
V_TWPC_COL	Column Definition	Versions before ERP 2005
V_TWPC_COL_ERP	Column Definition	ERP 2005
V_TWPC_COLHEAD	New Definition of Column Headers	All versions
V_TWPC_COLHEAD_C	New Definition of Column Headers — Customer	All versions
V_TWPC_COLHTYP	Definition of Column Header Types	All versions
V_TWPC_COLMERGE	Grouping Columns	All versions
V_TWPC_DATAVW	Data View	ERP 2005
V_TWPC_DATAVWG_P	Group of Data Views — Position	ERP 2005
V_TWPC_DATAVWGRP	Group of Data Views	ERP 2005
V_TWPC_FRIEND	Definition of Coherence Relationships	All versions
V_TWPC_HIERATP	Hierarchical Column Groups	All versions
V_TWPC_HIERATP_C	Hierarchical Column Groups — Customer	All versions
V_TWPC_NAV	Define Navigation Types	Versions before ERP 2005
V_TWPC_NAVOTP_C	Object Types Eligible for Navigation — Customer	Versions before ERP 2005

Table 8.2 Inventory of Table Views for OADP

Table View	Table View Name	Release Applicability
V_TWPC_NAVOTYPE	Object Types Eligible for Navigation	Versions before ERP 2005
V_TWPC_OBJSEL	Object Selection	ERP 2005
V_TWPC_OBJSELRUL	Rule for Object Selection	ERP 2005
V_TWPC_OBJTYPERS	Restriction of Permitted Object Types for Object Selection	ERP 2005
V_TWPC_ORGVW	Organizational View	ERP 2005
V_TWPC_ORGVWG_P	Group of Organizational Views — Position	ERP 2005
V_TWPC_ORGVWGRP	Group of Organizational Views	ERP 2005
V_TWPC_OTYPES	Object Types to be Displayed in the List	Versions before ERP2005
V_TWPC_OTYPES_C	Object Types to be Displayed in the List — Customer	Versions before ERP2005
V_TWPC_PARAMG_P	Parameter Group — Position	ERP 2005
V_TWPC_PARAMGRP	Parameter Group	ERP 2005
V_TWPC_V	View Definition	Versions before ERP2005
V_TWPC_V_C	View Definition — Customer	Versions before ERP2005
V_TWPC_VG	Grouping the Views	Versions before ERP2005
V_TWPC_VG_C	Grouping the Views — Customer	Versions before ERP2005

Table 8.2 Inventory of Table Views for OADP (Cont.)

In Table 8.3 are four table view clusters (new as of ERP 2005). Each table view cluster is accompanied by its name and its release applicability. All OADP view clusters begin with the prefix VC_TWPC*. These views can be maintained through configuration or via Transaction SM34 "View Cluster Maintenance."

Table View Cluster	Table View Cluster Name	Release Applicability
VC_TWPC_DATAVWGRP	Group of Data Views	ERP 2005
VC_TWPC_OBJSELRULE	Rule for Object Selection	ERP 2005
VC_TWPC_ORGVWGRP	Group of Organizational Views	ERP 2005
VC_TWPC_PARAMGRP	Parameter Group	ERP 2005

Table 8.3 Inventory of Table View Clusters for OADP

In our experience, it is often easier to work directly in these tables rather than via the IMG. If you work often enough in these tables, you will see that you will start to memorize their names and it usually becomes easier to access these views directly via Transactions SM30 and SM34.

Now's let's discuss how OADP configuration is set within the portal iViews properties. We have talked a lot about the backend configuration, but the portal iViews also need reference to the underlying configuration.

8.1.12 OADP within Portal Configuration

Now that we have performed the configuration on the backend, it is likely that frontend updates are needed as well. For example, if you have created a new organizational view group or data view group, the portal iView will need to know to look at your customizations and not the standard. To do this, you must work with your portal resources to configure the properties of the iViews that you will use in your implementation. Your portal content administrator has access to the Portal Content Directory (PCD), which contains all of the parameters that are used by the iView. Within the iView, these parameters influence its behavior, including where to source the data from in the SAP system. For example, if you wanted to add another organizational view to the Compensation Planning iView, a new organizational view group would need to be created and assigned to the iView via its iView properties. Figure 8.24 shows an example of organizational view group MSS_ECM_SEL defined as a portal parameter labeled "OADP Organizational View Group for Object Selection." If a custom organizational view group were created, you would need to enter your own custom entry in this field in order for the iView to realize its implementation.

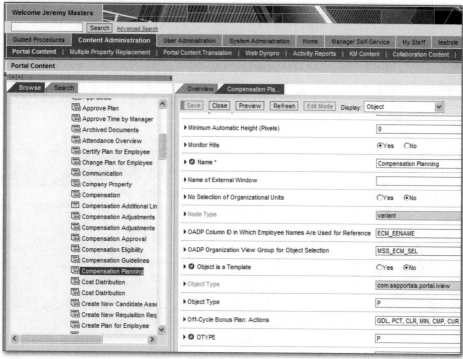

Figure 8.24 Configuration of Properties within Compensation Planning iView

Because the OADP is not new functionality, some customers who implemented a previous version will need to configure new tables with the framework. To do this, SAP has provided some migration steps. Let's discuss those now.

8.1.13 Migration from Old OADP Tables in Previous SAP Versions

For those of you currently using OADP and upgrading to ERP 2005, some migration steps need to be performed so that you can use the new functionality. The software includes a standard program RP_OADP_MIGRATE_CUSTOMIZING to migrate the customizing performed in older tables to the newer ones. This standard program allows you to leverage the OADP work done from previous implementations.

The report (pictured in Figure 8.25) can be accessed directly from Transaction SE38 or SA38 or via the IMG under the path: INTEGRATION WITH OTHER MYSAP.COM COMPONENTS • BUSINESS PACKAGES / FUNCTIONAL PACKAGES • MANAGER SELF-SERVICE (MYSAP ERP) • OBJECT AND DATA PROVIDER • TRANSFER EXISTING CUSTOMIZING SETTINGS. This procedure should be performed in your development system first, assigned to a transport, and moved up your landscape based on your company's established transport procedures. Although a standard SAP utility, proper testing should be conducted to ensure all organizational views and organizational view groups are working per business requirements. You will also need to work with your portal resources to ensure that any new iViews you are implementing are pointing to the right back-end views, as many of the newer Web Dynpro iViews require the newer OADP configuration.

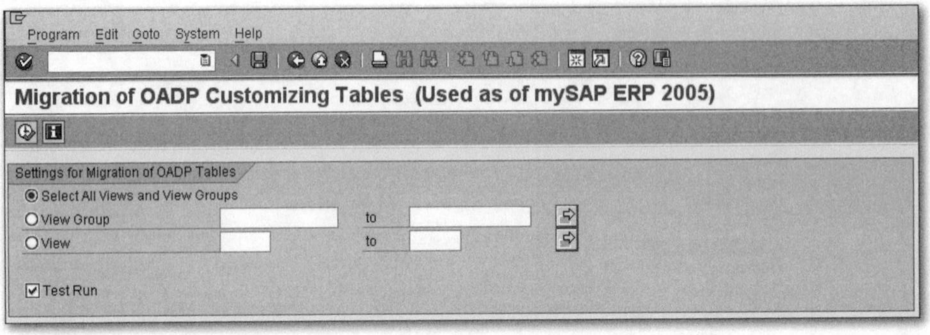

Figure 8.25 Selection Screen for Program RP_OADP_MIGRATE_CUSTOMIZING

The report migrates view groups (in table view V_TWPC_VG) and views (in table view V_TWPC_V) that lie in your customer name space to the new OADP table views. For view groups and views delivered by the SAP system, a dialog box is displayed in which you can transfer the view group/view to the customer name space (by default, a Z is added in front of the view/view group but can be changed based on your naming convention). If the name you enter in this dialog box already exists in the new tables, the system informs you that you must enter a different name. If you terminate this operation, the view group/view is not migrated to the new tables.

You can also choose to only migrate select views or view groups. To do this, simply identify only those specific tables in the selection screen of the program. Before you can migrate view groups, you must remember to first migrate all of the views that belong to that particular view group. Like any other report, we advise that you first run the report in test mode.

Figure 8.26 shows the output of the report RP_OADP_MIGRATE_CUSTOMIZING showing views and view groups being migrated and those that will not. As with many report logs, the program associates red balls with those views or view groups that have not been transferred, yellow triangles with those views or view groups that have been transferred successfully but with warnings, and green squares for those views or view groups that have been transferred successfully.

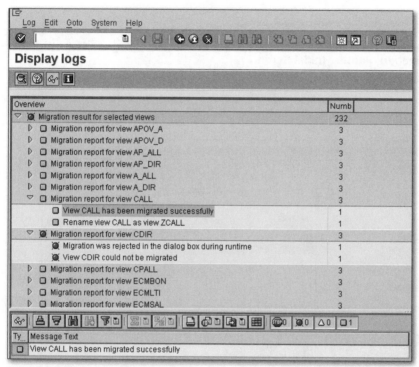

Figure 8.26 Migration Log for Report RP_OADP_MIGRATE_CUSTOMIZING Identifying Views and View Groups Being Migrated

Let's now discuss how to test OADP configuration from the SAP backend.

8.1.14 Testing OADP Configuration

OADP configuration can be tested via standard function module HRWPC_OADP_TEST. To test your OADP configuration, execute Transaction SE37 (Function Builder). Input HRWPC_OADP_TEST as the Function Module and click the Test/ Execute button on the application toolbar (it is an icon that looks like a wrench). The Test Function Module:Initial Screen appears (see Figure 8.27) where you can input various parameters such as the organizational view in parameter ORGVIEW, the object selection in parameter OBJSEL, the data view in parameter DATAVIEW, the begin date in parameter BEGDA, the end date in parameter ENDDA, and the user in parameter USER. Other import parameters including search settings are available as well for input.

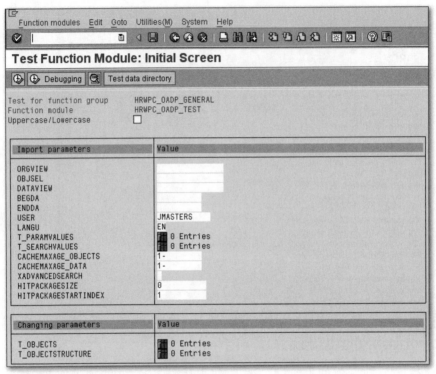

Figure 8.27 Function Module HRWPC_OADP_TEST

You may need to test this function module, for example, if you are experiencing errors on the portal. Oftentimes, changes to OADP views and columns can cause a portal Java runtime error if the configuration is wrong or if an underlying development object (e.g., a custom function module for a custom column on a data view) is throwing an error. In some cases, the error is not informative or even misleading. To debug the issue, either an external breakpoint or a session breakpoint can be set within the source code. You will need to work with an ABAP-skilled resource in either case so that they can go through the code to diagnose the issue.

This concludes the OADP portion of the chapter. Let's now discuss another advanced topic within MSS — workflow.

8.2   Advanced Workflow Topics

SAP Workflow has been around for a long time with much storied success. The workflow engine has consistently received high marks from industry experts who contend SAP Workflow is one of the best — if not the best — workflow tools that exist today in the marketplace. Workflow is one of the most powerful mechanisms to drive processes and their timely completion. It has become even more powerful as work items can now be exposed on the SAP Portal via the Universal Worklist (UWL) (think of it as the online workflow inbox). Now, all employees within the enterprise can participate in workflow-enabled processes regardless of their role within the organization. Online workflow functionality has allowed approval-based processes, such as transfer/promotion requests and leave and travel requests, to be exposed on the portal. Results have been dramatic, as many customers are finding tremendous value in driving these types of processes to the lowest "tier" of service delivery — self-service. Holding employees and managers accountable for their own data and tasks has begun to reduce HR's administrative role and positioned them more as business partners within the organization.

Although more and more companies are workflow-enabling their processes on the portal, implementing such processes has proven harder than conceptualizing them. Processes involving workflow are challenging to implement partially because of the skill set involved in deploying and supporting them. Functional resources are needed to understand the process flow and functional requirements, while technical resources, are needed to build the workflow and write the underlying ABAP functions. Portal specialists are needed for knowledge of the UWL, which is key to web-enabling workflow online.

Let's now cover some of the core workflow principles within self-service. We will highlight what we believe to be are the key challenges with delivering workflow on the portal.

8.2.1   Core Workflow Principles for Self-Service

We have established what we consider to be good operating principles when implementing workflow-enabled processes in a self-service environment. The principles that follow are recommendations to work from. Our experience throughout the years on workflow-enabling processes online — coupled with recent enhancements to SAP's Portal and UWL functionality — has helped us establish these important themes. The following six principles are meant to aid you in your implementation. You will need to take the information here and apply it to your unique situation.

► Keep your organizational structure up to date. As discussed in Chapter 4, the organizational structure forms the "backbone" of MSS and workflow routing rules. It is essential that the OM procedures (e.g., organizational restructuring due to reductions in force, position management procedures such as vacancies) are adhered to. If not already established, formal standard operating procedures, business process procedures, and desktop procedures should be drafted, agreed upon, and finalized for all OM processes.

► Ensure the "chief" relationship is implemented and kept current. Without the identification of chiefs within the enterprise, workflow routing becomes difficult — if not impossible — to achieve. Also, as discussed in detail in Chapter 4, be consistent with your definition of chief.

► Update authorizations and security profiles as needed. Adding additional online workflow responsibilities will inevitably affect the authorizations needed for your managers (and possibly) for your employees. Be sure to consider both front-end (SAP Portal) and backend (SAP ECC) authorizations and roles. The next chapter, Chapter 9, discusses authorizations in detail.

► Consider substitution as a viable means to complete a process. Some processes will work best when there is an opportunity for the manager to delegate some or all of his responsibility (e.g., a manager delegates the ability to approve leave requests to an administrative assistant). Delegation is covered in detail later in this chapter.

► Take a firm stance on work item notifications versus email notifications. When are managers alerted and how are they alerted during the process? Which managers should be notified during approvals and which should be notified during rejections? Should email notifications be sent to the company's corporate email (e.g., Outlook, Lotus Notes) or should alerts be driven to the UWL on the Portal? There is no right answer for this, as every company's culture is different. Stay consistent with your messaging and your employees and managers will be more receptive to the decision.

► Invest time in understanding all of what the UWL has to offer. SAP has made some major improvements over the years on its portal workflow inbox. SAP Note 676253 (EP 6.0: Central Note for Universal Worklist (UWL)) contains a running list of improvements, bug fixes, and general updates on the functionality. Very detailed documentation on the UWL can be found by going to *http://service.sap.com/netweaver* and navigating the path: MEDIA LIBRARY HOW-TO GUIDES • PORTAL, KM AND COLLABORATION • ALL • CONFIGURING THE UNIVERSAL WORKLIST. If you experience problems with the configuration of the UWL, support component EP-BC-UWL is available. Also, visit the SAP Developer Network (SDN) website at *https://www.sdn.sap.com/irj/sdn/wiki?path=/x/ehU* to view the latest FAQs for the UWL. You will need to partner with a portal-knowledgeable resource during its setup and when updates are needed.

> **Note**
>
> Detailed information on the UWL can be found in Darren Hague's ESSENTIALS Book, *Universal Worklist with SAP NetWeaver Portal* (SAP PRESS; 2008).

Now that we have covered some core principles of online workflow, let's take a closer look at how to approach approvals within your web-enabled processes.

8.2.2 Approval Levels

Many portal-enabled processes involve either a one-step or multistep approval. In a one-step approval, a manager-initiated transaction is typically routed to that manager's manager. The process flow may go something like this: A manager initiates an off-cycle pay increase via a personnel change request for one of his direct reports. The manager's manager (i.e., the chief of the initiating chief) receives a work item in his UWL in the SAP Portal (and perhaps a notification email to their corporate inbox as well). This work item is reviewed by the approving manager. If the approving manager approves the request, the work item is sent to HR for processing or for direct update into the system (this depends on the business requirements and your technology choice). Both managers would be notified on successful processing of the action. If the request were to be rejected by the approving manager, the work item would be passed back down to the initiating manager for resubmission. An email notification to the corporate email inboxes of both parties would also be sent.

Multistep approvals would involve multiple approvals and may even involve special approvals from an HR Generalist, a Division Vice President (VP), a Cost Center Manager, or a Compensation Professional. In a multistep approval scenario, a manager-initiated transaction would typically route first to that manager's manager (let's say, in this case, the personnel change request includes an increase for a Division VP proposed to make $265,000). The manager's manager (i.e., the chief of the initiating chief) receives that work item in his UWL in the SAP Portal (and perhaps a notification email to his corporate inbox as well). This work item is reviewed by this first approving manager. If the manager approves, the work item is then sent to the approver's own chief manager (who will then need to conduct the same review of the request). After approval from this manager, the work item is routed to the Compensation Professional who manages the affected employee's functional area. This additional layer of approval is needed due to a "special rule," stating that any pay change involving base salary over $250,000 needs review from the Compensation Department. After Compensation approval, the work item routes to HR for processing or for direct update into the system. All managers involved in the decision would be notified on successful processing of the action. At any time during the routing process, if the request were to be rejected, the work item would be passed back down to the initiating manager for resubmission. An email notification to the corporate email inboxes of all parties would also be sent.

As you can see, a multilevel approval can be challenging to implement efficiently. Oftentimes, highly complex approvals become a burden to managers and HR Professionals because approvals "get stuck" within the approval chain. Simplifying the approvals needed for manager-initiated transactions will streamline online transaction processing and enhance the overall experience for the manager, executive management, and HR. Although we do understand that certain rules are non-negotiable (e.g., the handling of pay for bargaining unit or union employees), other rules should be looked at critically. In the U.S., for example, are different/additional approvals necessary for your exempt versus nonexempt employee population?

Some additional complexities within approvals can be specific to a process. For example, within the transfer process, the approvals may be different depending on whether you subscribed to a "push" vs. "pull" philosophy for out-of-span transfers. Does the sending manager initiate the process by "releasing" the employee to the receiving manager (i.e., "push"), or does the receiving manager initiate the process by requesting the release of the employee from the sending manager (i.e., "pull")? Answers to this question will impact the effectiveness of your online process.

An additional example of a process-specific complexity concerns the processing of a request for off-cycle promotions, pay increases, and special payments (e.g., spot awards). If the increases within these processes are tied to a budget, how and where does this information get tracked? Assuming you have decided that a personnel change request (or an HCM form) is to be used for the processing, what (if any) information gets updated on the Enterprise Compensation Management (ECM) side? Approvals may be based on available budgets funds but if no tracking is done, how will the workflow know how to process the approval routing if certain business rules apply? This example illustrates some of the challenges when dealing with complex processes that are highly integrated within HCM.

There is no silver bullet to any of these situations. The answer varies from company to company, based on business decisions and Information Technology's (IT) appetite for customizations. One of the core questions during all system implementations is: Is this process step or requirement business critical or is there opportunity for change or a manual workaround? Regardless of the technology decision or business process implemented, our recommendation would be to streamline and simplify workflow processes by reducing the amount of approvals needed wherever possible.

8.2.3　Escalation Procedures

One important topic to mention is that of deadline monitoring — SAP's answer to workflow escalation. Work item escalation is essential to any workflow — especially if the process contains multistep approvals. With deadline-monitoring functionality activated, the SAP workflow system "watches" the process against predefined, time-sensitive business rules that are built into the workflow template. For example, you might build an escalation rule that states that if any work item is left dormant in the approver's portal inbox for more than three business days, the workflow should move the work item to the approver's manager. This way, the work item is escalated to a higher authority who can transact and move the process along.

Another example of a deadline monitoring rule could state that, if after seven business days a work item is not actioned on within the approver's portal inbox, the work item terminates and the requester is notified. Figure 8.28 shows an example snippet from a workflow diagram showing how a missed deadline would result in the termination of the work item.

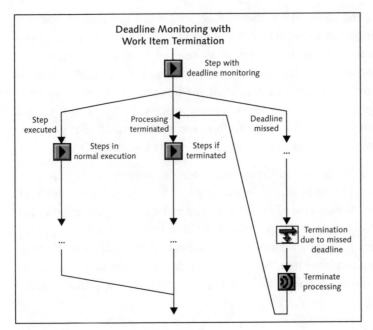

Figure 8.28 Example of Deadline Monitoring

Some escalation scenarios can be curbed if delegation is implemented. By doing so, additional opportunity is afforded to the process as more than one user can action on the request. Using delegation in this way is also consistent with the service delivery model by not giving higher level management additional responsibilities. Escalation to higher level managers needs to be considered carefully because these managers are usually busier than the manager for whom the request came to.

Now that we have an understanding of workflow and its escalation capabilities, let's review what workflows are delivered as standard.

8.2.4 Standard Self-Service Workflows Available

SAP delivers many standard workflow templates related to self-service processes. Most workflows are triggered by manager-initiated process but some (such as leave and travel requests) are employee-initiated. Most of these standard workflows scenarios offer a baseline template. You will need to understand the details of the delivered scenario and adapt it to your own business rules. It is more common than not to adjust a delivered workflow, as each company is bound to have different business rules for approval routing, escalation, and backend updates. As is typical with all workflow implementations, you will want to copy the standard workflow template into your own template within your customer name space.

In the section that follows, all available workflows for ESS and MSS are listed. All workflows are organized by functional area.

Performance Management

Performance Management workflows are more notification-based than approval-based workflows. They are triggered within the appraisal when the user selects a push button. The following 15 workflows are available within Performance Management: 12300109 (Info to Appraiser–Display), 12300110 (Info to Appraiser–Change), 12300113 (Info to Appraisee–Display), 12300114 (Info to Appraisee–Change), 12300115 (Info to Appraiser–Approve), 12300116 (Info to Appraisee–Approve), 12300117 (Info to Appraiser–Approved), 12300119 (Info to Appraiser–Rejected), 12300120 (Info to Appraisee–Approved), 12300121 (Info to Appraisee–Rejected), 12300122 (Info to Higher Level Manager–Approve), 12300124 (Info to Next Part Appraiser–Change), 12300125 (Info to Appraiser–Review), 12300126 (Info to Appraisee–Review), and 12300127 (Info to Appraiser–Change in Period).

Enterprise Compensation Management

At the time of this book's publishing, there are no standard workflows available within the ECM component. However, there is talk of a standard workflow coming in a future Enhancement Package.

For information on implementing your own workflow, reference SAP Note 802992 (Standard workflow not available for ECM).

Working Time

For the approval of leave requests, workflow template WS12300111 (General Workflow for Documents) is used. Enhancements can be implemented based on your customer-specific requirements within Enhancement Spot PT_ABS_REQ (Method GET_WORKFLOW_ATTRIBS) to control the processing of leave requests. An Enhancement Spot is the "next generation" BAdI. Documentation on Enhancement Spots can be found on the SAP Help site or on SDN. Enhancement Spots can be viewed via Transaction SE18. You will need to work with an ABAP programmer to implement any logic.

Cross-Application Timesheet (CATS) approval is managed via standard task TS31000007 (there is no associated workflow). Manipulation of the CATS approvals can be achieved via Enhancement Spot APPR_CUST.

Both workflows are employee-initiated and are tightly coupled with their respective ESS transaction (Leave Request and CATS Approval iViews, respectively).

Travel Management

Approval of travel requests is handled in standard workflow template WS20000050 (Approve Travel Request). Workflow template WS01000087 (Approve Travel Plan) allows the manager to approve travel plans. Travel expense approval is managed via workflow template WS20000040 (Approve Trip).

Additional information on these workflows can be found in the Finance (FI) component. The support application component for travel management is FI-TV.

Personnel Change Requests

There are three workflows available for PCRs based on the number of approvals needed. Workflow template WS50000042 (Process Change Request (0)) does not include an approval step. It is linked to the following scenarios out-of-the box: Change Employee Group/Subgroup, Change Personnel Area/Subarea, and Change Working Time. Workflow template WS50000041 (Process Change Request (1)) includes a one-up approval step. It is linked to the following scenarios out-of-the box: Request Special Payment, Change Position, Change Position (Enhanced), Request Promotion, Request Separation, and Request Separation (Enhanced). Workflow template WS50000031 (Process Change Request (2)) includes an approval with two steps. It is linked to the following scenarios out-of-the box: Request for Transfer and Request for Transfer (Enhanced).

Ensure that you do the proper customizing for the tasks for these workflows. Task customizing can be performed in IMG under the path: INTEGRATION WITH OTHER mySAP.COM COMPONENTS • BUSINESS PACKAGES/FUNCTIONAL PACKAGES • MANAGER SELF-SERVICE (mySAP ERP) • PERSONNEL CHANGE REQUESTS • SET UP WORKFLOWS FOR PERSONNEL CHANGE REQUESTS.

Two BAdIs (BAdI HRWPC_PCR_APPR_FORM and HRWPC_PCR_APPR_NEXT) within the personnel change requests functionality allow you to control the workflow rule resolution for the receiving manager and one-up manager, respectively. Logic can be implemented within the workflow to manipulate the "actors" of the workflow based on any unique requirements for how the workflow should route.

Workflows available within HCM Processes and Forms are outside the scope of this book.

Recruitment Requisition Requests

Within the E-Recruiting functionality, a few templates are available to allow the manager to create a requisition. Workflow template WS12200021 (E-Recruiting (1)) initiates a requisition with one approval step. It is linked to the following scenario out-of-the box: Simple Requisition Request. Workflow template WS12200022 (E-Recruiting (2)) initiates a requisition with two approval steps. It is linked to the following scenario out-of-the box: Extended Requisition Request.

As with the PCRs, there are two BAdIs (BAdI HRWPC_RQ_APPR_FORM and HRWPC_RQ_APPR_NEXT) within the recruitment area that allow you to control the workflow rule resolution for the receiving manager and one-up manager, respectively. Logic can be implemented within the workflow to manipulate the "actors" of the workflow based on any unique recruitment requirements for how the workflow should route.

We have now covered workflow as it pertains to self-service. Let's now discuss one of the most interesting topics being addressed in the marketplace — the delegation of managerial duties.

8.3   Delegation

Delegation within a self-service context is one of the hottest topics in HR service delivery today. This is because a formal process for the delegation of managerial duties is needed in many organizations today. The practice of managers sharing their user name and password with their administrative assistants is being highly scrutinized by IT Security and Compliance teams. It is thought that, besides the legal implications of an unauthorized employee transaction, this practice is an expensive problem for many companies because the transaction is sometimes done in error or needs re-processing due to missing or incorrect data. In an attempt to stop these bad habits in the workplace, many organizations are looking for ways to formally delegate manager's tasks to a selected, "authorized" employee. This proxy would then be formally responsible for any work item that he approved or any transaction that he initiated.

There are several scenarios where delegation is needed within line management. Delegation could be needed for a short-term scenario in the case where a manager goes on vacation or on a short leave of absence and needs some coverage. Delegation could also be needed for a more long-term scenario. For example, a manager may need ongoing assistance from an administrator or peer due to his heavy day-to-day workload. It may make better business sense to permit a manager's administrative staff to take on some of these activities.

How you address each of these scenarios will depend on your company's policies for delegation management. In more specific terms, not all companies will permit their entire employee population base to be suitable for delegation (take a company with a large union population, for example). Depending on the organization and the policies established there, those employees suitable for delegation could be "chief" managers only, all employees (managers and non-managers), or perhaps certain employees based on specific criteria (e.g., salary grade 16 and above only).

> **Note**
>
> Another important concept within delegation concerns the "life span" of the proxy. Most companies do not leave delegation privileges without an end date. Typically, after a set interval (e.g., six months), a delegation would end and become obsolete — until requested again by the manager. Although this does increase work for managers on a periodic basis, providing a maximum end date to delegation privileges and requiring the manager to request the delegation again does provide added safeguards to a process badly needing extra controls.

Once elected, the delegate should never be granted full access to the manager's functionality on the portal. Delegating does not mean you are "mimicking" or "impersonating" the manager. All processes initiated or approved by the delegate will have the delegate's name behind the transaction (with date and time stamp). This will comfort auditors who may feel uncomfortable with releasing proxy functionality to the organization. A delegate should be held accountable for his decisions and will have to justify them if questioned by HR, IT Security, Compliance, or a third party.

Defining the exact scope of delegation within your company will depend on a number of factors, including how many processes you have web-enabled and how mature your processes are. Common processes where delegation is used include PCRs, Leave Request, Travel Request, and Time and Expense Requests. Less common processes where delegation is used include Performance Management and E-Recruiting (e.g., hiring manager activities such as interviewing). There are some processes — such as Compensation Management and Succession Planning — that are rarely delegated due to the sensitive nature of the matter.

It is also important to distinguish delegation between two types of authority: transactional and approval. Some managers want the delegate to have:

▶ the ability to view employee information only;

▶ the ability to view employee information and initiate transactions but not approve workflow items;

▶ the ability to view employee information and approve workflow items but not initiate transactions; or,

▶ the ability to view employee information, initiate transactions, and approve workflow items

There are important differences between granting a delegate approval versus transactional authority. Let's first discuss approval delegation authority first.

8.3.1 Approval Authority

Approval authority permits delegates to review and action on work items that have been routed to the manager's UWL. Approval authority for delegates can be achieved via standard "substitution." There are two types of substitution within the SAP system: user-based (or "personal") substitution and position-based substitution.

With personal substitution, two SAP user IDs are directly associated in table HRUS_D2. The user name of the substitute (i.e., delegate) is assigned directly to the user name of the delegator. Figure 8.29 shows table HRUS_D2 with the delegator, the delegate, the start date, the end date, the substitution profile, and an active indicator. Personal substitution is the substitution that the SAP system uses on the UWL, as part of its standard functionality. In this example, user JMASTERS has delegates with user names AMEYER, GHANSON, and ZNILSON.

Each relationship can also hold a substitute profile. This substitute profile enables you to delegate certain workflow tasks but not others. For example, you could delegate leave and travel approval requests but restrict the proxy from approving requests for promotion and change in pay PCRs. This way, certain approvals can be filtered out for a delegate based on the assigned substitute profile.

New substitution profiles can be customized under the following IMG path: SAP NETWEAVER • APPLICATION SERVER • BUSINESS MANAGEMENT • SAP BUSINESS WORKFLOW • BASIC SETTINGS • SUBSTITUTE PROFILE • DEFINE SUBSTITUTE PROFILE.

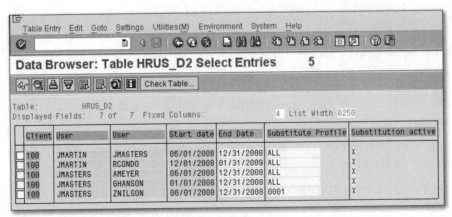

Figure 8.29 Table HRUS_D2 for Personal Substitutions

Position-based substitution is also available and is based on standard organizational management relationship A/B 210 "Substitutes with profile." With position-based substitution, a relationship is established between the position (S) and the employee (P) objects. Figure 8.30 shows position Senior VP, Human Resources substituting (i.e., delegating) approvals to employee Greg Hanson. When Greg Hanson logs into his UWL, he should be able to access the work items in the inbox of this VP.

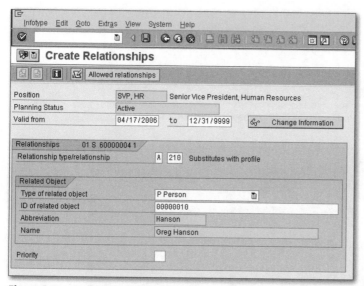

Figure 8.30 Position-based Substitution via OM Relationship A/B 210

Help

Substitutions maintained at the position level can reduce maintenance. However, you should research position-based substitution on SAP help to understand its implications for the processing of work items. The differences between the two are outside the scope of this book.

As with personal substitution, you can specify a substitute profile within position-based substitution. Figure 8.31 shows substitute profile ALL associated with the position-based substitution relationship. An active flag is also available to turn the substitution functionality off and on.

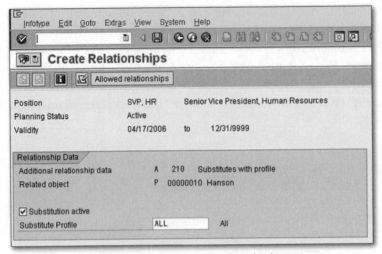

Figure 8.31 Substitute Profile within Position-based Substitution

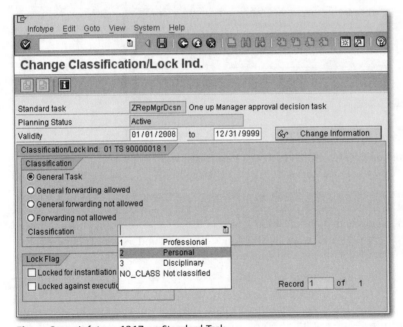

Figure 8.32 Infotype 1217 on Standard Task

Each task within a workflow can specify a classification. Infotype 1217 (Classification/Lock Indicator) is created within the Workflow Builder or via Transaction PP01. Figure 8.32 shows options for classification (1-Professional, 2-Personal, 3-Disciplinary, and NO_CLASS-Not Classified) within the dropdown of the task. Task classifications are configured in the IMG under the path: SAP NETWEAVER • APPLICATION SERVER • BUSINESS MANAGEMENT • SAP BUSINESS WORKFLOW • BASIC SETTINGS • MAINTAIN TASK CLASSES.

Work items are filtered in the UWL for the delegate depending on whether the task classification is associated to the substitute profile assigned to the substitution of the delegate. Each substitute profile is mapped to a classification under the IMG path: SAP NETWEAVER • APPLICATION SERVER • BUSINESS MANAGEMENT • SAP BUSINESS WORKFLOW • BASIC SETTINGS • SUBSTITUTE PROFILE • ASSIGN SUBSTITUTE PROFILE.

Once an approval delegate is established in the system, the delegate's UWL will appear different. Above the configured tabs, a selection "Work on:" with several radio buttons will allow the substitute to review work items that are sitting in his inbox, his substitute's inbox, or in both inboxes. The dropdown box next to the label Items on Behalf Of allows the substitute to switch between the inboxes of more than one delegate (if needed). Figure 8.33 shows a user's inbox with an activated approval substitution. The logged on user is a delegate for James Martin.

The substitute can now action on any work item available in the UWL — assuming that the proper backend security is set up for him to do so. Additional security roles may need to be provisioned to the substitute depending on your authorization design. You will need to work with your security team to ensure that all appropriate authorizations are granted to the substitute so that they can do their work.

You have now seen how to set up and utilize approval delegation, sometimes called work item substitution — both personal and position based. Let's next discuss delegation from a transactional perspective.

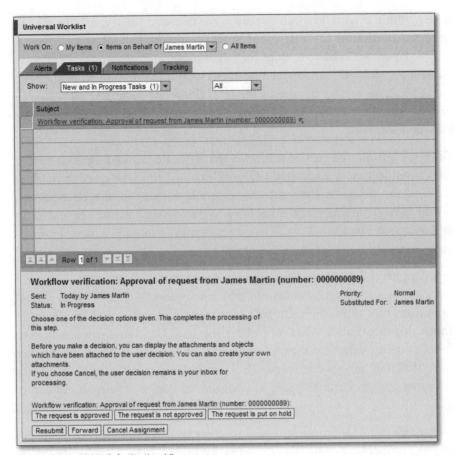

Figure 8.33 UWL Substitution View

8.3.2 Transactional Authority

Transactional authority permits delegates to view data within standard iViews and initiate processes ordinarily only performed by the manager. Although there is no standard transactional delegation available within the SAP HCM solution, the OADP framework can be enhanced to provide this functionality. In this section, we detail how to set up transactional delegation in a five-step process.

Please note that it is not easy to establish transactional access for all processes. For example, while personnel change requests and compensation management are relatively easy processes to enable transactional delegation for, performance management and CATS approval prove more challenging to implement due to the functionality available in the standard iViews. This is not to say that transactional delegation is not achievable for these processes; rather, standard iViews using the OADP framework will more easily integrate into transactional delegation scenarios.

Note

Higher level managers are typically regarded as "natural delegates." Due to their span-of-control, any manager higher in the organizational hierarchy will typically have abilities to view and transact on any lower level manager's functionality. This way, many of the standard iViews using the OADP framework provide higher level managers with "natural" proxy capability.

If you are interested in enabling transactional delegation in your self-service environment, follow these five basic steps:

Step 1: Create a custom relationship (e.g., ZDT) that will identify a delegate within your organization. Configuration for this custom relationship is performed under the IMG path: PERSONNEL MANAGEMENT • ORGANIZATIONAL MANAGEMENT • BASIC SETTINGS • DATA MODEL ENHANCEMENT • INFOTYPE MAINTENANCE PERSONNEL MANAGEMENT • ORGANIZATIONAL MANAGEMENT • BASIC SETTINGS • DATA MODEL ENHANCEMENT • RELATIONSHIP MAINTENANCE • MAINTAIN RELATIONSHIPS. Figure 8.34 shows custom relationship ZDT. Employee (P) has relationship A/ZDT Is a delegate for... (trx) to the position (S) object while the inverse relationship is identified via relationship B/ZDT Is delegated by... (trx). Once established, these custom relationships will identify the delegation agreement between the manager and his proxy.

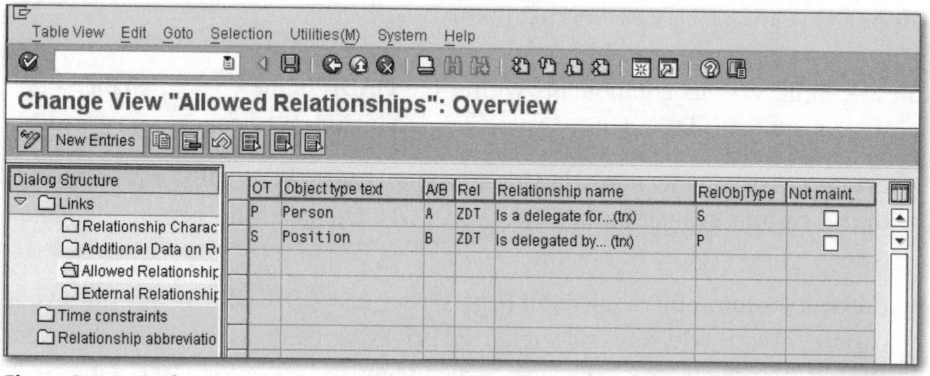

Figure 8.34 Configuration of Custom Relationship ZDT

Step 2: Create custom subtypes for the transactional delegation. You will need to configure two custom subtypes on Infotype 1001 for objects P and S. Custom subtypes (e.g., AZDT and BZDT) are configured under the IMG path: PERSONNEL MANAGEMENT • ORGANIZATIONAL MANAGEMENT • BASIC SETTINGS • DATA MODEL ENHANCEMENT • INFOTYPE MAINTENANCE PERSONNEL MANAGEMENT • ORGANIZATIONAL MANAGEMENT • BASIC SETTINGS • DATA MODEL ENHANCEMENT • INFOTYPE MAINTENANCE • MAINTAIN SUBTYPES. Be sure to specify a time constraint for each subtype as well.

Step 3: Create a custom evaluation path for the delegate. Custom evaluation paths are created in Transaction OOAW. You can base your custom evaluation path (e.g., ZDLGTRX) off the standard evaluation path, MANASS. See Figure 8.35. Integrate the new custom relationship (e.g., ZDT) created in Step 1 into the evaluation of your custom evaluation path. The user (US) or employee (P) with an A/ZDT relationship to the position (S) will provide the linkage needed between the delegate and the manager. This custom evaluation path will return all organization units for which the delegate has responsibility for.

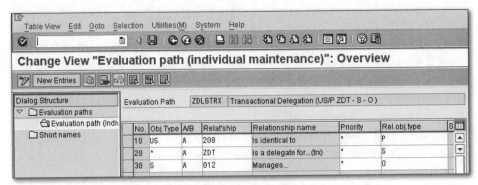

Figure 8.35 Custom Evaluation Path ZDLGTRX for Delegation

Step 4: Build various components within the OADP framework to enable a delegate to view their delegated reports. This step includes the following tasks:

▶ Create a custom objection selection rule (e.g., ZMSS_ECM_DEL) with reference to the custom evaluation path (e.g., ZDLGTRX) created in Step 3. See Figure 8.36.

▶ Create a custom object selection (e.g., ZMSS_ECM_DELG) that identifies your custom object selection rule (e.g., ZMSS_ECM_DEL) as its Rules for Root Objects. See Figure 8.37. Be sure to also identify a Rule for Target Objects in order to fill your data view.

▶ Create a custom organizational view that references the custom object selection.

▶ Create a custom organizational view group and include the custom organizational view.

You will also want to explore the use of BAdI HRWPC_EXCL_MANAGERS (discussed earlier in the chapter). Based on your business requirements, it may be necessary to exclude certain managers from the delegate's span-of-control (e.g., the manager who is delegating).

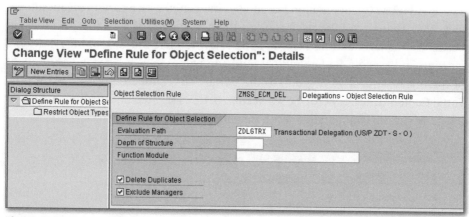

Figure 8.36 Custom Object Selection Rule with Custom Evaluation Path for Delegation

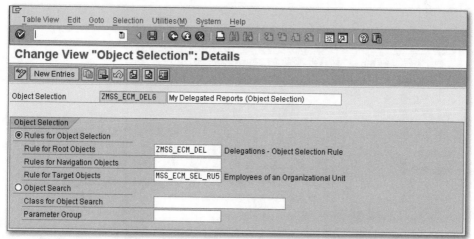

Figure 8.37 Custom Object Selection with Custom Object Selection Rule for Delegation

Step 5: Prepare your portal environment to ensure the delegate can view all appropriate portal content objects (iViews, pages and worksets). The delegate should be granted access to appropriate portal content containing their delegation tasks. If you delegate to non-managers, you will most likely need to create a new "nonmanager delegate" portal role to house the content for those employees. For managers, it is common to integrate delegation functionality into their existing MSS portal role. Where to integrate the delegation functionality into your existing self-service roles is a decision that should be made in concert with the business.

Figure 8.38 shows an example implementation of a transactional delegation whereby a standard iView (Compensation Planning) is integrated with a custom organizational view (My Delegated Reports) based on the assignment of a custom relationship between a manager and his delegate. The iView renders the custom organizational view group based on underlying backend configuration as well as the assignment of the organizational view group to the portal iView properties (made within the Portal Content Directory (PCD)). See Section 8.1.12 for more information on how to integrate custom configuration into iView properties on the portal.

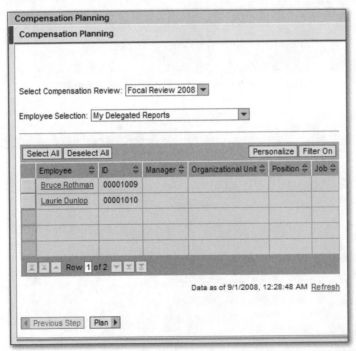

Figure 8.38 Compensation Planning with Custom View My Delegated Reports

Now that the mechanics behind the delegation are established and configured within the system, we still need to discuss how to manage these relationships. (This is true more for transactional delegations, as approval delegations are standard within the UWL.) Some companies choose to handle a manager's request for a proxy via an email to HR, through an online form, or even resorting to a paper-based process. Under these scenarios, when all approvals are cleared, HR would set up the appropriate access in the SAP backend (including creating the custom relationship and the assignment of security roles) as well as the portal front end (issuing the additional delegate portal role).

As an alternative, an online mechanism could allow managers to request a proxy by conducting a search. In the request, the manager would specify whether approval or transaction authority is required and propose a validity period for the delegation. Once submitted, a workflow would route based on specific business rules. For example, the workflow could route to the proposed delegate's inbox. Within this work item, the proposed delegate may be required to read some policies on delegation before accepting the assignment. By doing so, you have established a system control and provided the necessary training required before taking on such a responsibility.

Figure 8.39 shows Worklogix's Proxy Manager iView, which contains this online delegation request and tracking functionality. The iView is organized into three tabs. The first tab, My Delegates, tells the manager who his current approval and transactional delegates are. The I am a Delegate For tab identifies any managers for whom that manager is a delegate. The last tab, Pending Delegates, enables the manager to track the work items for those employees who are pending the manager's delegation request. This iView could exist on the home page of MSS or in an otherwise prominent place on your portal.

An iView such as this — or a manual process — to track and manage transactional (and approval) delegation is critical to the success of the project. The management of delegation should be straightforward so the manager can understand it. Without clear visibility to the managers' delegation responsibilities, confusion is bound to occur and disgruntled calls will be made to HR.

Finally, let's review some lessons learned for the implementation of delegation within self-service.

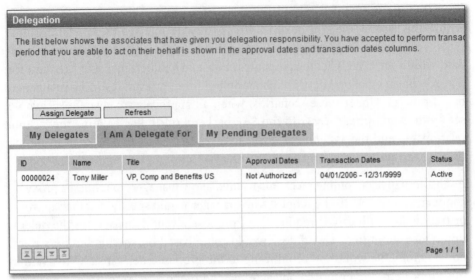

Figure 8.39 Worklogix's Proxy Manager iView for Delegation Management

8.3.3 Delegation Implementation "Gotchas"

There are few common challenges when implementing delegation within the SAP self-service platform. The following list attempts to address a few of the more important issues that you may encounter as well as recommendations to mitigate the risks associated with them.

First, ensure that the delegate cannot view or transact himself and that the delegate cannot view or transact on the manager. By using the enhanced features within the OADP functionality, unwanted "objects" (such as employees) being returned from the result set can be manipulated or removed based on logic, either through the standard configuration or through minor enhancements via function modules or BAdIs.

Second, ensure that all audit trails (including infotype and workflow logging) are activated. You will need the proper logs to reflect when a delegate initiates transactions and approves work items. This is an important factor in ensuring adherence to your auditing policies. Make your auditors happy!

Third, address data privacy and access control concerns with any international constituents. Directives from bodies such as the European Union or from local governments, for example, can influence if and how much delegation is permissible within your company. Also, understand how cultural norms within certain countries can influence how much information a delegate is permitted to view or transact upon.

Fourth, consider the additional security complexities involved if you are using (or going to use) structural authorization. Specifically, the nature of transactional delegation will have an impact on your structural profiles because it's based on OM objects and relationships.

Despite these challenges, implementing delegation functionality within your self-service environment will go a long way to enhance its overall service delivery. Let's now turn to our final topic in this chapter: employee checklists and guided procedures.

8.4 Checklists and Guided Procedures

Guided Procedures are SAP's framework for delivering personalized work and life event checklists within their self-service platform. Checklists are used to guide employees, managers, and HR Professionals through a process from the user's perspective. Instead of being presented with a disparate list of transactions that are grouped somewhat ambiguously, the user can provide intent by initiating a checklist based on a real-life event. The checklist is monitored and can be tracked until completion.

The main purpose of an online checklist is to aid the employee, manager, or HR Professional in the completion of a process — whether it be related to work, family, or a company event or process. Any process or series of tasks can be made into a checklist. Typically, however, checklists are built to assist with the completion of a common life or career event. Table 8.4 lists some examples of popular implemented checklists made available in self-service. For each checklist, a list of possible users of that checklist is listed. In many cases, a checklist may be shared between an employee, manager and HR Professional (e.g., Leave of Absence), but the tasks/activities within that checklist would differ depending on the role of the user.

Checklist	Users
Birth/Adoption of a Child	Employee, Manager, HR
Voluntary/Involuntary Separation	Employee, Manager, HR
Retirement	Employee, Manager, HR
Relocation	Employee, Manager, HR
Prehire	Employee, Manager, HR
Hire/Rehire	Employee, Manager, HR
Change in Position or Pay	Employee, Manager, HR
Moving/Change of Address	Employee
Expatriation/Inpatriation	Employee, Manager, HR
Marriage/Domestic Partner Union	Employee
Loss of Family Member	Employee, HR
Leave/Return from Leave	Employee, Manager, HR
Legal Separation/Divorce	Employee
Disability	Employee, Manager, HR
Employment Verification	Employee
Beneficiary Change	Employee
Death of Employee	Manager, HR

Table 8.4 List of Common Checklists for Employees, Managers, and HR Professionals

Checklists provide a holistic approach to HR. Events experienced by the employee and manager can have profound impacts on the employees' psyche. Providing a mechanism to capture and track progress during this important event is a powerful and concrete way of HR providing assistance to their employees.

8.4.1 Guided Procedures

Guided Procedures are part of SAP's Composite Application Framework (CAF), a framework that extends well beyond HCM checklists. Guided Procedures enable a platform on which to render and track personalized checklists. Tasks on these checklists can access multiple systems (SAP and non-SAP), multiple technologies (Web Dynpro for Java, Web Dynpro for ABAP, BSP, Adobe, etc.) and multiple services types (transactional, non-transactional, internal and external website content, etc.).

The recent move from ITS-based life and work events to Guided Procedures is part of SAP's attempt at improved usability. SAP Note 859061 addresses the transition from ITS-based life and work events framework and the new one based on Guided Procedures. The life and work event iViews discussed in Chapter 7 provide a good starting place for you to integrate into your self-service environment.

There are three main roles within the framework — runtime, design time, and administration. The runtime role is designed for so-called "process contributors." Within a self-service context, a process contributor would be an employee, manager, or HR Professional. The iViews and pages within the runtime role would be placed within a self-service role. The design time role provides functions to create actions, process templates, and interactive Adobe forms. The administration role allows for the monitoring and housekeeping activities needed by process administrators.

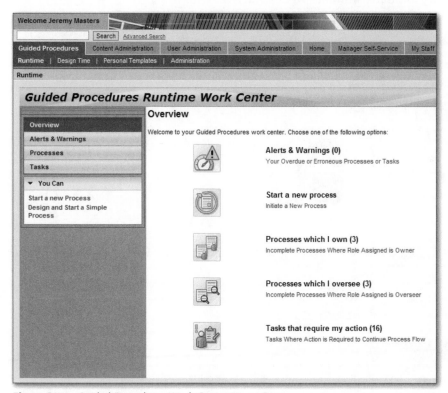

Figure 8.40 Guided Procedures Work Center Home Page

Figure 8.40 shows the home page to the Guided Procedure runtime. Within the runtime environment, the user can do one of several tasks, including start a new process, view a process that he owns or oversees, or take action on a task already in process. There is also an "Alerts & Warnings" section that summarizes those processes and tasks that are either overdue or processed incorrectly.

The start page for a process instance of the standard "My First Days" checklist is seen in Figure 8.41. A list of process activities is organized by "blocks." These blocks contain links to various "actions." Most actions in the standard are either transactional in nature (e.g., Maintain Bank Information) or content-based (e.g., benefit information on an internal/external website). As the employee completes each action, he selects the Read or Complete button. A green box is then seen next to the action indicating its completion. The employee could work through all remaining checklist items until completion. After completion, the checklist would show in the "Completed Process" subsection of the "Process" section within the Guided Procedures Runtime Work Center.

Figure 8.41 The Home Page for the My First Days Checklist

Figure 8.42 shows an action (i.e., the Web Dynpro for Java transaction for updating bank information) within process block Payment Information. After completing the transaction, the employee would select the Complete button and move to the next action.

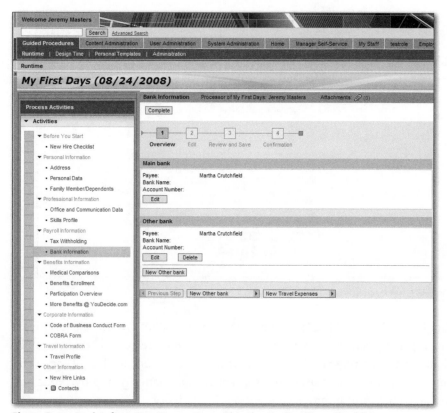

Figure 8.42 Bank Information Transaction within the My First Days Checklist

The Guided Procedures framework has received mixed reviews in its role as the platform for supporting work and life event checklists. Some companies have been eager to embrace its robust design and runtime environments, while others feel the tool's user interface is too complicated for end users.

Some third-party companies provide alternatives for checklists not based on Guided Procedures hoping to provide users with a more intuitive interface. Figure 8.43 shows an example of such a checklist. A Marriage checklist for an employee from Worklogix's Process Server is shown. The left panel allows the employee to select from a list of work and life events. The tasks of the chosen checklist appear on the main (right) panel. Clicking on a task's Do It button would take the user to a transaction, internal /external website, policy/training document, or some other type of service.

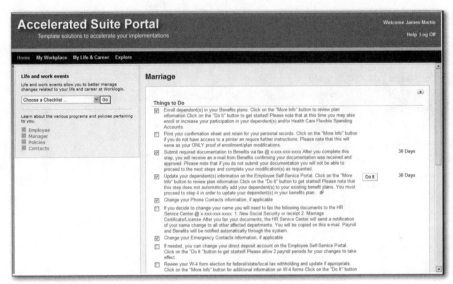

Figure 8.43 Marriage Checklist from Worklogix's Process Server

Without a doubt, checklists offer important functionality within self-service for employees, managers, and HR Professionals. Work and life event checklists can be implemented to empower the end user with a process-centric view of the event. Basing the experience of a user on his intent will dramatically improve your portal's effectiveness and improve your HR service delivery.

8.5 Summary

In this chapter, we explained some of the more advanced topics within self-service. The OADP framework provides important functionality to make MSS iViews more user friendly. SAP Workflow and delegation capabilities also offer the robust ability to deliver complex solutions within the SAP Portal. Last, we saw how work and life checklists provided within the Guided Procedures framework can drive the completion of important processes for employees, managers, and HR Professionals.

Next, we will cover Authorization Management within self-service. Both standard and structural authorizations on the ECC backend are discussed as well as portal-level security.

Security authorizations within Manager Self-Service (MSS) and Employee Self-Service offer enhanced abilities for restricting user access. Both standard and structural authorizations on the ERP Central Component (ECC) backend are discussed within the context of its use within the self-service framework. Portal-level security, in the form of permissions, is reviewed, and awareness on data privacy is also discussed.

9 Authorization Management

Authorization management plays a crucial role within SAP ERP HCM self-service functionality, as sensitive Human Resources (HR) data — including employee's personally identifiable information (PII) — becomes more accessible to employees, managers, and HR Business Partners online. Managers and HR gain access to more HR information for their employees. Exposing HR data on the SAP Portal underscores the importance of having a bullet-proof security plan, because providing web access to your underlying HR information inevitably extends the security risk. All too often, successful ESS and MSS deployments turn sour when a security breach is encountered post go-live. Don't let this happen to you!

The SAP system has added several layers of security to prevent such a circumstance from occurring. Besides the standard security authorizations available within the HCM component, new authorization objects S_RFC and S_SERVICE offer enhanced security necessary to support the new Web Dynpro functionality. Using authorizations available within the standard backend role assignment, the functions called by the front end (i.e., the portal) are secured according to your unique business requirements. These new authorization objects — coupled with the existing standard objects (from PLOG to P_ORGIN to P_PERNR) and structural authorizations — allow for tremendous flexibility in your security design.

We will also look at the standard ECC backend roles that are provided by the SAP system. The SAP system offers both country-specific and generic roles that customers can use as a model for their own self-service roles. Both composite and single roles are available within standard delivery for ERP 2005, Enhancement Packages 1, 2, and 3. Keep in mind that just as with other standard roles, copies should be made into your customer name space and edited based on requirements.

We will discuss portal-level security by covering the topic of portal permissions. Portal permissions are important within self-service as they allow portal content, such as worksets, pages, iViews, etc., to be visible to the end user. Without this important step, users would not be able to view any content or access any iViews on the portal.

Finally, we will cover data privacy and its implication on your project. The most successful projects consider data privacy and access control issues from the start, especially if your project has global scope.

It is imperative that you work with your security and portal resources when designing the authorizations needed for your implementation. Many of the authorization objects will be familiar to your security resource, but special attention should be paid to some of the nuances when delivering self-service functionality. Your portal resource should be able to assist you with portal permissioning.

> **Note**
>
> For a more comprehensive look at security in the HCM component, please refer to the SAP PRESS book *Authorizations in SAP ERP HCM* by Martin Esch and Anja Junold.

9.1 Important Authorizations within ECC for Self-Service

We recommend that a security resource familiar with HCM authorizations spend a sufficient amount of time architecting the security design to support your self-service implementation. This is especially true if your organization has implemented structural authorizations. Structural authorizations offer an additional way to apply security via organizational management objects, relationships, and structures. Before discussing the benefits and challenges associated with integrating structural authorizations with your overall security model for self-service, we will first cover an overview of the standard authorization objects. All core HR authorization objects, such as P_PERNR and P_ORGIN, are needed to implement ESS and MSS, and will be reviewed in detail.

Several new authorization objects in HCM are now available to further control access within self-service. These include S_SERVICE, S_RFC, and P_HAP_DOC. Almost every function on the portal calls the same backend authorizations used throughout the HCM component. This is because the same infotypes are being updated in HCM but just through a different medium. For example, Infotype IT0006 (Address) information is updated regardless of whether an HR administrator updates the employee's address in Transaction PA30 or whether this update is performed by the employee himself on the SAP Portal.

In the sections that follow, each authorization object is described with examples and tips for use in your customer-defined scenarios. We will review all authorization objects within a self-service context. The first authorization object, S_SERVICE, will be discussed first.

9.1.1 S_SERVICE

Authorization object S_SERVICE is needed to authorize access to external services, including Web Dynpro applications. When Web Dynpro applications are started, the authorization S_SERVICE is called. Only if authorization has been granted to the service will the Web Dynpro application start. Just as authorization objects S_TCODE and P_TCODE grant access to transaction codes, authorization object S_SERVICE grants access to external services, such as Web Dynpro applications.

The following authorization fields comprise the S_SERVICE authorization object. Each field is described separately and highlighted with important information on usage.

- *Service Program, Transaction, or Function* (SRV_NAME)
  Determines what external service is available to start.

- *Type of Check Flag and Authority* (SRV_TYPE)
  Determines the type of external service.

Figure 9.1 shows the detail behind these two authorization fields. Each external service is defined with a 30-character string (e.g., A54F8385A9868919E-A0F952DE7452E) along with its more popular name (e.g., *sap.com/ess~us~fam/Per_Family_US*). Also, the "service type" dropdown identifies the external service as type Web Dynpro.

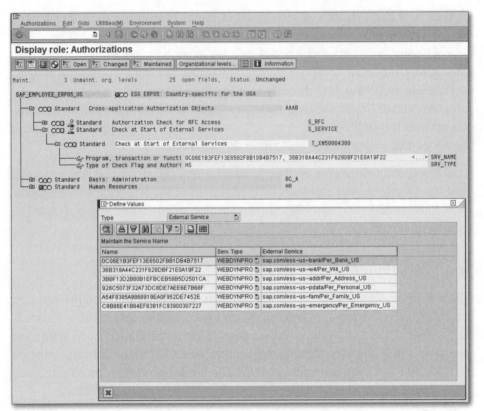

Figure 9.1 External Services Available for Start Within a Sample Authorization Using S_SERVICE Authorization Object

If you enter value * for the authorization object S_SERVICE, you will grant users the authorization to start all external applications, including Web Dynpro. Some customers that do this believe that the portal will do all of the security "naturally." This is because portal roles can be constructed in such a way as to limit what Web Dynpro services a user can access based on portal page and iView design. Although this approach is viable, we recommend that you assign authorizations explicitly for the external services you introduce into your profiles.

Next, let's discuss authorization object S_RFC, an authorization object equally as critical to self-service functionality as S_SERVICE.

9.1.2   S_RFC

Without providing access to the backend ABAP functions, data cannot be saved in the SAP system from the Web Dynpro applications on the portal. Using authorization object S_RFC, access to program components (via function groups) can be granted. The following authorization fields comprise the S_RFC authorization object. Each field is described separately and highlighted with important information on usage.

▶ **Activity** (ACTVT)
  Determines the activity level the user has access to. In the standard delivery, the only value is 16 (Execute).

▶ **Name of Remote Function Call (RFC) to be protected** (RFC_NAME)
  Contains the names of function groups granted access to. This authorization field can have a maximum of 18 characters. For example, function groups HRXSS_PER_EMERGENCY_US, HRXSS_PER_P0002_US, HRXSS_PER_P0009_US, HRXSS_PER_P0021_US, and HRXSS_PER_P0210_US are included within the RFC_NAME field of authorization S_RFC for the role SAP_EMPLOYEE_ERP05_US.

▶ **Type of RFC object to be protected** (RFC_TYPE)
  Contains the type of RFC to be checked. In the standard system, only function group (type FUGR) is available.

Figure 9.2 shows an example of the standard SAP role SAP_EMPLOYEE_ERP05_US containing the values of an authorization using authorization object S_RFC. Technically, only one authorization would be needed within your ESS and MSS roles because both the activity (ACTVT) and RFC type (RFC_TYPE) authorization fields are always constant.

The SAP system delivers over 200 function groups beginning with HRXSS*. The group of function groups starting with HRXSS_PER* contain over 190 function groups that support the following applications: personal data (IT0002), emergency contact (IT0006/IT0021), address (IT0006), bank details (IT0009), and family/dependent information (IT0021). Other country-specific applications are also supported by their own function groups.

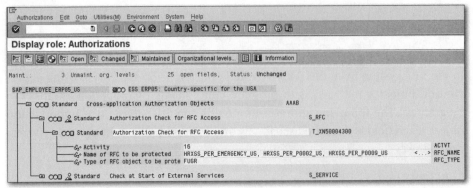

Figure 9.2 Example Authorization Using Authorization Object S_RFC Within Standard Single Role SAP_EMPLOYEE_ERP05_US

We have covered two of the most important authorization objects. Next, let's discuss one of the most important authorization objects for ESS — P_PERNR.

9.1.3   P_PERNR

Authorization object P_PERNR is used to control access to a user's (i.e., employee's) own HR data. P_PERNR restricts access based on infotype and subtype. If you have already implemented ESS, this authorization object is part of your existing ESS role. Based on the ESS functionality you are rolling out, this authorization object may need updating.

The following authorization fields comprise the P_PERNR authorization object. Each field is described separately and highlighted with important information on usage.

▶ **Authorization Level** (AUTHC)
Determines what level of authorization a user has. The following values are permissible: M (read with entry helps), R (read), S (write locked record; unlock if the last person to change the record is not the current user), E (write locked record), D (change lock indicator), W (write data records), and * (all operations).

▶ **Infotype** (INFTY)
Determines which infotypes a user has access to. The group of Infotypes 0002, 0006, 0009, and 0021 are common infotypes used for this authorization field to support ESS functionality. Only infotypes from Personnel Administration (PA) are available within this authorization field. Infotypes available for inclu-

sion within this field include 0000 to 0999 (for employee master data), Infotypes 2000-2999 (for time management data), and Infotypes 9000-9999 (for customer-specific data, if applicable).

▶ **Interpretation of Assigned Personnel Number** (PSIGN)
This field defines how the user logged in should be "interpreted" when authorization checks of HR infotypes are performed (i.e., whether to include or exclude). Only values "I" and "E" are permissible: the value "I" means that authorizations for the assigned personnel number are included within the authorization while the value "E" means that authorizations for the assigned personnel number are excluded. If both authorizations I and E are entered, authorization E will be given preference. Please note that the value * is not allowed in this field.

▶ **Subtype (**SUBTY**)**
Determines which subtypes a user has access to. Values for subtype go hand-in-hand with those infotypes identified in your infotype authorization field (INFO-TYP). For example, inclusion of subtype 1 for Infotype 0021 signifies that the "Spouse" record is available within the authorization.

Let's look at an example. The following authorization would indicate that the employee has full authorization to update any subtype on their Infotype 0002 (Personal Data), Infotype 0006 (Address), Infotype 0009 (Bank Details), and Infotype 0021 (Family Members/Dependents). (Infotype 0106 appears as a subscreen on U.S. versions of IT0021.)

Authorization level: *

Infotype: 0002, 0006, 0009, 0021, 0106

Interpretation of assigned personnel number: I

Subtype: *

In Figure 9.3, this authorization is depicted. In this example, only one authorization is listed. It is more likely, however, that you will have more than one authorization for P_PERNR.

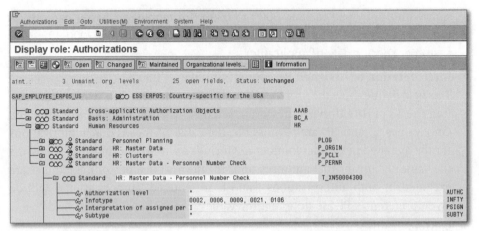

Figure 9.3 Example Authorization using Authorization Object P_PERNR Within Standard Single Role SAP_EMPLOYEE_ERP05_US

Authorization object P_PERNR represents a fundamental element of your ESS security design. Without it, employees would not be able to update any of their own data. Be sure to spend sufficient time and energy on designing P_PERNR authorizations because your audience for this is your entire employee population.

Next, we discuss another important authorization, PLOG, which allows us to control components within the organizational management and personnel development areas.

9.1.4 PLOG

For most ESS and MSS implementations, updates will be needed to authorizations provided by authorization object PLOG. Authorization object PLOG provides access to Organizational Management (OM) and Personnel Development (PD) objects, infotypes, and relationships. Any iView within MSS and ESS that reads or writes data to OM or PD objects, such as position (object type S), organizational unit (object type O), course (E), appraisal (VA), budget unit (object type BU), etc., will need to incorporate authorizations within the PLOG authorization object.

The following authorization fields comprise the PLOG authorization object. Each field is described separately and highlighted with important information on usage.

▶ **Infotype** (INFOTYP)

Determines which infotypes a user has access to. The group of Infotypes 1000 (Object), 1001 (Relationships), and 1002 (Description) contain the core infotypes of any OM or PD object. Without read authorization to these infotypes, no information from the configuration can be read. Infotypes in PLOG only refer to those infotypes within PD (and not PA). Other relevant infotypes commonly used in ESS and MSS include 1005 (Planned Compensation), 1007 (Vacancy), 1008 (Account Assignment Features), 1011 (Work Schedule), and 1013 (Employee Group/Subgroup).

▶ **Planning Status** (ISTAT)

Determines which planning statuses a user has access to. The vast majority of objects are typically set in status 1 (Active). The exception to this is appraisal documents, which can be either in status 3 (Submitted) or status 4 (Approved).

▶ **Object Type** (OTYPE)

Determines which object types a user has access to. Objects commonly found in authorizations for ESS and MSS roles include P (employee), S (position), O (organizational unit), and C (job). Other objects include: VA (appraisal template), VB (criteria groups), and VC (criteria) for Performance Management (PM). For personnel and competency management, QB (Qualification Block) and QK (Qualifications Catalog), and Q (qualifications). For LSO, DC (Curriculum Type), EC (Curriculum), E (Course), F (Location), and G (Resource). For development planning, BL (Development Plan Group) and B (Development Plan). For Compensation Management, and BU (Budget Unit).

▶ **Plan Version** (PLVAR)

Determines which plan versions a user has access to. Plan version 01 (Active plan) is the default plan version for most objects and should be the only plan version used. Using other plan versions should be avoided. Plan versions ** and .: should never be used.

▶ **Function Code** (PPFCODE)

Determines what permissions the user has Ð read, write, delete, and so on Ð for the object. Most likely, you will use one or more of the following function codes in your implementation: AEND (Change), DEL (Delete), DISP (Display), and INSE (Insert).

▶ **Subtype** (SUBTYP)

Determines which subtypes a user has access to. Values for subtypes go hand-in-hand with those infotypes identified in your infotype authorization field (INFOTYP), discussed earlier. Subtypes in PLOG only refer to subtypes within PD (and not PA).

In Figure 9.4, the depicted authorization provides the user the ability to view all relationships (subtypes) of objects job (C), organizational unit (O), employee (P), qualification (Q) and position (S) in the active plan version (01) and in any planning status.

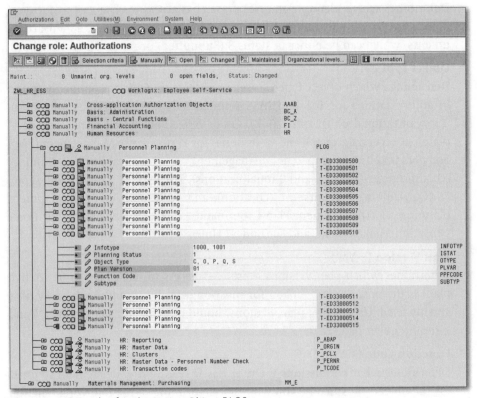

Figure 9.4 Example of Authorization Object PLOG

Now, let's turn our focus to another very important authorization, P_ORGIN.

9.1.5 P_ORGIN/P_ORGINCON

P_ORGIN and P_ORGINCON are very important authorization objects because they permit users to access HR data on other employees. Both provide the same function but differ in one important way: P_ORGINCON includes an authorization profile. For those clients seeking a context-sensitive solution, P_ORGINCON enables the use of structural authorizations in the overall profile. Discussion on the use of context-sensitive authorizations is described in a later section of this chapter.

Both objects provide a way to restrict access based on infotype, subtype, personnel area, personnel subarea, and organizational key. The following authorization fields comprise the P_ORGIN and P_ORGINCON authorization object.

- **Authorization Level** (AUTHC)
  Determines the access level a user is granted. Available options are M (search help), R (read record), S (write locked record; unlock if the last person to change the record is not the current user), E (write locked record), D (change lock indicator), W (write record), and * (all operations).

  Please note that within the Enterprise Compensation Management (ECM) component, additional authorization levels are needed in order to allow users to create or change records on Infotype 0759 (Compensation Process). Authorization levels "P" (for planning and submitting compensation process records) and "A" (for approving or rejecting compensation process records) have been added to authorization object P_ORGIN. Additionally, the standard authorization levels R (read) and W (write) are required for line and higher managers involved in the online planning process.

- **Infotype** (INFTY)
  Determines which infotypes a user has access to. This is the infotype in question. Infotype range 0000 to 0999 is used for employee master data, Infotypes 2000 to 2999 for time data, Infotypes 4000 to 4999 for applicant data, and Infotypes 9000 to 9999 are customer specific.

- **Personnel Area** (PERSA)
  Determines which personnel areas a user has access to. This is the personnel area (field PERSA) that is located on an employee's IT0001 (Organizational Assignment) record.

- **Employee Group** (PERSG)
  Determines which employee groups a user has access to. This is the employee group (field PERSG) that is located on an employee's IT0001 (Organizational Assignment) record.

335

▶ **Employee Subgroup** (PERSK)
Determines which employee subgroup a user has access to. This is the employee subgroup (field PERSK) that is located on an employee's IT0001 (Organizational Assignment) record.

▶ **Organizational Key** (VDSK1)
Determines which organizational keys a user has access to. This is the organizational key (field VDSK1) that is located on an employee's IT0001 (Organizational Assignment) record.

Additionally, P_ORGINCON includes one other very important field:

▶ **Authorization Profile** (PROFL)
Identifies the authorization profile to be used. If structural authorizations are used in your organization, you can integrate an authorization profile directly in P_ORGINCON through this authorization field. Any profile defined in table T77PR can be used (accessed through Transaction OOSB).

Figure 9.5 show an example of authorization P_ORGIN, which provides the user with read and matchcode (or search) access to Infotypes 0000, 0001, and 0002.

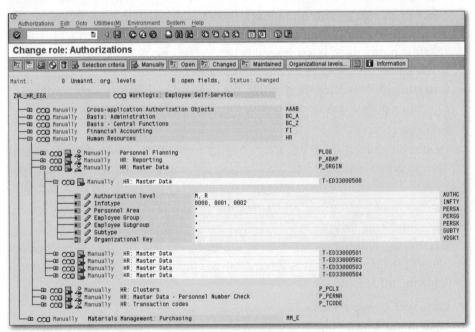

Figure 9.5 Example P_ORGIN Authorization with Read and Search Access to Infotypes 0000, 0001, and 0002

Next, we discuss a new authorization object used exclusively within the PM component (Objective Setting and Appraisals). If you are not implementing SAP's PM functionality, this section is not pertinent for you.

9.1.6 P_HAP_DOC

P_HAP_DOC is a new authorization object within the Objective Setting and Appraisals functionality. P_HAP_DOC is a mandatory authorization for implementing appraisals and must be used in conjunction with P_PERNR, PLOG, and P_ORGIN or P_ORGINCON. Figure 9.6 shows an example implementation of authorization object P_HAP_DOC.

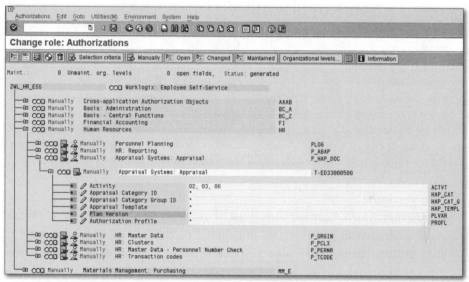

Figure 9.6 Authorization Object P_HAP_DOC Used Within PM

The following authorization fields comprise the P_HAP_DOC authorization object:

▶ **Activity** (ACTV)
Determines what operations (or "activities") a user can perform on an appraisal form. Available options are 02 (Change), 03 (Display), and 06 (Delete). Notice there is no Create activity. Without change authorization, an appraisee or appraiser is unable to create an appraisal.

▶ **Appraisal Category ID** (HAP_CAT)
Determines which catalog ID a user has access to. The appraisal category ID is the eight-digit ID category defined in your configuration. In addition to Trans-

action PHAP_CATALOG, you can also view your categories via Transaction OOHAP_CATEGORY.

▶ **Appraisal Category Group ID** (HAP_CAT_G)
Determines which catalog group ID a user has access to. The appraisal category group ID is the eight-digit ID category group defined in your configuration. In addition to Transaction PHAP_CATALOG, you can also view your category groups via Transaction OOHAP_CAT_GROUP. Standard out-of-the-box SAP software delivers category groups 1 (Personnel Appraisals), 10 (Learning Solution), and 100 (E-Recruiting).

▶ **Appraisal Template ID** (HAP_TEMPL)
Determines which appraisal template ID a user has access to. The appraisal template is the eight-digit ID defined in your configuration. The appraisal template ID is the same as the VA object ID of the form.

Tip

Using the appraisal template ID in the P_HAP_DOC authorization object is a common approach many clients choose for defining authorization to different forms. For example, if you configured one form for exempt employees and another form for non-exempt employees or one form for executives and another for non-executives, this authorization field can provide a way to identify which templates can be accessed by which users.

▶ **Plan Version** (PLVAR)
Determines which plan versions a user has access to. Plan version 01 (Active plan) is the default plan version and should be the only plan version used in your process. Using other plan versions should be avoided. Again, plan versions ** and .: should never be used under any circumstances.

▶ **Authorization Profile** (PROFL)
Identifies the authorization profile to be used (this is optional). If structural authorizations are used in your organization, you can integrate an authorization profile directly in P_HAP_DOC through this authorization field. Any profile defined in table T77PR can be used (accessed through Transaction OOSB).

We have completed our review of the main authorization objects used within ESS and MSS.

9.1.7 Summary of Main Authorization Objects Used in ESS and MSS

Table 9.1 contains a list of the most important authorization objects used with the MSS and ESS application. Each authorization object is listed with its primary use. Most of these objects will not be new to your organization if you are already running HCM.

Authorization Object(s)	Use
S_SERVICE	Used to check whether an external service (such as a Web Dynpro application) can be started by the user.
S_RFC	Used to specify if the user has access to RFCs (i.e., function groups). For example, S_RFC with a value of HRXSS_PER_P0002_US would allow the user access to IT0002 (Personal Data) in the U.S.
P_PERNR	Used to control access to the user's own HR employee data, such as Basic Pay (IT0008), Personal Data (IT0002), and Address (IT0006). This object is critical within the ESS functionality.
PLOG	Used to control access to OM objects, such as O (organizational unit), S (position), and C (job) as well as PD objects, such as Q (qualification), E (course), VA (appraisal template), VB (criteria group), and VC (criterion)
P_ORGIN / P_ORGINCON	Used to control access to other employee's infotype data, including actions (Infotype 0000), organizational assignment (Infotype 0001), and personal data (Infotype 0002). Can also include authorization profiles (i.e., structural authorizations) if P_ORGINCON is used.
P_HAP_DOC	Used within PM only. Used to control access to appraisal documents, configured in the Appraisal Catalog.

Table 9.1 Authorization Objects for Self-Service and Their Intended Use

There are a few other authorization objects that are used within ESS and MSS applications. Table 9.2 contains a list of some of the other authorization objects used with the MSS and ESS application.

Authorization Object(s)	Use
P_ABAP	Used to allow access to HR reports.
P_PCLX	Used to determine access to PCLx cluster tables, including payroll data per country.

Table 9.2 Authorization Objects for Self-Service and Their Intended Use

P_PCR	Used to determine access to payroll control records, based on payroll area.
P_TRAVL	Used to determine authorization for accessing trip data within the Travel Management component. (Technically, part of the Finance component.)
B_NOTIF, I_QMEL, S_USER_GRP, S_BDS_DS	Used for supporting the Personnel Change Request (PCR) functionality. B_NOTIF for controls notifications, I_QMEL for notification types, S_USER_GRP for user groups, and S_BDS_DS for access to documents.
P_ASRCONT	Used within HCM Process and Forms. Controls whether the user can start, approve, reject, and process a form.
S_SER_ONBE	Used to grant Employee Interaction Center (EIC) agents the authorization to execute a particular self-service application on an employee's behalf. It is the S_RFC (service) equivalent for EIC agents.
S_MWB_FCOD	Used to restrict function codes within a manager's desktop. Also used within the reporting iView functionality on the portal.
P_LSO_FOUP, and P_LSO_TU	Used in authorizations for Learning Solution (LSO). P_LSO_FOUP controls participation follow-up and P_LSO_TU controls LSO content management.
P_HRF_INFO, P_HRF_META and P_CERTIF	Used in authorizations for HR Forms and Statements. P_HRF_INFO and P_HRF_META control Infodata and Metadata for HR Forms, respectively. P_CERTIF controls statements (but not SAPScript).
P_RCF_ACT, P_RCF_APPL, P_RCF_POOL, P_RCF_STAT, P_RCF_VIEW, and P_RCF_WL	Used in authorizations for E-Recruiting to control activities, applications, talent pool access, object status, status overview, and worklists.

Table 9.2 Authorization Objects for Self-Service and Their Intended Use (Cont.)

We have now covered the majority of the authorization objects that you will most likely need for your ESS and MSS implementation. Of course, there may be situations where you have a custom authorization object or objects. If this is the case, you will need to work with your security team to ensure that the new functionality on the portal is taken into consideration. Often times, poorly documented custom authorization objects get in the way of progress.

9.1.8 Activation Switches in T77S0

To activate authorization objects P_PERNR, P_ORGIN, and P_ORGINCON for use in your system, you must ensure that the proper switches have been activated in system table T77S0. Please note that these switches have probably already been configured, as they are paramount to the basic design of HCM authorizations. Do not change this configuration without first checking with your security resource.

For P_PERNR, switch AUTSW/PERNR needs value 1 to activate; for P_ORGIN, switch AUTSW/ORGIN needs value 1 to activate; and for P_ORGINCON, switch AUTSW/INCON needs value 1 to activate. Figure 9.7 shows authorization objects P_PERNR and P_ORGIN being used, but not P_ORGINCON.

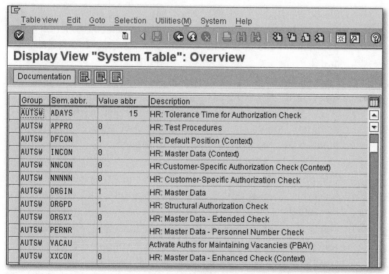

Figure 9.7 Authorization Switches Within System Table T77S0, Group AUTSW

We have now covered all relevant authorization objects within an ESS and MSS context. Now let's understand what the SAP system has provided out of the box from an SAP security role perspective.

9.2   Standard Roles in Self-Service

SAP delivers several backend ECC security roles for ESS that can be copied to your customer name space and altered according to your specific security requirements via Transaction PFCG (Role Maintenance). Depending on your own security practices you may or may not use composite roles within your ESS functionality. Table 9.3 lists both standard single and composite roles. A new set of standard roles for ESS were delivered with the ERP2005 platform, Enhancement Package 3. See SAP Note 1129412 for more information on security roles issued with Enhancement Package 3.

SAP Standard Role	Description
SAP_ESSUSER	Single role that comprises all non-country-specific functions. Only relevant for the older ESS functionality, including all Internet Transaction Server (ITS) components, such as PZ02 (Address), PZ13 (Personal Data), PZ03 (Bank Details), and PZ12 (Family Member/Dependent). Relevant for those on earlier platforms, such as version 4.6C.
SAP_ESSUSER_ERP05	Single role that comprises all non-country-specific functions. Relevant for the ERP2005 platform, Enhancement Packages 1 and 2.
SAP_EMPLOYEE_ERP05	Composite role that comprises all country-specific functions. Relevant for the ERP2005 platform, Enhancement Packages 1 and 2. Includes all country-specific single roles, such as SAP_EMPLOYEE_ERP05_CA for Canada, SAP_EMPLOYEE_ERP05_JP for Japan, SAP_EMPLOYEE_ERP05_US for the U.S., SAP_EMPLOYEE_ERP05_VE for Venezuela, etc.
SAP_EMPLOYEE_ERP_13	Composite role that comprises all non-country-specific functions. Relevant for the ERP2005 platform, Enhancement Package 3.
SAP_EMPLOYEE_ERP05_xx	Single role comprising country-specific functions. A separate role exists for each country version (xx = country ID). The corresponding composite role is SAP_EMPLOYEE_ERP05. Relevant for the ERP2005 platform, Enhancement Packages 1 and 2. See Table 9.4 for a complete list available by country.
SAP_EMPLOYEE_ERP_13_xx	Single role comprising country-specific functions. A separate role exists for each country version (xx = country ID). The corresponding composite role is SAP_EMPLOYEE_ERP_13. Relevant for the ERP2005 platform, Enhancement Package 3.

Table 9.3 Authorization Objects for Self-Service and Their Intended Use

Table 9.4 lists the all country-specific single roles and their descriptions available within the ERP 2005 system, Enhancement Packages 1 and 2. A similar listing by country (not shown) is available for those on Enhancement Package 3. These single roles (e.g., `SAP_EMPLOYEE_ERP05_ES` for Spain) already contain default values for the S_RFC authorization object (in this example, `HRXSS_PER_EMERGENCY_ES`, `HRXSS_PER_P0002_ES`, `HRXSS_PER_P0009_ES`, and `HRXSS_PER_P0021_ES`) and the `S_SERVICE` authorization object (e.g., `sap.com/ess~es~addr/Per_Address_ES`, `sap.com/ess~es~pdata/Per_Personal_ES`, `sap.com/ess~es~bank/Per_Bank_ES`, `sap.com/ess~es~fam/Per_Family_ES`, and `sap.com/ess~es~emergency/Per_Emergency_ES`). Each single role per country listed provides the necessary access for the basic self-service transactions that are country specific.

Single Role Name	Single Role Description
SAP_EMPLOYEE_ERP05_AR	ESS ERP05: Country-specific functions for Argentina
SAP_EMPLOYEE_ERP05_AT	ESS ERP05: Country-specific functions for Austria
SAP_EMPLOYEE_ERP05_AU	ESS ERP05: Country-specific functions for Australia
SAP_EMPLOYEE_ERP05_BE	ESS ERP05:Country-specific functions for Belgium
SAP_EMPLOYEE_ERP05_BR	ESS ERP05: Country-specific functions for Brazil
SAP_EMPLOYEE_ERP05_CA	ESS ERP05: Country-specific functions for Canada
SAP_EMPLOYEE_ERP05_CH	ESS ERP05: Country-specific functions for Switzerland
SAP_EMPLOYEE_ERP05_CN	ESS ERP05: Country-specific functions for China
SAP_EMPLOYEE_ERP05_DE	ESS ERP05: Country-specific functions for Germany
SAP_EMPLOYEE_ERP05_DK	ESS ERP05: Country-specific functions for Denmark
SAP_EMPLOYEE_ERP05_ES	ESS ERP05: Country-specific functions for Spain
SAP_EMPLOYEE_ERP05_FR	ESS ERP05: Country-specific functions for France
SAP_EMPLOYEE_ERP05_GB	ESS ERP05: Country-specific functions for Great Britain
SAP_EMPLOYEE_ERP05_HK	ESS ERP05: Country-specific functions for Hong Kong
SAP_EMPLOYEE_ERP05_ID	ESS ERP05: Country-specific functions for Indonesia
SAP_EMPLOYEE_ERP05_IE	ESS ERP05: Country-specific functions for Ireland
SAP_EMPLOYEE_ERP05_IT	ESS ERP05: Country-specific functions for Italy
SAP_EMPLOYEE_ERP05_JP	ESS ERP05: Country-specific functions for Japan

Table 9.4 Table of Country-specific Security Roles

Single Role Name	Single Role Description
SAP_EMPLOYEE_ERP05_KR	ESS ERP05: Country-specific functions for South Korea
SAP_EMPLOYEE_ERP05_MX	ESS ERP05: Country-specific functions for Mexico
SAP_EMPLOYEE_ERP05_MY	ESS ERP05: Country-specific functions for Malaysia
SAP_EMPLOYEE_ERP05_NL	ESS ERP05: Country-specific functions for the Netherlands
SAP_EMPLOYEE_ERP05_NO	ESS ERP05: Country-specific functions for Norway
SAP_EMPLOYEE_ERP05_NZ	ESS ERP05: Country-specific functions for New Zealand
SAP_EMPLOYEE_ERP05_PH	ESS ERP05: Country-specific functions for the Philippines
SAP_EMPLOYEE_ERP05_PT	ESS ERP05: Country-specific functions for Portugal
SAP_EMPLOYEE_ERP05_SE	ESS ERP05: Country-specific functions for Sweden
SAP_EMPLOYEE_ERP05_SG	ESS ERP05: Country-specific functions for Singapore
SAP_EMPLOYEE_ERP05_TH	ESS ERP05: Country-specific functions for Thailand
SAP_EMPLOYEE_ERP05_TW	ESS ERP05: Country-specific functions for Taiwan
SAP_EMPLOYEE_ERP05_US	ESS ERP05: Country-specific functions for the U.S.
SAP_EMPLOYEE_ERP05_VE	ESS ERP05: Country-specific functions for Venezuela
SAP_EMPLOYEE_ERP05_ZA	ESS ERP05: Country-specific functions for South Africa

Table 9.4 Table of Country-specific Security Roles (Cont.)

It is a good practice to copy these standard roles for ESS into your customer name space and modify them as needed based on your requirements. For MSS, it is quite different as the SAP system does not delivery any standard ECC backend roles. It is expected that customers either create a new role for managers from scratch or update/augment their existing MSS roles if they have already implemented. Regardless of this difference, the process for maintaining roles in the backend ECC system (as described in the next section) is the same for both ESS and MSS, as all Web Dynpro services are managed in a similar fashion via the profile generator. Some help for implementing MSS roles is included in SAP Note 844639.

Next, we discuss some mechanics on how to build and enhance the standard security roles with external services (e.g., Web Dynpro applications). The manner in which external services are edited differ than the normal procedure within Transaction PFCG. Understanding how to edit and enhance the pre-delivered roles will speed up implementation time and reduce security-related defects during your testing phase.

9.2.1 Editing Roles and Authorizations for Web Dynpro Services

With the new Web Dynpro functionality, you are able to default security authorizations based on selections made on the Menu tab within the profile generator. See the following steps to create a new role and assign the required Web Dynpro services to that role.

First, create a new role or copy an existing standard role using Transaction PFCG (profile generator). Second, assign the required services to this role. To do this, choose the "Menu" tab and then click on the button "Authorization Default." A dialog box will appear, choose the "External Service" radio button. Select Web Dynpro from the dropdown as the type of external service. In the service field, select the Web Dynpro service that you require from the dropdown (this list should contain the full inventory of the services available in your installed ESS and MSS business packages). Save your changes. The added service should appear under the folder entitled "Role menu" on the "Menu" tab. See Figure 9.8 for a screenshot of this step. Repeat until you are sure that you have selected all Web Dynpro services you want this role to have access to. The last step is to assign the required authorizations per your requirements. Choose the "Authorizations" tab to maintain the authorization objects. For most services, you will see authorizations S_RFC and S_SERVICE already pre-populated with valid values.

Where do the authorizations from these services get defaulted in from? Great question! Authorizations from these services are defaulted based on the information in Transactions SU22 and SU24 (these are the same transactions used for transaction code authorization assignments as well). These two transactions allow you to maintain the assignments of authorization objects to applications (including Web Dynpro services) and their authorization default values. This data then forms the basis for the creation of role authorizations with the profile generator (Transaction PFCG).

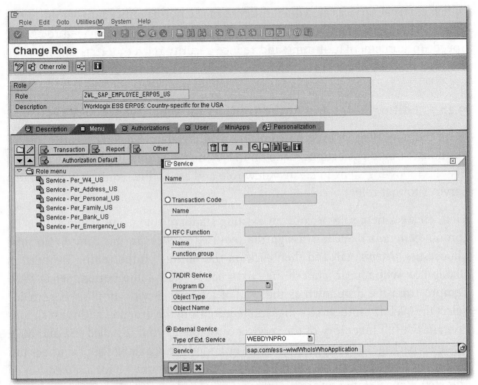

Figure 9.8 Adding a Web Dynpro Service from the Menu Tab

Note

SU22 displays and updates the values in tables USOBT and USOBX, while SU24 does the same in tables USOBT_C and USOBX_C. The _C stands for Customer. The profile generator (Transaction PFCG) sources data from the _C tables. In tables USOBT and USOBX, the values are the SAP standard values as shown in SU24. With SU25 one can (initially) transfer the USOBT values to the USOBT_C table. SAP Note 612585 has more detailed information on this topic.

Figure 9.9 shows an example of the details behind service *sap.com/ess~us~bank/Per_Bank_US* (Bank Details ESS for the United States) via Transaction SU22. SU22 is set up in three panels — a left navigation panel and an upper and lower main screen. The navigation panel on the left lists all of the external services available in the system based on the implemented business packages for ESS and MSS. The inventory of authorization objects are listed on the top right; each with an indicator on whether it is maintained (green icon) or not maintained (red icon). Also, the proposal status of each authorization object defines whether or not an authorization default value for the object is to be added to the authorizations of the role when the application is added to a role when using the profile generator.

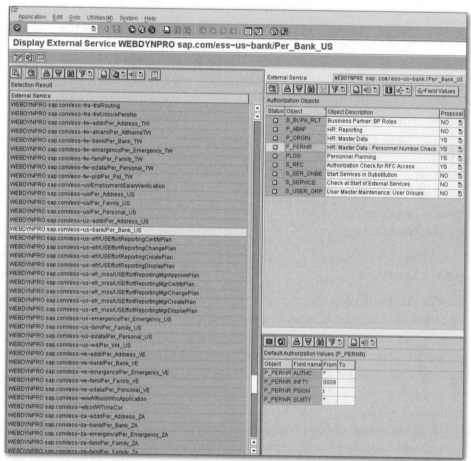

Figure 9.9 Details for External Service Web Dynpro *sap.com/ess~us~bank/Per_Bank_US*

If you understand how the Web Dynpro services are defaulted within the profile generator and used within the application, you have learned the essence of the new security functionality within the self-service framework. All other authorizations objects use the same standard HCM authorizations (PLOG, P_PERNR, etc.) that your team is most likely already using within the rest of HCM.

We have now concluded the discussion on the available standard authorizations. Let's now discuss structural authorizations — to learn its basics and its place within ESS and MSS.

9.3   Using Structural Authorizations with Self-Service

This section discusses implementing structural authorization security in addition to the standard authorization. Implementing structural authorizations is not a requirement for the deployment of ESS or MSS. Rather, it serves as additional means of securing data. Some SAP customers are under the mistaken belief that structural authorization is a prerequisite for self-service functionality — particularly MSS — on the portal. Although structural authorizations offer benefits that standard authorization alone does not, it should only be considered when there is a strong business reason to do so. In this section, we review structural authorizations — including an overview, its place within self-service and some best practices for implementation.

9.3.1   Overview

Structural authorization allows you to restrict authorizations based on underlying structures (organizational structures, business event hierarchies, qualification catalogs, etc.). Structural authorization access — in the form of authorization profiles — is granted at the position or user level. Access to organizational objects (organizational units, positions, jobs, etc., from SAP OM) is granted based on this access. A root object (e.g., organizational unit) is sometimes explicitly specified along with an evaluation path (e.g., SBESX Staffing Assignments Along Organizational Structure) to return all objects in a given time period (all, today, current month, current year, past, and future). Other times objects can be determined dynamically based on a function module set in the authorization profile. The SAP system delivers two standard function modules for this purpose: RH_GET_MANAGER_ASSIGNMENT (which determines all organizational units for which the user is the chief manager) and RH_GET_ORG_ASSIGNMENT (which determines which organizational unit the user is assigned to). From any root node that is returned from these functions, an evaluation path (such as SBESX) can be used to retrieve all objects (organizational units, positions, and employees) underneath that user's "span-of-control." These returned objects are used in conjunction with the user's standard authorizations to present a complete authorization check from both the standard authorization side (that uses authorization objects P_ORGIN, PLOG, P_PERNR, etc.) and from the structural authorization side (using the "structures hierarchy" previously mentioned). The intersection of these authorization checks provides SAP customers with added security.

Although structural authorizations provide an additional level of security, some customers decide against using structural authorizations in their design. Many of these customers have full self-service functionality but do quite well without implementing structural authorizations. We recommend that you establish a sound business case if you want to use structural authorizations.

Let's discuss function module RH_GET_MANAGER_ASSIGNMENT in greater detail and learn how it can be used within an MSS context. We can get a better idea of how and why this authorization can be used.

9.3.2 Function Component RH_GET_MANAGER_ASSIGNMENT

As part of the manager's structural authorization profile, standard function module RH_GET_MANAGER_ASSIGNMENT (or a customized version of it) is typically granted. As previously mentioned, this function retrieves all organizational units for which the user is the chief manager. If the manager is a chief of multiple organizational units, all organizational units will be returned as "root nodes." The manager can sit anywhere in the organizational structure; it's the 012 "Manages" relationship on his position to an organizational unit that drives the identification of organizational units managed. Within this function component, standard evaluation path MANASS is used to retrieve the organizational units.

Once the root node (or nodes) is retrieved, an evaluation path is used to identify all underlying objects that should be available for the user's authorization. Figure 9.10 shows an example authorization profile Z_MANAGER with evaluation path SBESX. The following parameters are used to fully define the authorization profile.

- Authorization Profile: Z_MANAGER
- No.: (sequence number of your choice)
- Plan Version: 01
- Object Type: O
- Object ID: (leave blank)
- Maintenance Flag: (unchecked)

- Evaluation Path: SBESX
- Status Vector: 12 (where 1=Active and 2=Planned)
- Depth: (blank, meaning no restriction in depth)
- Sign: (blank, meaning process objects "top down" and not "bottom up")
- Period: (blank, meaning no time period restriction)
- Function Component: RH_GET_MANAGER_ASSIGNMENT

Additional authorization profiles can be built and assigned to users in a similar fashion.

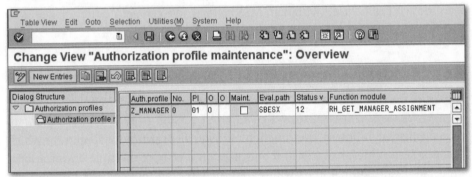

Figure 9.10 Authorization Profile Z_MANAGER Within Table T77PR Containing Function Component RH_GET_MANAGER_ASSIGNMENT

According to authorization profile Z_MANAGER, a manager would be able to view his whole organizational structure (i.e., full span-of-control, including organizational units, positions, and employees). This profile — together with the authorizations from his standard authorization — would form the total picture of backend security for the user.

In some cases, a combination of standard and structural authorizations is not enough. Some customers need to implement context-sensitive authorizations to handle their complex requirements. Context-sensitive authorizations are discussed next.

9.3.3 Context-Sensitive Authorizations

A context-sensitive solution is required when you need to associate individual standard and structural authorization profiles together within the same "context."

A classic example is that of a payroll manager. The payroll manager has certain responsibilities for the organization in his role as a manager of corporate payroll and certain responsibilities for his direct and indirect reports in his role as a people manager (i.e., "chief"). This segregation of duties is typical within the HR function. Other examples, include compensation managers, HR Generalists, and HR Administrators. In order to handle this issue, you can either issue two separate user IDs for this employee or implement context-sensitive authorizations.

In Figure 9.11, authorization P_ORGINCON contains read and search access to Infotypes 0000, 0001, and 0002 but only for the objects (i.e., employees) available within structural authorization profile Z_MANAGER. Another P_ORGINCON authorization could give this user access to update Infotype 0002 for a different contextual scenario.

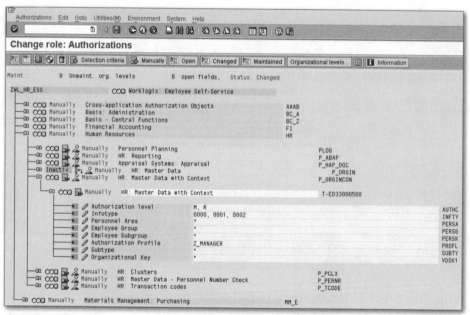

Figure 9.11 Example of Context-sensitive Authorization P_ORGINCON

We have seen how context-sensitive authorizations can provide a segegration of duties without the need for creating duplicate user IDs. By maintaining context-sensitive authorizations, you can more tightly integrate standard and structural authorizations together. This might be pertinent to your MSS implementation if the same manager using MSS functionality will also be using backend HR transactions (e.g., payroll manager).

9.3.4 Structural Authorizations in PM

If you are implementing PM, the handling of structural authorizations is unique in that you have the option of activating the functionality for this component only. In other words, structural restrictions can be made for accessing appraisals only, but in the PA component, no checks are performed. To do this, you must activate switch HAP00/AUTHO in table T77S0 by placing an X as the value (see Figure 9.12). Additionally, because no structural authorization checks need to be performed in PA, you use authorization object P_ORGIN for your infotype checks (and not P_ORGINCON, which includes an authorization profile).

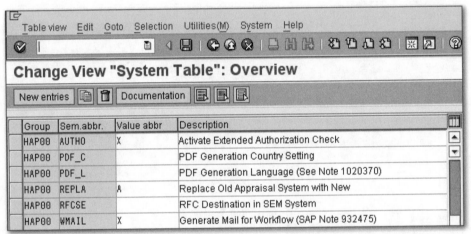

Figure 9.12 System Table T77S0, Group HAP00 Showing Semantic Abbreviation AUTHO, Used for Determining Structural Profile Use

When the HAP00/AUTHO switch is turned on, a structural profile must be entered in the authorization field PROFL for authorization object P_HAP_DOC. Additionally, the user must have an entry in table T77UA. Also, be sure that the correct authorization profile is defined in P_HAP_DOC itself. If the HAP00/AUTHO switch is turned on, and no authorization profile (or a wrong authorization profile) is defined in P_HAP_DOC, users with the identified authorization profile will be unable to access appraisals.

> **Note**
>
> More information on structural profiles within PM can be found in the SAP PRESS Book, *SAP ERP HCM Performance Management* by Christos Kotsakis and Jeremy Masters.

It's clear that structural authorizations provide a more robust way to handle complex, context-sensitive security requirements. If structural authorizations will be used for your implementation, give yourself additional testing time for unexpected challenges to surface. Implementing structural authorization is a major shift in the backend security approach. There is also additional maintenance with supporting a security design with structural authorizations.

Now that we have discussed both standard and structural authorizations, let's shift focus to the portal where another level of authorization is managed. SAP Portal permissions provide a key layer of added security for your ESS and MSS components.

9.4 Portal Permissions

Permissions set within the portal administrator console are important so that all end users can access the content served up from the iViews, pages, and worksets available within the ESS and MSS packages. Without this access, this content cannot be viewed by the end user. There are two basic ways the portal sets permissions on this content: via security zones and via the Portal Content Directory (PCD) object (pages, iView, etc.) itself. You should work with your SAP Portal administrator on ensuring that these permissions are set for the iViews within the ESS and MSS. These resources should already be familiar with these concepts. We will first discuss the Permissions Editor — a tool available to your portal administrators to enable proper permissioning for content viewing.

9.4.1 Permission Editor

The Permission Editor allows you to set authorization permissions on portal objects, components, and services to portal users, groups, or roles. The editor allows an administrator to search for and assign users, groups, and roles with appropriate permissions. Basic inheritance principles reduce maintenance for portal administrators, as permissions set at higher levels are used as defaults for lower-level objects unless overriden.

As seen in Figure 9.13, permissions are composed of two flags — one which identifies an "Administrator" setting. Settings can be one of the following: Read, Read/Write, Owner, Full Control, or None. This administration setting defines the access level for that user, group, or role. The other flag (the "End User" permission setting) is a checkbox that tells the system whether or not the object is available to the user during the portal runtime (when the user is logged in to the portal). Both values are important to fully define the permission level of the user, group, or role.

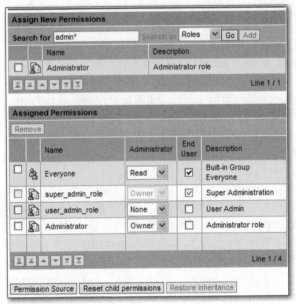

Figure 9.13 Permission Editor Example with Role and Groups Identified with "Administrator" and "End User" Flags

Also, it is important to note that roles and folders have an extra selection in the Permission Editor called "Role Assigner," which grants authorization to users or groups to the role in question. The role assigner is not available at the workset, page, or iView level.

These settings form the basis for the permissions granted for the security zones and PCD security discussed next. Let's discuss security zones first.

9.4.2 Setting Up Permissions to Security Zones

All portal applications and services available in the portal are assigned to a security zone. Security zones are assigned to portal applications and services in their portalapp.xml file (part of its deployment on the portal). Upon deployment, their respective security zones are then created in the portal. The portal's system administrator is responsible for verifying that the appropriate roles, groups, or users are assigned to the new security zones using the Permission Editor, and then making the necessary adjustments. If new components are deployed in your portal (e.g., custom applications), you must ensure that the proper security zones are identified within the portalapp.xml file. You can open security zone permissions as a system administrator if you navigate the path: SYSTEM ADMINISTRATOR • PERMISSIONS • PORTAL PERMISSIONS. Here, you can open the permissions of the high, medium, and low safety zones. As with other objects in the PCD, you can right-click and select the "Open Permissions" option to view and edit the permissions using the Permission Editor. The start page of the Permission Editor is shown in Figure 9.14.

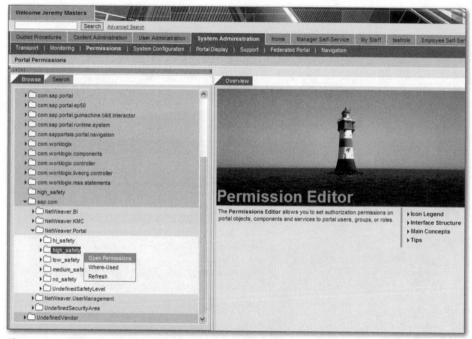

Figure 9.14 Permissions Editor Under System Administrator

Note

For more information on portal permissions, please refer to the document "How To Configure Permissions for Initial Content in SAP NetWeaver Portal," which is available as an SAP How-to Guide at *https://www.sdn.sap.com/irj/sdn/howtoguides*.

Now that we have discussed permissions with respect to security zones, let's discuss persmissions on the actual portal content — worksets, pages, iViews, and other content objects.

9.4.3 Setting Up Permissions to Portal Content

Once you have made the recommended changes to the security zone permissions, you need to configure the permissions content stored in the PCD. This content includes objects used by the portal, such as iViews, pages, worksets, and roles. Permissions assigned to content objects also enable you to determine which templates are available to users in the portal's content creation wizards. By default, the "Super Admin" role has Owner administrator permission to the entire collection of content that resides in the portal. The Super Admin permission settings cannot be modified.

You can open any PCD object's permissions as a content administrator if you navigate the path: CONTENT ADMINISTRATOR • PORTAL CONTENT. Here, you can either browse or search for the object and open its permissions by right-clicking and selecting the path: OPEN • PERMISSIONS to view and edit the permissions using the Permission Editor (see Figure 9.15).

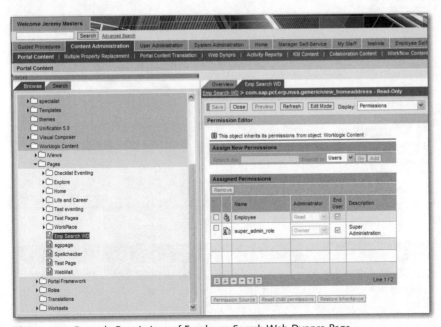

Figure 9.15 Example Permissions of Employee Search Web Dynpro Page

The SAP Portal catalog folders inherit the permissions of their parent folder. If the permissions of a folder are modified in any way, the folder will no longer inherit the permissions of its parent folder. You can use the "restore inheritance" feature in the Permissions Editor to restore inheritance between folders. However, keep in mind that folders are not the only objects that pass inheritance to suborindate objects. For example, pages pass their permissions to the iViews contained in them. Worksets and roles also pass their permissions to the pages and iViews contained in them.

Tip
When you assign a user or group to a role, that user or group is automatically given access to the role and its content, regardless of the role's existing permissions. However, if some of the components in the role (such as a page or workset) call an iView outside the role hierarchy, a permission denial error will result if the user does not have "End User" authorization to the external iView.

We have covered both authorization areas in which portal permissions play a factor in the overall security set up for deploying ESS and MSS transactions. Now, let's discuss some important SAP Notes relevant for self-service authorizations.

9.5   Important SAP Notes

Tabel 9.5 lists important SAP Notes relevant for typical ESS and MSS implementations. Most are categorized under application components BC-SEC-AUT-PFC (ABAP Authorization and Role Administration) or CA-ESS-WD (ESS Web Dynpro). We recommend that you read through these Notes to ensure that you are aware of any that pertain to your implementation. Please be aware that several Notes are release dependent (e.g., relevant for ERP2005 Enhancement Package 3, but not Enhancement Package 1 and 2).

Please note that SAP Notes related to the Permission Editor can be found in application component EP-PIN-SEC-ACL (ACL Editor).

As with other areas within the SAP system, it is best to periodically check the Service Marketplace for updated or new SAP Notes related to authorization and role management for ESS and MSS functionality.

SAP Note	SAP Note Description
1129412	ESS: Authorizations and roles for WD services in ERP EHP3
1054355	MSS: Authorizations & roles for WD services in SAP ERP PS-FS
857431	ESS: Authorizations and roles for WD services in ERP 2005
844639	MSS: Authorizations and roles for WD services in ERP 2005
785345	Copying authorization default values for services
754207	PFCG: Missing authorization check with menu change
745655	PFCG: Various errors in the authorization data maintenance
642359	PFCG: Authorization checks in role maintenance
622632	MSS: R/3 roles for business package MSS (My team)
612585	New: Authorization default values for external services

Table 9.5 Important SAP Notes Relevant for Typical ESS and MSS Implementations

Let's switch gears and talk about data privacy and its importance within an ESS and MSS context. More and more, data privacy and access control requirements are driving a self-service project's success, especially with global implementations.

9.6 Data Privacy

Data privacy considerations are quickly becoming an important part of ESS and MSS projects today, especially with global implementations. Many firms that are headquartered or have subsidiaries in Europe or Asia may need to consider local regulatory or legal requirements. Work councils, unions, bargaining units, and other groups of "represented" employees may influence what data can be made available for employee and manager updates as well as what data can "cross" international borders. This is especially interesting when a particular function, such as supply chain or information technology, is global in nature. There may be challenges, for example, if a manager in the United States manages employees in Ireland, China, and South Africa. Data privacy statutes, local laws, or bargaining unit rules may place certain restrictions on what employee data can be seen by whom and from where.

Personally Identifiable Information, such as national identification, private address, credit card data as well as sensitive HR data, such as benefit elections and family member data, must be protected as well. Some countries, like the United States, regard birth dates and race with extreme sensitivity versus some European countries, for example. European countries, in contrast, are typically more concerned with data privacy directives as they are part of the European Union. These directives, for example, typically claim important rights on sensitive data including:

▶ a right of access to that data

▶ a right to know where the data originated (if such information is available)

▶ a right to have inaccurate data rectified

▶ a right of recourse in the event of unlawful processing

▶ a right to withhold permission to use their data in certain circumstances

Based on our experience implementing global projects, we have established some best practices with respect to data privacy and access control that include the following:

▶ Ensure proper guidelines are in place with cross-border data transfers to ensure compliance with directives from regulatory or legal laws.

▶ Apply data masking of sensitive data wherever possible and whenever appropriate.

▶ Ensure appropriate segregation of duties with online processes (such as performance and compensation management) and audit regularly.

▶ Ensure data privacy is maintained when communicating sensitive information to third-party vendors.

▶ Limit, authorize, and track electronic and physical exchange of sensitive data, such as compensation data.

▶ Categorize data on its level of sensitivity in one of the following areas:

    ▶ "Confidential" — Information that is highly sensitive and critical to the operation of the organization. Information of this type is for use only within the organization or a department within an organization. Examples of this information include sealed bids from vendors, software code, or sensitive employee information.

    ▶ "Internal" — Information that is used within the organization but which is of a less-sensitive nature. Information of this type, while not publicly exposed, would not create a significant loss if it were to become exposed. Examples of this information include employee phone directories and organizational charts.

▶ "Public" — Information that has a negligible level of sensitivity. Information that has no potential for causing harm to the organization and can be distributed freely internally or externally. Examples of this information include mission statements and product lines.

With the preceding areas in mind, it is important to work with the IT Security, Legal, and Compliance teams within your organization to ensure that proper attention is given to the data being sourced from your ESS and MSS system. PII, such as home address and benefits information, must be kept secure. Data privacy provisions must be respected and complied with or uncertain consequences may be had from local regulatory and legal laws.

9.7 Summary

We have covered a wide range of authorization, security, and data privacy topics in this chapter. We hope we have provided you with the information you need to ensure that proper system controls are implemented to support your self-service functionality. Regardless of scope size, implementing security for ESS and MSS is complex because of the various layers involved, including standard and structural backend authorizations, as well as front-end security (SAP Portal permissions). In addition, data privacy and access control requirements may mean that additional controls are necessary to secure your employee's HR data based on local regulatory or legal legislature.

In the next chapter, we discuss how to set up your development environment so that you can make enhancements to the standard ESS and MSS Web Dynpro applications. We will walk you through the process with relevant examples and lessons learned provided.

Continuous improvement is reliant on the flexibility of the people, processes, and underlying systems to accommodate change.

10   Enhancing Self-Service Applications

Delivering robust and intuitive self-service applications is the fundamental building block to gaining the necessary adoption that delivers business value. If your users do not use the applications you deliver, you will not reap the benefits of self-service.

Earlier versions of SAP self-service technology were fairly difficult to enhance. You could make enhancements in the SAP development environment for most pages and publish to Internet Transaction Servers (ITS) for testing and production, but this was only part of the equation. Some of the framework files and other components were not available in the SAP development environment and had to be changed directly on the server, making it difficult and expensive to maintain.

With the latest versions of self-service, the SAP system has delivered a robust platform for developing applications and enhancing existing Employee Self-Service (ESS) and Manager Self-Service (MSS) applications. In this chapter we will discuss the various components involved in getting access to, enhancing, building, and deploying applications into production.

10.1   Terminology

Before we get started, let's review some of the concepts and terminology that have been introduced with the new versions of SAP software and Web Dynpro development. It is helpful to understand these terms as you start to learn about the new technology.

▶ **Product:** An application that you can deliver to an end user or an existing product provided by a vendor.

▶ **Development Component (DC):** A DC represents a software unit you develop and is always contained within a Software Component (SC). A DC contains the source code that you develop for the unit of software and also maintains relationships with other DCs and the associated metadata.

▶ **Software Component (SC):** SC is an installable application that combines development components and can be reused in products. The SCs have references to their dependencies, which includes other SCs.

▶ **Component Model:** Software projects are divided into components allowing you to organize them into reusable units. The component model is the underlying technology that allows components to interact and consists of SCs and DCs.

▶ **Design Time Repository (DTR):** The DTR serves as a source code similar to concurrent Versions System (CVS). The DTR is integrated into the SAP NetWeaver Development Studio and gives developers the ability to collaborate during development cycles by providing version control, concurrent development by multiple developers, and release processes.

▶ **Central Build Services (CBS):** The CBS allows development teams and build masters to centrally build the product. The CBS checks to see if all of the requirements of the components are met (dependencies, shared resources, etc.) and then creates all of the runtime objects. The CBS provides a smart build process that builds the dependent development components incrementally and synchronizes the runtime objects as a central build process.

▶ **Change Management Service (CMS):** The CMS allows you to configure your environment to manage the release process.

▶ **Track:** A track is an abstraction that allows you to segregate a set of source code and control what changes and when it gets pushed to other environments, such as consolidation or production. You define and label a track and then you import or develop source code into it.

▶ **NetWeaver Development Studio (NWDS):** NWDS is the Integrated Development environment (IDE) for developing JAVA-based applications.

These are just a few of the new terms that are used within the SAP NetWeaver development infrastructure. The learning curve can sometimes be steep, but most development teams relate to these concepts and developing applications using NWDI in a remarkably short timeframe.

10.2 Supporting Enhancements to Standard Applications

It is important to start with supporting your enhancements prior to setting up your environment so that you can get a better understanding of the reasons why setting up multiple tracks and processes are necessary.

In current SAP ERP Central Component (ECC) development, developers are able to make a copy of the source programs in the customer space (as denoted by renaming the program with the Z prefix). Once the copy is made, the program can be enhanced and maintained separately. This process is very reliable and cost effective until it is time to upgrade, and then each program in the customer space that has been enhanced has to be reviewed and tested to make sure it still works.

It is no different for self-service applications designed using Web Dynpro technology. The source code is delivered to companies as software components that can be imported into the CMS, making them available for enhancement.

The current support of the enhanced source code requires that the environment be set up in a specific way. It is very important to set up your environment so that future SAP software support packs can be applied and compared to the enhanced source code for conflicts.

The initial setup requires that you create two tracks and that the latest self-service software components and support packs be imported into both. This will give you two identical environments to work from. Figure 10.1 shows the initial state of your environment with the creation of two tracks.

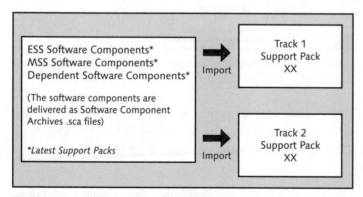

Figure 10.1 Initial State of Your Landscape

Once you have created the two tracks, you will use one of the tracks (Track 1) to make all your enhancements, leaving Track 2 to represent your starting point. With two tracks available, you can use the compare tool (Web Dynpro Diff Tool) to evaluate the changes that you made from the base software components.

You need to go through the upgrade process once a new support pack is released by SAP software and it is determined that it needs to be applied to your environment. The support pack contains needed enhancements and bug fixes and you will want to identify and merge your changes into the new version.

To apply the new support package, you need to download the file package from SAP software, create a new track, and import the latest support package into the newly created track. At this point you will have three tracks as shown in Figure 10.2.

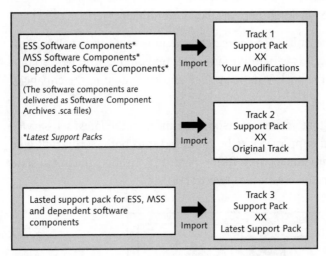

Figure 10.2 The State of Your Environment After Making Enhancements and Importing the Latest Support Pack

Once you have imported the last support pack, you are ready to start comparing the tracks to determine how and what needs to be merged so that you can create a new merged track that will include the updates from the SAP support pack and your enhancements.

The process to create a merged track requires that you compare your track (Track 1) that contains modifications to the original track (Track 2) so that you can determine what has been modified. You will also make the same comparison between the tracks containing the new support pack and determine what has been modified and how it will impact your applications. After determining the modifications that need to be merged, you re-create your modifications into a new track.

Figure 10.3 shows the process of comparing the tracks and creating a new track.

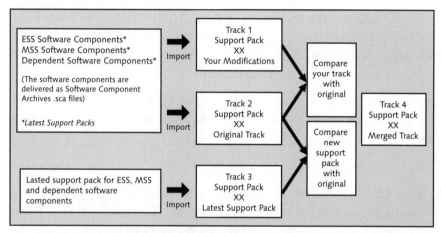

Figure 10.3 The State of Your Environment After Completing the Merged Track That Contains Your Enhancements and the Latest Support Packs

Once you have isolated and merged all of the changes into your merged track you can start to move your software components into the consolidation environment for integration testing. Your Quality Assurance (QA) team will need to confirm that the previous enhancements are working as designed and that the latest support package has not introduced new issues or unwanted functionality.

Upon the successful completion of testing, you discard the original track containing your modifications and your merged track will be copied to your original track. This will leave you with your merged code in your new original track and the latest code in your track containing your modifications. You can continue to work on the track for modifications until you need to repeat the process to support a future support package.

10.3 Setting Up the Environment

As described in the previous section, you need to create an environment that is suitable for making the necessary configuration and enhancements. The following process describes what you need to complete prior to the start of any development. Before starting to configure your system, please refer to SAP Note 872892 and related notes.

10.3.1 Define a Domain

You need to create a domain and a track in the CMS. By creating the domain and the track, you define the transport environment that your applications will follow to be released to production. Typically, you will have your development, consolidation, test (QA) environment, and production.

Configuring your system is accomplished via web applications installed on the NWDI server. To gain access to these tools, open a browser and input the following address:

http://<your server hostname>:5<instance number>00/devinf

The browser will ask you to log in. You can use the admin user that you have created for managing your environment. If you have not completed this step, please review the post installation procedures for your NWDI environment.

After logging in, you will see options to the various applications shown in Figure 10.4.

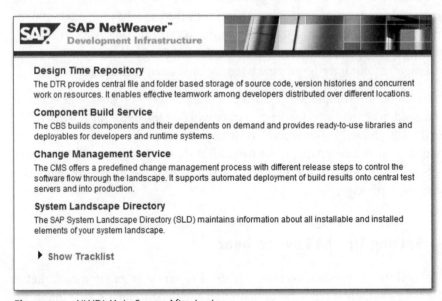

Figure 10.4 NWDI Main Screen After Login

Select the CMS and log in if prompted. Once you have logged into the CMS, you can select the Landscape Configurator, which will enable you to create a domain (see Figure 10.5).

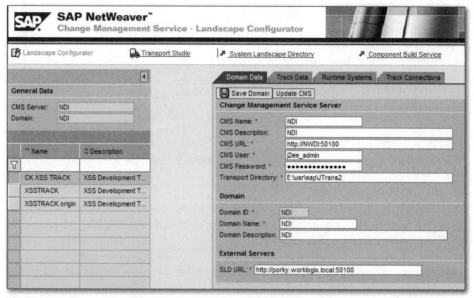

Figure 10.5 Screen After Selecting the Landscape Configurator and the Domain Data Tab

To understand what is needed to complete the fields, you can refer to the following SAP online documentation:

http://help.sap.com/saphelp_nw04/helpdata/en/b9/086b4066d9bf49e10000000a155 0b0/frameset.htm

10.3.2 Create a New Track

As discussed in Section 10.2, you need to create a track to hold your development. To create a track, navigate to the Track Data tab and complete the information as shown in Figure 10.6. Your DTR and CBS will need to be specifc to your environment.

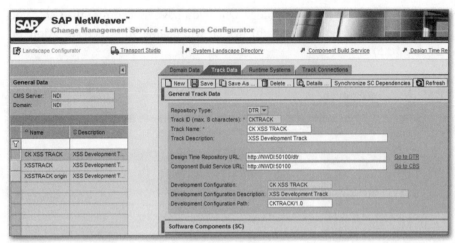

Figure 10.6 Creating the Track

Table 10.1 lists the specific values needed to create a track. Substitute your values to create your track, keeping in mind that the name of your track must be meaningful so that its purpose is clear.

Track Data	Value
Repository Type	DTR
Track ID	Unique ID for your track
Track Name	Name your track
Track Description	Track for Software Component Technology
DTR URL	http://<host name>:<port number>/dtr Replace <host name> and <port number> with the host name and port of the Java 2 Enterprise Edition (J2EE) Engine on which the DTR is installed.
CBS URL	http://<host name>:<port> Replace <host name> and <port number> with the host name and port of the J2EE Engine on which the CBS is installed.
Development Configuration	This value is copied from the track name and cannot be modified here.
Development Configuration Description	This value is a copy of the track description and cannot be changed here.
Development Configuration Path	Your TrackID/1.0

Table 10.1

10.3.3 Add Software Components to Track

We need to add the software components that will be maintained in this track. You add software components in the section below the General Track Data that was completed earlier. You will see a Software components section as shown in Figure 10.7.

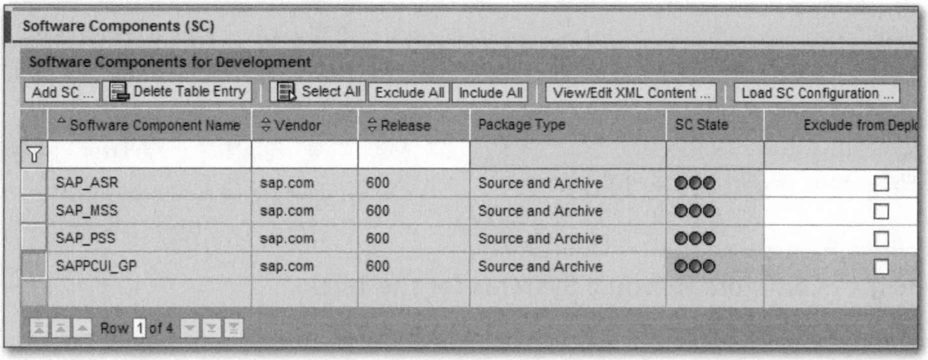

Software Components (SC)					
Software Components for Development					
Add SC ... Delete Table Entry Select All Exclude All Include All View/Edit XML Content ... Load SC Configuration ...					
⌃ Software Component Name	⇕ Vendor	⇕ Release	Package Type	SC State	Exclude from Depl
▽					
SAP_ASR	sap.com	600	Source and Archive	●●●	☐
SAP_MSS	sap.com	600	Source and Archive	●●●	☐
SAP_PSS	sap.com	600	Source and Archive	●●●	☐
SAPPCUI_GP	sap.com	600	Source and Archive	●●●	☐
Row 1 of 4					

Figure 10.7 Software Components Section Below General Track Data

To add your software components, you need to select the Add SC... button, which will give you a pop-up window with all of the available software components. You can filter to find the components, select them, and hit the Add button. Figure 10.8 shows the list being filtered by SAP_ESS and the software component selected.

Add Software Component					
✓ Add ✖ Close Select All Deselect All **General Package Type** Source and Archive ▼					
⌃ Name	⇕ Vendor	⇕ Release	⇕ Caption	⇕ Description	Package Type
▽ SAP_ESS					
SAP_ESS	sap.com	100	SAP ESS 100	SAP ESS 100	Source and Archive ▼
SAP_ESS	sap.com	600	SAP ESS 600	SAP ESS 600 (Employee Self Services)	Source and Archive ▼

Figure 10.8 The Added Software Components Pop Up with SAP_ESS Filtered From the List

You want to add SAP_MSS for MSS applications and SAP_ESS for ESS applications depending on what you want to use the track for.

Below the Software Component section is the Required Software Components. As you add software components, you will notice that the system automatically determines the dependencies and adds them to that section. Figure 10.9 shows the required components section with the dependencies listed.

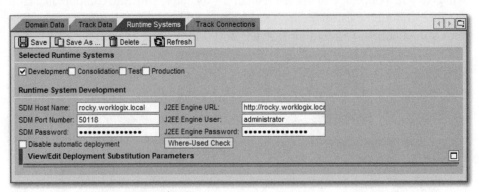

Required Software Components				
Software Component Name	Vendor	Release	SC State	Exclude from Deployment
BASELIBS	sap.com	7.00	⊙⊙⊙	☐
BASETABLES	sap.com	7.00	⊙⊙⊙	☐
CAF-UM	sap.com	7.00	⊙⊙⊙	☐
EC-ECLI-RE	sap.com	7.00	⊙⊙⊙	☐
EC-ECLIPSE	sap.com	7.00	⊙⊙⊙	☐

Figure 10.9 Required Software Components

10.3.4 Configure Runtime Systems for the Track

Once you have added the software components, you need to configure the runtime systems. You want to select the appropriate runtime systems that the track will be applicable to. For most tracks, you select all of the environments. Figure 10.10 shows the tab for configuring runtime systems.

Figure 10.10 Runtime Systems Tab

At this point, you can hit Save and you should get a message saying that the track was created successfully.

10.3.5 Import Software Components Into the Track

Once you have created your track, you can import the archives (source code) into your system.

Download Archives from SAP Software

The archives needed for ESS and MSS can be found on the SAP Service Marketplace. You can get to the marketplace via *http://service.sap.com/patches.*

Most systems use Solution Manager to find and download version-specific software from the SAP system. Please check with your basis administrator on what the best source for this software is.

Once you have downloaded the archive files (.sca software component archives), you will need to place them into your inbox folder on the CMS server. The location of the inbox will correspond to the domain settings that we made in Section 10.3.1.

You will need to download and place the following files into your inbox directory:

▶ SAP_JTECHS.sca

▶ SAP_BUILDT.sca

▶ SAP-JEE.sca

▶ SAPPCUI_GP.sca

▶ SAP_ESS.sca

▶ SAP_MSS.sca

The files may differ from the ones listed here because they will contain a string of numbers denoting the version number, etc.

Check-In and Import Archives Into the Development System

Once you have added the files to the CMS inbox, they will be available in the transport studio for check-in and importing into the development system.

Figure 10.11 shows the archives that are available for check-in. Select each one of the archives and hit the Check-in button to start the check-in process.

File Name	Component	Release	SP Number	PatchName	Version
EPPSERV15_0-10003474.SCA	sap.com_EP-PSERV	7.00	15	appl645VRcurU160208	SAP AG.20080218050539
EPBC15_0-10003473.SCA	sap.com_EPBC	7.00	15	appl645VRcurU160208	SAP AG.20080218050410
EPBC215_0-10003489.SCA	sap.com_EPBC2	7.00	15	appl645VRcurU260208	SAP AG.20080227064850
SAPEU15_0-10003026.SCA	sap.com_SAP-EU	7.00	15	APL70VAL.02151252	MAIN_APL70VAL_C.20080218055857
SAPJEE15_0-10003469.SCA	sap.com_SAP-JEE	7.00	15	645_VAL_REL.080216	SAP AG.20080216073456
SAPBUILDT15_0-10003479.SCA	sap.com_SAP_BUILDT	7.00	15	bpscore645VRcurU1602	SAP AG.20080216005300
SAPJTECHS15_0-10003467.SCA	sap.com_SAP_JTECHS	7.00	15	645_VAL_REL.080216	SAP AG.20080216073957
SAPMSS13_0-20000503.SCA	sap.com_SAP_MSS	600	13	ERP05VAL.05161019	MAIN_ERP05VAL_C.20080516101945
SAPPCUIGP13_0-20001215.SCA	sap.com_SAPPCUI_GP	600	13	ERP05VAL.05161019	MAIN_ERP05VAL_C.20080516101947

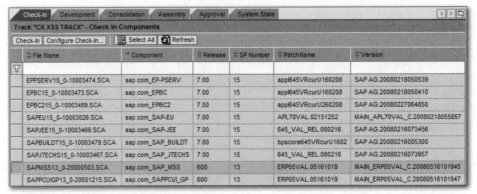

Figure 10.11 Archives Available for Check-in

Once the archives are checked in you will be able to import them into your environment. To import the archives, select the Development tab and you will see each archive that is waiting to be imported. The State column shows the current status. Figure 10.12 shows the status of an archive waiting to be imported.

Processed at (GMT)	Component	Label	Owner	State
2005/03/02 15:38:54	sap.com_SAP-JEE	6.40 Level 12 Update NIGHTBUILD.20050218	Make	Waiting for import

Figure 10.12 Archive Waiting to be Imported

Import each of the archives and track their status until they are all imported successfully. This may take several hours if you try to import all of the archives at once. So you may want to consider doing one at a time to determine how long they take to import into your system.

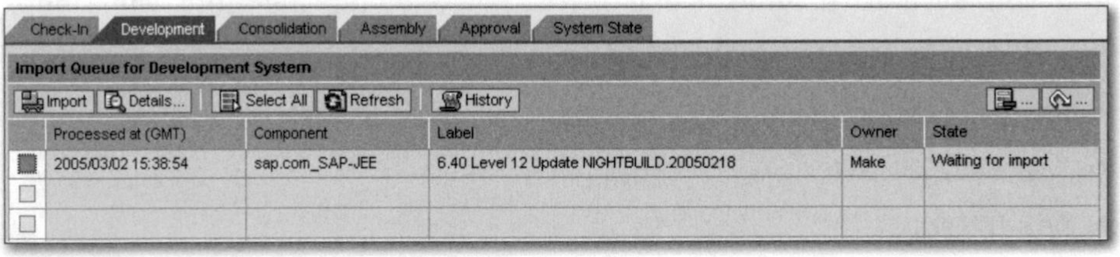

10.3.6 Importing the Development Configuration

Now that the servers are configured and the software components have been checked in, you can start to prepare your development environment. You will want to start your SAP NetWeaver Developer Studio and import an existing development configuration.

Here is the process for establishing a connection to your server and importing the development configuration:

- From the NWDS menu, choose the path: Window • Preferences • Development Infrastructure

- Choose the Landscape directory and specify the path to your System Landscape Directory (SLD) in the following format: *http://<hostname>:<port>*

- Ping the server to see if you can establish a connection

- Open the Development Infrastructure perspective in the IDE

- Log in to NWDI

- Choose the New Development Configuration icon

- Choose from where you want to import the development configuration (you will see a dialog box)

- Select the configuration to import and complete the import

You are now ready to start enhancing your self-service applications.

10.4 Summary

Building and delivering intuitive self-service applications is fundamental to user adoption and higher levels of productivity for your organization. Being able to support the applications and enhancements in a cost-effective manner determines if the productivity gains and solutions are sustainable.

The SAP system has expanded its already powerful software development platform by introducing a robust set of tools along with Web Dynpro technology. The platform enables you to quickly develop applications that leverage SAP ECC and integrate into your SAP NetWeaver Portal. Using this platform, the SAP system provides access to ESS and MSS applications, allowing you to enhance them to meet your business requirements and subsequently support those applications as SAP software releases updates.

Self-service processes and technologies enable companies to move from a business unit/geography basis to a highly standardized central operation that reduces costs, increases operational efficiency, and improves the quality of Human Resource (HR) services. In this chapter we will review a case study about a company in which a major HR transformation project was launched to help the company transform HR into an organization that would deliver consistent and efficient HR services that were defined globally and executed locally.

11 Self-Service Case Study

Companies continue to find unique ways to solve complex business challenges, especially in the area of self-service. Self-service solutions empower users to take control of the process and conveniently, efficiently, and cost effectively complete a business transaction. In this chapter, we will study a large pharmaceutical company that transformed the way it does business and improved and strengthened its culture while adding more money to the bottom line. The company employs 40,000 people in over 30 countries around the world.

The project and transformation of HR were very large multiyear initiatives. In this case study, we will look at the overall project, but we will focus specifically on the adoption and rollout of the self-service technology.

11.1 Business Landscape

In the mid-nineties, major pharmaceutical companies realized and prepared for a change in their business models. They had to look forward and change the way they did business because many of the pipelines for blockbuster drugs had become smaller and the patents on existing drugs were due to expire. This created an awakening for many pharmaceutical companies as they started to see market share eroding to generic drug makers that prayed on those patents that were expiring and had started to sell to a more cost-conscience public via new channels, such as the Internet. At the same time, major pharmaceutical companies sought a more aggressive global expansion to both increase sales and to find new talented researchers that could find the next big blockbuster drug.

With this focus in mind, pharmaceutical companies focused on the emergence of biotech companies and also started to look at their network of sales people as a competitive advantage. At the same time, they focused inward on cost-cutting measures that could help them survive in a more competitive landscape.

Every major part of the company was being examined to determine what cost savings could be realized. HR was also evaluated, and it was determined that the level of service and competitive advantage that was derived from the function was not highly correlated to the high costs that it carried.

The company had a history of mergers and acquisitions as well as organic growth that allowed it to expand globally. This also left the company with inefficient and high-cost legacy processes and the technologies that delivered them.

After lengthy reviews and analysis, it was determined that the organization was not in a good position for the future and faced the following key issues:

- ▸ HR was a paper-intensive and locally focused organization
- ▸ Most processes were inefficient and required too many approvals
- ▸ Processes were inconsistent accross business units resulting in inconsistent execution
- ▸ Policies were not effective and often not widely communicated
- ▸ HR could not accurately determine headcount locally or globally
- ▸ HR had become overly administrative dealing with simple transactions and was less consultative with their clients
- ▸ HR had become decentralized, growing too large with too many HR professionals for the amount of employees that each HR professional served
- ▸ HR was unable to leverage existing data to provide strategic value to the organization

The future had to be aggressively defined. With that in mind, a major HR transformation project was launched that would help the company transform HR into an organization that would deliver consistent and efficient HR services that were defined globally and executed locally.

11.2   Business Challenges

Undertaking an HR transformation project that would implement a global service delivery model and reduce the size of HR at the end was not something that could be carried out in a short period of time. The company had aging systems, complex paper processes that were not consistent across the organization, and did not have the ability and the resources to help define the future.

The business had also grown into a decentralized model, so creating governance committees that could come to agreement and enforce change was nearly impossible.

Furthermore, it was difficult to convince key stakeholders outside of HR that the HR organization could become a strategic partner and that the changes in the service delivery would push administrative work back into the enterprise, but in a way that was both intuitive and efficient.

Another challenge that became evident early on in the project was the fact that the objective of downsizing HR became evident and many of the employees in the HR organization and HR field started to disengage, and in some cases leave the company. This posed a serious risk to the project and to the overall objectives of transforming the HR organization.

11.3   Transformation Objectives

The company adopted self-service as the main strategy to achieve a higher level of efficiency and as a key initiative in the overall transformation of HR. Self-service enabled the transformation to take place by allowing for an improved service delivery model.

The business was undergoing a change and HR needed to provide services in ways that made it easy for the business to execute. Controls around hiring, transferring, and third-party resources had to become tighter and be managed aggressively. HR had become decentralized in how it delivered services, creating many silos that replicated parts of the organization causing redundancy and higher costs.

The HR organization was determined to right size the organization by providing HR generalists tools and processes that allowed them to handle a larger span of control. Additionally, the tools and analytics provided new functionality empowering HR with data that could help shape the organization and partner with the business to make key decisions.

Processes had to move away from paper and become standard across the globe. Process efficiency needed to be improved by removing unnecessary handoffs and reducing approvals to one-up managers, for example. Policies had to be defined globally and adapted locally to allow for the application of policies to be consistently applied.

Figure 11.1 shows the transformation objectives for the HR functions associated with the project.

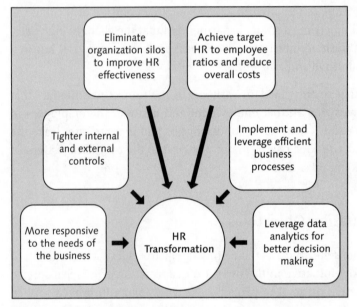

Figure 11.1 HR Transformation Objectives

Achieving the transformation objectives would provide HR and the organization with streamlined processes and a simplified, consistent, and more efficient organization that operated cost effectively and provided strategic value to the business.

11.4 Project Scope for Self-Service

The scope for self-service was determined by looking at various statistics. During the creation of the business case, a summary of all of the transactions that

HR completed on behalf of employees and managers was collected and evaluated to determine which transactions would yield the greatest benefits. Based on the transaction volumes and potential return on investment through direct cost savings or efficiency gains, specific self-service components were selected as part of the initial phase.

11.4.1 Employee Self-Service (ESS) Scope

ESS transactions were logically grouped into service categories, such as Personal Information, Pay and Taxes, Total Rewards, Benefits, Time Management, Life Events, and Career Planning. Grouping the transactions and delivering them to employees via the portal provided for an intuitive experience and simplified adoption. Figure 11.2 shows the detailed scope of ESS.

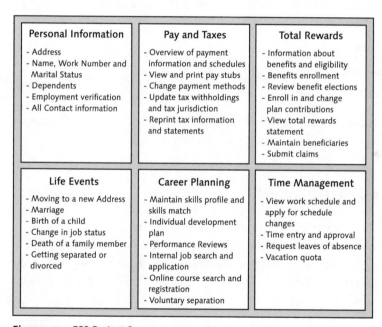

Personal Information
- Address
- Name, Work Number and Marital Status
- Dependents
- Employment verification
- All Contact information

Pay and Taxes
- Overview of payment information and schedules
- View and print pay stubs
- Change payment methods
- Update tax withholdings and tax jurisdiction
- Reprint tax information and statements

Total Rewards
- Information about benefits and eligibility
- Benefits enrollment
- Review benefit elections
- Enroll in and change plan contributions
- View total rewards statement
- Maintain beneficiaries
- Submit claims

Life Events
- Moving to a new Address
- Marriage
- Birth of a child
- Change in job status
- Death of a family member
- Getting separated or divorced

Career Planning
- Maintain skills profile and skills match
- Individual development plan
- Performance Reviews
- Internal job search and application
- Online course search and registration
- Voluntary separation

Time Management
- View work schedule and apply for schedule changes
- Time entry and approval
- Request leaves of absence
- Vacation quota

Figure 11.2 ESS Project Scope

11.4.2 Manager Self-Service (MSS) Scope

Manager Self-Service posed a new set of challenges though, because managers perceived that the transactions would add more work and shift administrative work from HR to themselves. After reviewing which processes would benefit from extending them to managers, each individual process was reengineered to remove unnecessary steps, approvals, and limit the data needed to complete the transaction.

The reengineering of the transactions and approval steps allowed for the necessary process improvements and standardization that enabled the successful adoption of MSS. The following transactions were selected for the initial phase. Each could be initiated by the manager via the portal:

▸ Transfers, promotions, demotions, and other position/job changes

▸ Separation requests (voluntary and involuntary)

▸ Special payment requests, such as spot bonuses

▸ Salary and compensation adjustments (off-cycle and administration of annual compensation changes)

▸ New hire requisitions

▸ Time correction and approval

▸ Management of work schedules

Along with the transactions, managers could also view up-to-date information about their employees and view key data about their organization.

11.5 Service Delivery Model

As we discussed in Chapter 2, "Self-Service Overview," the HR service delivery model describes how the HR organization delivers services to its customers, which include employees, managers, executives within the organization as well as candidates seeking to join the company. In some organizations, it also includes retirees if they have not outsourced that service.

Each approach for service delivery has its tradeoffs. Many companies have decentralized models that they have grown into over the years but suffer from higher costs and inconsistent service levels. Business units prefer decentralized service models because they are more responsive and closer to the business.

While some companies have completed HR transformations, they may still be in between service delivery models as the company caters to various business units that are important to the company's growth. Figure 11.3 shows the characteristics common to a specific service delivery model and the underlying tradeoffs.

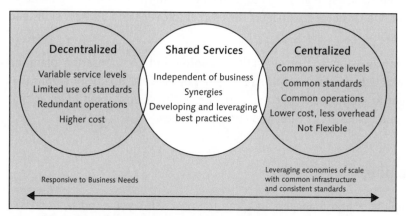

Figure 11.3   Characteristics of Service Delivery Models

The goal of the transformation project was to optimize the service delivery model by centralizing the function to regional service centers and leverage key technologies to streamline the processes. To accomplish this objective, the company radically shifted from a decentralized approach to an internally staffed central-service center located regionally. In this model, corporate and field HR were consolidated and focused on providing key HR services and HR strategy.

The regional employee shared-service centers were created to support the new changes and achieve better service levels while reducing HR staff. The service centers were now staffed with specialists for tier 1, 2, and 3, which could answer questions from employees and managers as well as open cases that needed to be escalated.

The service delivery model included tier 0 due to the adoption of self-service, which shifted over 70% of the transactions to the employees and managers, allowing for more accurate data and timely completion of transactions.

11.6   Role of the HR Generalist

With the HR transformation taking hold, the role of the HR generalist had to be adapted to realize the benefits outlined in the business case.

HR generalists focused more on employee relations and change management while assisting managers with staffing strategies and organizational planning. Additionally, HR generalists assisted all levels of management in the performance management process, which helped managers develop employees and address skills and resource gaps.

HR generalists also focused on diversity planning and compensation planning strategies with a focus on retention. HR generalists were finally in a role that enabled them to strategically partner with the business and assist in areas that directly affect revenue generation and customer issues.

11.7   Training

Training employees and managers to adopt the new self-service transactions was accomplished using several methods. Along with online materials, employees and managers were able to attend live online guided training sessions hosted by HR. Employees and managers could log in to web meeting sessions held at defined times and experience a guided tour of the portal along with an in-depth discussion of what changed and why.

Managers were also provided a "manager kit" that had all of the information about the new processes and contact information to resources that could provide assistance with any questions.

11.8   Results

In the first full year, the company realized approximately $15 million in cost savings associated to the adoption of self-service. The transformation of HR was completed with the employee and manager contact centers that now accounted for 70% less administrative transactions and enabled the company to reduce HR resources by over 30%.

The complete transformation of HR was completed after approximately three years, however, many of the self-service transactions yielded gains in process efficiency as well as a reduction in costs as soon as they were introduced.

11.9 Critical Success Factors

To achieve dramatic results with the introduction of self-service technologies in the context of a larger transformation project, it is important to have the support of every business unit leader globally and the support of senior leadership. Without the necessary support, many of the key decisions will not be made in a timely manner and adoption will be poor resulting in project delays, unrealized business objectives, and lost opportunity.

Additional critical success factors include:

▶ Creation of a global governance committee that meets frequently and has the authority to make decisions about processes, policies, timelines, and risks

▶ The right team of people with extended team members participating from every country

▶ A clear project charter with a defined scope and guiding principles for the delivery of HR services

▶ Provide training in SAP software technogies for the teams and dedicated training for employeess and managers prior to the launch of new applications and processes

11.10 Summary

The consolidation of technologies and HR systems into one centrally managed Enterprise Resource Planning (ERP) enabled a solid platform for implementing self-service process. With key technology in place and process improvement completed, the transformation project yielded tremendous results at the pharmaceutical company. More important, HR was now positioned to tackle key organizational issues, such as employee retention and recruiting, that would provide the company strategic benefits.

The company was able to focus on key business model changes and leverage HR as a strategic partner. HR had reduced its delivery costs, implemented consistent controls, and improved the quality of its services across the organization. Although its services are not necessarily core to the business, HR was able to focus on the critical aspects that aided the company strategically and gave it a competitive advantage.

A transformation such as this could not have been accomplished without the direct involvement of key business units. The assignment and dedication of the right resources was critical. Without the right people focused on this effort, the business case would have never been realized.

In the next chapter, we share some additional lessons learned that we have gathered while implementing SAP ESS and MSS functionality.

If you approach things the way you have always approached them, you will always end up with the same results.

12 Lessons Learned

This chapter presents a summary of the lessons learned from various companies that have implemented Employee Self-Service (ESS) and Manager Self-Service (MSS), either independently or as part of a larger SAP HCM implementation. We selected lessons learned that have applied across implementations. Although not all project circumstances are the same, we can draw many parallels from one implementation to the next.

We have organized the lessons learned by topic. We wanted to cover both system and non-system aspects of a self-service implementation. The following topics are covered:

▶ ESS processes and applications

▶ MSS processes and applications

▶ Change management

▶ System implementation.

Each lesson learned is documented in a way that outlines the underlying issue or challenge as well as a recommendation on how the risk associated to that issue or challenge can be mitigated. You will need to judge how relevant the underlying issue is in your company and if the recommendation applies. There are many cases where only part of the issue or challenge may pertain to your project. We hope you glean whatever aspects are most relevant for your project to make it the most successful.

12.1 Self-Service Processes and Applications

Self-service applications and processes have been around for many years with both the processes and underlying technology evolving. Companies choose to implement the process differently but many of the core concepts and approaches remain the same. An effective self-service process relies on more than the implementation of a system; rather it needs a holistic mix of a rich system implementation, simple processes, change management, and intuitive user interfaces. We will first discuss the interplay between systems and process, and we will attempt to answer the question "What is the best way to deliver harmonized, end-to-end self-services while implementing best-practice processes, all in an intuitive, user-centric manner?"

12.1.1 ESS Processes and Applications

Our first topic focuses on ESS. Due to its expanded growth within most companies, lessons learned for ESS applications are particularly crucial for an effective self-service campaign and successful go-live.

Wrap Transactions and Content into Life and Career Events

Adoption of self-service applications is difficult when they are presented in an unstructured manner. Most implementations attempt to group applications into a navigation structure that makes sense to the employee or manager. The result is an intuitive navigation to applications.

However, most users will probably be trying to execute the transactions based on a life or career event that requires the execution of a series of transactions. An example of a life event is the birth of a child or marriage. Career event examples include a position transfer or going on an international assignment. Career events are sometimes referred to as work events.

After many usability studies, we have concluded that making the relevant transactions available under a life or career event delivers a better adoption and user experience for the employee and reduces calls to Human Resources (HR) or the service center. Investing the time up front in developing and vetting content appropriate for your ESS transactions will be well worth it. Your customers (your employees!) will expect nothing less.

Some clients have also found that additional process efficiencies can be gained if "process checklists" are used to highlight all of the related steps in a life or career event. Transactions associated to that event are grouped together in these logical steps (and often related with specific timeframes). The content that accompanies the transactions offers a flow of advice that traditional ESS cannot provide alone. The checklists should contain informational steps and be created from an employee's point of view. Checklists can be catered to specific users, such as employees, managers, and even HR Professionals.

The same life or career event may mean different things to different people. For example, an employee taking a leave of absence will necessitate actions by the employee (e.g., benefits and payroll choices/activities) that are different from the manager (e.g., potentially backfilling for the position or shifting work from others). Furthermore, there may be action needed from the HR side to assist the employee before and during their leave. This means three different checklists for the same life event.

Create an Area in the Portal Dedicated to ESS and Related Content

Most companies adopt the standard navigation imposed by the ESS and MSS roles (via the standard Homepage Framework covered in previous chapters). Although this navigation is fairly simple, it has its drawbacks when coupled with additional functionality presented in the portal. Some employees and managers have a difficult time with the standard portal's two-level navigation and how it is broken down.

After conducting usability studies on this topic with several clients, we found that you can dramatically improve the user experience if you subdivide the navigation into four or more categories. An example would be *Home*, *My Workplace*, *My Life and Career*, and *Explore*. Let's explain the breakdown and how it is frequently regarded as being more intuitive and user-friendly than the standard layout.

The home page, or "landing page," usually contains information that is relative to all users in the organization and can be tailored by taking into account geography, subsidiary, etc., and whether the user is an employee, manager, HR Professional, or even a vendor. The home page would exist on the first tab of the portal (perhaps called "Home"). It would be the place where you could broadcast certain finite, time-sensitive messages to a selected audience. For example, if your company is rallying managers to plan for their annual merit focal review, a message (appearing for managers only) could indicate that the planning window is open. Also, this message could include a link to the actual transaction for compensation planning. The more important and relevant the messaging is on the portal home page, the more likely users will get in the habit of checking for company messages there. Much like Internet users have repeatable habits (e.g., first checking their Gmail and then checking Yahoo! News, etc.), behaviors can also be shaped on your intranet portal by offering rich content that is relevant for their day-to-day operations.

A second tab, perhaps called "My Workplace," may contain information, links, and applications related to executing transactions within the enterprise. Users may find applications such as expense management, procurement, and company directories in this area of the portal. If the user is also a manager, they may have access to MSS transactions, such as personnel change requests, as well as information about the organization. Exposure to an organizational structure is often common for managers (and now employees as well), so as to raise awareness and provide transparency to management changes and organizational hierarchies. Many third-party tools are available in the marketplace to add on to the SAP software to provide more robust views of the organization.

The portal workflow inbox (i.e., the Universal Worklist) is functionality that would most likely live in this section of the portal. The trend now is to provide workflow actioning capability for all users of the portal and not just managers. This is because there are more and more approvals requiring employee involvement. For example, employees who are part of your company's performance management process may need access to their portal inbox to receive updates on the process or even to take action to move the performance management process forward.

We also discovered that providing the portal with a "My Workplace" section enabled a broader set of applications to be intuitively positioned in one convenient location, thereby limiting the amount of end-user training needed. The ultimate aim here is to provide portal users an experience that increases efficiencies and reduces questions. For example, managers should know how to navigate to the "My Workplace" tab to initiate performance evaluations for their direct reports. It wouldn't make much sense if this information was found in the "My Life and Career" tab.

The "My Life and Career" pages could be dedicated to information and applications that revolve around the employee's life and career. Employees would find opportunities to manage their personal information, enroll in benefits, request vacation time, and view their career development. You would typically put most ESS transactions under this umbrella, including any employee checklists you have implemented.

The "Explore" tab would be relevant for those whose companies have SAP Knowledge Management (KM) implemented or another mechanism to search for documents and content. Information on policies, procedures, and guidelines would be accessible quickly based on the user's search criteria. Providing robust search capability on a portal is now considered a necessary part of self-service, as online help and documentation are seen as critical components to an end user's portal experience. Collecting and organizing company documents — as well as keeping them current — is one of the more challenging exercises, especially with content that changes frequently. A sound content management strategy is paramount to keep your content fresh and your users happy. Rich content will always attract your users back to the portal.

Using the tabbed approach mentioned earlier creates a simple, yet powerful navigation structure that users can quickly understand at a glance. Anything related to work activities would be found under the "My Workplace" umbrella. Items related to employees' life events or careers would be found under "My Life and Career."

We have found that using this approach has increased adoption of the application and benefits the overall business case by having employees obtain information and manage data without calling a service center or related support function. Self-service as a delivery channel becomes more intuitive and widely accepted within the organization.

12.1.2 MSS Processes and Applications

Now let's focus on some lessons learned we have picked up while implementing MSS. Whether you are a large, multinational company or a small organization, we feel these same principles apply universally for a successful implementation.

Roll out MSS in Multiple Phases

Organizations that introduce MSS for the first time tackle the functionality in a variety of ways. Some companies first implement MSS by introducing functionality around a particular process, such as Performance Management or Compensation Management. This approach works well, as it often displaces existing functionality with an already-defined process. Introducing employee transactions and employee data via personnel change requests (PCRs) or HCM Processes and

Forms has not been as successful, especially when managers have not been accustomed to having the responsibility for initiating HR transactions online. You may encounter pushback and hear from managers that feel they are "doing HR's job." There may be a perception within the organization that MSS will add additional administrative work to the manager with little or no direct benefit. Although this is not the case, it can negatively impact the ease of implementation and the rate of adoption. It is important that proper change management is applied to address these important issues. Stakeholder management, including your most important stakeholders — managers — will be discussed later in the chapter when we cover change management.

One of the ways we have been able to overcome these issues is to plan MSS projects in (at least) two phases. The first phase targets the delivery of information about employees and the organization. This approach gives managers easy access to robust information (such as compensation and work history, career information, etc.) that has typically been hard to obtain without HR manager involvement. This approach engages and excites managers and gets them accustomed to using these tools online.

Once the first phase is completed and managers have adopted the portal and its offerings, you can launch a phase two, which might have more process-oriented transactions, such as Performance Management, Compensation Management, or PCRs/forms. Future phases can be built on the functionality of this second phase based on feedback from previous phases.

Using this approach will not only increase manager acceptance of the portal but will also decrease the learning curve by allowing managers to focus on subsets of functionality instead of overwhelming them with many self-service applications all at once.

Simplify Manager Transactions and Avoid Multiple Layers of Approval

A common issue we have encountered while designing and implementing self-service applications is the desire to "over engineer" a process, especially with regard to manager-initiated transactions for their employees. It is common to want to capture every possible variation of a transaction in order to improve productivity and deliver a more robust system; however, it often leads to a very complex process that managers and HR do not understand and that Information Technology (IT) cannot support effectively.

This same principle applies to workflow approvals. The unlimited capability of SAP software's workflow engine enables many designs to become overly complicated with multiple approval steps and notifications that often prove to actually reduce the effectiveness of the system and overall process. Also, it will almost certainly frustrate users and distract them from their daily activities. Having their inboxes inundated with emails from transactions spawning from SAP processes is a recipe for an irritable staff.

Let's first revisit the topic of PCR/forms. As a general rule, these forms should be limited to no more than two pages with many of the transactions only requiring one page. Transactions should have clear titles and be limited in scope to make them easy to understand and simple to complete (the new Adobe functionality goes a long way in providing that capability). If there are decisions to be made that are outside the knowledge of the manager, it may be best to move that work onto the appropriate subject matter expert. Having managers guess whether an employee move should be coded as a promotion or lateral could be outside their realm of HR knowledge. Educating managers on the process or driving the transaction to incorporate the subject matter expert in the workflow later in the process may be a better option, depending on your corporate philosophy.

Let's talk workflow — an often nebulous concept for many SAP software professionals. Although being one of the most robust functionalities within the software, workflow and its inherent approval processes should be designed with the utmost basic process in mind. Where possible, manager transactions needing approval should have a flow consisting of one-up manager approval and an escalation path to the next level after three to five days of inaction. These "escalation procedures" should be included in your workflow rules through the use of SAP software's "deadline monitoring" concept. Deadline monitoring and its Best Practice were discussed in Chapter 8, "Advanced Concepts in Employee and Manager Self-Service."

Exception cases should be examined and dealt with offline. Designing approval processes with these exception cases in mind could be dangerous and cost-prohibitive. Try to apply the "80/20" rule to your online workflow processes. In many organizations, these exceptions are the first to change from year to year, so baking them into your approval process may be a waste of effort.

We are not suggesting that complex approval processes cannot be handled by the SAP software. However, approval processes that are more complex should be designed with care and monitored for impacts to productivity. Complex routing rules based on relationships established in the SAP software are achievable and sometimes necessary, but should be architected with a future state in mind. You can do some amazing things with workflow, but the question you should ask yourself is: What is the business need for the workflow's complexity and are there ways to simplify the process such that the technology can more effectively support the business requirement?

Determine if Delegation Is Required and Implement a Solution That Is Both Functional and Intuitive

A common requirement requested in many MSS implementations is the ability to delegate transactional or approval authority to a peer or administrative assistant. In the absence of this functionality, managers often give administrative assistants or peers their own portal user name and password so that they can login and act on their behalf. These bad habits endanger the security of the system and introduce huge liabilities for data leakage — particularly with sensitive employee information, such as personally identifiable information (PII). Exposing PII, such as employees' national identification, address, and credit card data can lead to grave consequences. It is critical to determine if this is an issue in your organization and provide an intuitive solution that safeguards the system.

Providing delegation capability within the SAP environment is not a trivial task but it is feasible to implement. We have implemented delegation functionality many times over on the SAP Portal and believe it is a viable and important option to offer the organization. Discussion on delivering delegation functionality was covered in Chapter 8, but it is worth summarizing again.

Steps for implementing delegation in your system are listed here:

▶ A delegate portal role and a backend SAP role need to be implemented to enable managers and non-managers (such as administrative assistants) to have delegation-relevant access to MSS functionality. Both roles will be needed in order to provide delegate functionality on the SAP Portal.

▶ Custom relationships using SAP Organizational Management (OM) objects need to be created in order to manage delegation of responsibilities from a transaction perspective. Like all OM objects and relationships, the effective dates of the relationships can limit the duration of the delegate relationship.

▶ Optionally, you can provide a workflow that enables the delegate to approve the responsibility. The workflow process provides a robust audit trail. The workflow will allow the delegate to approve the request in the portal's universal worklist as well as inform the manager via an email once the responsibility has been accepted.

▶ Automate the assignment of the required SAP roles once the delegate has approved the request. A custom program can be created that can assign the appropriate roles to the delegate for the period of time that the delegation relationship is required.

The preceding steps provide a quick snapshot of the system readiness procedures needed to deliver delegation functionality on the portal. However, the other half of the equation is organizational readiness. It is important to educate your workforce about what delegation is and what it isn't. Setting expectations and concrete business rules around delegation practices is as important as a sound technical solution.

12.2 Change Management

Perhaps the most important element of a successful self-service project, organizational readiness is typically talked about a lot but rarely executed effectively. In our eyes, change management is seen as a "game-changer" — those projects without a dedicated change management team frequently fail to execute to their fullest potential. When adoption suffers, the self-service platform is at risk. Senior leaders — some of whom experienced the tool firsthand — may rethink their service delivery approach. This is not meant to scare you, but rather underscore the importance of having dedicated, full-time resources on the project that can help you transform the organization to think about service delivery from a new perspective.

12.2.1 Adoption and Compliance

One of the key steps in change management is to ensure adoption across the business, and then to test that the systems are working as planned.

Conduct Usability Labs as Early as Possible with a Representative Set of Users

Having the best user experience possible is one of the most important components of a successful project. Providing end users with an intuitive flow, "look-and-feel," and layout within self-service applications enables efficiencies within the service delivery, unparalleled elsewhere. Avoiding experiences that cause confusion and frustration for your users will go a long way in securing self-service as a viable and effective means of delivery in the future.

During the realization phase of the project, we suggest that you find a point when your self-service applications are working as expected (or as close to as expected). Then, create a user group that can test the application(s). Conduct individual sessions where you provide the user with a scenario and ask them to complete that part of the process. Do not provide them too much instruction on how to complete the transaction. Observe where they get stuck. If the user is at a dead end and can no longer navigate, ask them to explain what did not make sense on the screen and what they would expect in order to continue.

Once all of the users have completed the usability lab, collect the results and isolate the common issues. It is best to address these issues before rolling out the process in order to gain the maximum acceptance and adoption of the new functionality. Depending on the quantity of the changes, you may need to get creative with timelines considering where you are in the build or testing of the application.

You may be surprised at how consistent the responses are. The challenge will be deciding which changes can be (or should be) incorporated given the timeframe of the project. In some cases, changes that are rejected or delayed until a later phase can, at minimum, be incorporated into the training materials.

Communicate Terms That May Not Be Evident To the Employees and Managers

A common challenge that is encountered when rolling out self-service information and transactions is the language that the underlying system imposes. Many of us have heard of "SAPanese" and other cute terms to describe the language and semantics used within the SAP system and portal. It is common for users to not be familiar with the new terminology.

Many companies roll out self-service and then spend time answering questions about the data that is presented. For example, managers may not understand what personnel area means. Additionally, if this is the first venture into self-service for your organization, managers and employees may not be familiar with concepts such as organizational units, positions, and jobs or how they interrelate.

One approach to mitigate the impact is to introduce the unfamiliar terminology with a frequently asked questions (FAQ) document that is readily accessible on the portal for users to easily access during the transaction. Educating users on new terminology helps to remove the apprehension associated with the new technology or products you are implementing.

Another more costly approach is to do some level of translation for the manager on the actual portal screens. Labels within iViews could be updated to reflect the business-appropriate term for your company. For example, the term "Position Title" could be re-labeled "Job Title" to properly reflect the "business card" title of the employee. "Pay scale group" could be changed to read "Salary Grade." These are just a few examples, but as you can see, attempting to implement these changes portal-wide comes with its challenges, especially if keeping to standard SAP software is desired. In some cases, this verbiage can be changed via standard configuration but, at other times, an enhancement to the application is needed. The decision on whether to make these changes is an informed decision from the appropriate HR and IT stakeholders.

12.2.2 Communication

Obviously effective communication will be essential for a successful adoption, so you want to be sure to establish a communication plan that is efficient and straightforward.

Limit the Number of Automated Emails Generated From the System

Automated, system-generated communication can sound like a great idea during blueprinting, but we advise that email automation be kept to a minimum in your self-service design. Emails work well to kick-off a process, but we have found that they can quickly become overwhelming if they are used to notify employees and managers too often. Frequently, these emails become ignored and deleted by the recipient.

As discussed before, SAP software's workflow functionality can be leveraged for approval processes and notifications. Some of these notifications are portal based.

In other words, out-of-the-box notifications will come to the user's inbox on the portal and not to their corporate email (Outlook, Lotus Notes, etc.). Companies have been reluctant to drive notification to the portal, because the concern is that users won't check their portal inbox as frequently as their corporate email (clearly a valid statement). However, this doesn't necessarily warrant a flux of processes that introduce additional emails to the corporate email as employees and managers today are already flooded with unread emails. Portal inbox notifications should be considered and used whenever it makes good business sense. Over time, behaviors will change and employees and managers will start checking their portal inbox if they realize there is value in doing so. This change does not happen overnight, but with the right campaign and communication, users will start to adopt the portal as an information cockpit.

Another alternative is to manage certain notifications centrally from HR. In some companies, this is not a change. Emails have always been distributed manually. Many HR folks are eager to look at the system to assist them with these administrative tasks. It is important, though, to understand that the SAP software is not meant to be an email system. Whether or not an email should be autogenerated by the system really depends on the process and circumstances of notification. For example, with one-off approvals, such as promotions and other pay changes, a system-generated email notification may make good business sense to facilitate and expedite the approvals of the request. However, during your annual compensation planning time, it is probably a good idea to manually manage communication from the compensation department or HR as it is a condensed period of time when system-generated emails could prove overwhelming for your users.

At the end of the blueprinting phase, it is important to review the various communications that employees and managers will receive throughout the process to ensure they will not be confused by repeated messages. Look at alternatives such as using portal work items (via the UWL) or manage notification in bulk centrally from HR or from the appropriate business function.

12.2.3 Stakeholder Management

Be sure to have a plan for managing the progress and include key stakeholders in the plan.

Form a Steering Committee to Review Project Progress and Resolve Project-Level Issues

A steering committee should be formed during the project to review project status and to provide advice on key, outstanding issues. Typically, this committee is comprised of senior-level management and other key stakeholders of the process. The project sponsor or his representative is usually on the committee as well. It is not uncommon to have Vice President (VP) and even C-level involvement at this stage. HR and IT representation is normal, as self-service functionally affects stakeholders in both functions of the organization.

The frequency of these meetings will depend on the group's availability, but the project's timeline and status should be considered. As the project ramps into the deployment phase, it may be necessary to hold more meetings to ensure a smooth transition. Also, if a project reaches a critical point anytime during the implementation, it may be necessary to increase the number of meetings or call impromptu meetings to resolve issues and remove any roadblocks along the way.

In your average project, it is not uncommon for the steering committee to meet biweekly. In these meetings, it is important that your project leaders are in attendance to provide direct feedback to senior leaders and raise issues if needed. A steering committee must be able to make quick decisions when necessary in order to not impede the progress of the project.

The steering committee also can exist after go-live. Their role transforms more into an advisory on operational issues and future enhancements rather than advisory in a typical project implementation. This is not as common, but we have seen many companies implement a post go-live committee or review board in order to provide some continuity between the project and operations associated to it post-implementation.

Review Any Changes to Online Forms, Transactions, and Processes with the Affected Business Units and Functions

Process reengineering should not be performed in a vacuum, especially when it impacts the entire organization. For example, migrating personnel change request forms from a paper-based process to an online, workflow-enabled process should prompt a review from other areas in the company that may have critical dependencies or feedback about how the new forms and processes will impact them.

We have seen a project team complete their blueprint and then delay the project because they could not obtain the required signoff when other functions did not agree with a redesigned process. Making processes and forms too complicated may prevent you from using them company-wide, if business rules and user interfaces cannot be reconciled or standardized between the groups.

12.3 System Implementation

The following technical considerations represent findings from years of working through customers' pain points to achieve a more successful implementation. Most lessons learned here are version independent, though our focus has inevitably gravitated toward the latest SAP NetWeaver functionality.

12.3.1 System Considerations

There will be many things to think about in terms of the system itself, including access modes, required security, application versions, and system testing.

Handle Employee Locking Issues that Prevent Payroll and Other Processes from Running

The power of ESS transactions is attributed to the real-time access to data that resides in the SAP ERP Central Component (ECC) backend. Employees are able to access current information and make updates directly in the backend system. When users make changes to their personal information, the SAP system will lock the employee's record to prevent other users (such as HR) from modifying the same information. This functionality is important in order to preserve the system's data integrity. It can also cause issues for other system functions such as SAP payroll (if you are running that in-house).

If managers or employees are locking records from the portal and the Payroll Department attempts to run payroll in the system, the latter process is interrupted because the payroll processing cannot get exclusive access to employee information. This problem is exacerbated if payroll is being run during the day. Depending on how many employees in the company and how many of those employees are conducting portal transactions, this process could be very time-consuming.

We have handled this a few different ways depending on the size of the company. In smaller organizations, where the Payroll group is familiar with most employees, the payroll group has been given access to SAP Transactions AL08 or SM04. These transactions allow payroll to see exactly which users or employees are locking records as well as the ability to terminate a user's session (if warranted). The Payroll department would typically run these transactions prior to running payroll to determine which users, if any, are locking their records. They could call these users (if they were at their desk) and ask them to complete their work and exit the transaction and the portal. In the event that users cannot be found (if they are in the field, for example) or if they simply don't respond, payroll could terminate the session using one of the two transactions mentioned earlier (given they have the appropriate security access).

In larger organizations it is best to automate the process. The following is a successful approach that we have implemented for several clients.

The solution centered on a custom portal application that took into account the employees' payroll area and mapped it against a payroll calendar. A custom table was configured with dates and times that indicated when the Payroll department would run their payroll processing. The portal application would be placed in front of every transaction that could potentially lock a record for a prolonged period of time and, if it determined that payroll was about to run or was running, it would generate a message to the user indicating that the system was not currently available due to payroll processing (or a message of your choice). Every other condition would seamlessly forward the employee to the transaction.

This approach would enable payroll administrators to control periods of time that payroll needs to execute payroll processes. Blocking users from making changes to underlying data during certain times is a clean solution for those companies that run payroll (or even time evaluation) in-house. Another positive impact from automating this "blackout period" is that it allows payroll administrators to set a threshold period around the time of payroll processing that prevents users from updating personal data that could adversely impact payroll results.

Online Access to Remuneration Statements and Controlling When They Appear

We have encountered many instances when we are asked the question: "When will the paystubs appear in the portal?". This is very important once you are live in production when you want to make sure that the paystub will show up to employees on a specific day after running payroll. SAP software has provided the ability to change the standard setting to meet your requirements. Business Add-In (BAdI) XSS_REM_INTERFACE can be enhanced to change the default settings (method PROVIDE_FILTERED_RGDIR provides this ability). We recommend that you keep some grace period between when payroll is run and when the paystub should appear to employees. A delay in when employees can see their own paystub will enable the Payroll Department to ensure that they have accounted for any corrections.

Exposing the SAP Portal and Self-Service Functionality Over the Internet Can Enable Employees to Gain Access from Remote Locations

Many corporate portals are designed to be accessible while the employee is in the workplace or through the use of a virtual private network (VPN) using company-supplied computers. This approach limits employees that want to access their personal information and enterprise applications from home or remote locations because some do not have a laptop or are not using a company computer. Providing self-service access from the Internet gives employees and managers the necessary tools, transactions, and content — even when they are not in the office.

Today, the SAP Portal and the applications that it hosts are becoming fundamental to service delivery. From an employee's perspective, certain information and transactions that relate to life events or life decisions are best viewed at home with a spouse, partner, or loved one. This is especially true when most of the information that was sent to employees' homes is now contained within the portal, such as pay stubs and benefits statements. The best example of a process needing remote access is annual benefits enrollment, which is often a decision taken between the employee and spouse or domestic partner.

With the advanced security inherent in the latest SAP NetWeaver platform, it is feasible to deliver portions or all of the functionality contained within the portal to users over the Internet. Our experience has shown that the SAP Portal becomes a more viable and well-adopted tool for employees and managers if it is available over the Internet, because it dramatically increases the ability to deliver information and transactions to all employees, regardless of where they are physically located.

**Provide Kiosk Access for Employees Who Do Not Have
Access to a Computer in the Workplace**

Another common challenge that we encounter in most self-service applications is that online access is not always readily accessible to everyone in the organization. Considerable effort and investments are made to drive content and functionality to the portal, yet the target audience is limited to corporate and mobile users. It is important to consider employees that may not already have access to computers within the enterprise or at their home. These users will often be found in production facilities, factories, retail locations, and warehouses. In many companies, these "workers" comprise the bulk of the employee population.

A common approach to include this important population into the self-service world is to implement a simple kiosk. This kiosk is typically either a desktop computer or laptop that is designed to limit the access to the underlying operating system and only offer users the ability to access the SAP Portal. Less common are kiosks with touch screens and trackballs with third-party kiosk software and interactive screens. These types of operations using computer terminals are more advanced and not as fully integrated into the SAP NetWeaver platform.

We have found that the location of the kiosk is dependent on the environment. In most situations when employees are in an environment such as a factory or warehouse, the kiosk should be located in a quiet area that can provide privacy to users when they are working with their personal information. Depending on the location and number of users, you may also want to consider sign-up sheets that allow employees to reserve time to use the kiosk.

In these cases, IT security procedures and practices are extremely important to follow. Crucial concepts, such as password strengths and kiosk timeouts, need to be implemented in order to protect the personal data of your employees.

**Conduct Performance Tests That Take into Account Peak Periods in
Processes, Such as Benefits Enrollment and Compensation Planning**

Performance of your applications is a major contributor to the rate of adoption and user experience. Applications that respond quickly are more likely to be adopted by users. Self-service applications add another dimension because the overall process depends on a user being able to access the system and complete the work in a timely manner. In several implementations, we have observed that a slow and unresponsive SAP Portal has contributed to delays in the overall process. HR would need to continually extend dates for employees to complete the process.

When you consider that some processes, such as performance management, benefits enrollment, and compensation management, affect large user populations, you can conclude that delays in the process cost a considerable amount of money to the company.

Performance testing (sometimes called, "stress testing") is not a new concept and most companies conduct performance tests prior to rolling out any Internet or intranet application to assess how the application will behave under a heavy load. The challenge is to run performance tests indicative of peak usage that the applications will be subjected to and determine an acceptable response time. Some strongly believe that an acceptable response should be one or two seconds between clicks, while others do not hold such high standards.

An effective way to approach performance testing is to use existing data from legacy applications that perform similar functionality. If this data does not exist in your system, then you need to step back and look at the key processes that are being rolled out and the behavior of the user population. For example, we have observed that over sixty percent of employees complete benefits enrollment in the last week of the open enrollment period. It is human nature that your employee base (as well as managers) will procrastinate.

When you consider processes like benefits enrollment and the dynamics of how users complete this process, you can design appropriate performance tests that can reveal potential issues in your implementation. There are several testing software tools in the marketplace to assist you in automating this process.

The outcome of your performance tests could a) verify that you have a proper environment/landscape on which to roll out your functionality; b) cause you to make tweaks within the ECC backend and SAP Portal configuration to enhance performance; or c) force a second look at how the system landscape and components are setup. Outcomes a) and b) can be expected, but if outcome c) is reached, you may need to re-evaluate your deployment plan.

**Install and Configure NetWeaver Development Infrastructure to Manage
Team Development and Enhancements to Self-Service Applications**

SAP software has introduced a powerful set of tools within the SAP NetWeaver
Developer Studio (NWDS) and NetWeaver Development Infrastructure (NWDI).
These tools enable your development team to work collaboratively in the development of rich applications for your SAP NetWeaver Portal while, at the same time,
providing the rigorous controls in place to ensure that the software development
process is managed and easily promoted to multiple environments for testing and
production.

The suite of tools and processes that the SAP software provides are powerful but
can also carry a steep learning curve for developers. If your team is relatively new
to the Java 2 platform, Enterprise Edition (J2EE) development, and source code
control tools, it is recommended that you send your team for training where they
can get hands-on experience and, at the same time, learn the SAP software–specific
components needed to develop and deliver these solutions.

In addition to training your team, you will want to consider your technology
direction. SAP software has stated several directions in the past couple of years.
However, the SAP software is starting to set its own technology direction with
Web Dynpro. You will want to consider what your team's strengths and weak-
nesses are before selecting a technology and setting the direction. Once you have
defined your technology direction, you can make the necessary investments in
your development team.

NWDI is also intended to facilitate and manage the enhancement of any XSS Web
Dynpro application. It is recommended that you update all your systems to the
latest versions of your System Landscape Directory (SLD) and the Component
Build Service (CBS). It is critical to have the latest version in order to upload the
XSS packages.

**Enforce a Security and Data Privacy Stance Prior to
Rolling out Self-Service Functionality**

Security has become a major concern for many organizations in the past few years.
Many high-profile companies have had security breaches that have generated system down time, loss of confidential information, and eventual loss of revenue.

Self-service applications are designed to enable employees and managers to gain access to key HR information that is highly sensitive and can easily be used to cause damage to the employee or the enterprise. It is advised that security policies be reviewed when releasing self-service for the first time. Your IT Security team — as well as legal and compliance teams — should be involved and aware of your project. Specific policies that govern the length and complexity of passwords, when passwords should be changed, sharing of passwords, and access controls should be reviewed and reinforced by your IT Security organization.

Data privacy is also of chief concern to many users in Europe and other areas. Data origin and the viewing of this data across borders are of principal concern, as many companies with offices in Europe need to conform to local work councils and regulatory laws. If your implementation is global in nature, be sure to involve your legal and compliance organizations when you localize your self-service applications.

Automate the Hiring Process to Include Creating a User and Assigning the Appropriate Security Roles

Depending on the size of your organization, you may want to analyze the effort required in administering security and access controls. Larger organizations invest considerable resources to this effort. Both the SAP Portal and the backend ECC system provide all of the necessary information and controls to administer security and access controls without needing to introduce new processes and additional resources. In many of our implementations, we have opted to automate the process of administering security by embedding it into the user lifecycle.

Consider an example of this automation when an employee is hired into the SAP system. The security and maintenance associated for granting access to this new hire can be expedited by implementing an automated process such as the following:

An employee is hired into the organization. After the hiring action is complete, a background process is started that creates the user ID. After the user ID is created, it is then linked to the employee's Infotype 0105 record (subtype 0001, SYUNAME) and, based on the position that the employee is hired into, additional roles are assigned to the user. User creation, user assignment, and authorization assignments are now complete in ECC.

Once this process is complete, the information is synchronized with the company's Lightweight Directory Access Protocol (LDAP) server, which your portal (most likely) uses for authentication and authorization. (You will have to work with your portal and networking group if these concepts are not familiar to you.)

In this example, little to no manual intervention is required for the administration of security. The employee was hired into the system and basic access was available (in near real time) after the hiring action was completed. We have created many of these extensions to the employee lifecycle — automating everything from the initial creation of the user to the final deactivation of the account upon employee termination. The result has been extensive cost savings and a reliable process that provides (or removes) access in a timely manner.

Test Your Self-Service Solution with Multiple Browsers

With the SAP Portal supporting more and more browsers and the trend to allow employees access from home, it becomes critical to test the various browsers during the testing phase of the project. It is more and more mainstream that browsers, such as Firefox, are used to access the Internet. We have also seen many companies set the standard to Internet Explorer version 6.x or 7.x.

It is also important to understand the Adobe Acrobat versions you have within your company, especially if the Adobe Form technology is being used for change requests. Regardless of the version of your Adobe software (6.x, 7.x, 8.x, or 9.x), testing should be performed on the version(s) supported.

Implement a Testing Strategy that Takes Self-Service into Consideration

Testing integrated systems can sometimes be challenging as it requires comprehensive data to be created in support of the various business scenarios. Self-service applications can also add an additional layer of complexity because they introduce the SAP Portal as its front end. A portal layer adds complexity and makes the testing effort more challenging.

Table 12.1 lists some of the most common testing issues that we have faced in SAP self-service implementations. Next to each issue, we list the approach on how we have dealt with this issue in the past.

Issue	Approach
Self-service applications require an extensive set of data with many employees set to a particular state. As you cycle through each test case, new employees are needed. For example, if you are terminating employees as a manager, you will need other employees that are not terminated to continue to test.	Create a "build up" and "tear down" approach to testing based on what components you are implementing. You can create scenarios that hire employees as part of the test script and then use that employee to complete an entire lifecycle that tests every self-service component. Also, consider moving your production master data to your staging system and decide which organizations you will use for your test data. Separate your test data from your testing scripts so that the testing scripts can be reused to accommodate different employees within different business scenarios. Some customers opt to conduct client refreshes to "reset" employee data for the test cycles. This will return the testing environment data to a previous snapshot, which can prove valuable before each cycle of testing.
Not enough portal users to complete test scenarios. Also, a complicated set of users with varying passwords slows progress.	When selecting an organization and employees, request that the Basis team (your SAP system administrators) create user IDs based on what is assigned within Infotype 0105. Request that every user have a common password to limit confusion when testing. However, be sure that your HR master data is scrambled if there is sensitive information (i.e., birth date, salary, and benefits data). There are programs that can be created or software for purchase that can perform this task.
Workflow notifications and system emails are being sent to active employees.	Testing system notifications, such as emails, can be an issue and could expose the wrong people to HR data that they should not have access to. Request that a script be created by Basis that will set all user email addresses to a group email box that the testing team can access. Using this approach will make it easier to test system notifications and will reduce the possibility that data in emails is sent to the wrong email address. Queuing emails in Transaction SOST and manually sending requests is one approach, but could be dangerous if an email is sent to a production user by accident.

Table 12.1   Common Testing Issues and Approach for Mitigation

Issue	Approach
Many self-service transactions can affect payroll processing. Lack of payroll testing could result in project delays or issues with completing testing.	If SAP payroll is performed in-house, allocate a payroll resource to your testing cycles that can run payroll for a specified period. Payroll should be run at the end of a testing cycle and verified against the business scenarios that are being tested.
	Ensure that all payroll-related ESS transactions get tested and approved by the payroll department. Services, such as online pay stubs, bank information, and W4 should be tested by a subject matter expert in the payroll group.

Table 12.1 Common Testing Issues and Approach for Mitigation (Cont.)

Leverage Testing Cycles to Train Service Center Personnel and the HRIS Team

Testing a system and being able to experience the resolution of issues has proven to be a powerful mechanism for getting the HRIS team trained and prepared to support the system after go-live. We have also found that if you allow the service center personnel (or appropriate HR support organization) to participate in the testing cycles, you may be able to reduce training time by upward of fifty percent. There's nothing quite like "on the job" training and by participating in the testing cycles, your support teams will experience "day-in-the-life" scenarios that will soon become second nature to them.

12.4   Summary

We hope you will find these lessons learned helpful in your own effort for delivering a usable self-service solution with a high adoption rate. We encourage you to use these lessons learned and to connect and benchmark with other companies that have implemented self-service functionality in the SAP system.

We believe the main objective when implementing ESS and MSS is to provide an intuitive interface and seamless integration of information and transactions that empower the employee to manage life, career, and work events. By hearing the experiences of others — both success stories and implementation struggles — your own implementation should see immediate benefit and eventual success.

In the next chapter, we will discuss some resources to assist you and your project team. These resources — some provided by SAP software — are literally at your fingertips and should be leveraged whenever possible.

Knowing where to look for answers is perhaps one of the single most important skills of a project team. This is especially true when implementing self-service applications, given the complex mix of technologies (both frontend and backend). Resourcefulness is crucial in implementations such as Employee Self-Service (ESS) and Manager Self-Service (MSS). This chapter helps you become aware of the resources available to assist you before, during, and after your implementation.

13 Resources

This chapter lists recommended websites, information repositories, and user communities that may help you gain a better understanding of SAP's ESS and MSS functionality. The following sections comprise a thorough inventory of resources you can leverage before, during, and after your implementation.

13.1 Solution Documentation on SAP Service Marketplace

Solution documentation for ESS and MSS is available on SAP's Service Marketplace website for registered users as shown in Figure 13.1. (For those that do not have a Service Marketplace username and password, speak to one of your project leaders or Basis resources on how to obtain a username and password for the Service Marketplace.) A lot of solution documentation is available in the Media Library sections of Service Marketplace for ESS and MSS.

To peruse and download ESS product documentation in the Media Library, do the following:

Go to *http://service.sap.com/ess* in your web browser.

On the left navigation panel, under the path: SAP ERP • END-USER SERVICE DELIVERY • EMPLOYEE SELF-SERVICES (ESS), click on Media Library for access to documents such as:

▶ ESS Services and Country Availability

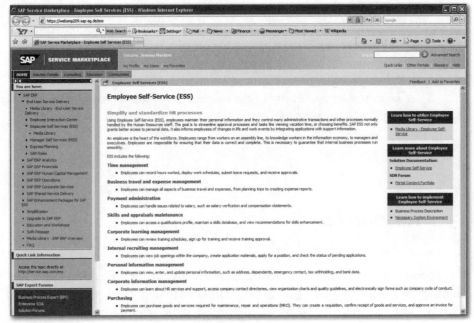

Figure 13.1 ESS within SAP's Service Marketplace

To peruse and download MSS product documentation in the Media Library (see Figure 13.2), do the following:

Go to *http://service.sap.com/mss* in your web browser.

On the left navigation panel, under the path: SAP ERP • END-USER SERVICE DELIVERY • MANAGER SELF-SERVICES (MSS), click on Media Library for access to documents such as:

▶ MSS SAP Help documentation

▶ Detailed documentation on topics such as Object and Data Provider (OADP), Business Intelligence (BI) content, and portal integration

▶ Frequently Asked Questions (FAQs)

▶ Overview Presentations on Functionality

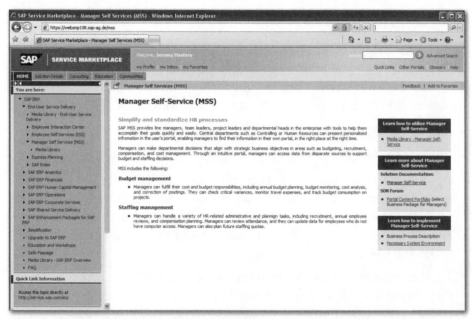

Figure 13.2 MSS within SAP's Service Marketplace

Within the Media Library, the link "Manager Self-Service Documentation" under the heading "Documentation" provides the following topics related to MSS:

▶ SAP Notes on Documentation

▶ Business Package Documentation

▶ Release Notes

▶ Installations Guides

▶ Upgrade Guides

▶ Security Guides

▶ Configuration Guides

▶ Technical iView Documentation

▶ Documentation on Tools

We strongly recommend that you bookmark this link and refer to it frequently. SAP software keeps this section of the Service Marketplace the most current for MSS matters.

13.2 SAP Online Help

SAP's online help is often overlooked as a great resource for documentation. It is always helpful to ground yourself with the standard documentation from SAP. SAP posts the latest, revised help documentation online on this site. To read the documentation on SAP's help website, do the following:

► Go to *http://help.sap.com* in your web browser.

► On the SAP Solutions tab, click on SAP ERP.

► Open the documentation by clicking on the available language you prefer. (The latest documentation as of this book's release is SAP Enhancement Package 2 for SAP ERP 6.0 available in English and German.) If you are on an Enhancement Package, click on the link underneath SAP ERP Central Component (ECC) called SAP ERP Enhancement Packages.

► Another window will launch with the SAP Library. Click on SAP ERP Central Component in the left navigation panel.

► Expand the Cross-Application Components folder in the left navigation panel.

► Expand the Self-Services folder in the left navigation panel.

► Click on the Business Package for Employee Self-Service (SAP ERP) 1.x folder to open up the help documentation on ESS or click on Business Package for Manager Self-Service (SAP ERP) 1.x to open up the help documentation on MSS, where x is the Enhancement Package number.

13.3 SAP Notes on SAP Service Marketplace

The SAP Notes section of the Service Marketplace is typically where SAP software customers go when they are looking to troubleshoot an issue. This site, previously called the Online Service System (OSS), provides important bug fixes for SAP software customers as well as consultative advice on workarounds for known product issues. It is the lifeline to a lot of project implementations.

The SAP Notes section of the Service Marketplace can be accessed directly by going to *http://service.sap.com/notes* in your web browser. You will be prompted for a username and password as you will need to be a registered user.

Most ESS SAP Notes are categorized under application area PA-ESS or CA-ESS. Under the PA-ESS application area, sub-application PA-ESS-DE is for Germany-relevant transactions, PA-ESS-US is for US-relevant transactions, and PA-ESS-OCY is for transactions related to all other countries. PA-ESS-XX (for "Common Parts") is a generic application that is pertinent to all countries while PA-ESS-XX-CE is reserved for Concurrent Employment–related transactions. Under the CA-ESS application area, CA-ESS-ITS (services for the Internet Transaction Server) and CA-ESS-WD (services for Web Dynpro services) are the two sub-application components available.

Most MSS SAP Notes are categorized under application area EP-PCT-MGR-HR. Other components relevant for MSS functionality include CA-TS-IA-XS for the Cross-Application Timesheet (CATS) application and PT_RC_UI_XS for Leave Requests. The Composite SAP Note for MSS functionality is SAP Note 903319. Reference this note to obtain an inventory of the important SAP Notes pertinent to deploying and maintaining MSS.

- SAP Note 1151791 — ATO & ROD: Erroneous static locale setting
- SAP Note 1146203 — ECM: No statistics calculated for ineligible employees
- SAP Note 1134378 — MSS E-Recruiting: Wrong functional area text
- SAP Note 1015231 — MSS: Properties for period spec missing in generic iViews
- SAP Note 1007341 — SAP ERP 2004/2005: Supported ESS/MSS system landscapes
- SAP Note 1004528 — SAP Self-Services: Business packages and components
- SAP Note 997351 — ERP2005: Profile Matchup new parameter enhancement
- SAP Note 994934 — ERP: MSS E-Recruiting Remote Function Call (RFC) connection authorization
- SAP Note 979914 — MSS: Incorrect date may appear in Attendance Overview
- SAP Note 977362 — MSS OADP: Incorrect format of the time stamp
- SAP Note 952693 — MSS: Interactive forms and HCM processes and forms
- SAP Note 952692 — Transfer of SAP MSS functions to mySAP ERP 2005
- SAP Note 949625 — ERP: MSS E-Recruiting new standard workflow templates
- SAP Note 940906 — Fields removed from Forms to request requisitions
- SAP Note 931836 — ERP: Requisition object creation fixed-workflow task update

- ▶ SAP Note 931794 – SAP HR Interface for Organizational Charting (HR-OCI) 6.0
- ▶ SAP Note 925549 – ERP: MSS Recruiting forms: accessible enhancements.
- ▶ SAP Note 925129 – ERP2005: Profile Matchup course details link activated
- ▶ SAP Note 907524 – ERP2005-SP02: Status Overview for Personnal Change Reports (PCRs) and Requisitions
- ▶ SAP Note 905132 – MSS Reporting: Customizing entries for Business Warehouse (BW) reports
- ▶ SAP Note 903370 – Missing Customizing leads to failures in employee profiles
- ▶ SAP Note 896964 – ERP2005: MSS Recruiting development fixes (please disregard)
- ▶ SAP Note 865439 – ERP2004: Recruitment Officer dropdown restricted
- ▶ SAP Note 861261 – ERP2005: No PCR Direct Launch links in Rel.Activities iView
- ▶ SAP Note 790629 – PCR: Manager Search does not handle middle names
- ▶ SAP Note 720460 – ESS-in-MSS: Process all employees in the Team Viewer
- ▶ SAP Note 568576 – Composite SAP note: MSS (HR Management)

There is no composite SAP Note for ESS functionality. However, some important SAP Notes for ESS include:

- ▶ SAP Note 939412 – Missing Permissions for the Enduser: Everyone
- ▶ SAP Note 929447 – Adopting life and work events for countries other than the US
- ▶ SAP Note 837215 – Switching Caching on/off in area Homepage Framework
- ▶ SAP Note 824847 – ESS: UI Customizing of ESS 60.1 (Web Dynpro)
- ▶ SAP Note 1159911 – Correction in view V_T7XSSPERBIZFLD
- ▶ SAP Note 870126 – ITS-based ESS services in SAP ERP2005
- ▶ SAP Note 761266 – Self-services patches
- ▶ SAP Note 808111 – ESS/MSS: Changes in self-service homepage causes errors
- ▶ SAP Note 746396 – ESS PersInfo: "Mandatory field" error

▸ SAP Note 1032194 — Confirmation screen links type: Call PCD page, not displayed

▸ SAP Note 773684 — Error calling a dynamic XSS from another XSS application

▸ SAP Note 1007341 — SAP ERP 2004/2005: Supported ESS/MSS system landscapes

▸ SAP Note 1030552 — BP ESS 60.2 (ERP 2004): Travel with ECC 600 (SAP ERP 2005)

▸ SAP Note 968360 — Configuring generic enrollment action in ESS LWE

▸ SAP Note 818958 — ESS PersInfo: Important configuration tables

There are many other SAP Notes pertinent to ESS that are not listed, especially SAP Notes within the CA-ESS-WD, PA-ESS-XX, and PA-ESS-OCY application areas. Be sure to check the full inventory of SAP Notes on the Service Marketplace when trying to troubleshoot an issue (see Figure 13.3).

Figure 13.3 SAP Notes Main Search Page

13.4   SDN (SAP Developer Network)

SDN is an online community and network of SAP practitioners, developers, configurators, and other project team members. SAP software is now branding it as the *SAP Community Network* because the site has a lot to offer other resources besides developers. Registration is free. Members can post, respond to, and view questions found in the Forum. The Forum is the most popular spot on the website (see Figure 13.4), but there are other great features, including free eLearning classes, interesting blogs, and downloads.

Figure 13.4   Forum Search on SAP's SDN Website

A new community, called the Business Process Expert Community (BPX), is a repository for business process expertise and knowledge sharing. Both SDN and BPX are online communities worth participating in.

13.5   HR Expert

Wellesley Information Services also publishes HR Expert — a magazine that covers essential SAP HCM concepts, tips, and Best Practices. There is a focus on case studies and "real-world" experiences in the articles (see Figure 13.5). You can find a lot of good material on the website as well (it is a paid subscription). The website is *http://www.hrexpertonline.com/*.

Table 13.1 lists several articles within the *HR Expert* archive that are relevant to ESS and MSS.

Article	Volume # / Issue # / Month
"Restricting Changes by ESS Users"	Volume 01 / Issue 02 / May
"Manager Self-Service Now Allows Enhancements Without Programming"	Volume 01 / Issue 07 / November
"ESS A to Z: How One Company Planned, Deployed, Tested, and Trained for Its ESS Implementation"	Volume 02 / Issue 06 / July
"Use Standard SAP to Restrict Access in a CATS Implementation"	Volume 02 / Issue 08 / October
"An Easy Way to Create Custom Services in ESS"	Volume 02 / Issue 10 / December
"Create an ESS Implementation That Users Will Love"	Volume 03 / Issue 04 / May
"Improve Efficiency of HR Service Request Processing with SAP Personnel Change Requests"	Volume 04 / Issue 01 / January and February
"Build Your Organizational Structure to Support SAP's Manager Self-Service"	Volume 04 / Issue 01 / January and February
"Improve Data Entry Efficiency with CATS User Exits"	Volume 05 / Issue 03 / April
"Part 1: Prepare Your Team for a Successful ESS/MSS Implementation"	Volume 05 / Issue 10 / December
"SAP HCM Processes and Forms — A Better Alternative to PCRs"	Volume 06 / Issue 03 / April
"Navigate ESS with Ease"	Volume 06 / Issue 04 / May

Table 13.1   List of HR Expert Articles Pertinent to ESS and MSS

Figure 13.5 Example Article on the HR Expert Website

13.6 Annual Conferences

The two conferences that are the most popular for SAP HR practitioners are the annual SAP HR conference and SAPPHIRE.

Every year, Wellesley Information Services (the publisher of *SAP Insider*) sponsors the HR conference where SAP software partners, exhibitors, and customers come to listen to speakers, share Best Practices, and see what new functionality is coming down the road. The conference is a great place to network, hear what others are doing, and have fun. The website for the HR 2009 conference is *http://www. saphr2009.com/*.

Each year, SAP software hosts a SAPPHIRE event that is geared for both current and prospective clients. It is an opportunity for SAP software to show their cutting-edge solutions to its customer base. As you might expect, SAPPHIRE events include speaker presentations, demos, and an exhibitor area. For more information on the conference, visit *http://www.sapsapphire.com/*.

13.7 User Communities

Two SAP HCM user communities are popular for networking events, knowledge sharing/harvesting, and roundtable discussions:

▶ Americas' SAP Users' Group (ASUG) is a customer-driven community of SAP software professionals and partners. There are more than 45,000 individuals and 1,700 companies represented within the community. It is a great place for networking. Visit their website at *http://www.asug.com/*.

▶ The Society for Human Resource Management (SHRM) is the world's largest association devoted to HR management. Founded in 1948 and representing more than 225,000 individual members, SHRM currently has more than 575 affiliated chapters and members in more than 125 countries. Visit their website at *http://www.shrm.org/*.

13.8 Internet Search Engines

It may sound silly, but don't forget about your Internet search engines!

Google, Yahoo!, and Microsoft Live, among many others, provide a great mechanism for answers to SAP software questions. You know what to do. Simply type in your question or keyword and see what you get — you may be surprised!

13.9 Summary

In conclusion, there are many resources you can embrace to research answers to your ESS and MSS questions. Some of these resources, such as SDN, SAP Service Marketplace, and Internet search engines such as Google and Yahoo!, are free of charge and provide a wealth of information at your fingertips. Just remember: if you are stuck on something, there are probably fellow SAP HCM practitioners who are struggling or have struggled with the same or similar challenge. Go out there and take advantage of all of the wonderful resources at your disposal!

The Authors

Christos Kotsakis is Vice President of Information Technology at Starwood Hotels and Resorts Worldwide, which together with its subsidiaries, operates as a hotel and leisure company worldwide. Prior to joining Starwood Hotels and Resorts, Mr. Kotsakis was an associate partner in the Human Capital Management practice at IBM Global Business Services where he led the design and implementation of large-scale, global HR transformation projects using SAP HR. In the past 10 years, Mr. Kotsakis has managed more than a dozen project teams, spanning across HR functionality, including Performance Management, Compensation Management, and eRecruitment. He also has extensive experience in software development; self-service technology; enterprise portal implementations; including the SAP NetWeaver Portal, and related technologies. You can reach him via email at christos.kotsakis@emedianet.com.

Jeremy Masters is an author, speaker, and SAP HR subject matter expert. Mr. Masters is also the cofounder and managing partner of Worklogix, which provides SAP HR professional services and software solutions to fortune 1000 companies. Mr. Masters has been an SAP HR practitioner for over 10 years, spending his early years with Price Waterhouse, PwC Consulting, and IBM. He has been involved in over 16 projects, many of them global in scope. Mr. Masters has been helping clients implement performance management systems for the past 6 years. Besides Performance Management, he has worked with much of the new self-service functionality, including Compensation Management, Personnel Cost Planning, Succession Planning, and eRecruitment in both the SAP R/3 system and the SAP Enterprise Portal. You can reach him via email at jmasters@worklogix.com.

Index

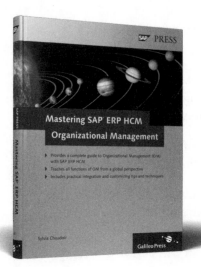

Provides a complete guide to Organizational Management (OM) with SAP ERP HCM

Teaches all functions of OM from a global perspective

Includes practical integration and customizing tips and techniques

Sylvia Chaudoir

Mastering SAP ERP HCM Organizational Management

This book teaches the HCM team how to maximize the organizational management (OM) component of SAP ERP HCM. It takes readers beyond the basics, by delving into all aspects of the component as well as the little-known concepts. It teaches all of the key OM functions, their purpose, and how to use and customize them. Numerous examples from customers are used to provide context for decisions and to explain the benefits of the choices that can be made. And in-depth explanations and practical examples are used to help readers leverage the many available organizational objects to get the most out of their SAP HR implementation.

348 pp., 2008, 69,95 Euro / US$ 69.95
ISBN 978-1-59229-208-0

>> www.sap-press.de/1796

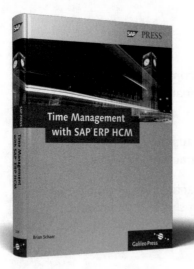

Learn how to set up the
Time Management to meet
your business needs

Explore configuration and
customization options

Find out how to use Infotypes and
BAdIs to streamline and integrate
cost-intensive processes

Brian Schaer

Time Management with SAP ERP HCM

This book provides a detailed guide to understanding, implementing, and
configuring the Time Management component of SAP ERP HCM. It teaches
readers the core topics of Time Management and provides the foundational
information they need for implementing and configuring the business
requirements. It also provides insight into some of the more advanced
topics, such as process flows.

approx. 500 pp., 69,95 Euro / US$ 69.95
ISBN 978-1-59229-229-5, Dec 2008

>> www.sap-press.de/1848

 **PRESS**

Provides a complete guide to
the functionality of E-Recruiting

Teaches how to configure and
use E-Recruiting with other
HCM components

Uses a real-world workflow
approach

Ben Hayes

E-Recruiting with SAP ERP HCM

This book provides a practical guide to configuring and using SAP E-Recruitment effectively
in the real-world. It is written to teach SAP ERP HCM users and the implementation team
what the E-Recruiting tool is so that they can use it effectively in their recruitment process
and integrate it easily with other HCM components. Beginning with an overview, the book
progresses through the configuration process from a real workflow perspective. And all of
the processes are covered in the order in which they are used in a real recruiting project.
The book also details how to integrate E-Recruiting with other SAP components, and, as
applicable, examples of companies using E-Recruiting successfully will be integrated
throughout.

approx. 320 pp., 69,90 Euro / US$ 69.95
ISBN 978-1-59229-243-1, Jan 2009

>> www.sap-press.de/1957

Covers standard SAP reports, queries, SAP NetWeaver BI, and the creation of customer reports

Provides practical examples for report creation in the different SAP ERP HCM components

Examines reports in area menu, HIS, MDT, and SAP NetWeaver Portal formats

Up-to-date for SAP ERP 6.0

Hans-Jürgen Figaj, Richard Haßmann, Anja Junold

HR Reporting with SAP

This comprehensive book describes how you can use the powerful reporting tools of the SAP system efficiently and in a goal-oriented manner. You will first get to know the details of the reporting tools, Standard SAP Report, Query, SAP NetWeaver BI, and Customer Report. The book then describes various real-life examples in order to demonstrate how you can use the tools in the different HCM modules in the best-possible way. You will get to know selected standard reports as well as the SAP NetWeaver BI Standard Content for each module. In addition, you will learn how you can make the reports available to users. The book is based on SAP ERP 6.0 and can be used with Release R/3 Enterprise or higher.

435 pp., 2008, 69,95 Euro / US$ 69.95
ISBN 978-1-59229-172-4

>> www.sap-press.de/1638

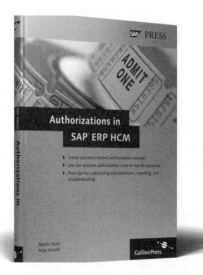

Learn how to create and implement a process-oriented authorization strategy for your company

Discover how to use the complex authorization tools of SAP ERP HCM in real-life scenarios

Explore practical customizing and extensions, reports, and error analyses examples

Martin Esch, Anja Junold

Authorizations in SAP ERP HCM

Design, Implementation, Operation

This book describes how you can create and implement an appropriate authori–zation strategy for your company in SAP ERP HCM. It answers all of your potential questions, from the differences and areas of usage for general, structural, and context-sensitive authorization checks to the specific challenges involved in using performance management functions. In addition, you'll learn about the typical problem areas and discover how to resolve them. The book contains many useful tips that support you in implementing the authorization system for the first time or in your daily work.

336 pp., 2008, 69,95 Euro / US$ 69.95
ISBN 978-1-59229-165-6

>> www.sap-press.de/1602

Prepare for, design, implement, and configure your HCM implementation

Increase employee and company productivity by using HCM Performance Management efficiently

Learn to enhance performance management based on business best practices

Jeremy Masters, Christos Kotsakis

SAP ERP HCM Performance Management

From Design to Implementation

This comprehensive book is an indispensable reference for HR professionals, analysts, and consultants learning how to implement SAP ERP HCM Performance Management. The book teaches you everything you need to know about the Objective Setting and Appraisal (OSA) module within SAP so that you can identify and retain key talent within your organization. You'll take a step-by-step journey through the design and implementation of your own performance management application that will help you improve your companies' performance and talent management processes. The book covers all the latest releases, including the R/3 Enterprise Release (4.7), SAP ERP 2004 (ECC 5.0) and SAP ERP 2005 (ECC 6.0).

302 pp., 2008, 69,95 Euro / US$ 69.95
ISBN 978-1-59229-124-3

>> **www.sap-press.de/1421**

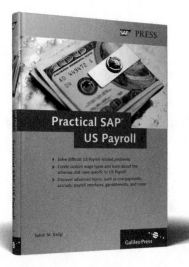

Solves difficult US Payroll-related problems

Create custom wage types and learn about the schemas and rules specific to US Payroll

Discover advanced topics, such as overpayments, accruals, payroll interfaces, garnishments, and more

Satish Badgi

Practical SAP US Payroll

„Practical US Payroll" has everything you need to implement a success–ful payroll system. Readers will learn how to create custom wage types, process deductions for benefits and garnishments, handle accruals, report and process taxes, and process retroactive payrolls.
From the hands-on, step-by-step examples to the detailed wage type tables in the appendix, this book is your complete guide to the US Payroll system.

332 pp., 2007, 69,95 Euro / US$ 69.95
ISBN 978-1-59229-132-8

>> www.sap-press.de/1450

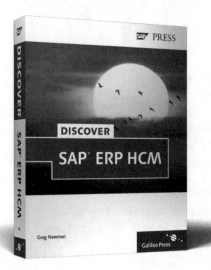

Teaches readers what SAP ERP HCM is and how it can benefit their company

Provides a detailed overview of all core functionality

Includes practical insights and real-world case studies to show HCM at work

Greg Newman

Discover SAP ERP HCM

This book is an insightful, detailed guide to what SAP ERP HCM is all about and how it can make companies more effective in managing their own HR processes. The book details all of the major components of SAP HCM, explaining the purpose of the components, how they work, their features and benefits and their integration with other components. It uses real-world examples throughout to demonstrate the uses, benefits, and issues encountered by existing SAP HCM users to ground the book in reality rather than just marketing hype. After reading this book, readers will have a broad understanding of SAP's HCM offering and insight into existing customer experiences with the product.

approx. 400 pp., 39,95 Euro / US$ 39.95
ISBN 978-1-59229-222-6, Dec 2008

>> www.sap-press.de/1846